SMOKING BEHAVIOR:
MOTIVES AND INCENTIVES

EDITED BY WILLIAM L. DUNN, JR.

V. H. WINSTON & SONS

1973   Washington, D.C.

DISTRIBUTED BY THE HALSTED PRESS DIVISION OF

JOHN WILEY & SONS
New York   Toronto   London   Sydney

SMOKING BEHAVIOR:
MOTIVES AND INCENTIVES

V. H. Winston & Sons, Inc., Publishers
1511 K St. N.W., Washington, D.C. 20005

Distributed solely by Halsted Press Division, John Wiley & Sons, Inc., New York.

Library of Congress Cataloging in Publication Data:

Dunn, William L.
    Smoking behavior.

    Includes bibliographies.
    1. Smoking–Psychological aspects. I. Title.
[DNLM: 1. Behavior. 2. Nicotine–Poisoning.
3. Smoking. QV 137 D923s 1973]
BF789.S6D85   615'.78   72-13271
ISBN 0-470-22746-X

Printed in the United States of America

CONTENTS

viii   CONTENTS

LIST OF CONTRIBUTORS

Numbers in parentheses indicate the pages on which the authors' contributions begin.

A. K. Armitage, Tobacco Research Council Laboratories, Harrogate, England (83)

Barbara B. Brown, Veterans Administration Hospital at Sepulveda, California (67)

Albert Damon, Harvard University, Cambridge, Massachusetts (219)

Edward F. Domino, University of Michigan, Ann Arbor, Michigan (5)

William L. Dunn, Jr., Philip Morris Research Center, Richmond, Virginia (93)

Grace S. Emley, Fort Custer State Home, Augusta, Michigan (171)

Walter B. Essman, Queens College of the City University of New York, Flushing, New York (51)

Hans J. Eysenck, Institute of Psychiatry, University of London, Denmark Hill, London, SE 5, U.K. (113)

Anita Kassen Fischer, College of Physicians and Surgeons, Columbia University, New York, N.Y. (255)

Lucy N. Friedman, Columbia University, New York, N.Y. (243)

Evelyn B. Harner, University of Pennsylvania, Philadelphia, Pennsylvania (267)

Norman W. Heimstra, University of South Dakota, Vermillion, South Dakota (197)

Richard J. Hickey, University of Pennsylvania, Philadelphia, Pennsylvania, (267)

Ronald R. Hutchinson, Fort Custer State Home, Augusta, Michigan (171)

Murray E. Jarvik, University of California, Los Angeles Center for the Health Sciences, Los Angeles, California (33)

Seymour S. Kety, Harvard Medical School and Massachusetts General Hospital, Boston, Massachusetts (287)

Paul F. Lazarsfeld, Columbia University, New York, N.Y. (243, 283)

Joseph D. Matarazzo, University of Oregon Medical School (215)

Alan S. Meyer, Columbia University, New York, N.Y. (243)

Neal E. Miller, The Rockefeller University, New York, N.Y. (209)

Francis J. Ryan, Philip Morris Research Center, Richmond, Virginia (231)

Stanley Schachter, Columbia University, New York, N.Y. (147)

Hans Selye, University of Montreal, Montreal, Canada (1)

Leo Srole, College of Physicians and Surgeons, Columbia University, New York, N.Y. (255)

Caroline B. Thomas, The Johns Hopkins University School of Medicine, Baltimore, Maryland (157)

PREFACE

Early in his career some 50 years ago, Clark L. Hull, foremost among American psychologists, described his ongoing research efforts as a search for ". . . a clue to the charm which tobacco has for those accustomed to its use." Hull never found that clue.

When I first became associated with the cigarette industry in 1961, I came across a contractual survey in which one of the questions asked of the smoker respondents was "Why do you smoke?" Of those whose reply went beyond the cliche, "It's a habit," about half of them said "It stimulates me." The other half said "It relaxes me." How to reconcile the remarkable polarity of these responses has intrigued but escaped me over the years.

In January, 1972, a representative group of life, behavioral and social scientists convened on St. Martin Island of the Lesser Antilles to reflect upon human cigarette smoking behavior. It was hoped that such a conference would redirect the scientific community's interest to the fundamental motivational question which has gone unanswered since Clark Hull posed it a half century ago, and which has not been given the priority it deserves during the past decade.

It was further hoped that the conference would correct for a dearth of interdiscipline cross talk among those conducting research on smoking. The pharmacologists were bent upon understanding the modifying effect of nicotine and other smoke constituents upon biochemical processes. The psychologists were seeking to fit their observations into theoretical models of learning and personality, looking chiefly at the differences between smokers and nonsmokers. The sociologists were documenting the refractoriness of the habit in face of massive dissuasion campaigns. The anthropologists were still recording the brushfire-like geographic diffusion of cigarette smoking and its integration into the cultural patterns of technology-remote peoples. Common to all of these efforts was the relevance of the data to the problem of smoker motivation, yet little was happening in the way of idea exchange.

This, then, is the question that was put to the St. Martin conferees: "What are the motivational mechanisms sustaining cigarette smoking behavior?" Their replies make up this volume. These published proceedings do not of themselves correct for the aforementioned cross talk deficiencies among the disciplines. Nevertheless the contributors have been well rubbed against each other in the course of this exercise. Only with time will we know if cross-fertilization occurred.

The conference was sponsored by The Council for Tobacco Research—U.S.A., Inc.

William L. Dunn, Jr.

December, 1972

SMOKING BEHAVIOR:
MOTIVES AND INCENTIVES

1
SOME INTRODUCTORY REMARKS

Hans Selye
University of Montreal

We are greatly indebted to the organizers of this volume for bringing together the work of a group of scientists having the most diverse points of view on smoking. This has afforded us opportunity to present our respective ideas on the factors motivating people to smoke.

As this is the first and therefore keynote chapter, I would like first to present a brief outline of my ideas on stress.

Stress is the nonspecific response of the body to any demand made upon it. The state is a physiological reaction, an effort to bring about internal bodily adaptation to changed external conditions. There are three phases to the response. The alarm reaction is the first phase, consisting of a series of related and appropriate physiological phenomena. The stage of resistance, the second phase, is reached when these adjustments have stabilized and the adaptation is optimal. If the organism is exposed to continued stressor stimulation sustained over time, the third stage, the stage of exhaustion, may be reached. Adequate appropriate response is no longer possible. I refer to this three-stage sequence as the General Adaptation Syndrome.

Life in an advanced technological society such as ours exposes the individual to a barrage of excessive stimulation, often of stressor intensity, and to assault after assault of stressor situations. Circumstances usually preclude simple animal flight. Under these conditions, individuals turn with varying fervor to activities promising respite from a stressor environment or relief from a stressed state, however transient the effect may be.

I view this universal tendency in man as a defensive mechanism, and I have labeled these activities inclusively as deviational or diversional tendencies. I prefer the latter of the two labels because there is a misleading implication of a value judgement in the former. These activities vary in degree of disruptiveness or intrusiveness upon ongoing life styles, ranging from innocuous mannerisms such as pencil or foot tapping at the one extreme to devastating heroin or alcohol addiction at the other.

I view cigarette smoking as being of the class of diversional activity. It is but one of a host of choices at the disposal of the individual, and I would emphasize that the choice man faces is not one of "Yes" or "No," but one of "Which." The choice is not "to smoke or not to smoke," but whether to smoke, or to overeat, to drink, to drive on polluted and crowded highways, or merely to fret and bite our fingernails to avoid boredom and give vent to our pent-up energy. Man must weigh the pros and cons of any diversional activity; he must undertake his own benefit/risk analysis, and act accordingly. If you take aspirin, you accept its potentially dangerous effect on platelet adhesiveness in exchange for the relief of pain. A woman using contraceptives accepts their undesirable side effects in exchange for protection against an unwanted pregnancy and the risks of childbearing. The value of diversion has been well shown by various forms of "nonspecific therapy," many of which (insulin shock, metrazol shock, electroshock, extreme hot or cold bath, etc.) are unpleasant or even highly dangerous.

Few investigators have made a point of the possible benefits of smoking; yet, as I have said in my testimony before the Canadian Senate, there would be no need to create a committee on smoking if nobody found cigarettes advantageous or desirable. Certainly smoking is one of the diversional activities which, to many people, has proved to be so much more useful than complete rest after exposure to severe stress.

I offer cigarettes to postgraduate candidates when they present themselves for interviews, because I find that it relaxes them and they speak more easily.

The soldier will smoke before battle.

A salesman I met on a plane told me that he always smokes when he has an important conversation with a potential buyer.

It is hardly necessary to enumerate more examples of conditions under which people naturally turn to cigarettes as a means of diversion. They do so instinctively, as it were, whenever one organ system or the other is under excessive and unbalanced stress in proportion to the rest of the body.

As a preview of what is contained in this volume, let me just quote at random remarks from a few chapters which I believe fit in very well with my own thoughts as just outlined.

Eysenck in Chapter 8 suggests that "different people smoke for different reasons, some to arouse and others to quiet themselves, under stress."

Hutchinson and Emley, in Chapter 11, state that the intake of nicotine "produces a differential reduction in the tendencies toward aggressiveness, hostility, and irritability."

Heimstra, in Chapter 12, states, "The data from these studies strongly suggest that smoking will modify mood states, or, more specifically, will tend to reduce fluctuation or change in mood."

Thomas, in Chapter 10 writes, "It therefore seems not unreasonable to conclude that adolescents who are outgoing and desire to obtain social acceptance are often aware of anxiety and anger in situations of stress, and that cigarette smoking, particularly heavy cigarette smoking, stems in large part from the inner need to cope with their negative affect."

Ryan, in Chapter 16, states, "We have also noticed that, under stress conditions in our laboratory, highly anxious subjects tend to smoke more than nonanxious subjects, with the interval between their puffs reflecting the state of tension they are experiencing."

Brown, in Chapter 5, states, "There is growing evidence that nicotine, and/or possibly an integral part of the smoking act, exerts a tranquilizing action on the central nervous system."

All of these passages allude to smoking as a response occurring in the context of a stressed state or a stressor situation. Perhaps no one explanatory model will suffice to account for all smoking behavior, but whatever the ultimate explanation or explanations, we can certainly say at this point in time that the smoker finds smoking a gratifying experience.

2

NEUROPSYCHOPHARMACOLOGY OF NICOTINE AND TOBACCO SMOKING[1]

Edward F. Domino
University of Michigan, Ann Arbor
Lafayette Clinic, Detroit

INTRODUCTION

The reasons people smoke tobacco are complex, involving psychological, social, pharmacological, and economic factors. Economic, psychological, and social factors clearly determine which brands of cigarettes are most popular in the United States. One only needs to plot the amount of money the American tobacco industry spent on advertising in 1970 (Advertising Age, 1971) versus estimated domestic cigarette consumption by brand and company (Maxwell Report, 1971) to realize (see Figures 1 and 2) that money spent on advertising is better correlated with domestic cigarette consumption than is nicotine or tar content (U. S. Department of Health, Education, and Welfare, 1970). Data for 1970 were chosen because of the TV ban on cigarette advertising in 1971.

Even before the days of mass advertising, man managed to smoke hundreds of different substances, either by accident or on the recommendation of fellow men. It is remarkable that of the many substances humans have smoked in the past, relatively few have been sufficiently reinforcing to cause the behavior to persist. The few plants which are consistently smoked by humans contain very potent, pharmacologically active chemicals, such as morphine in opium, nicotine in tobacco, and tetrahydrocannabinol in marijuana. A common postulate is that it is the peculiar pharmacology of each of these compounds that reinforces smoking behavior. All tobacco-containing cigarettes which are widely sold in the United States have sufficient nicotine—0.2 to 2.2 mg per cigarette (U.S. Department of Health, Education and Welfare, 1970)—to produce definite pharmacological effects. Apparently there is an optimal dose of nicotine, for too little or too much is rejected by tobacco smokers. Some therapeutic programs to induce smokers to

[1] Supported in part by the Council for Tobacco Research, U.S.A., Inc.

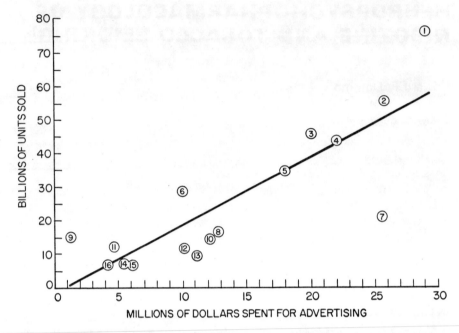

FIG. 1. Relation of money spent on advertising to total sales of top 16 cigarette brands in the United States in 1970. Each point is numbered and represents the following: 1–Winston; 2–Pall Mall; 3–Marlboro; 4–Salem; 5–Kool; 6–Camel; 7–Kent; 8–Viceroy; 9–Lucky Strike; 10–Tareyton; 11–Raleigh; 12–L&M; 13–Benson and Hedges; 14–Bel Air; 15–Lark; 16–Chesterfield. The data were obtained from Advertising Age (1971) and Maxwell (1971).

stop include nicotine injections (Ejrup & Wikander, 1959; Ejrup, 1965) and nicotine substitutes (Ejrup & Wikander, 1959; London, 1963).

There are several studies however, which indicate that there is more to tobacco smoking than the intake of nicotine. Lucchesi, Schuster, and Emley (1967) infused nicotine intravenously into normal tobacco smokers who were unaware of the true nature of the experiment or the drugs given. Subjects performed a number of psychological tests throughout a 6-hour experimental session. Several physiological parameters, such as blood pressure and heart rate, were also monitored. Commercial tobacco cigarettes (each subject's own brand) were easily available as part of the "care" provided to make the subjects as comfortable as possible. In actual fact, the number of cigarettes smoked during saline or nicotine infusion was the critical variable being measured. With saline, five subjects smoked 6 to 18 cigarettes for a 6-hour period. Assuming each subject received about 20 μg/kg of nicotine per cigarette, this would be about 1.4 mg total of nicotine per cigarette. Pierce (1941) and Harlan and Mosekey (1955) estimated the mainstream smoke of an "average" tobacco cigarette in those days contained 1.2 to 3 mg of nicotine. Perhaps the 1.4 mg calculated is too high these days. In any event, it would mean that the subjects in the Lucchesi et al. (1967) study voluntarily inhaled 8.4 to 25.2 mg of nicotine for the total 6-hour period under saline infusion. During the course of the 6-hour test period when nicotine was infused, each subject received intravenously 22 mg of nicotine (2 mg per hour for the first hour, and 4 mg per hour for the next 5 hours). Nicotine infusion significantly decreased the number of cigarettes smoked. The decrease averaged about 2.7 cigarettes per subject. In additon to a reduction in the total number of cigarettes smoked, there was a decrease in the amount each cigarette was smoked. Intermittent infusions of nicotine (1 mg per 14 minutes) to mimic cigarette smoking were also effective in reducing cigarette smoking in three of four subjects tested. A dose of 12 mg of nicotine over the 6-hour test period was effective in the fourth subject.

Jarvik, Glick, and Nakamura (1970) reached similar conclusions to Lucchesi et al. (1967) using oral nicotine. Seventeen paid chronic tobacco smokers were given capsules containing 10 mg of nicotine tartrate and identical-looking placebos. The subjects were unaware of the content of each. Five capsules were taken per day. Nicotine was taken on the first and fourth days by half of the subjects, and on the second and third days by the other half. All subjects smoked their own brands of cigarettes ad libitum. Subjective estimates of "strength" and "quality" were obtained, number of cigarettes smoked was recorded, and butt length was measured. Oral nicotine produced a small but significant (8%) decrease in the number of cigarettes smoked. There was no change in the average strength and quality of cigarettes smoked. Smokers who tended to smoke more of a cigarette showed a greater decrease by oral nicotine than those with a high butt weight. In a related study, Goldfarb, Jarvik, and Glick (1970) measured smoking rate and

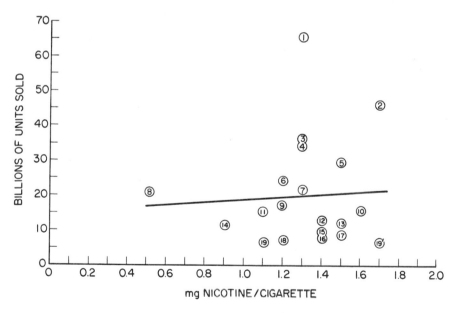

FIG. 2. Relation of nicotine content per cigarette to total sales of top 20 cigarette brands in the United States in 1970. Each point is numbered and represents the following: 1–Winston (soft pack); 2–Pall Mall; 3–Salem; 4–Kool; 5–Camel; 6–Marlboro (king, hard pack); 7–Marlboro (king, soft pack); 8–Kent; 9–Viceroy; 10–Lucky Strike; 11–Tareyton; 12–Winston (100s); 13–Raleigh; 14–L&M; 15–Pall Mall (100s); 16–Benson and Hedges; 17–Salem; 18–Bel Air; 19–Lark; 19'–Chesterfield. The data were obtained from Maxwell (1971) and U.S. Department of Health; Education, and Welfare (1970).

obtained subjective estimates of "strength" and "quality" of cigarettes of varying nicotine content in 15 chronic smokers. The subjects were divided into three different groups and were asked to smoke and to rate their own brand of tobacco versus lettuce cigarettes of 0, 1.26, and 2.25 mg nicotine added per cigarette. Each week the groups smoked a different batch of cigarettes. They had no knowledge of the content of the experimental cigarettes. All groups showed a decrease in smoking rate for all experimental cigarettes compared to smoking their own brand, regardless of nicotine content. Most subjects could detect the nicotine added to the lettuce cigarettes as measured by the "stronger taste," but "strength" measures were very close. The "quality" ratings showed that all of the experimental lettuce cigarettes were aversive, irrespective of nicotine content. Interestingly, when the subjects finished all of the experimental cigarettes, they also showed decreased satisfaction and rate of smoking with their own brand of cigarettes as well. Especially important is that even though the subjects disliked the experimental cigarettes, they continued to smoke them at a high rate. Either there is a high degree of dissociation of smoking behavior from nicotine content, or the subjects are unconsciously attempting to achieve "adequate" dose levels of nicotine by smoking more. Evidence for the latter is provided by Ashton and Watson (1970). These investigators studied the smoking behavior of 36 subjects who were given cigarettes with filters of differing nicotine-removal efficiency. The subjects were observed during performance on a driving simulator and at rest. During both behavioral situations, smokers of cigarettes with high-retention filters took more frequent puffs and therefore obtained nearly the same amount of nicotine as smokers of cigarettes with low-retention filters. The results support the notion that smokers automatically adjust the nicotine dose from cigarettes to an "optimal" level. The findings, consistent with much behavioral data in animals indicate that the operant rate of self-administration of a large variety of reinforcing drugs, as different as alcohol, amphetamine, barbiturates, cocaine, and morphine, is related to an optimal total daily intake.[2] Animals adjust their rate of self-administration of positively reinforcing drugs depending upon the dose per injection. Because of its commercial importance to the tobacco industry and because of its medical implications, it is of special importance that with low concentrations of a reinforcing drug, operant rate of responding is increased. In fact, Schuster and Lucchesi (personal communication, 1971) have some unpublished data indicating that subjects will smoke more low- than high-nicotine cigarettes of the same type of tobacco. It appears that the current fashion to switch to low-nicotine cigarettes, within limits, will promote an increased consumption of such cigarettes! This may explain the continued economic success of the tobacco industry in the face of publication of nicotine and tar content of various brands. The studies by Lucchesi et al. (1967) and by Jarvik and associates (1970) support the earlier findings of Johnston (1942) that nicotine administration influences human tobacco-smoking behavior. Finnegan, Larson, and Haag (1945), Herxheimer, Griffiths, Hamilton, and Wakefield (1967), and Goldfarb et al. (1970) have shown that one can detect

[2] C. R. Schuster. Self-administration of CNS stimulants. In J. E. Villarreal & C. R. Schuster (Eds.), *Reinforcement mechanisms and drugs.* In preparation.

differences in nicotine content in various cigarettes on the basis of psychological and physiological measures. Nevertheless, nicotine played only a small role in determining smoking rate under the experimental conditions of Finnegan et al. (1945), Lucchesi et al. (1967), and Goldfarb et al. (1970). The role of tachyphylaxis to intravenous or oral nicotine, the aversive nature of lettuce cigarettes, and the role of abstinence all confound the relative importance of nicotine content. Under conditions of tobacco deprivation, conceivably the role of nicotine might be much greater. Obviously, other highly significant factors contribute to the tobacco-smoking habit besides the pharmacology of nicotine (Larson, Haag, & Silvette, 1961). These include (a) psychological, (b) social, and (c) economic considerations, as well as (d) stimulation of the senses by other constituents of tobacco smoke. However, as a pharmacologist, my own bias is to study the pharmacological factors, and especially those affecting the brain.

The pharmacology of nicotine and tobacco smoking is very complex (Larson et al., 1961; DiPalma, 1971; Goodman & Gilman, 1970). Nicotine acts on the cardiovascular, nervous, gastrointestinal, and endocrine systems. Armitage, Hall, and Morrison (1968) and Jarvik (1970) have provided evidence for nicotine as the pharmacological basis of tobacco smoking. It is obvious that we need much more research to unravel the relative importance of the multiple actions of nicotine in doses inhaled during tobacco smoking. In agreement with these investigators, it is my basic premise that one of the many reasons people smoke tobacco is that it contains nicotine. An extension of that premise is that the doses of nicotine inhaled produce definite, mild, and transient neuropsychopharmacological effects which are positively reinforcing and thus promote repetition of smoking. These effects include: (a) modulation of conditioned behavior; (b) mixed depression and facilitation of the neural substrates of reward; (c) transient (in minutes) EEG and behavioral arousal crudely reminiscent of d-amphetamine but pharmacologically quite different; and at the same time (d) skeletal muscle relaxation. This chapter will describe the evidence, both animal and human, which has been accumulated in our laboratory to support these notions.

BEHAVIORAL EFFECTS IN ANIMALS

Effects of Nicotine on Conditioned Behavior in Rats

Since the review by Silvette, Hoff, Larson, and Haag (1962) on the actions of nicotine on the central nervous system, many behavioral studies have been performed which support the generalization that nicotine, depending upon dose, may facilitate or depress behavior. In our experience (Domino, 1965), small doses of nicotine have no consistent effect on established conditioned pole-jump behavior in the rat (less than 250 µg/kg subcutaneously) or shock-avoidance behavior in monkeys (40 µg/kg intravenously). Acquisition of pole-jump behavior in the rat was very slightly facilitated by 40 µg/kg and depressed by 80 µg/kg of nicotine, subcutaneously. Nicotine in doses above 250 µg/kg consistently depressed established pole-jump avoidance behavior, producing a more selective depression of avoidance than of escape behavior (Figure 3). These selective effects of large doses of nicotine on avoidance behavior are reminiscent of the actions of neuroleptic

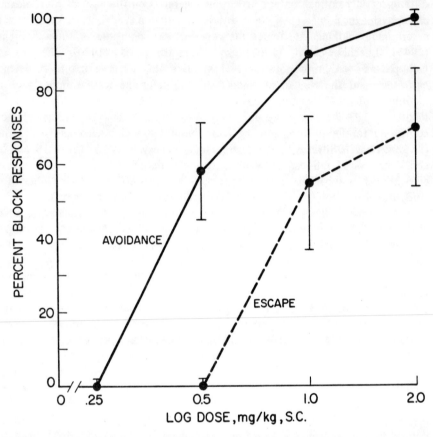

FIG. 3. Effects of nicotine on established conditioned pole jumping in rats. Each point represents the mean avoidance responses ±s.e. of six different rats given five trials each. The effects were measured 5 minutes after subcutaneous (s.c.) nicotine. (From Domino, 1965.)

agents like chlorpromazine, and of narcotic analgesics like morphine, or tetrahydro-cannabinol, the putative active ingredient of marijuana. Interestingly nicotine is much more potent. It would appear that large doses of nicotine have some of the animal behavioral properties attributed to a "tranquilizer." The relevance of such large doses of nicotine given subcutaneously to the much smaller doses inhaled by man certainly is to be questioned.

Effects of Nicotine on the Neural Substrates of Reward

In view of the fact that rat pole-jumping is a relatively crude behavior, we subsequently studied the effects of nicotine on self-stimulation behavior. Our first study (Olds & Domino, 1969a) was on the differential effects of cholinergic agonists and antagonists on self-stimulation in rats with chronically implanted electrodes in the lateral posterior hypothalamus. Drug doses were given subcutaneously as base of readily available salts. Nicotine tartrate (25 to 600 μg/kg) caused biphasic effects. The initial depression was sometimes followed by facilitation, but the actions were much less consistent. The peak effects of nicotine were observed within 8 minutes after subcutaneous injection. The mean data for groups of six or more self-stimulating rats given increasing doses of nicotine are summarized in Figure 4 and Table 1. The effects were variable and transient but usually depressant. Unexpected biphasic effects were observed at 0.6 mg/kg of nicotine, although the overall trend of increasing doses of nicotine was to depress self-stimulation. Marked individual variation was observed. This is illustrated in Figure 5, where a dose of 600 μg/kg is shown to have caused a slight increase in bar pressing without the preceding depression in one animal (C) but not in another (D). After the transient depressant effects, there was some facilitation of responding at a dose of 0.2 mg/kg (Figure 4). At the higher doses an increase in responding was observed in some cases. However, the mean data show an overall depressant effect. The effects of various cholinergic antagonist pretreatments were determined against 600 μg/kg of nicotine given subcutaneously. Mecamylamine (5.0 mg/kg) and scopolamine (0.5 mg/kg) blocked the transient depressant effects of nicotine, whereas methscopolamine (0.5 mg/kg) and trimethidinium (5.0 mg/kg) did not.

It should be noted that Pradhan, Bowling, and Roth (1967), Bowling and Pradhan (1967), Pradhan and Bowling (1971), and Newman (1972) have consistently observed facilitating effects of nicotine on self-stimulation behavior in the rat. In fact, Newman was sufficiently impressed with the fact that nicotine

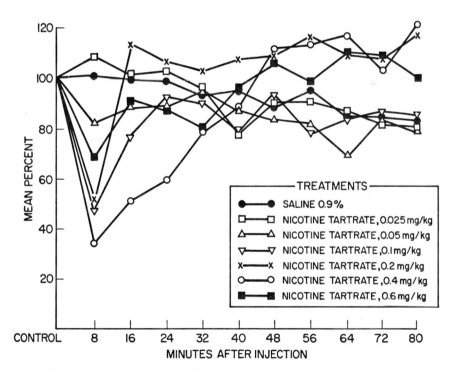

FIG. 4. Dose effect relationship of nicotine on posterior lateral hypothalamic stimulation. Note that a maximal depressant dose of nicotine was 0.4 mg/kg s.c. (From Olds & Domino, 1969a.)

TABLE 1

Dose-effect Relationship of Nicotine on Self-Stimulation Behavior in the Rat

Drug	Dose (s.c.), µg/kg	N	Control rate of self-stimulation, mean % ± s.e.	p value[a]
0.9% NaCl				
8 min.		22	100.7 ± 3.7	
16 min.		22	100.2 ± 5.2	
32 min.		22	94.3 ± 6.2	
Nicotine	25	7	108.7 ± 31.6	.7
8 min.	50	12	81.8 ± 7.6	.02
	100	14	46.5 ± 11.4	.001
	200	7	51.4 ± 13.4	.001
	400	8	32.5 ± 14.4	.001
	600	16	69.1 ± 12.6	.02

[a]Compared to saline at the same time. Student's t test.

tartrate in doses of 100 to 800 µg/kg given intraperitoneally to rats self-stimulating on a variable-interval 30-second schedule caused sufficient facilitation that he suggested nicotine acts through a central "go" mechanism. Our own data, although not contradicting the results of these investigators, show a strong initial depressant component of nicotine as well. In our experience the main effect of nicotine on self-stimulation is depressant. Only occasional animals show a consistent facilitating effect. These mixed effects are also evident in the dose-effect relationships of nicotine in which doses in the order of 400 to 600 µg/kg produced a maximal transient depressant effect. It should be emphasized that our studies involved highly overtrained, high-rate self-stimulators in which facilitating effects would be less likely to be observed because the animals were bar-pressing at almost maximal levels. However, even in animals which self-stimulated at relatively lower rates, no consistent facilitatory effects of nicotine were observed. The fact that mecamylamine and scopolamine, in contrast to trimethidinium and methscopolamine, were effective in blocking the depressant action of nicotine would suggest that the effects of nicotine involve primarily central cholinergic components. These studies should be compared to those described above in which nicotine appears to have a primary central depressant effect on established pole-jump behavior (Domino, 1965). This depression also was significantly blocked by mecamylamine, but not by trimethidinium. Furthermore, self-stimulation behavior was much more sensitive to nicotine than is either pole-jump or escape behavior from aversive stimuli to the midbrain (Olds & Domino, 1969b). Total doses of nicotine as low as 25 and 50 ug/kg subcutaneously showed effects on self-stimulation. This dose range is quite similar to doses smokers inhale. Of course, one must be cautious in generalizing that nicotine modifies the neural substrates of reward in the human brain. Clearly it does in the rat! The action of nicotine differs from the effects of d-amphetamine inasmuch as the latter produces a clear dose-effect increase in self-stimulation, with only large doses causing rate-depressant effects (Domino & Olds, 1972).

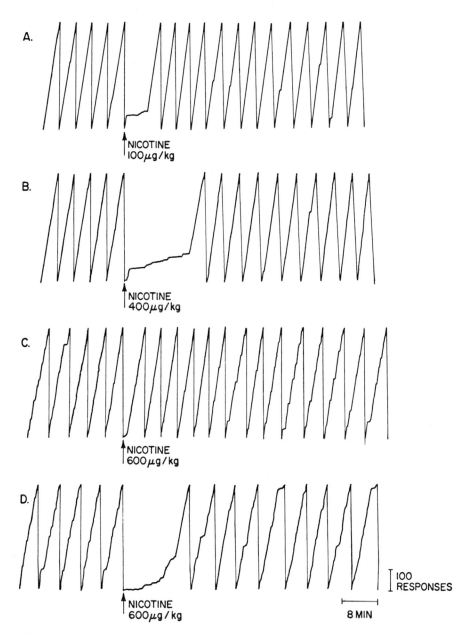

FIG. 5. Sample records of the effects of increasing doses of nicotine on self-stimulation. A through D represent the records of individual animals. Note that animals C and D were given the same dose of nicotine with markedly different effects. (From Olds & Domino, 1969a.)

Effects of Nicotine on Operant Responding as a Function of Rate

It is well known that baseline rate is an important determinant of the direction and extent of rate changes produced by certain drugs. Amphetamine is the most well known agent with important rate-dependent actions. At appropriate doses, amphetamine stimulates responding maintained at low baseline rates and depresses responding maintained at high baseline rates, irrespective of the type or schedule of reinforcement generating these rates (Kelleher & Morse, 1968). Morrison (1967), Morrison and Armitage (1967), and Bovet-Nitti (1965) pointed out the apparent similarity between the effects of nicotine and amphetamine on operant behavior. A differential effect of nicotine on low and high response rates within the same animal would be a powerful test of its possible amphetamine-like, rate-dependent effects. Therefore, we studied the effects of nicotine on operant responding maintained in rats by a fixed-interval 88-second schedule of water reinforcement (Stitzer, Morrison, & Domino, 1970). Nicotine was given subcutaneously immediately prior to the experimental session in doses of 0.05 to 0.4 mg/kg. The drug produced an initial cessation of responding, the duration of which was dose-related. The length of this depression initially decreased over successive injections of 0.4 mg/kg of nicotine. After the initial depression, local rates of fixed-interval responding were altered during nicotine sessions. Baseline rates below 20 responses/minute were variably affected; whereas, rates above 30 responses/minute were reliably depressed. The degree of rate depression was dose-related. The actions of 0.4 mg/kg of nicotine were compared to equal doses of d-amphetamine. At this dose, nicotine produced more depression of high rates than did d-amphetamine, whereas d-amphetamine was more effective than nicotine in elevating low rates. The relationship between baseline rate and the effect of nicotine was not invariant. In particular, rate elevation could not be predicted entirely from baseline rates of responding. The nature of the factors which determine whether elevation or depression of rates follows nicotine administration and the type of interactions that exist between these nicotine responses is not clear. It appears that baseline response rate is at least one determinant of the behavioral action of nicotine. In some animals, nicotine's rate effects were shown to be qualitatively similar to those produced by 0.4 mg/kg of d-amphetamine. It is perhaps surprising that these two drugs with distinctly different pharmacological properties should have produced similar rate changes in behavior maintained by a fixed-interval schedule. However, elevation of low rates and depression of high rates is a characteristic effect of several other pharmacologic agents including imipramine, cocaine, and chlordiazepoxide.

NEUROLOGICAL EFFECTS IN ANIMALS

Actions on the Brainstem Activating System

Nicotine in small doses equivalent to those inhaled in tobacco smoke has a marked but short-lasting stimulant effect on the brainstem-activating system of various animals (Knapp & Domino, 1962). This effect on the EEG is illustrated in Figure 6. Within 1 minute after the intravenous injection of 20 μg/kg of nicotine, EEG activation rapidly occurs in acute-midbrain-transected animals. Within 4

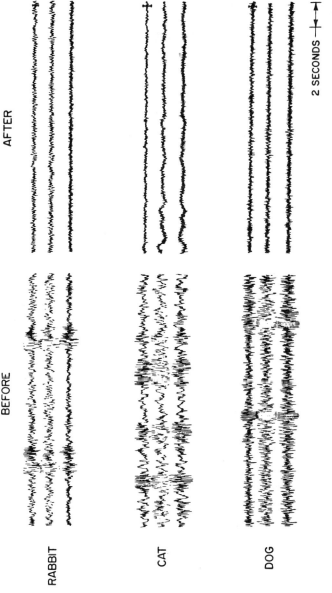

FIG. 6. Effect of nicotine upon the EEG of the midpontine rabbit, cat, and dog. Intravenous injection of 20 μg/kg of nicotine produced EEG activation within one minute after injection in all species tested. Channels 1, 2, and 3 are respectively monopolar right somatosensory area, monopolar left somatosensory area, and bipolar right to left somatosensory areas. Vertical calibration bars, 100 microvolts. (From Knapp & Domino, 1962.)

minutes spindle bursts return, often more prominent than before nicotine injection.

Evidence that EEG activation involves an action of nicotine directly on the brainstem reticular formation has been summarized previously (Domino, 1967; Kawamura & Domino, 1969). A critical area of the midbrain reticular formation is involved. In a high-rostral-midbrain-transected cat, 20-40 μg/kg of nicotine does not produce significant activation in the hippocampus, although similar doses cause marked activation of both neocortex and hippocampus in the intact-or caudal-midbrain-transected cat. In the high-rostral-midbrain-transected preparation without trimethidinium pretreatment, 20 μg/kg of nicotine induces a marked hypertension associated with sporadic sharp waves localized to the hippocampus. After 1 mg/kg of trimethidinium, the pressor response to nicotine is completely blocked and no EEG change is seen in the hippocampus. With large doses of 200 to 500 μg/kg, hippocampal sharp waves are sometimes followed by seizure discharge.

If the midbrain is transected caudally at the junction of the pons, nicotine induces neocortical desynchronization as well as hippocampal regular slow "arousal" waves. Such EEG activation is induced by nicotine even when blood pressure remains constant by pretreatment with trimethidinium. Whenever a blood pressure change has been observed, the EEG changes have been of longer duration and have consisted of waves of higher frequency. After bilateral lesions of the midbrain tegmentum, the EEG-activating effect of nicotine is completely blocked. Figure 7 illustrates this phenomenon in a preparation in which the caudal midbrain was transected. To further eliminate from the periphery afferent impulses which might cause activation, the optic nerves and olfactory tracts were cut bilaterally in three cats. Similar results were obtained indicating that these afferents have no effect on forebrain activation induced by nicotine or arecoline.

In intact animals nicotine, in doses of 20 μg/kg intravenously, induced marked hypertension (up to 200 mm Hg) with bradycardia, simultaneous desynchronization of the neocortical EEG, and enhancement of hippocampal regular slow "arousal" waves, as illustrated in the recording in the upper panel of Figure 7. After pretreatment with 1 mg/kg) of trimethidinium 1 hour previously, a second dose of nicotine (20 μg/kg) produced no change in blood pressure, but neocortical desynchronization and hippocampal "arousal" waves still appeared. However, the duration of activation and the frequency of the EEG waves were lower than before trimethidinium. Bilateral electrolytic lesions of the midbrain reticular formation in such preparations completely prevented the EEG actions of nicotine even in doses of 100 μg/kg. This finding indicates that the reticular formation is critical to the action of nicotine on the EEG. In agreement with this is the observation of Bradley and Wolstencroft (1967) that iontophoretic injection of nicotine in the brainstem activates some neurons. It should be remembered that both EEG activation and acetylcholine release can occur following systemic nicotine, although the two phenomena can be dissociated (Armitage, Hall, & Sellers, 1969).

The EEG-activating effect of nicotine superficially resembles that of d-amphetamine, but differs from it in regard to its shorter duration of action, specificity of antagonists and extent of brainstem involved. Furthermore, in cats with chronic indwelling electrodes, nicotine EEG activation is accompanied by a brief behavioral arousal and followed by a subsequent increase in REM sleep (Domino & Yamamoto, 1965; Yamamoto & Domino, 1965, 1967). Although d-amphetamine

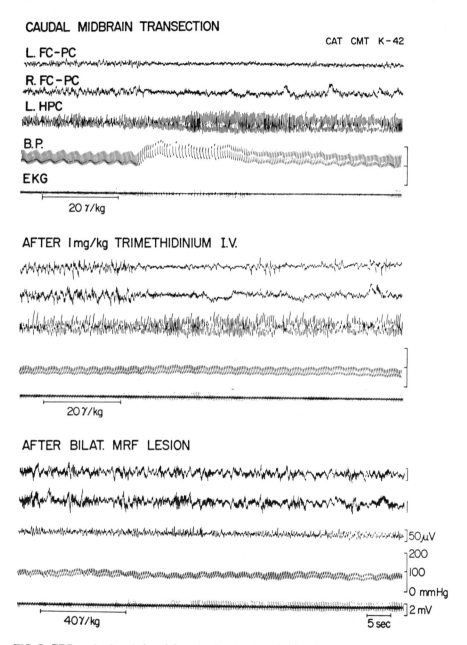

FIG. 7. EEG activation induced by nicotine in the caudal-midbrain-transected cat. Upper panel: the i.v. injection of 20 μg/kg of nicotine produced marked hypertension and dramatic EEG activation both in the neocortex and hippocampus. Middle panel: 1 hour after 1 mg/kg of trimethidinium i.v., the same dose of nicotine still produced EEG activation in the absence of a change in blood pressure. The intensity of EEG activation was not as great, although still clearly evident. Lower panel: after bilateral lesions of the midbrain reticular formation, even a larger dose of nicotine (40 μg/kg) did not activate the EEG. This was true even though the interval between nicotine injections was more than 1½ hours to avoid tachyphylaxis. (From Kawamura & Domino, 1969.)

also increases behavioral arousal, this lasts much longer. Furthermore, d-amphetamine decreases REM sleep. Thus the two drugs have only superficial neuropharmacological similarities.

Action on the Lateral Geniculate Nucleus of the Visual System

Phillis (1970) has recently summarized the data that acetylcholine has neurotransmitter role at the lateral geniculate nucleus. Our own experiments[3] suggest that both muscarinic and nicotinic cholinergic mechanisms are involved. With Matsuoka (Matsuoka & Domino, 1972) we studied the effects of intravenous nicotine (25 μg/kg) on the activity of single lateral geniculate neurons in acute cats. Most of the lateral geniculate neurons selected were P-cells. These increased their responses to ipsilateral optic tract and midbrain reticular formation stimulation. Nicotine in doses equivalent to those obtained from tobacco smoking significantly increased the spontaneous firing rate of single geniculate neurons. Spontaneous firing rates of unit responses were recorded 2 minutes after 25 μg/kg of nicotine. After nicotine, the mean arterial blood pressure rose rapidly to about 60 to 88 mm Hg above control levels and lasted for about 60 to 80 seconds. Nicotine caused 14 units to increase their mean spontaneous firing rate ± s.e. to 38.0 ± 4.2/second. This value was significantly higher than for the control group (22.3 ± 1.9, $p < 0.001$). The effects of nicotine were blocked by mecamylamine (2 mg/kg), but only reduced by trimethidinium, suggesting that this effect was mediated primarily through the central nervous system. Of course this could be either a direct or an indirect effect of nicotine on lateral geniculate neurons. Therefore, we investigated the direct effects of nicotine applied iontophoretically to lateral geniculate neurons (Roppolo, Kawamura, & Domino, 1970). Cats were anesthetized with pentobarbital or were locally anesthetized, decamethonium-paralyzed, and artificially ventilated. The characteristic effect of iontophoretically applied nicotine was a long-lasting neuronal discharge after a latency of 30 seconds to 1 minute. Tachyphylaxis was observed when nicotine was applied repeatedly to the same cell. This is illustrated in Figure 8. A rate meter counted the firing of the lateral geniculate cell. The output of the rate meter was recorded on a polygraph. An upward deflection indicates an increase in neuronal firing. Note that acetylcholine, glutamate, and nicotine all produced an increased rate of firing. Repeated applications of nicotine showed rapid tachyphylaxis, but glutamate did not. The fact that nicotine can directly excite lateral geniculate neurons indicates still another locus of action of this remarkable drug.

Action on Renshaw Interneurons in the Spinal Cord

Recently Phillis (1970) has summarized the extensive investigations on the nicotinic and muscarinic cholinergic receptors on Renshaw inhibitory neurons in the spinal cord. The recurrent collateral-Renshaw cell synapse is of special significance, for it represents one of the first sites where there is convincing evidence that acetylcholine is a neurotransmitter in the central nervous system. This

---

[3] E. F. Domino. Evidence for a functional role of acetylcholine in the lateral geniculate nucleus. In H. C. Sabelli (Ed.), *James E. P. Toman memorial volume*. In preparation.

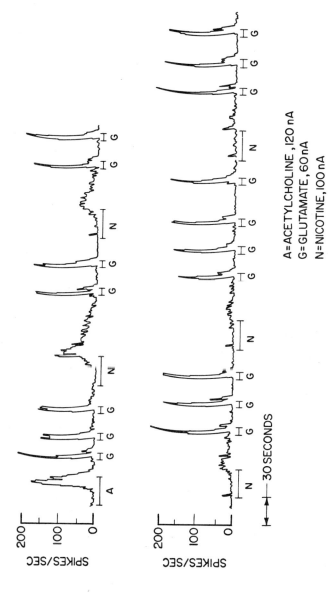

FIG. 8. Tachyphylaxis to iontophoretically applied nicotine to a lateral geniculate neuron. An upward deflection of the polygraph pen indicates the number of neuronal spikes/second recorded. The lengths of the horizontal lines indicate the duration of acetylcholine (A), glutamate (G) and nicotine (N) application. The iontophoretic current is given in nanoamperes (nA). Time base is as shown. Note that all three chemicals cause excitation of this neuron. However, repeated administrations of nicotine show rapid tachyphylaxis, but glutamate does not.

19

neuronal system in the spinal cord is also of great significance to those interested in the pharmacology of tobacco smoking, because very small intravenous doses of nicotine are capable of exciting Renshaw neurons. We have shown that these effects of nicotine are blocked by mecamylamine (Ueki, Koketsu, & Domino, 1961). In pentobarbital-anesthetized cats, normally minimal to no spontaneous Renshaw cell discharges are seen. After the intravenous administration of 20 μg/kg of nicotine, a very marked increase in spontaneous cell discharge occurs. This is illustrated in Figure 9. In panel A, before nicotine, no spontaneous discharge of a Renshaw cell was seen. Within 2 minutes after nicotine, marked spontaneous Renshaw cell activity was observed (Figure 9, panel B). Mecamylamine in doses of 1 mg/kg was very effective in reducing the spontaneous discharge, as illustrated in panels C, D, and E. This effect of mecamylamine was very rapid, occuring within 1 minute. Hexamethonium in doses of 5 to 10 mg/kg intravenously was less effective than mecamylamine in reducing Renshaw cell discharge, suggesting central but also some peripheral components of action.

EFFECTS OF TOBACCO SMOKING AND NICOTINE ON THE PATELLAR REFLEX IN MAN

Tobacco Smoking

Some time ago the author attempted to record the EEG of a very tense and anxious patient. After the patient smoked a tobacco cigarette, the amount of EMG artifact was dramatically reduced. This anecdotal experience plus our previous data (Ueki et al., 1961) indicating that nicotine stimulated Renshaw cell discharge (which would inhibit motor anterior horn cells) prompted a review of the literature. We were impressed that Webster (1964) reported that cigarette smoking causes a dramatic and transient reduction in skeletal muscle tone in spastic patients. We decided to reinvestigate the effects of tobacco smoking on skeletal muscle tone. This was measured quantitatively by the amplitude of the patellar reflex and the EMG of the quadriceps femoris muscle (Domino & von Baumgarten, 1969). A similar study was reported independently by Clark and Rand (1968). It is well known that low doses of nicotine produce a dramatic reduction of the patellar reflex in animals. The mechanisms are complex, involving both central and peripheral components (Ginzel, 1967; Ginzel, Eldred, Watanabe, & Grover, 1970; Ginzel, Watanabe, & Eldred, 1970).

In our first study, the experiments were performed on 115 healthy men between 17 and 29 years of age. The experimental sessions were carried out in the morning. The subjects were asked not to smoke for 12 hours before the experiment. Those who did not comply were excluded from testing. The volunteers were classified as nonsmokers, light smokers (one to three cigarettes a day), moderate smokers (3 to 20 cigarettes a day), and heavy smokers (more than 20 cigarettes a day). Prior to the study, a complete medical examination was given to exclude those with physical or mental abnormalities. Four subjects were rejected because of hyporeflexia. Subjects taking drugs within 2 weeks of the experimental sessions were also excluded. Most of the subjects had breakfast several hours before. The experiment consisted of smoking two cigarettes with an interval of 25 minutes between. The

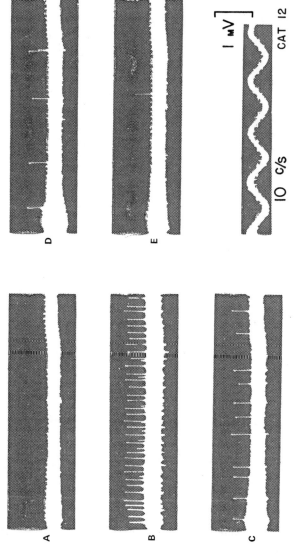

FIG. 9. Effects of nicotine and mecamylamine on spontaneous Renshaw cell activity. Panel A: no spontaneous discharges are noted. Panel B: 2 minutes after 20 µg/kg of nicotine given intravenously. Panel C: 15 seconds after 1.0 mg/kg of mecamylamine given intravenously. Panel D: 30 seconds later. Panel E: 1 minute after mecamylamine. The effect of nicotine is rapidly antagonized by mecamylamine. (From Ueki et. al., 1961.)

21

patellar reflex was elicited with a mechanical rubber-tipped hammer and was monitored before, during, and after smoking by recording simultaneously the isometric contraction with a Grass Model FT 10 strain gauge and the electromyogram of the quadriceps muscle by surface electrodes attached to the overlying skin. A polygraph was used for the recordings. Three different cigarettes with varying nicotine content were used. These were lettuce cigarettes which contained no nicotine, and tobacco cigarettes with a nicotine content of 0.80 and 1.69 mg per cigarette. In the beginning of the experimental series before nicotine-free cigarettes were available, sham smoking was performed by taking puffs from an unlighted cigarette or by inhaling air through a cotton-filled glass tube. A typical experiment consisted of a control period of 10 minutes during which the subject relaxed in a horizontal position with the use of pillows to make him as comfortable as possible. Smoking was started after 10 minutes or later, when relatively constant patellar reflex responses were obtained. The subject was advised to smoke each cigarette in a series of deep inhaling puffs within a period of 4 minutes. Each cigarette was smoked to approximately 2.5 cm butt length. The second cigarette was smoked 25 minutes after the first.

The patellar reflex was elicited mechanically every 2 seconds. The hammer exerted a pressure of about 0.5 kg upon hitting the patellar tendon. The knee joint was flexed to about 90 degrees during the resting state. The distal part of the lower leg was connected by a chain to the strain gauge. The surface electromyogram was recorded bipolarly with Grass EEG electrodes. One electrode was placed above the quadriceps muscle in the middle of the upper leg, and the other one was placed 1 cm proximal to the patella. The ground electrode was placed in the middle. An ac differential amplifier with a time constant of 0.1 millisecond and 100 microvolts per cm amplitude was used. Because the amplitude of the patellar reflex showed marked individual variation, all data were transformed as percentage of control. Only experiments in which a steady state of reflex responding was maintained for at least 5 minutes before tobacco smoking were included in these studies.

At the beginning of the experiment, marked variability of the patellar reflex was observed. With time, as the subject relaxed, a more constant reflex amplitude was obtained. Several subjects showed an actual increment during the first 10 minutes of recording. The experiments with sham smoking and with nicotine-free cigarettes revealed that when a steady state was reached within the first 10 to 15 minutes, no further habituation or accommodation appeared during the following 60 minutes of reflex recording.

The amplitude of the EMG of the quadriceps femoris was highly correlated with the amplitude of the mechanical response. Alteration of the respiratory pattern when smoking started led to slight changes in reflex activity. In most cases, an early slight facilitation of the patellar reflex was observed beginning almost immediately after smoking. However, the facilitation was quite variable. Some individuals showed an early slight depression instead. The mean of 20 cases showed an increase of about 11 % reflex activity during the first 15 seconds after beginning smoking.

Subjects who smoked nicotine-containing cigarettes invariably obtained a marked depression of the patellar reflex as recorded mechanically, as well as in the EMG response, as illustrated in Figure 10. A portion of the actual record from a typical subject is shown to illustrate the response to both types of cigarettes.

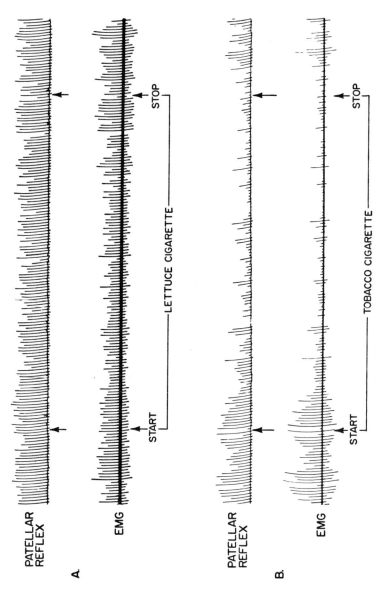

FIG. 10. Portions of a typical polygraph tracing of the isometric recording of the patellar reflex and the EMG response of the quadriceps femoris muscle to smoking a tobacco and a lettuce cigarette. Note the marked corespondence of the amplitude of muscle tension and EMG. The time base represents the tapping of a patellar tendon automatically every 2 seconds. During the 4-minute period, the two cigarettes were smoked to approximately the same butt length of 2.5 cm.
(From Domino & von Baumgarten, 1969.)

Following a nicotine-containing cigarette, depression of the patellar reflex was observed about 30 seconds after the initial facilitation (if there was any). The depression of the patellar reflex was progressive and reached its peak at the end of smoking. The depression was always greater during the first minute than during the last 3 minutes of smoking. After smoking, the patellar reflex remained depressed at the same level or increased slightly for a period of 30 to 120 seconds. Following this period of depression, progressive recovery was observed. The curve of recovery was steeper within the first 10 minutes than later. Twenty-five minutes after the end of smoking, the reflex response in all but one case returned toward control levels. When full recovery was obtained, the subject was asked to smoke a second cigarette of the same nicotine content. The induced depression of the patellar reflex

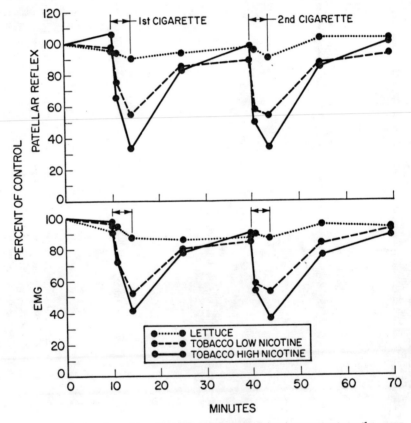

FIG. 11. Effects of smoking cigarettes of differing nicotine content on the mean patellar reflex and EMG. *Above:* mean patellar reflex. The dotted line represents the mean amplitude of 22 subjects smoking lettuce cigarettes. The dash line represents the mean amplitude of 19 subjects smoking low-nicotine-containing cigarettes. The solid line represents the mean amplitude of 16 subjects smoking high-nicotine-containing cigarettes. *Below:* electromyogram of the quadriceps femoris muscle. The data on the same subjects are plotted as above. (From Domino & von Baumgarten, 1969.)

quickly reappeared and resembled closely the depression following the first cigarette. The mean data of all subjects is illustrated in Figure 11. Marked mean differences in the depression of the patellar reflex were found according to the nicotine content of the cigarettes smoked. Nicotine-free cigarettes caused no more depression than that of normal habituation of the reflex during sham smoking. Cigarettes with a nicotine content of 0.80 mg produced about 45% depression of the patellar reflex. Cigarettes with a nicotine content of 1.69 mg produced 67% depression of normal.

In our experiments with sham smoking and nicotine-free cigarettes, no significant depression was noted in the majority of subjects. Inasmuch as one inhales a very large number of miscellaneous chemicals including CO, CO_2, etc., during smoking, the observed depression of the patellar reflex could be due to a large variety of substances other than nicotine. However, smoking nicotine-free lettuce cigarettes, which also cause the release of many products of pyrolysis, did not produce reflex depression. This makes unlikely an effect of such miscellaneous compounds. The fact that the high-nicotine-containing cigarettes were also more effective further supports the conclusion that the depression of the patellar reflex is due to the nicotine. Still, it would be nice to demonstrate that this effect can be seen with pure nicotine. Therefore, we began another study using a nicotine aerosol.

Nicotine Aerosol

The aerosol used was similar to that of Herxheimer et al. (1967) in their cardiovascular study. The experiments were performed on 10 healthy men between the ages of 23 and 56 years old. They were asked not to smoke at least 1 hour before the experiment. Subjects who proved in previous tests to be unable to inhale the aerosol, who showed signs of physical or mental unfitness, or who took any drugs or medication within the previous week were discarded. Others had to be rejected because a significant patellar reflex could not be recorded with our mechanical method. All subjects had breakfast several hours before the experiment. When the subjects felt pharyngeal irritation during inhalation of the aerosol, they were allowed to drink some water in order to overcome the tendency to cough. All subjects were smokers or had smoked cigarettes earlier, so they knew how to inhale. The recording method was identical to that described above. The subjects were placed in a recording chair rather than in a horizontal position as in the first study.

The patellar reflex was elicited until a steady-state amplitude was reached after approximately 10 minutes. Subjects who had a highly irregular patellar reflex or showed rapid habituation were discarded. Nicotine aerosol or an aerosol free of nicotine was used in a single blind design. The nicotine aerosol was obtained through the courtesy of Dr. W. F. Kirk, Head of Pharmaceutical Development of the Riker Laboratories in Leicestershire, England. Each plastic-coated glass vial contained not less than 12 ml (13.5 g) of a solution of nicotine alkaloid in aerosol propellent.

	Contents, mg/ml	mg/50-µl dose
Nicotine alkaloid B.P.C. 1934	1.25	0.0625
Ethanol B.P. (98%)	375.00	18.7500
Dichlorotetrafluorethane B.P.C. (Propellent 114)	448.75	22.4375
Dichlorodifluoromethane B.P.C. (Propellent 12)	300.00	15.000
Total	1125.00	56.2500

The specific gravity of the preparation was 1.125 at 20° C. The solution contained 1.25 mg/ml of nicotine alkaloid. The vials were fitted with metering valves which deliver 50 µl per shot. Each shot, therefore, contained 62.5 µg of nicotine alkaloid. The amount available from the adapter was about 50 µg due to loss in the adapter. The nicotine-free aerosol contained the same ingredients minus the nicotine. The subjects were instructed to inhale each shot and to take them at regular time intervals of 30 seconds. The total period of aerosol inhalation was 7 minutes and corresponded to a nicotine intake of 700 µg. The top 20 cigarette brands in 1970 delivered from 500 to 1,700 µg of nicotine (U.S. Federal Trade Commission, 1970). After nicotine inhalation, the patellar reflex was recorded for approximately 20 minutes more. At the end of this period, when the patellar reflex reached control levels, the inhalation experiment was repeated once more but this time with a placebo aerosol. This was unknown to the subject.

The inhalers caused subjective discomfort and had to be used over a longer period (7 as opposed to 4 minutes) than cigarette smoking. Subjects by far preferred cigarette smoking. Most coughed once or several times following inhalation of the aerosols. Synchronization between the release of the spray and inspiration was difficult. One subject complained of becoming ill during inhalation of the nonnicotine control spray, and the experiment had to be terminated prematurely. Most subjects complained more about pharyngeal irritation when the nicotine aerosol was used than when the placebo spray was used, even though they did not know which was which.

In typical experiments the amplitude of the patellar reflex decreased to about 70% of the control value within 1 minute after application of the nicotine aerosol, and to 60% of the control value 4 minutes after inhalation was started. One subject showed a depression to 40% within the first minute and another to 40% within 4 minutes. Figure 12 shows the mean data for 5 to 8 subjects. The complete data are summarized in Table 2. The reduction of the patellar reflex paralleled closely the depression of the EMG of the quadriceps femoris muscle. Recovery of the reflex began in all cases after aerosol inhalation stopped. Control amplitudes were usually reached 20 minutes after nicotine aerosol inhalation.

Inhalation of the nicotine-free aerosol also caused depression of the patellar reflex, but caused a much shallower depression of shorter duration. The differences between the effects of the two aerosols were clearly significant ($p < .05$).

In order to obtain data that the inhaled nicotine was pharmacologically effective, heart rate was recorded via Lead II of the electrocardiogram. After nicotine aerosol inhalation was started, the heart rate increased slightly in seven out of eight cases, and reached the control values after nicotine inhalation was stopped somewhat earlier than the patellar reflex.

The results of this study with a nicotine aerosol are very similar to the data obtained in the first study in which tobacco cigarettes were used. The data strongly suggest that the depression of the patellar reflex after cigarette smoking was caused by the nicotine content and not by the tar, CO, or CO_2 or other compounds present in tobacco smoke. Our first study also showed that the depression of the

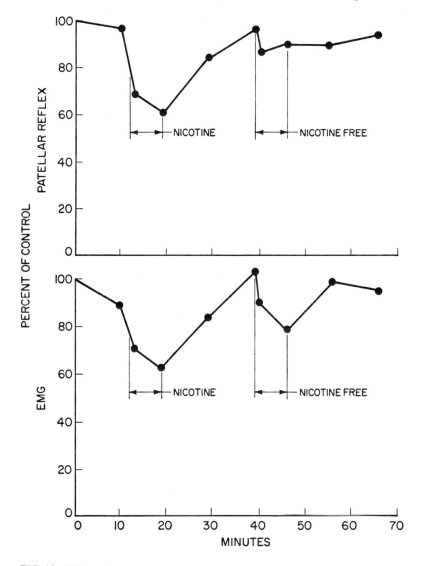

FIG. 12. Effects of inhaling a nicotine aerosol and nicotine-free aerosol on the mean patellar reflex and EMG. The mean patellar reflex is shown above, and the EMG of the quadriceps femoris muscle below. Both represent 100% as the control for five to eight subjects. Note that inhaling the nicotine aerosol gave a greater depression than the nicotine-free aerosol.

TABLE 2

Percent Change in Mean Amplitude of the Patellar Reflex and EMG of the Quadriceps Femoris
Muscle at Various Times After Inhaling Nicotine Aerosol and Nicotine-free Aerosol
in Normal Volunteers

Treatment	Parameter	Number of subjects	1st min. of inhalation	7th min. of inhalation	10th min. after inhalation	20th min. after inhalation
			Mean ± s.e.	Mean ± s.e.	Mean ± s.e.	Mean ± s.e.
Nicotine aerosol	PR	8	68.0 ± 6.3	61.5 ± 5.4	85.0 ± 14.4	97.9 ± 21.4
	EMG	6	71.4 ± 12.7	62.4 ± 12.8	83.9 ± 18.5	103.7 ± 30.1
Nicotine-free aerosol	PR	7	88.8 ± 17.3	91.2 ± 27.7	90.9 ± 11.8	94.1 ± 14.3
	EMG	5	90.1 ± 29.6	78.9 ± 25.5	98.8 ± 25.6	95.5 ± 25.5

patellar reflex was greater after smoking cigarettes with a high compared to a low nicotine content. There was a significant depression of the patellar reflex after inhalation of nicotine-free aerosol. However, it was smaller and of shorter duration. The mechanism of this aerosol-induced depression is unclear but may be related to the marked irritation and altered respiratory patterns caused by the aerosol. Also, one cannot exclude completely a one-trial conditioning effect as a possible cause of induced depression by the nicotine-free aerosol. After the nicotine aerosol, the patellar reflex was depressed less than after smoking a cigarette of high nicotine content. This can be explained by the nicotine dose given by aerosol (700 μg). This is only about half the content of the high-nicotine-containing cigarette (1600 μg). Our attempts to increase the inhaled nicotine dosage of the aerosol by increasing the number of applied puffs failed because of the discomfort caused. However, there is no doubt whatsoever that pure nicotine can reproduce the depression of the patellar reflex with tobacco smoking, and that this occurs in doses usually inhaled by the average tobacco smoker. The depression of the patellar reflex and probably of other myotatic reflexes involves phasic skeletal muscle responses. It would be important to determine if tonic muscle activity is reduced as well.

CONCLUSIONS

Besides the economic, psychological, and social factors which motivate people to smoke, there are pharmacological factors as well. The present report summarizes data for the neuropsychopharmacological effects of nicotine and tobacco smoking. These include mixed stimulation and depression of (a) conditioned behavior, (b) the neural substrates of reward, (c) transient EEG and behavioral arousal due to stimulation of the brainstem activating system, and (d) skeletal muscle relaxation.

REFERENCES

Advertising Age, 30 August 1971, 22.

Armitage, A. K., Hall, G. H., & Morrison, C. F. Pharmacological basis for the tobacco smoking habit. *Nature* (London), 1968, **217,** 311-334.

Armitage, A. K., Hall, G. H., & Sellers, C. M. Effects of nicotine on electrocortical activity and acetylcholine release from the cat cerebral cortex. *British Journal of Pharmacology,* 1969, **35,** 152-160.

Ashton, H., & Watson, D. W. Puffing frequency and nicotine intake in cigarette smokers. *British Medical Journal,* 1970, **3,** 679-681.

Bovet-Nitti, F. Action of nicotine on conditioned behavior in naive and pretrained rats. Part II. Complex forms of acquired behavior: Discussion. In U.S. von Euler (Ed.), *Tobacco alkaloids and related compounds.* New York: Macmillan, 1965.

Bowling, C., & Pradhan, S. N. Interaction of some drugs on nicotine-induced facilitation of self-stimulation in rats. *Pharmacologist,* 1967, **9,** 201.

Bradley, P. B., & Wolstencroft, J. H. Effects of acetylcholine, nicotine, and muscarine on brain stem neurons. *Annals of the New York Academy of Science,* 1967, **142,** 15-20.

Clark, M. S. G., & Rand, M. J. Effect of tobacco smoke on the knee-jerk reflex in man. *European Journal of Pharmacology,* 1968, **3,** 294-302.

DiPlama, J. R. (Ed.) *Drill's pharmacology in medicine.* (4th ed.) New York: McGraw-Hill, 1971.

Domino, E. F. Some behavioral actions of nicotine. In U.S. von Euler (Ed.), *Tobacco alkaloids and related compounds.* New York: Macmillan, 1965.

Domino, E. F. Electroencephalographic and behavioral arousal effects of small doses of nicotine: A neuropsychopharmacological study. *Annals of the New York Academy of Science,* 1967, **142,** 216-244.

Domino, E. F., & Olds, M. E. Effects of *d*-amphetamine, scopolamine, chlordiazepoxide, and diphenylhydantoin on self-stimulation behavior and brain acetylcholine. *Psychopharmacologia,* 1972, **23,** 1-16.

Domino, E. F., & von Baumgarten, A. M. Tobacco cigarette smoking and patellar reflex depression, *Clinical Pharmacology and Therapeutics,* 1969, **10,** 72-79.

Domino, E. F., & Yamamoto, K. I. Nicotine: Effect on the sleep cycle of the cat. *Science,* 1965, **150,** 637-638.

Ejrup, B. The role of nicotine in smoking pleasure, nicotinism, treatment. In U.S. von Euler (Ed.), *Tobacco alkaloids and related compounds.* New York: Macmillan, 1965.

Ejrup, B., & Wikander, P. A. Forsok med nicotin, lobelin och placebo. *Svenska Laekartidningen Forhandlingar,* 1959, **56,** 32.

Finnegan, J. K., Larson, P. S., & Haag, H. B. The role of nicotine in the cigarette habit. *Science* (Washington), 1945, **102,** 94-96.

Ginzel, K. H. Introduction to the effects of nicotine on the central nervous system. *Annals of the New York Academy of Science,* 1967, **142,** 101-120.

Ginzel, K. H., Eldred, E., Watanabe, S., & Grover, F. Drug-induced depression of gamma efferent activity. Part I. Peripheral reflexogenic effect of nicotine. *Neuropharmacology,* 1970, 9, 151-167.

Ginzel, K. H., Watanabe, S., & Eldred, E. Drug-induced depression of gamma efferent activity. Part II. Central action of nicotine. *Neuropharmacology,* 1970, **9,** 369-379.

Goldfarb, T. L., Jarvik, M. E., & Glick, S. D. Cigarette nicotine content as a determinant of human smoking behavior. *Psychopharmacologia,* 1970, **17,** 89-93.

Goodman, L. S., & Gilman, A. (Eds.) *The pharmacological basis of therapeutics.* (4th ed.) New York: Macmillan, 1970.

Harlan, W. R., & Mosekey, J. M. Tobacco. *Encyclopedia of Chemical Technology,* 1955, **14,** 242.

Herxheimer, A., Griffiths, R. L., Hamilton, B., & Wakefield, M. Circulatory effects of nicotine aerosol inhalations and cigarette smoking in man. *Lancet,* 1967, **2,** 754-755.

Jarvik, M. E. The role of nicotine in the smoking habit. In W. A. Hunt (Ed.), *Learning mechanisms in smoking.* Chicago: Aldine, 1970.

Jarvik, M. E., Glick, S. D., & Nakamura, R. K. Inhibition of cigarette smoking by orally administered nicotine. *Clinical Pharmacology and Therapeutics,* 1970, **11,** 574-576.

Johnston, L. M. Tobacco smoking and nicotine. *Lancet,* 1942, **2,** 742.

Kawamura, H., & Domino, E. F. Differential actions of *m* and *n* cholinergic agonists on the brainstem activating system. *International Journal of Neuropharmacology,* 1969, **8,** 105-115.

Kelleher, R. T., & Morse, W. H. Determinants of the specificity of behavioral effects of drugs. *Ergebisse der Physiologie, Biologischen Chemie und Experimentellen Pharmakologie,* 1968, **60,** 1-56.

Knapp, D. E., & Domino, E. F. Action of nicotine on the ascending reticular activiating system. *International Journal of Neuropharmacology,* 1962, **1,** 333-351.

Larson, P. S., Haag, H. B., & Silvette, H. *Tobacco: Experimental and clinical studies.* Baltimore: Williams & Wilkins, 1961.

London, S. J. Clinical evaluation of a new lobeline smoking deterrent. *Current Therapeutic Research: Clinical and Experimental,* 1963, **5,** 167-175.

Lucchesi, B. R., Schuster, C. R., & Emley, G. S. The role of nicotine as a determinant of cigarette smoking frequency in man with observations of certain cardiovascular effects associated with the tobacco alkaloid. *Clinical Pharmacology and Therapeutics,* 1967, **8,** 789-796.

Matsuoka, I., & Domino, E. F. Cholinergic modulation of single lateral geniculate neurons in the cat. *Neuropharmacology,* 1972, **11,** 241-251.

Maxwell, J. C., Jr. Maxwell's report for 1971: How the brands ranked in 1971. *Tobacco Reporter,* November 1971, 20-23.

Morrison, C. F. Effects of nicotine on operant behavior of rats. *International Journal of Neuropharmacology,* 1967, **6,** 229-240.

Morrison, C. F., & Armitage, A. K. Effects of nicotine upon the free operant behavior of rats and spontaneous motor activity of mice. *Annals of the New York Academy of Science,* 1967, **142,** 268-276.

Newman, L. M. The effects of cholinergic agonists and antagonists on self-stimulation behavior in the rat. *Journal of Comparative and Physiological Psychology,* 1972, **79,** 394–413.

Olds, M. E., & Domino, E. F. Comparison of muscarinic and nicotinic cholinergic agonists on self-stimulation behavior. *Journal of Pharmacology and and Experimental Therapeutics,* 1969, **166,** 189-204. (a)

Olds, M. E., & Domino, E. F. Differential effects of cholinergic agonists on self-stimulation and escape behavior. *Journal of Pharmacology and Experimental Therapeutics,* 1969, **170,** 157-167. (b)

Phillis, J. W. *The pharmacology of synapses.* New York: Pergamon Press, 1970.

Pierce, I. H. The absorption of nicotine from cigarette smoke. *Journal of Laboratory and Clinical Medicine,* 1941, **26,** 1322-1325.

Pradhan, S. N., & Bowling, C. Effects of nicotine on self-stimulation in rats. *Journal of Pharmacology and Experimental Therapeutics,* 1971, **176,** 229-243.

Pradhan, S. N., Bowling, C., & Roth, T. Some behavioral effects of nicotine in rats. *Federation Proceedings, Federation of American Societies for Experimental Biology,* 1967, **26,** 289.

Roppolo, J. R., Kawamura, H., & Domino, E. F. Effects of cholinergic agonists and antagonists on lateral geniculate nucleus neurons. *The Pharmacologist,* 1970, **12,** 270.

Silvette, H., Hoff, E. C., Larson, P. S. J., & Haag, H. B. The actions of nicotine on central nervous system functions. *Pharmacological Reviews,* 1962, **14,** 137-173.

Stitzer, M., Morrison, J., & Domino, E. F. Effects of nicotine on fixed-interval behavior and their modification by cholinergic antagonists. *Journal of Pharmacology and Experimental Therapeutics.,* 1970, **171,** 166-177.

Ueki, S., Koketsu, K., & Domino, E. F. Effects of mecamylamine on the Golgi recurrent collateral-Renshaw cell synapse in the spinal cord. *Experimental Neurology,* 1961, **3,** 141-148.

U.S. Department of Health, Education, and Welfare. (USPHS, GPO: 1970-0-410-207). National Clearinghouse for Smoking and Health. November, 1970.

U.S. Federal Trade Commission. Tar and nicotine content of cigarettes. Washington, D.C.: U.S. Government Printing Office, November, 1970.

Webster, D. D. The dynamic quantitation of spasticity with automated integrals of passive motion resistance. *Clinical Pharmacology and Therapeutics,* 1964, **5,** 900-908.

Yamamoto, K. I., & Domino, E. F. Nicotine-induced EEG and behavioral arousal. *International Journal of Neuropharmacology,* 1965, **4,** 359-373.

Yamamoto, K. I., & Domino, F. E. Cholinergic agonist-antagonist interactions on neocortical and limbic EEG activation. *International Journal of Neuropharmacology,* 1967, **6,** 357-373.

3

FURTHER OBSERVATIONS ON NICOTINE AS THE REINFORCING AGENT IN SMOKING[1]

Murray E. Jarvik[2]
Albert Einstein College of Medicine

Although there is much circumstantial evidence supporting the role of nicotine as the chemical underlying the smoking habit, there is no conclusive evidence as yet which proves that it is the sole or a contributing agent that reinforces smoking (Jarvik, 1970). To prove that nicotine is the essential ingredient in cigarettes, it would be necessary to show that cigarettes from which the nicotine has been removed are not smoked, and, conversely, that nicotine alone can substitute for cigarettes. Although these experiments are simple in principle, there are formidable difficulties in actually carrying them out. Before describing our attempts to approximate these experiments, I should like to indicate why I think that nicotine is the reinforcing agent in smoking and why competing hypotheses are inadequate.

Tobacco was apparently first used by the American Indians as cigars and in pipes. Subsequently, snuff taking and tobacco chewing had a rather long-lasting vogue, particularly in Europe. Finally, in this century, cigarettes became immensely popular and tended to displace all other forms of tobacco usage. Although many psychological theories have been proposed to explain why people smoke, they fail to account for the use of tobacco in its nonsmoked forms (Larson & Silvette, 1968). Thus, theories based upon oral gratification, pulmonary eroticism, satisfaction of manipulative tendencies, or visual or olfactory stimulation from fire or smoke cannot be applied to snuff taking or tobacco chewing. Although cigarette smoking is the most popular form of tobacco usage, there is some evidence that the various habits are interchangeable. Thus, for example, when cigarette smokers come to work in lumber mills where smoking is forbidden for fear of fire, they readily take to chewing tobacco.

[1] This research was supported by The American Cancer Society TH-IC.
[2] Sincere thanks to Mrs. Toni Goldfarb for help in preparing this paper.

What these various forms of tobacco use seem to have in common is nicotine absorbable in a parenteral fashion. Obviously, there are many other products present in tobacco and some extra ones in tobacco smoke, such as carbon monoxide and pyrolysis products. But it is very doubtful whether any of them have significant effects on the organism which could conceivably be pleasant or reinforcing. Nicotine, on the other hand, is a powerful and well-studied pharmacological agent, and it is absorbed into the body from all these methods of using tobacco in amounts which are strong enough to cause measurable degrees of physiological change. It is known that the smoking of a single cigarette and the injection of an equivalent amount of nicotine both produce the same increase in blood pressure, in heart rate, and of catecholamines and free fatty acids in the blood (Kershbaum, Bellet, Jiminez, & Feinberg, 1966; Schievelbein & Werle, 1967). It would be a remarkable coincidence if the effects of this powerful pharmacological agent had nothing to do with why people smoke. But in the absence of proof, it remains a possibility.

It is therefore quite remarkable that nicotine's reinforcing property has not yet been unequivocally demonstrated. An analogy and a contrast might be drawn between another plant product that is widely self-administered, opium. For over 150 years, it has been known that the active ingredient in opium is morphine, and the individuals who are addicted to opium can generally be satisfied with morphine or any of several opioid drugs. The abstinence syndrome, particularly in heavy users, may be very severe, and can be precipitated by antagonistic drugs. However, to my knowledge, no studies have been made of the ability of morphine injections to adequately substitute for opium *smoking*.

The experiments I will describe were conducted with animals (monkeys and rats) and with humans. These are all concerned with the behavioral or psychological effects of nicotine or of drugs that interact with nicotine. The basic premise underlying this research is that smoking is really nicotine-seeking behavior, and that nicotine directly or indirectly stimulates the reward centers in the brain and therefore facilitates behavior associated with its use. Furthermore, if the action of nicotine is blocked, then the extinction of nicotine seeking behavior should occur.

For some years now, we have been using monkeys as subjects in smoking experiments. They are the only species we have succeeded in getting to exhibit a type of behavior that resembles smoking in humans. Our general procedure has been to first have monkeys suck water through a straw and, once this behavior is established, to substitute cigarette smoke, or its equivalent, for water. With this procedure, we have succeeded in inducing about half of the monkeys to smoke. Many of the animals will go on to smoke spontaneously with no other reward. However, the smoking behavior differs from human cigarette smoking in that the smoke is apparently drawn only into the mouth, held there, and then expelled from the mouth and nose. It is not inhaled. The only animals we have seen inhale voluntarily are two chimpanzees at the Yerkes Laboratory of Primate Biology in Orange Park, Florida. These animals were adept at cadging cigarettes from animal keepers, and they smoked them with great relish and obviously inhaled quite deeply. Unfortunately, they were never systematically studied for this behavior.

One of the problems with the free smoking behavior in monkeys was that it was rather erratic compared with human cigarette smoking. In order to produce a more uniform rate to study the action of other drugs, we modified the procedure so that monkeys had to puff cigarette smoke or air in order to obtain their drinking water (Glick, Canfield, & Jarvik, 1970). In order to further stabilize the puffing rate, water was delivered only on a fixed ratio of one drink of water per 30 cigarette puffs.

Four mature rhesus monkeys that had been trained to smoke were used in these experiments (Glick, Jarvik, & Nakamura, 1970). The first drug to be tried was mecamylamine, which is known to block both peripheral and central actions of nicotine. Mecamylamine in doses of 0.4 to 3.2 mg/kg was given intramuscularly 15 minutes before the beginning of a puffing session. Each dose was repeated on 2 to 5 other days, with at least 3 days between successive injections. In Figure 1 can be seen the depression of preference induced by mecamylamine. Our explanation of the decline is that mecamylamine blocked the action of nicotine, precluding its rewarding effect, and thus resulted in a loss of preference for the smoke. Without the rewarding effect of nicotine, the smoke became relatively aversive, perhaps because of its irritating properties.

Further experiments were conducted with two of the same monkeys to assess the actions of a variety of other drugs on smoke preference. These results are shown in Table 1. Pentobarbital, a sedative-hypnotic, decreased the overall puffing rate but did not change the smoke-air preference. Hexamethonium, a nicotinic blocking agent with only peripheral actions, reversed the smoke-air preference with large doses while decreasing the overall puffing rate. Scopolamine, a cholinergic blocking agent, and d-amphetamine, an adrenergic agonist, also reversed the smoke-air preference, and overall puffing rates were greatly decreased. Mecamylamine, again, reversed the smoke-air preferences, with a small decrease in overall puffing rates.

The pentobarbital results indicate that a preference reversal is not just an artifact caused by decreased overall puffing. The hexamethonium results suggest that a peripheral action of nicotine may be part of the smoking incentive. Alternatively, in view of the much lesser potency of hexamethonium as compared with mecamylamine, perhaps a small amount of hexamethonium entered the brain.

A comparison of the patterns of puffing with the various drugs suggests that the scopolamine and d-amphetamine results may have been an artifact of decreased overall puffing.

These results tend to support the view that nicotine is doing something special in the brain. None of the other agents could be expected to block the nicotinic cholinergic receptors in the brain, and their depressant effects were probably due to other actions.

The drug that might be expected to have the most reliable influence on smoking is nicotine itself. In the next situation, monkeys were given varying quantities of nicotine tartrate dissolved in their drinking water. The amounts shown are only relative since they drank about half of the water given to them. What Table 2 shows is that for each monkey, there was a dose of nicotine which was capable of lowering the smoke preference ratio without changing the puffing rate appreciably. Presumably, the ingested nicotine substituted for the nicotine in the smoke or else

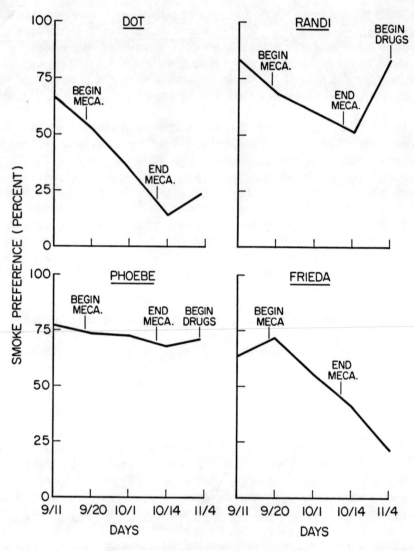

FIG. 1. Changes in smoke preference, on nondrug days, induced by mecamylamine. (From Glick, Jarvik, and Nakamura, 1970.)

blocked its action so that the aversive properties of the smoke were unmasked and became prepotent. In one monkey, Phoebe, a combination of nicotine and mecamylamine produced a further depression of preference. It was surprising to obtain an additive rather than a competitive action of these two drugs, and it may be that we were observing the blocking action of nicotine, which is in the same direction as that of mecamylamine.

Although we have never succeeded in inducing rats to smoke or to self-inject nicotine, it was of some interest to us to determine whether they might develop tolerance to nicotine. The evidence that tolerance develops in humans is now fairly solid (Larson, Haag, & Silvette, 1961; Larson & Silvette, 1968). Nicotine tolerance has not been systematically observed in animals, although Domino (1965) noted acute tolerance to nicotine in pole-climbing rats. Work on nicotine tolerance in rats was conducted in my laboratory by Dr. Ian Stolerman. He used a method of measuring activity in rats devised by Hannah Steinberg (Steinberg, Rushton, & Tinson, 1961). Rats are placed in a Y-maze, and the number of entries into alleys and of rearings on their hind legs in a given period of time is recorded.

TABLE 1

Drug-Induced Changes in Smoke Preference in Monkeys

Drug	Drug (mg/kg)	Randi		Phoebe	
		Total puffs	Percentage smoke pref.	Total puffs	Percentage smoke pref.
Control		4,618	82.7	4,537	74.6
Pentobarbital	10	4,496	87.1	2,822*	78.6
	20	3,514*	68.8	2,635*	77.4
	30	2,028*	71.6	1,347*	78.7
Hexamethonium	1	4,491	80.0	4,016	80.9
	2	4,492	78.8	3,821	75.7
	4	4,243	27.4*	4,092	80.5
	8	2,084*	1.0*	4,008	69.6
	12			3,013*	39.4*
Scopolamine	0.025	2,043*	19.6*	2,902*	65.3
	0.05	741*	38.6*	3,136*	76.5
	0.1			2,530*	55.6*
	0.2			1,554*	44.7*
D-Amphetamine	0.2	1,614*	71.3	3,813	66.6
	0.4	114*	24.2*	1,143*	14.8*
Mecamylamine	1.6	3,844	14.1*	4,553	15.2*

*Significantly less than control at $p < 0.05$.

TABLE 2

Changes in Smoke Preference Induced by Oral Nicotine

Nicotine dose (mg)	Phoebe		Alex		Ivan		Dot	
	Total puffs	% pref.	Total puffs	% pref.	Total puffs	% pref.	Total puffs	% pref.
Control	6108	88.7	4844	86.4	2786	87.2	4322	91.1
50	6509	87.5			2594	87.0	3666	88.3
75	6466	91.0	5191	90.0	3465	87.0	4437	86.0
100	6440	92.0			3453	75.0	4754	81.5
125	5784	64.1*	4789	91.9	2589	41.7*	4308	14.8*
175			4973	75.0				
225			4623	56.7*				

*Significantly less than control at $p < 0.05$.

The dose of nicotine used throughout these tolerance experiments was 1.0 mg/kg unless otherwise indicated. This is a fairly large dose, but one similar to that used by other investigators to depress motor activity in rats.

In Figure 2 can be seen the effect of giving two injections of nicotine separated by different intervals in different animals. Note that the greatest tolerance seems to occur at the two-hour interval. This acute tolerance or tachyphylaxis may somehow represent the occupation of receptors by nicotine or it may be a secondary effect involving some biogenic amine such as norepinephrine. In a supplementary experiment, rats were tested at different times after challenge with nicotine, and it was found that the depressant effect on motor activity largely dissipated by 30

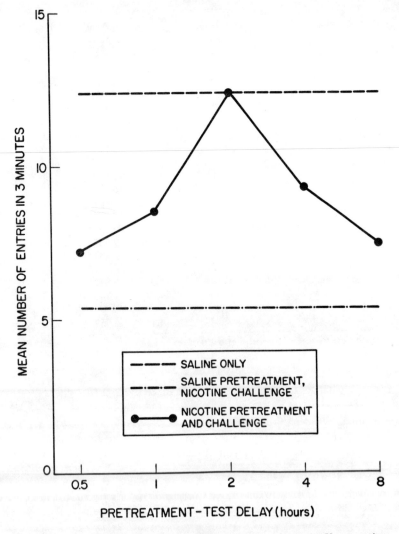

FIG. 2. Nicotine depression of spontaneous activity of rats in Y-maze: time course of block following single previous dose of nicotine (nicotine tartrate 1 mg/kg l.p., $n = 10$, throughout).

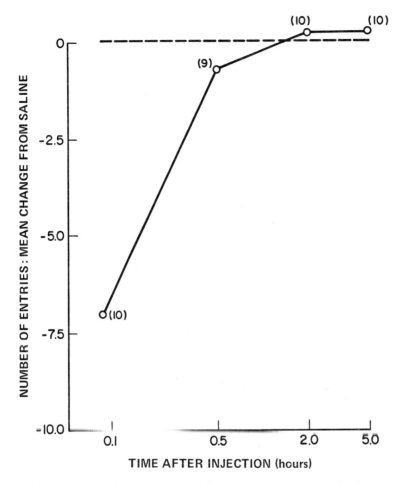

FIG. 3. Depression of spontaneous activity in rats in Y-maze after nicotine tartrate (1 mg/kg i.p.).

minutes after administration of the drug and that, at the dose used, no stimulant action could be detected subsequently (see Figure 3).

The next experiment was designed to test the possibility that multiple injections of nicotine given over a longer period of time would have a greater ability to produce tolerance than a single injection preceding the challenge dose. In order to demonstrate this, it was necessary to choose a pretreatment interval other than that (2 hours) which would produce complete insensitivity. An interval of 5 hours from the last dose of nicotine was selected. In Figure 4, it can be seen that the degree of tolerance was indeed a function of the number of pretreatments. In Figure 5, it may be seen that extending the duration of the period of nicotine pretreatment to 8 days produced tolerance for as long as 80 days after the end of pretreatment (60 days after the last single dose of nicotine).

The fact that tolerance to nicotine can be induced in rats is not necessarily related to dependence on nicotine seen in man. However, the possible relationship

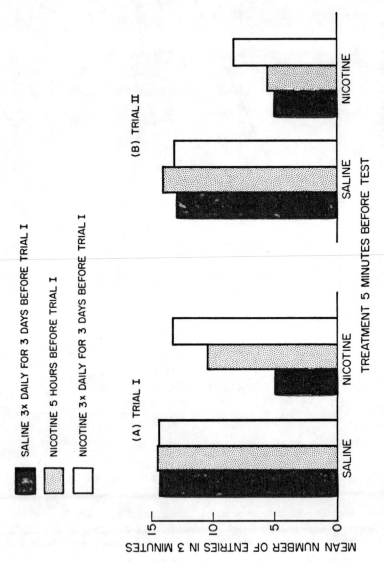

FIG. 4. Nicotine depression of spontaneous activity of rats in Y-maze (1 mg/kg i.p., $n=8$ throughout).

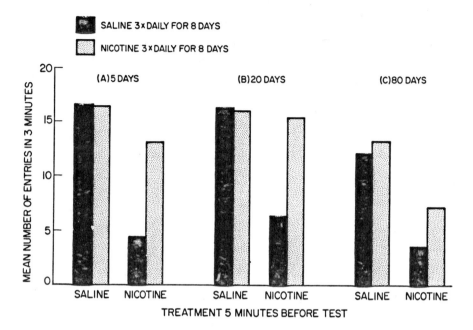

FIG. 5. Nicotine depression of Y-maze activity in rats ($n = 11$-12, 1 mg/kg i.p.): tolerance at three different times after nicotine pretreatment ended.

between drug dependence and tolerance has been stressed by some theorists such as Goldstein (Goldstein, Aronow, & Kalman, 1968). If some mechanism such as enzyme induction is responsible for tolerance, it might also be responsible for physical dependence and the production of a withdrawal syndrome.

For many purposes, man is the best subject in which to study smoking behavior, even though there are obvious ethical limitations to the variety of pharmacological and physiological studies which can be performed with this species. One rather obvious approach is to see whether the psychological nonnicotine theories of smoking are adequate to account for this behavior. The first approach is to remove nicotine from cigarettes and then see how much heavy cigarette smokers like them. However, nicotine-free tobacco cigarettes are exceedingly difficult to obtain and, therefore, we resorted to lettuce cigarettes (Bravos). When these were given to heavy smokers over a three-week period (Goldfarb, Jarvik, & Glick, 1970), smoking rate tended to decrease for most but not all subjects (see Table 3). When smokers were allowed to smoke their own brands during the fifth week, the low rate of smoking persisted.

The measures of strength and quality do show that subjects could discriminate difference in the three experimental cigarettes which were artificially fortified with nicotine, as shown in the table. The higher nicotine cigarettes were reported to be stronger than the lower. The quality ratings indicate that none of the subjects liked the experimental cigarettes more than their own brands and, indeed, complained about the taste of the lettuce cigarettes throughout the experiment. That considerable smoking did occur in the absence of both tobacco and nicotine

TABLE 3

Cigarette Nicotine Content as a Determinant of Human Smoking Behavior:

Measures of Rate, Strength, and Quality of Experimental Cigarettes Versus Subjects' Own Brands[a]

Subject		Cigarettes smoked[b]			
	Own	0% nico.	2% nico.	3% nico.	Own
Group 1					
RN	23	20	20	25	24
RP	24	24	27	29	24
JG	17	18	17	15	14
Group means: rate	20	19	19	19	19
strength	2.3	2.0	2.3	2.9	2.5
quality	1.8	2.4	1.8	1.9	2.4
	Own	2% nico.	3% nico.	0% nico.	Own
Group 2					
BF	13	11	11	9	9
RH	21	16	15	13	15
NK	24	12	6	7	20
Group means: rate	20	13	11	10	15
strength	2.3	2.1	2.3	1.8	2.0
quality	1.7	2.5	2.6	2.7	2.0
	Own	3% nico.	0% nico.	2% nico.	Own
Group 3					
PL	25	13	11	10	11
AL	13	6	9	5	10
DG	37	27	35	27	29
AK	34	14	12	5	6
Group means: rate	25	15	17	12	14
strength	2.0	3.8	3.1	3.5	2.1
quality	0.9	3.6	3.3	3.6	1.1

[a]Numbers represent mean cigarettes per day smoked by each S during each experimental week. Strength continuum: 0 (very weak) to 4 (extremely strong). Quality continuum: 0 (great satisfaction) to 4 (extreme dissatisfaction).
[b]Columns indicate type of cigarette smoked by each group in order of presentation in the experiment.

indicates that the smoking habit comes to display considerable functional autonomy (Allport, 1937). I would guess that smoking, like most overlearned habits, favors the development of conditioned reinforcers or secondary reinforcement and becomes thereby very resistant to extinction. These results resemble those of Finnegan, Larson, & Haag (1945).

An alternative approach is to administer nicotine to subjects in addition to that self-administered through spontaneous smoking, and to see whether it depresses their smoking. Seventeen heavy smokers received five doses per day of 10-mg nicotine tartrate orally administered in capsule form. On the first and last of 4 days, half the subjects were given nicotine, and placebos on intermediate days. The procedure was reversed for the other subjects. The results are summarized in Table 4 (Jarvik, Glick, & Nakamura, 1970). These results are similar to those of Lucchesi, Schuster, & Emley (1967), who found that intravenously administered nicotine produced a decrease in number of cigarettes smoked, which, though significant, was quite small. Again, the negative side of these results points to the important role played by secondary conditioning and functional autonomy in the maintenance of a long-standing habit such as cigarette smoking. Of course, the alternative hypothesis, that nicotine plays little role in smoking behavior must also be entertained, though we are reluctant to accept this conclusion.

Another experiment involved the reaction to restricted tobacco smoke intake in cigarette smokers (Goldfarb & Jarvik, 1972). Smoking behavior was studied for 4 weeks in 18 volunteers given cigarettes cut to half their normal length for one week, and marked with a red line at the halfway point for another week. As may be seen in Table 5, there was a small tendency for smokers to light up more of the half cigarettes than the normal cigarettes, but none of the subjects fully compensated for decreased nicotine intake by proportionately increasing the number of cigarettes they smoked. Most subjects in this study, in effect, decreased their tobacco use by almost half. No attempts were made to measure long-term effects with this procedure. These findings are similar to the above, in which the sensory-motor patterns involved in smoking behavior are exceedingly resistant to change and appear to exhibit functional autonomy.

Our final group of studies was concerned with the effect of nicotinic blocking agents upon smoking behavior in human smokers. Six groups of subjects were tested, twice each after a placebo or a dose of drug. The order of drug or placebo treatment was balanced out except at the largest dose of mecamylamine, which was always given after the placebo. It can be seen in Table 6 that mecamylamine consistently increased the number of cigarettes smoked during the observation period. Pentolinium, a peripherally acting nicotinic blocking agent tended, by contrast, to decrease the number of cigarettes smoked. Our explanation is that subjects tried to overcome the central blockage of mecamylamine by smoking more cigarettes. With pentolinium, the imbalance between the unobstructed central effects of nicotine and the lowered peripheral effects was peculiar and perhaps unpleasant, causing decreased smoking.

TABLE 4

Smoking Behavior of Subjects When Administered Nicotine and Lactose

	Nicotine	Lactose	$p*$
Average number of cigarettes per day	22.35	24.14	<0.02
Average butt weight per cigarette	0.375 Gm.	0.373 Gm.	N.S.**
Average strength of each cigarette	2.25	2.13	N.S.
Average quality of each cigarette	1.60	1.46	N.S.

Note.—Adapted from Jarvik, Glick, and Nakamura (1970).
  *p = level of significance.
**N.S. = not significant.

TABLE 5

Smoking of Control Versus Experimental Cigarettes[a]

Test group	Mean cigarettes smoked							Weekly mean cigs/day	Weekly mean strength	Weekly mean quality
	Day 1	Day 2	Day 3	Day 4	Day 5	Day 6	Day 7			
Control (week 1)	24.5	25.0	26.0	27.8	26.8	23.9	24.5	25.5	2.1	1.5
Lined cigarettes	29.4	22.5	27.3	27.7	27.4	28.4	27.5	27.2	2.1	1.4
Cut cigarettes	30.4	25.7	28.6	28.4	28.7	27.7	30.4	28.6	2.2	1.7
Control (week 4)	29.5	25.3	26.2	27.2	26.9	29.0	27.1	27.3	2.0	1.5

Note.—Adapted from Goldfarb and Jarvik (1972).
[a]Mean number of cigarettes smoked per day ($N = 18$).

TABLE 6

Mean Numbers of Cigarettes Smoked in Two-Hour Sessions

Group	N	Drug treatment	Cigarettes after drug	Cigarettes after placebo	p
1	8	Mecamylamine 7.5 mg	4.38	3.38	<0.05
2	14	" " 12.5 mg	4.75	3.25	<0.05
3	10	" " 17.5 mg	3.85	3.45	
Mean	32		4.33	3.36	<0.01
4	6	Mecamylamine 22.5 mg	5.00	3.83	
5	10	Pentolinium 100 mg	3.60	3.80	
6	10	" " 150 mg	3.30	4.30	<0.05
Mean	20		3.45	4.05	

In the subjects tested in our laboratory with these drugs, it appears that mecamylamine produced the expected drop in blood pressure, but pentolinium did not (Figure 6). Hand steadiness was improved by mecamylamine but not by pentolinium in smokers (Figure 7), with no effect on nonsmokers. Both drugs increased the time taken to complete a Digit Symbol Substitution Test, presumably an effect of feeling ill (Table 7). Results from an adjective check list indicated undesirable effects were induced by these drugs, and a reasonable dose-effect curve based on a dysphoria index can be seen (Figure 8).

SUMMARY STATEMENT

We have described a series of experiments on monkeys, rats, and people, all aimed at studying the role of nicotine in smoking. The monkey studies are in line with previous ones done in my lab that indicate monkeys might smoke tobacco freely and prefer cigarette smoke to air. Both mecamylamine and oral nicotine reduced the preference for tobacco smoke, and an explained additive rather than competitive effect occurred in one animal. The negative side of the story is that it has been difficult to get monkeys to smoke consistently in humanoid fashion. In future studies, we hope to be able to measure the amount of nicotine actually absorbed by the animals to give us a more meaningful baseline.

A series of experiments by Dr. Ian Stolerman showed that tolerance could be induced to large doses of nicotine in rats. Some theorists of drug dependence invoke tolerance as a necessary ingredient (e.g., Goldstein et al., 1968), but, of course, dependence was not measured in rats.

Experiments in man indicated that lettuce cigarettes were partially rejected but nevertheless smoked by smokers when no others were available. Adding nicotine to the lettuce cigarettes did not increase their acceptability. A week of smoking these treated cigarettes reduced the rate at which the smokers smoked their customary cigarettes. A similar experiment done with low-nicotine tobacco cigarettes (Marvels, 0.1 mg nicotine per cigarette) produced similar results.

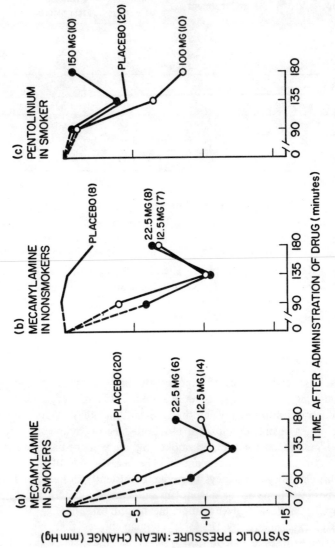

FIG. 6. Changes in systolic blood pressure after drugs.

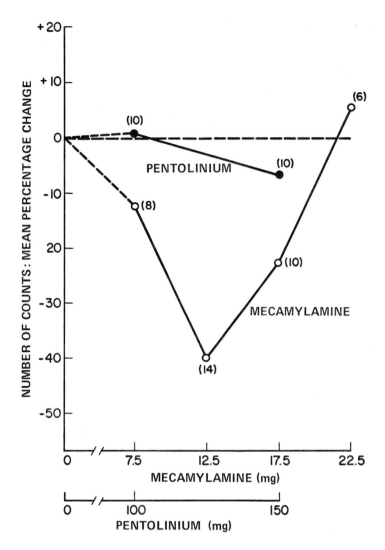

FIG. 7. Changes in tremor of smokers measured by stylus-in-hole apparatus.

A dose of 50 mg/day nicotine tartrate administered to smokers significantly reduced the number of cigarettes smoked, but the absolute magnitude of the reduction was small. If the orally administered nicotine resulted in high persistent blood levels, it was clear that the subjects were not compensating for the nicotine levels by a proportionate decrease in nicotine from their cigarettes. A similar surprising lack of titration was shown by a study in which only half the cigarette was smoked. In this experiment, it was possible that subjects might have compensated for the shortness of the cigarettes by longer or deeper puffs. Blood nicotine determinations should clarify such results.

Attempts to block nicotine effects with mecamylamine resulted in an increase in cigarettes smoked during the drugged interval; also, the number of puffs increased. This may be an attempt to overcome the mecamylamine blockade, but we could have also predicted extinction. There was a slight drop in blood pressure with mecamylamine, but not with pentolinium. Smoking tremor was reduced by optimal doses of mecamylamine. Mecamylamine itself produced dose-dependent dysphoria.

It is evident that smoking behavior is exceedingly resistant to extinction. This finding certainly supports the commonplace reports of heavy smokers that they have difficulty in relinquishing their habit. We have not yet adequately examined the other side of the coin, namely, that nicotine alone and devoid of tobacco may provide some measure of satisfaction or relief to smokers who are deprived of their cigarettes. These experiments with measures of subjective response are now in progress and should provide a more definitive answer to the question of whether nicotine is the reinforcing agent in smoking.

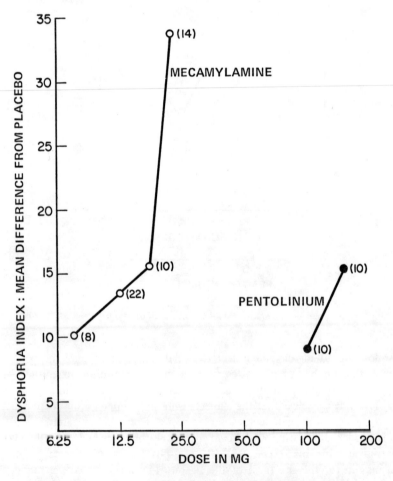

FIG. 8. Increases in dysophoria index after drugs (index 100 + "undesirable" adjectives checked/total adjectives checked).

TABLE 7

Time (Seconds) to Complete Digit Symbol
Substitution Test After Drugs

Group	N	Drug treatment	Time after drug	Time after placebo	p
1	8	Mecamylamine 7.5 mg	82.9	77.6	<0.05
2		" " 12.5 mg	85.6	83.0	
3		" " 17.5 mg	84.2	78.4	
Mean	32		84.2	79.7	<0.01
4	6	Mecamylamine 22.5 mg	95.0	75.2	<0.05
5	10	Pentolinium 100 mg	96.3	85.2	<0.05
6	10	" " 150 mg	95.5	90.3	
Mean	20		95.9	87.8	<0.05

REFERENCES

Allport, G. W. *Personality.* New York: Holt, 1937.

Domino, E. F. Some behavioral actions of nicotine. In U.S. von Euler (Ed.), *Tobacco alkaloids and related compounds.* Oxford: Pergamon Press, 1965,

Finnegan, J. K., Larson, P. S., & Haag, H. B. The role of nicotine in the cigarette habit. *Science,* 1945, **102,** 94-96.

Glick, S. D., Canfield, J. L., & Jarvik, M. E. A technique for assessing strength of a smoking preference in monkeys. *Psychological Reports,* 1970, **26,** 707-710.

Glick, S. D., Jarvik, M. E., & Nakamura, R. K. Inhibition by drugs of smoking behaviour in monkeys. *Nature,* 1970, **227,** 969-971.

Goldfarb, T. L., & Jarvik, M. E. Accommodation to restricted tobacco smoke intake in cigarette smokers. *International Journal of Addictions,* 1972, in press.

Goldfarb, T. L., Jarvik, M. E., & Glick, S. D. Cigarette nicotine content as a determinant of human smoking behavior. *Psychopharmacologia,* 1970, **17,** 89-93.

Goldstein, A., Aronow, L., & Kalman, S. M. *Principles of drug action: The basis of pharmacology.* New York: Harper & Row, 1968.

Jarvik, M. E. The role of nicotine in the smoking habit. In W. A. Hunt (Ed.), *Learning mechanisms and smoking.* Chicago: Aldine, 1970.

Jarvik, M. E., Glick, S. D., & Nakamura, R. K. Inhibition of cigarette smoking by orally administered nicotine. *Clinical Psychology and Therapeutics,* 1970, **11,** 574-576.

Kershbaum, A., Bellet, S., Jiminez, J., & Feinberg, L. J. Differences in effects of cigar and cigarette smoking on free fatty acid mobilization and catecholamine excretion. *Journal of the American Medical Association,* 1966, **195,** 1095-1098.

Larson, P. S., Haag, H. B., & Silvette, H. *Tobacco: Experimental and clinical studies.* Baltimore: Williams and Wilkins, 1961.

Larson, P. S., & Silvette, H. *Tobacco: Experimental and clinical studies,* Supplement 1. Baltimore: Williams and Wilkins, 1968.

Lucchesi, B. R. Schuster, C. R., & Emley, G. S. The role of nicotine as a determinant of cigarette smoking frequency in man with observations of certain cardiovascular effects associated with the tobacco alkaloid. *Clinical Pharmacology and Therapeutics,* 1967, 8, 789-796.

Schievelbein, H., & Werle, E. Mechanism of release of amines by nicotine. *Annals of the New York Academy of Science,* 1967, **142,** 72-82.

Steinberg, H., Rushton, R., & Tinson, C. Modification of the effects of an amphetamine-barbiturate mixture by the past experience of rats. *Nature,* 1961, **192,** 533-535.

4

NICOTINE-RELATED NEUROCHEMICAL CHANGES: SOME IMPLICATIONS FOR MOTIVATIONAL MECHANISMS AND DIFFERENCES[1]

Walter B. Essman
Queens College of the City University of New York

Some of the possible ways in which the pharmacological role of nicotine underlies the smoking habit have been reviewed by other investigators (Murphree, 1967; Larson and Silvette, 1968; Jarvik, 1970). The favored view holds that the motivational relevance of nicotine resides in its effects upon the central nervous system (Murphree, 1967). For the most part these effects have been resolved with a central catecholamine hypothesis (Burn, 1960). This chapter will redirect attention to the fact that, either directly or indirectly, nicotine also induces other biochemical changes in the brain, changes which could as well have motivational significance.

Work already reported by this writer has related changes in the motivated behavior of experimental animals to (*a*) changes in the concentration and turnover of 5-hydroxytryptamine (Essman, 1969), and to (*b*) changes in the central cholinergic system (Essman, 1971a). The relevance of the effects of nicotine to these reported relationships is to be found in the observation that nicotine induces changes in both the central indoleamine and cholinergic systems (Essman, Golod, & Steinberg, 1968; Essman, 1971a). These findings and the meagerness of evidence to support the central catecholamine effect of nicotine (Westfall, Flemming, Fudger, & Clark, 1967), suggest that any attempt to investigate motivation in human smoking should include a study focused upon the effects of nicotine upon the central indoleamine and cholinergic systems.

In order to study the central nervous system effects of nicotine, we have chosen 5-hydroxytryptamine (5-HT) and acetylcholine (ACh)—considered on a regional, cellular, and subcellular level. We have also investigated the possibility that differences in central amine level and metabolism are related to differences in the

[1] The research summarized in this paper was supported, in part, by a grant from The Council for Tobacco Research, U.S.A.

central uptake, distribution, and metabolism of nicotine. If the central correlates of a given motivational state were to be consistent with the pharmacological properties of agents that influence that state, then nicotine as a central stimulant would be expected to initiate predictable effects upon putative transmitters.

BRAIN INDOLEAMINE CHANGES

In previous experiments we have reported that several biologically active metabolites of nicotine can exert both behavioral and biochemical effects that often temporally overlap the central action of nicotine (Essman, 1971a). An initial study was concerned with the regional changes of 5-HT and its major metabolite, 5-hydroxyindoleacetic acid (5-HIAA) following nicotine treatment. Some other experimental observations (Wooley, 1965) would suggest reduction in motivated behavior in mice with lowered brain 5-HT content, and an increase in such behavior with 5-HT elevation. A change in brain 5-HT level following treatment with nicotine sulfate would be expected because of observed changes in brain 5-HT turnover following administration of that drug (1.0 mg/kg), most apparent by 45 minutes following i.p. injection in mice (Figure 1). A decreased turnover rate and increased turnover time (20 and 36%, respectively) are consistent with the increased 5-HT levels previously observed after nicotine and cotinine treatment, as shown in Table 1 (cotinine is a major intermediary metabolite of nicotine). It is apparent that cotinine did not affect 5-HT or 5-HIAA levels in the cerebral cortex, but did significantly elevate levels in the mesencephalon and diencephalon 15 minutes after

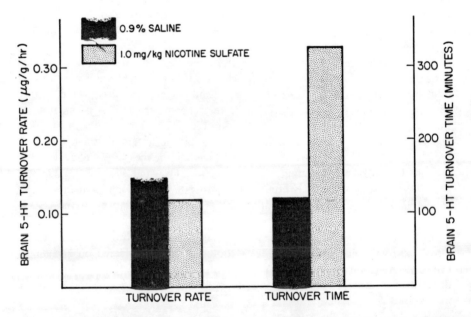

FIG. 1. Bring 5-hydroxytryptamine turnover rate (µg/g/hr) and turnover time (minutes) measured 45 minutes following injection of saline or nicotine sulfate.

TABLE 1

Mean ($\pm \sigma$) Regional Concentration ($\mu g/g$) of 5-Hydroxytryptamine (5-HT) and 5-Hydroxyindoleacetic Acid (5-HIAA) Following Saline or Drug Treatment

Brain area		Posttreatment time					
		15 minutes			45 minutes		
		Saline	Nicotine	Cotinine	Saline	Nicotine	Cotinine
Cerebral cortex:	5-HT	0.38 (0.06)	0.42 (0.01)	0.33 (0.04)	0.39 (0.04)	0.66 (0.04)	0.28 (0.03)
	5-HIAA	0.52 (0.19)	0.55 (0.06)	0.43 (0.05)	0.12 (0.02)	0.37 (0.02)	0.36 (0.04)
Mesencephalon:	5-HT	0.33 (0.04)	0.82 (0.02)	0.83 (0.05)	0.33 (0.04)	0.64 (0.06)	0.33 (0.05)
	5-HIAA	0.21 (0.02)	0.45 (0.02)	0.36 (0.04)	0.18 (0.03)	0.35 (0.06)	1.00 (0.12)
Diencephalon:	5-HT	0.33 (0.04)	0.96 (0.20)	0.56 (0.04)	0.33 (0.05)	0.90 (0.15)	0.28 (0.05)
	5-HIAA	0.15 (0.03)	0.45 (0.09)	0.29 (0.04)	0.14 (0.03)	0.45 (0.18)	1.07 (0.11)

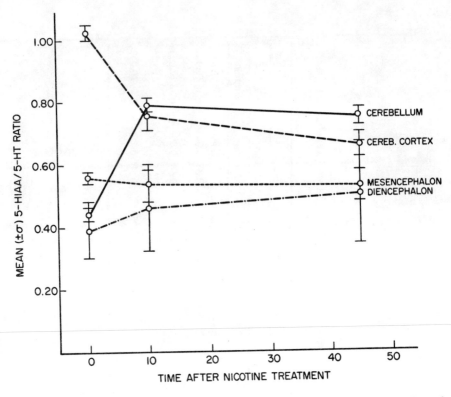

FIG. 2. Mean (+σ) 5-hydroxyindoleacetic acid/5-hydroxytryptamine ratio in several regions of the mouse brain following administration of nicotine sulfate (1.0 mg/kg, i.p.).

treatment, with a marked 5-HIAA elevation after 45 minutes. The effects of nicotine on the cerebral cortex were not apparent until 45 minutes after treatment, when 5-HT was elevated and 5-HIAA was decreased—again consistent with reduced turnover. In the mesencephalon and diencephalon, 5-HT was elevated after 15 minutes and remained elevated for at least 45 minutes following treatment.

Comparison of the 5-HT and 5-HIAA levels (the latter an index by which 5-HT turnover may be assessed) indicates that the rate of regional change induced by nicotine is greatest within the first 10 minutes following treatment (Figure 2). The clearly significant changes in the ratio 5-HIAA/5-HT occurred in the cerebral cortex and the cerebellar cortex, with a notable difference in the direction of change between these two regions. This finding agrees well with recent work (Essman & Heldman, 1972) suggesting regional differences in enzymatic regulation of biogenic amines.

If one accepts the premise that nicotine influences motivation via its effect(s) upon some central mechanism mediating positive reinforcement, termination of centrally regulated aversive stimuli, or mood alteration, then the matter of duration of effect becomes an important focus for future avenues of research. On what parameters, for example, can one best monitor the growth and decay of the effects of nicotine?

CELLULAR SPECIFICITY OF NICOTINE-RELATED CENTRAL EFFECTS

A previous communication (Essman, 1971b) indicated that in both the behavioral and biochemical spheres, nicotine acted pharmacologically in a manner reminiscent of the action of several psychoactive compounds having clinical antidepressant features. In order to observe effects at the cellular level, regional changes in populations of neuronally-enriched and glia-enriched cell fractions were assayed for 5-HT content 45 minutes following nicotine sulfate (1.0 mg/kg, i.p.) treatment. The cell fractions from five macrodissected areas of mouse brain, obtained with methods permitting verification of fraction purity with enzyme markers and phase-contrast microscopy (Essman, 1971b, 1972b), yielded the 5-HT concentrations summarized in Table 2. It may be of interest to observe that such areas as the corpus callosum, essentially free of neuronal cell bodies, did have 5-HT associated with the glia-enriched fraction. It is also apparent that, under control conditions, an appreciably larger proportion of the total 5-HT in several brain regions is accounted for in the glia-enriched fraction. The most apparent effect seen of nicotine is a generalized increase in regional 5-HT content, again consistent with previous data. The changes in 5-HT content observed following nicotine treatment suggest the possible trophic role of 5-HT, in addition to its potential transmitter role, especially in view of its localization in glia and its alterability within that storage pool by nicotine. The interference with neuronal and nerve ending metabolism through increased 5-HT availability (Essman, 1970b) and the possibly accelerated glial metabolism through increased 5-HT concentration (Murray, 1958; Essman, 1970a) suggest a mechanism whereby nicotine, acting at a cellular level, exerts its influence upon central motivational events. However, further work is needed on the chemical form, quantity, and frequencies of nicotine dosage and on the interval between semichronic or chronic treatment.

TABLE 2

Mean ($\pm\sigma$) Regional Concentration (μg/g) of 5-Hydroxytryptamine in Neuronally-Enriched and Glia-Enriched Cell Fractions

Brain area	Treatment			
	Saline (0.9%)		Nicotine sulfate (1.0 mg/kg)	
	Neuronally-enriched	Glia-enriched	Neuronally-enriched	Glia-enriched
Cerebral cortex	0.17 (0.07)	0.47 (0.16)	1.04 (0.26)	0.92 (0.18)
Corpus callosum	–	0.21 (0.08)	–	1.36 (0.34)
Diencephalon	0.71 (0.05)	0.41 (0.14)	1.60 (0.22)	1.78 (0.44)
Limbic system	0.97 (0.07)	0.91 (0.04)	1.68 (0.42)	1.28 (0.32)
Cerebellar cortex	0.17 (0.08)	0.21 (0.08)	0.68 (0.21)	0.36 (0.22)

NICOTINE-INDUCED CENTRAL CHOLINERGIC EFFECTS

The cholinergic action of nicotine, at least in the central nervous system, has been sparingly examined (Armitage and Hall, 1967; Essman, 1971a). Its action within the cholinergic system remains an intriguingly relevant phenomenon, particularly in view of the evidence for the excitatory properties of the drug and strong support for central cholinergic synaptic transmission. There are two relevant questions: Which ACh storage pool in the brain is affected by nicotine? And how can differences in cytoplasmic versus particle-bound ACh pools, as affected by nicotine, be relevant to the motivational influences of this agent? The release of stored ACh in the brain without appreciable alteration in free ACh turnover appears to have a bearing on strain-specific differences in nicotine effect (Bovet, Bovet-Nitti, & Oliverio, 1966). Perhaps the magnitude of the ACh storage pool ratio regulates the superimposed central states (Essman & Essman, 1971; Essman, 1971c).

The effects of nicotine sulfate (1.0 mg/kg, i.p.) upon the total, bound, free, and vesicular storage pools of ACh in the mouse cerebral cortex, 45 minutes following treatment, are summarized in Figure 3. The changes in bound ACh and the ACh

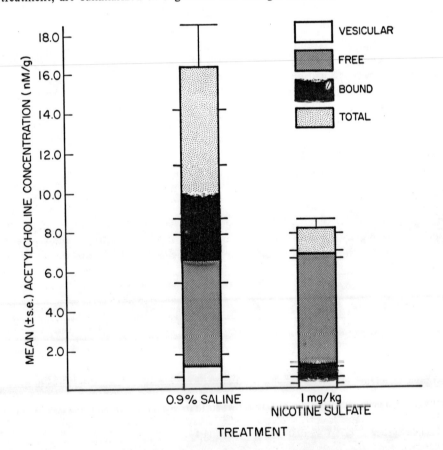

FIG. 3. Mean (±s.e.) acetylcholine concentration (nM/g) for saline- and nicotine-treated mice in several storage pools of the cerebral cortex.

content of isolated synaptic vesicles (vesicular) strongly support a nicotine-induced ACh release-from-storage hypothesis, but the tendency for free ACh levels to be maintained (probably within somatoaxonic structures) supports the view that the cholinergic effect of nicotine is limited to the nerve ending.

Those effects of acute nicotine treatment which appear to have consistently emerged thus far are: (a) reduced brain 5-HT turnover; (b) regionally increased brain 5-HT level; (c) a relationship between 5-HT changes and nicotine metabolite action; (d) a change, consistent for brain region, in the 5-HT content of neuronally-enriched and glia-enriched fractions; and (e) a decreased bound and vesicular ACh content without change in the free ACh pool concentration.

These observed nicotine-induced changes in brain chemistry and metabolism now require integration with models of mechanisms relating nicotine effect to smoking behavior. Such integration might be facilitated by recourse to another line of investigation. This involves the study of biochemical changes in the brain induced through the manipulation of environmental variables. It has already been established that differential housing of experimental mice can induce such changes (Essman, 1969, 1970a, 1971c). What follows is the report of a study of the effect of interaction between animal housing conditions and nicotine administration upon certain biochemical changes in the brain.

DIFFERENTIAL HOUSING: NEUROCHEMICAL STATUS AND NICOTINE UPTAKE

Although dose equivalence, in terms of administered quantity, is often assumed, dose differences in central drug uptake and form cannot be taken for granted. In the human smoking sphere, differences in a smoking habit or in the motivation to smoke may be dependent upon how much nicotine is derived from the smoke. If the central effect of the nicotine is at all a determinant of smoking behavior, then differences in central uptake and effect are important variables. We have explored a preliminary aspect of this question utilizing N-methyl-C-14 nicotine administered to adult mice (i.p.) that had been differentially housed (isolated housing vs. group housing) from weaning (21 days of age) for 180 days. The methodological details of the differential housing study design have been previously reported (Essman, 1969, 1971c). At 45 minutes following treatment, the four regions of the mouse brain were extracted and total radioactivity was determined. Nicotine uptake, expressed for isolated and for grouped mice, is shown in Figure 4. As may be observed, significantly more brain uptake of the drug (total dose = 0.7 mg/kg of alkaloid) occurred among the isolated mice in all sampled regions of the brain. When nicotine was separated chromatographically from its major metabolite, (-)cotinine, it was apparent that the latter was not incorporated in measurable quantity into any of the brain areas sampled within 45 minutes after nicotine treatment in group-housed mice (Figure 5). Among isolated animals the cerebral cortex and basal ganglia had measurable N-methyl-C-14 activity by 45 minutes after treatment. Specific N-methyl-C-14 nicotine activity was not derivable for the basal ganglia and cerebellar cortex of group-housed mice, whereas specific activity of nicotine was consistently and significantly present in the regions for the isolated animals.

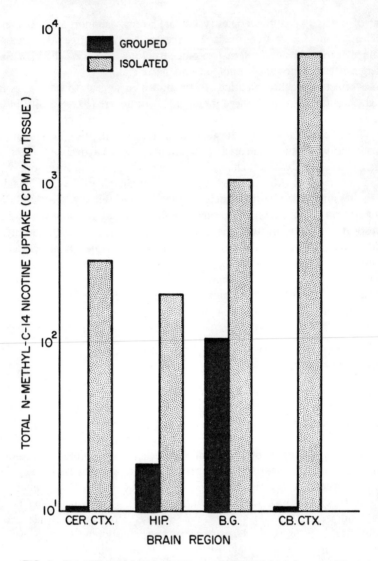

FIG. 4. Total N methyl C-14 nicotine uptake (C.P.M./mg) for several brain regions of differentially housed mice.

CHOLINERGIC EFFECTS OF DIFFERENTIAL HOUSING AND NICOTINE

In view of the possibility that the preferential rate of nicotine uptake into the central nervous system by isolation-housed mice may account for differences in the effect of this drug upon the endogenous level of relevant biologically active amines, animals differentially housed for 180 days were given a single i.p. injection of nicotine sulfate (1.0 mg/kg), 45 minutes following which the cerebral cortex was assayed for total, bound, and free ACh. The differences in ACh content, for each storage pool of this amine, between saline-treated control mice and nicotine-treated

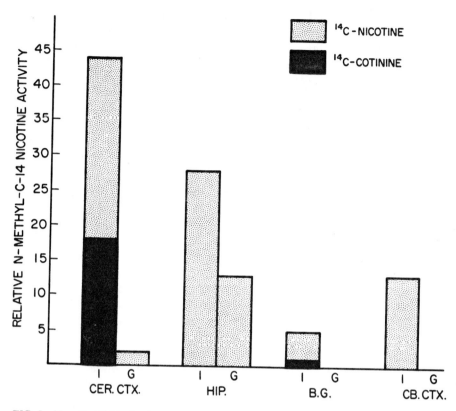

FIG. 5. N-methyl-C-14 nicotine activity recovery of nicotine or cotinine in several brain regions of differentially housed mice.

animals are summarized in Table 3. It is apparent from these data that the ratio of bound to free cortical ACh in group-housed mice (1.55) is significantly ($p < .01$) reduced in isolation-housed animals (0.33); furthermore, whereas nicotine reduces this ratio significantly ($p < .01$) in grouped mice (0.17), the same parenterally administered drug dose significantly ($p < .01$) elevates the ratio in isolated mice (1.06).

TABLE 3

Mean ($\pm\sigma$) Acetylcholine Concentration Difference Due to Nicotine Treatment in Several Storage Pools from the Cerebral Cortex of Differentially Housed Mice

Housing condition	Mean ($\pm\sigma$) acetylcholine concentration difference (nM/g)		
	Total	Bound	Free
Grouping	8.37 (1.39)*	8.78 (0.81)*	−0.41 (0.46)
Isolation	9.13 (1.13)*	0.42 (1.63)	8.71 (0.34)*

*$p < .01$.

It is of no mean significance that, in face of the positive findings reported, no consistent or obvious alteration in brain catecholamines was observed.

These findings can be summarized as follows: (a) endogenous ACh pool ratios (free ACh/bound ACh) were lower in isolated mice; and (b) nicotine and its metabolite cotinine were present in greater quantities in the brains of the isolated mice on assay following nicotine administration.

Thus, it would appear that the degree of pharmacological activity of nicotine may well be a function of the endogenous biochemical condition of the mouse brain at the time of nicotine administration. If such is indeed the case, then we have a highly plausible if but partial explanation for the wide interindividual variability in the pharmacological and behavioral effects of nicotine as reported so frequently in the literature. It would appear that we have identified a variable, a specified aspect of the endogenous biochemical substrate of the mouse brain, and manipulated that variable by means of differential housing upon weaning so as to produce a differential action of nicotine at the pharmacological level. The differentiation was also manifest at the behavioral level, for it was also observed in this study that nicotine administration usually produced locomotor excitation and activation among grouped mice, while the same dose given to the isolated animals, usually quite reactive, produced behavior typically observed in response to sedative drugs. These opposing behavioral patterns have been cited often in investigations of the effects of nicotine upon animal behavior, and have had the net effect of compounding data and obscuring relationships. The tendency has been to interpret the disparate responses as attributable to the biphasic action of the drug, although some investigators have suggested that genetic or developmental differences among the animals may be implicated. One would hardly wish to venture so far as to relate the findings of this study to the "Nesbitt paradox" as articulated by Stanley Schachter (this volume).

CEREBRAL PROTEIN SYSTNESIS: THE INTERACTIVE EFFECTS OF NICOTINE AND DIFFERENTIAL HOUSING

The relationship between some of those endogenous neurochemical systems upon which nicotine acts and the modulation of protein synthesis by substrates of these systems has been explored in previous work (Essman, 1970b, 1972a). It has also been reported (Essman, Heldman, Barker, & Valzelli, 1972) that isolation housing in mice can lead to changes in microsomal protein synthesis, perhaps consistent with changes observed after isolation housing, particularly in indoleamine metabolism (Essman, 1972b). The series of experiments summarized here were designed to: (a) determine the effect of a physiologically active dose of nicotine upon protein synthesis in several fractions derived from the mouse cerebral cortex; (b) compare the effects of nicotine with those of differential housing upon changes in cerebral protein synthesis; and (c) attempt to identify the characteristics of protein implicated in the cerebral effect of nicotine.

Since it has been indicated previously that (-) cotinine is not incorporated in significant quantity into the brain of group-housed mice by 45 minutes after nicotine injection, and that nicotine can alter at least two biogenic amines (5-hydroxytryptamine and acetylcholine) at this site, it seemed reasonable to hypothesize that effects upon cerebral protein synthesis by nicotine could be mediated by such amine changes.

In an initial experimental series male CF-1s strain mice were treated with either nicotine alkaloid (0.7 mg/kg, i.p.) or an equivalent volume of 0.9% saline. At 45 minutes after treatment, an intracranial injection of H^3-leucine was given; after a 15-minute labeling pulse, the animals were killed and the cerebral cortex, scraped of underlying myelin, was excised. From a total 10% homogenate in 0.32 M sucrose, differential and density gradient centrifugation procedures (Whittaker, 1969) permitted separation of several subcellular fractions including microsomes, myelin, synaptosomes, and mitochondria. Total protein was precipitated from each fraction, and the activity of the incorporated H^3-leucine and protein concentration were determined. The results have been summarized in Figure 6, wherein the determined differences in protein synthesis are given for each of the fractions isolated after treatment. It is apparent that nicotine treatment provided for an increase in protein synthesis, as compared with control animals, in every fraction except the myelin. For the myelin neither the time course nor the nature of the protein would indicate appreciable labeling of an effect of nicotine. It is clear ($p < .001$) that microsomal protein synthesis is increased by nicotine treatment ($< 52\%$), with smaller nicotine-related increments in the synaptosomal (8%) and mitochondrial (24%) fractions. There is always the possibility that the differences observed in the latter two fractions could represent microsomal contamination during the fractionation procedure, but this seems rather unlikely since one would expect the greatest microsomal contribution to appear in the lighter fractions

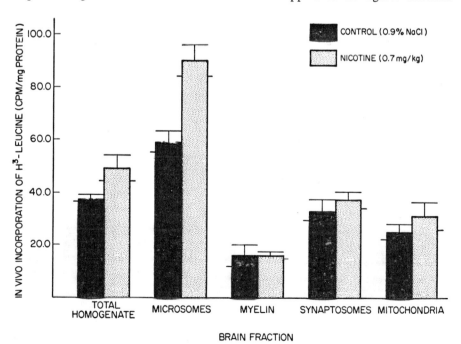

FIG. 6. Differences in protein synthesis for several fractions of mouse cerebral cortex 45 minutes following nicotine treatment.

(myelin) and the least in the more dense fractions (mitochondria). In the present data the reverse was observed.

In another experimental series the contributions of isolation and nicotine treatment to cerebral protein synthesis were compared. One group of male CF-1s strain mice had been individually housed for five weeks after weaning. Another group of the same strain was given nicotine alkaloid (0.7 mg/kg, i.p.) at 56 days of age. Appropriate control groups for each group respectively were group-housed mice and saline-treated mice. The differentially housed mice and the drug-treated animals (45 minutes after injection) were given intracranial H^3-leucine, for a 15-minute labeling pulse, and the cerebral cortex was excised and prepared, as previously described, for determination of specific activity of the incorporated amino acid. In Figure 7 the effects of isolation have been compared to those of nicotine for several fractions from the mouse cerebral cortex. Note that isolation resulted in reduced rates of protein synthesis (100% is the rate for each respective control group), and that nicotine treatment led to increased protein synthesis except in the myelin fraction. The effects of isolation upon cerebral protein synthesis may be associated with the elevation of cerebral 5-HT level and the reduction in 5-HT turnover also observed to be a consequence of isolation (Essman, 1969). Other observations have suggested that these 5-HT changes can inhibit brain protein synthesis (Essman, 1970a). A key difference between the effects of isolation and those of acute nicotine treatment is that nicotine, but not isolation,

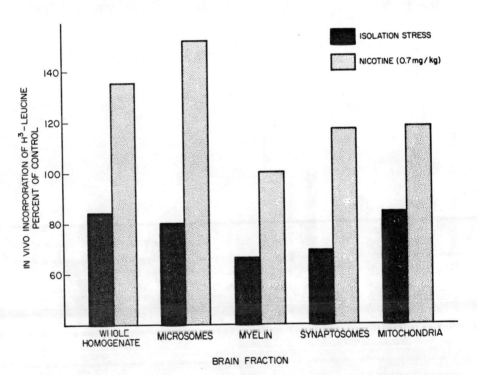

FIG. 7. Differences in cerebral protein synthesis for several cerebral fractions of the mouse brain. A comparison in the effects of isolation stress and nicotine treatment.

also produces 5-HT elevation and turnover changes, where both nicotine and isolation result in phasic alterations in other biologically active amines which can potentially modulate the synthesis of cerebral proteins. This difference between the effects of isolation and of nicotine raises the question of whether nicotine or its biologically active metabolites can oppose stress-induced changes in protein synthesis at specific cerebral sites, or can alter the synthesis of structural proteins regulating such cerebral processes as transport, diffusion, etc. Either or both such possibilities could provide a speculative base for an explanatory motivational mechanism for smoking behavior. Thus a reversal or attenuation of stress-induced reduction in site-specific protein synthesis could be occurring, and/or a unique protein specific to the central effects of nicotine could serve as a molecular substrate for reinforcement.

A final piece of work to be reported in this paper is a preliminary effort to observe the pattern of electrophoretically separated proteins obtained from a crude mitochondrial fraction composed of the insoluble proteins in the cerebral cortex. This latter fraction contained the insoluble proteins of the myelin, synaptosomes, and mitochondria, representing mainly structural proteins probably associated with organelle membranes. These proteins were solubilized by means of detergents. 200µg of such protein samples were obtained from three groups of animals; (*a*) saline treated (0.9%), (*b*) nicotine-treated, at 15 minutes after treatment, and (*c*) nicotine-treated at 45 minutes after treatment. Dosage of the latter two groups was 0.7 mg/kg, i.p., of nicotine alkaloid. These protein samples were run on polyacrylamide gel columns with appropriate current passed to cause migration of the protein constituents. The gels were stained with amido black and destained in acetic acid, to yield the electrophoretic patterns shown in Figure 8. There appear to be at least three protein bands unique to the insoluble protein fraction from the cerebral cortex of nicotine-treated mice—lb, 2a, and 3d. Additionally, there appear to be time-dependent protein bands among the nicotine-treated groups, 1a and 1c being observed at 45 minutes posttreatment, but not at 15 minutes. These could possibly represent differences in the migration of bands 1d and 1e observed in the control gels and not seen in the same position under treatment conditions. These data suggest qualitative differences among the constituent proteins comprising the insoluble protein pool of a crude mitochondrial fraction derived from mouse cerebral cortex. The differences appear to be a function of *in vivo* treatment with nicotine. These preliminary findings on the effect of acute nicotine treatment indicate the need for further evaluation of semichronic and chronic effects and the extent to which nicotine-related influences upon cerebral protein synthesis may be linked up with the appearance of apparently unique cerebral proteins after acute nicotine treatment.

SUMMARY

At points throughout this paper the implications of the reported findings for the general problem of accounting for the prevalence of the smoking habit have been so forceful that the temptation to suggest conceptual bridges between the observed biochemical effects of nicotine and the central correlates of the motivational mechanisms underlying smoking behavior has not been entirely suppressed. Model

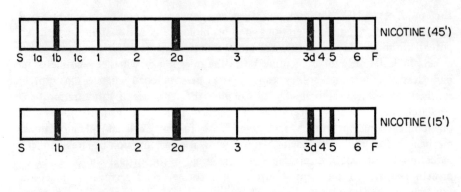

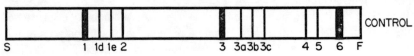

FIG. 8. Disc gel electrophoresis of insoluble proteins from a crude mitochondrial fraction of mouse cerebral cortex; effects of nicotine at two posttreatment times.

building is perhaps premature, but some speculation is nonetheless appropriate; if for no other reason than to direct our research efforts into the realm of relevance. We have pointed to some central biochemical changes effected by nicotine, and we have shown how certain conditions, known to alter specific drive states, can also modify the uptake, metabolism, and neurochemical effects of nicotine. It is our hope that these findings will stimulate further experimental effort to relate the motivation to smoking tobacco to the pharmacological effects of nicotine.

REFERENCES

Armitage, A. K., & Hall, G. H. Further evidence relating the mode of action of nicotine in the central nervous system. *Nature,* 1967, **214,** 977–979.

Bovet, D., Bovet-Nitti, F., & Oliverio, A. Effects of nicotine on avoidance conditioning in inbred strains of mice. *Psychopharmacologia,* 1966, **10,** 1–5.

Burn, J. H. Cardiovascular effects of nicotine and smoking. Part II. Pharmacological action of nicotine and tobacco smoke: The action of nicotine on the heart. *Annals of the New York Academy of Science,* 1960, **90,** 70–73.

Essman, W. B. "Free" and motivated behaviour and amine metabolism in isolated mice. In S. Garattini, & E. B. Sigg, (Eds.), *Biology of aggressive behavior.* Amsterdam: Excerpta Medica Foundation, 1969.

Essman, W. B. The role of biogenic amines in memory consolidation. In G. Adam, (Ed.), *The biology of memory.* Budapest: Akademiai Kiado Publishers, 1970. (a)

Essman, W. B. Some neurochemical correlates of altered memory consolidation. *Transactions of the New York Academy of Sciences,* 1970, **32,** 948-973. (b)

Essman, W. B. Metabolic and behavioral consequences of nicotine. In W. L. Smith, (Ed.), *Drugs and cerebral function.* Springfield, Ill.: Charles C. Thomas, 1971. (a)

Essman, W. B. Isolation-induced behavioral modification: Some neurochemical correlates. In M. G. Sturman, D. J. McGinty, & A. M. Adinolfi, (Eds.), *Brain development and behavior.* New York: Academic Press, 1971. (b)

Essman, W. B. Changes in cholinergic effects and avoidance behavior by nicotine in differentially housed mice. *International Journal of Neuroscience,* 1971, **2,** 199–205. (c)

Essman, W. B. Neuromolecular modulation of experimentally induced retrograde amnesia. *Confinia Neurologica,* 1972, in press. (a)

Essman, W. B. Contributions of differential housing to brain development: Some implications for sleep behavior. In C. Clemente, D. Purpura, & F. Mayer, (Eds.), *Sleep and the Maturing Nervous System.* New York: Academic Press, 1972, Pp. 99–107. (b)

Essman, W. B., & Essman, S. G. Cholinergic mechanisms and avoidance behavior acquisition: Effects of nicotine in mice. *Psychological Reports,* 1971, **29,** 987–993.

Essman, W. B., Golod, M. I., & Steinberg, M. Alterations in the behavioral and biochemical effects of electroconvulsive shock with nicotine. *Psychonomic Science,* 1968, **12,** 107–108.

Essman, W. B., & Heldman, E. Impairment of avoidance acquisition and altered regional brain amine levels in mice with uremic endotoxemia. *Physiology and Behavior,* 1972, **8,** 143-146.

Essman, W. B., Heldman, E., Barker, L. A., & Valzelli, L. Development of microsomal changes in liver and brain of differentially housed mice. *Federation Proceedings, Federation of American Societies for Experimental Biology,* 1972, **31,** 232.

Jarvik, M. E. The role of nicotine in the smoking habit. In W. A. Hunt (Ed.), *Learning mechanisms and smoking.* Chicago: Aldine, 1970.

Larson, P. S., & Silvette, H. *Tobacco: Experimental and clinical studies,* Supplement I. Baltimore: Williams and Wilkins, 1968.

Murphree, H. B. (Ed.). The effects of nicotine and smoking on the central nervous system. *Annals of the New York Academy of Science,* 1967, **142,** 1–333.

Murray, M. Response of oligodendrocytes to seratonia. In W. Windle (Ed.), *Biology of neuroglia.* Springfield: Charles C. Thomas, 1958.

Westfall, T. C., Flemming, R. M., Fudger, M. S., & Clark, W. G. Effect of nicotine and related substrates upon amine levels in the brain. *Annals of the New York Academy of Science,* 1967, **142,** 83 –100.

Whittaker, V. P. The synaptosome. In A. Lajtha (Ed.), *Handbook of neurochemistry.* Vol. 2. New York: Plenum Press, 1969.

Wooley, D. W. A method for demonstration of the effects of serotonin on learning ability. In M. Ya. Mikhel'son & V. G. Longo (Eds.), *Pharmacology of conditioning, learning and retention.* Oxford: Pergamon Press, 1965.

5

ADDITIONAL CHARACTERISTIC EEG DIFFERENCES BETWEEN SMOKERS AND NONSMOKERS[1]

Barbara B. Brown
Veterans Administration Hospital at
Sepulveda, California

INTRODUCTION

The habit of smoking cigarettes is difficult to assay in psychophysiological parameters. Despite the worldwide prevelance of cigarette smoking, despite the admission by most smokers that it is a habit of considerable strength, and despite the current movement designed to break the smoking habit, the question of why people smoke remains unanswered.

Knowledge of the pharmacological effects of cigarette contents contributes little to our understanding of this basic question. The effects of cigarette smoking on the central nervous system are extremely complex. Pharmacological studies in animals indicate that both nicotine and cigarette smoke produce different effects as a function of dosage, behavioral conditions, and the experimental animal (Brown, 1967; Domino, 1967; Armitage, Hall, & Morrison, 1968; Hall, 1970; Geller & Hartmann, 1969; Barnes, 1966). Effects in human beings of actually smoking cigarettes are also equivocal and variable. Some investigators have concluded that the effects arise from a type of conditioned response (Burch & DePasquale, 1961; Murphree, Pfeiffer, & Price, 1967; Hauser, Schwartz, Roth, & Bickford, 1958; Domino & von Baumgarten, 1969; Ulett & Itil, 1969). Doses of the constituents required to produce cleanly observable effects are usually much larger than those contained in an average cigarette or two. Further, there is little agreement about the nature of the physiological effects of inhaling the smoke. There are also problems in comparing different studies because of large differences in subject populations, such

[1] This study was supported by a grant from The Council for Tobacco Research, U.S.A.

as age, sex, length of smoking habit, and whether the subject inhales. Comparison of studies is further complicated by the life situation of the smoker at the time of observation.

Few studies have been directed specifically to the question of *why* people smoke cigarettes. A number of studies (Lawton & Phillips, 1956; Heath, 1958; Seltzer, 1963, 1967, 1968; Damon, 1961; Eysenck, Tarrant, Woolf, & England, 1960; Eysenck, 1963a, 1963b; Lawton, 1962; Schubert, 1958; James, Woodruff, & Werner, 1965; Smith, 1968; Matarazzo & Saslow, 1960) have documented striking psychological and physiological differences between individuals who tend to smoke cigarettes and those who do not, and it has been found that EEG patterns also differ between these groups of individuals (Brown, 1968; Hauser et al., 1958). These studies provide strong evidence that such differences arise from genetic or constitutional factors and that individuals who do adopt the smoking habit are perhaps predisposed to do so.

The present study is addressed to the relationship between degrees of smoking activity and manifest EEG patterns. Evidence is presented which suggests that individuals who tend to adopt the smoking habit possess inherently different EEG patterns from individuals who do not tend to adopt the smoking habit. Our findings suggest the following hypotheses: (*a*) a characteristic family of brain wave patterns represents a constitutional characteristic of heightened brain electrical excitability which may be associated with a fundamental *physiologic* predisposition to the smoking habit or to *some equivalent activity;* (*b*) a positive relationship exists between the amount of smoking activity and the degree of brain excitability; *and* (*c*) smoking rate is regulated to maintain an effective balance between the behavioral accompaniments of EEG synchronization and desynchronization.

A further outcome of these studies is that the strikingly different brain wave patterns between smokers and nonsmokers may be a factor of major importance in interpreting the relationships between EEG activity and behavior.

METHOD

Subjects

A cross-section of adults (ages 21 to 65, 45% males) was obtained from the hospital staff, from volunteer workers, and from both professional and nonprofessional workers at nearby colleges and industrial organizations. There were 88 subjects. In most cases the reason given for the EEG recordings was that they were part of a study to relate EEGs to type of work. It was necessary to seek out both heavy smokers and former heavy smokers, although *very* heavy smokers volunteered.

Subject categories are given in Table 1.

Recording

EEGs were recorded bipolarly from temporo-parietal, parieto-occipital, and occipital sites of both hemispheres. Eye movements were also recorded continuously to provide a monitor so that no EEG analyses were made during

TABLE 1

Subjects by Group

Category	Definition	Designation	Number
Never smoked	Self-defined	NS-1* (early group)	13
		NS-2 (later group)	13
Average smoker	3/4 to 1–1/4 packs/day	AS	13
Heavy smoker	2 to 3 packs/day	HS	13
Very heavy smoker	More than 3 packs/day	VHS	13
Former average smoker	AS but stopped at least 6 months ago	FAS	11
Former heavy smoker	HS but stopped at least 6 months ago	FHS	12

*NS−1 and NS−2 were run 18 months apart (at beginning and end of study).

major eye movement activity. EEG activity from the right parieto-occipital placement was used routinely for analysis. The EEG signals were recorded on a Grass Model 6 EEG machine and simultaneously on analogue tape. Recording sessions were run for at least 90 minutes. Data analysis was conducted for artifact-free samples of 5-minute durations from the temporal midpoint of the recording session. EEG analysis was also conducted for samples from midsections of the initial and final thirds of the recording session, but results did not differ significantly from the midpoint samples and are not reported.

Analysis

EEG analysis was conducted by filtering the taped records for alpha (8.5 to 13 Hz), beta (13 to 28 Hz), and theta (3.5 to 7.5 Hz) waves. Interval histograms were then derived for each frequency range by means of the amplitude discriminator and C.A.T. 400, using baseline voltages equivalent to 10 μV for alpha, 3.5 μV for beta, and 15 μV for theta frequencies. The abundance of each range was measured in terms of peak area of the histograms calculated by multiplying the peak height, measured in millimeters, by the width at one-half the peak height (giving an area equal to one-half the base of the triangle times its height). Mean frequencies in hertz were determined by measuring the interval from zero time to the peak of the histogram, converting to milliseconds and calculating the reciprocal. The variation of each dominant frequency was determined by measuring the intervals at both edges of the width of the histogram at one-half the peak height and by calculating the reciprocals in hertz. The Q of the peak ("peakedness" or degree of sharpness) was then calculated by dividing the mean frequency by the range of variation. Amplitudes were measured directly from the EEG records and were confirmed by measuring the amplitudes from tape playback by means of an oscilloscope.

Estimate of personality characteristics

Although evaluation of behavioral traits of the subjects was not an original objective of the study, a check list of some general personality dimensions was used as a guide for future work. Results were sufficiently different for at least two categories of subjects to warrant inclusion in this report. The experimental observers rated each subject on a scale of 1 to 10 for the following eight behavioral traits: aggression, anxiety, intelligence level for occupation, independence, physical activity, verbal activity, contentment, and sociability. Scores for each dimension were averaged across observers for each subject group. At least one observer for each experiment was unaware of the smoking history of the subject.

RESULTS

Values for characteristics of EEG alpha, beta, and theta frequency ranges are given in Table 2. Those EEG characteristics which provided the basis for significant discrimination between degrees of cigarette smoking activity and nonsmoking were:

TABLE 2

EEG Characteristics

Subject Group	No. Ss	Frequency Hz	Variation as "Q"	Amplitude μV	% Abundance[a]
			Alpha		
NS-1	13	10.01	4.8	20.2	47
NS-2	13	9.8	4.5	24.1	52
FAS	11	10.1	5.6	22.7	50
FHS	12	11.1*	4.2	21.6	39
AS	13	11.4*	3.6*	30.2*	54
HS	13	10.8*	4.3	26.2	43
VHS	13	11.0*	3.8*	16.3*	20*
			Beta		
NS-1	13	18.7	4.2	8.3	25
NS-2	13	19.2	3.7	10.3	32
FAS	11	20.4	4.3	8.4	37
FHS	12	19.0	3.6	8.6	39
AS	13	19.9	4.2	16.0*	37
HS	13	18.8	4.8	14.7*	35
VHS	13	18.8	3.9	13.7*	78*
			Theta		
NS-1	13	5.2	3.3	19.2	30
NS-2	13	5.5	3.1	19.3	19
FAS	11	5.3	5.2*	20.3	14
FHS	12	5.7	5.1*	18.5	25
AS	13	5.5	5.1*	23.5	14
HS	13	6.0**	4.7*	24.5	21
VHS	13	5.9	4.7*	22.3	3*

[a]% abundance of the summed three rhythmic activities (α, β, θ) only.
  *$p = .01$.
  **$p = > .02 < .05$.

alpha frequency and its variation, amplitude of alpha, amplitude of beta, and the frequency variation of theta. Values for relative abundance of the three frequency ranges indicated significant differences only between very heavy smokers and all other categories.

Alpha Activity

All active smoker subjects and the FHS group exhibited significantly higher frequency of alpha than did the nonsmoker and FAS groups. For average and for very heavy smokers, alpha frequency was significantly more variable (Q value). Variation appears to increase with increased frequency of alpha. The amplitude of alpha for the AS group was considerably larger than that of the NS groups, whereas that for the VHS group was significantly smaller. The abundance of alpha activity present in the EEG was similar for all groups except for the VHS group, which contained approximately half the amount of alpha per unit of time.

Beta Activity

One of the chief, visually distinguishing characteristics of heavy-smoker EEG records is the extraordinary amount of *rhythmic* beta activity. A further difference between smoker and nonsmoker groups in the beta frequency range was found in the amplitude characteristic, that for the smoker groups being nearly twice that for either the NS or the former-smoker groups. The total amount of beta activity present in the EEG (sum of both rhythmic and nonrhythmic) was similar for all groups except for the VHS group, which exhibited at least 50% more beta activity.

Theta Activity

Although not statistically significant for individual comparisons, the trend of differences suggests that the HS and VHS groups tend toward slightly higher than average frequencies of theta. The distinguishing characteristic, however, is shown by the surprisingly greater relative regularity of theta rhythm in all smoker and former-smoker groups as compared to the NS groups. Again, as for abundance of alpha and beta, the VHS group was distinguished by a markedly different relative content of theta in the EEG.

Number of Identifiable Frequencies

All active- and former-smoker subjects were found to have approximately 30% more distinguishable frequencies in the EEG than did the NS groups as identified by histogram peaks. These were spread throughout the frequency range analyzed, i.e., from 1 through 28 Hz, but were most evident in the beta frequency range. The average number of different specific identifiable EEG rhythms for the different groups were 2.75 for NS-1, 2.6 for NS-2, 2.25 for FAS, 2.55 for FHS, 3.3 for AS, 3.6 for HS, and 3.5 for VHS.

Muscle Artifacts

EEG records of heavy- and very-heavy-smoker subjects were commonly contaminated by high-frequency muscle artifacts in all EEG leads. This was rarely affected by changing electrode position, but in most cases the artifacts lessened after an

TABLE 3

Scores (on Scale of 1 to 10) for Personality Dimensions Averaged across
Observers for Each Subject Group

Dimension	Nonsmokers	Avg. smokers	Heavy smokers	Very heavy smokers
Aggression	5.0	6.0	7.1	9.8
Anxiety	4.5	7.1	7.8	8.5
Intelligence (for occupation)	6.2	6.3	7.3	8.1
Independence	3.5	5.2	6.6	8.4
Physical Activity	4.0	5.2	6.0	8.2
Verbal Activity	5.2	5.0	6.7	7.8
Contentment	8.5	7.1	5.2	3.0
Sociability	7.7	7.2	6.6	4.3

hour or so of recording. In a significant number of cases such artifacts continued in one or more leads throughout the recording session. Scalp muscle artifacts were rarely if ever encountered in nonsmoker subjects.

Personality Characteristics

Although notations of personality characteristics were originally not intended to be reported and were not well controlled, results suggest differences among subject groups and do provide a liaison between the EEG results and personality characteristics described in the literature for smokers. The results are tabulated in Table 3.

While no single factor can be used to demonstrate significant differences owing to the evaluation technique, nonetheless the consistency of differences between heavy and very heavy smokers and nonsmokers does indicate that heavy smoking relates to a quite different set of personality characteristics.

DISCUSSION

This report confirms and extends results of an earlier study (Brown, 1968) demonstrating marked differences in brain wave patterns between smokers and nonsmokers. A clear-cut relationship exists between pattern of EEG and degree of cigarette-smoking activity. EEG patterns of smokers and nonsmokers differ for all of the major characteristics, particularly in the frequency and amplitude of both alpha and beta activity. Nonrhythmic activity also differs markedly in that the desynchronized EEG of smokers appears to be chiefly a mixture of fast frequencies, and that of nonsmokers a mixture of slower frequencies.

The significance of the differences is more easily seen by comparing differences in EEG characteristics among the three most different categories—i.e., average smokers, very heavy smokers, and nonsmokers—to the differences in EEG patterns which occur over the continuum from activation to synchronous EEG activity. At first glance the EEGs of nonsmokers appear to resemble the average EEGs of rest and relaxation characterized by predominantly slow wave activity varying between theta and alpha rhythms and with nonrhythmic activity appearing as a mixture of relatively slow waves (Lindsley, 1960; Johnson, Lubin, Naitoh, Nute, & Austin, 1969; Volavka, Matousek, & Roubicek, 1967). The EEGs of very heavy smokers tend to resemble the EEG patterns of intense activation characterized by desynchrony comprised of fast, low-voltage activity (Lindsley, 1960; Volavka et al., 1967; Daniel, 1965); and the EEG patterns of average smokers contain the high-frequency rhythmic activity suggestive of intermediate degrees of activation usually indicated by fast (13 to 30 Hz) rhythmic activities (Volavka et al., 1967; Daniel, 1965; Gale; Dunkin, & Coles, 1969).

While these generalizations may reasonably well reflect the existing state of the EEG-behavior relationship among subjects with different degrees of smoking activity, the cause for the activated state appears to be one of considerable complexity. A persistent state of activation is quite different from one of momentary responsiveness; it is the complex resultant of behavioral characteristics, personality, and intelligence, and it may be further complicated by superimposed pharmacologic effects of the smoking habit.

Five outstanding and consistent EEG characteristics were found for individuals who had developed a habit of smoking cigarettes: (*a*) increased frequency of alpha activity, (*b*) increased amplitude of rhythmic beta activity between 13 and 28 Hz, (*c*) less variation in frequency of theta, (*d*) greater abundance of identifiably different frequencies within the range between 3 and 28 Hz, and (*e*) higher frequencies during desynchronization.

Reports relevant to the *set* of EEG characteristics found in the present study are virtually nonexistent; however, some literature reporting on one or two characteristics is available for comparison. Such reports relate EEG characteristics: (*a*) to short-term mental work or to arousal responses, i.e., effects related to EEG synchronizing mechanisms; (*b*) to rather specific personality traits; and (*c*) to effects of certain sedative-tranquilizer drugs. The significance of such relationships between EEG activity and behavior, to results of the present study will be discussed, albeit necessarily briefly, as they relate to elucidating the relationship between smoking activity and the EEG.

Relationship of Results to EEG Synchronizing Mechanisms

Numerous research reports have demonstrated that increased mental and emotional activities are characterized either by reduction in alpha activity (reported only in terms of abundance or amplitude) or by marked EEG desynchronization (Lorens & Darrow, 1962; Hofer & Hinkle, 1964; MacNeilage, 1966; Berlyne & McDonnell, 1965; Glass, 1966). Other studies have, however, demonstrated *enhanced* alpha activity and/or synchronization under similar experimental conditions (Legewie, Simonova, & Creutzfeldt, 1969; Giannitrapani, 1966; Morrell, 1966; Kreitman & Shaw, 1965). And still other studies have demonstrated shifts in EEG frequency spectra during mental, visual, emotional, and cognitive tasks (Legewie et al., 1969; Kreitman & Shaw, 1965; Berkhout & Walter, 1968; Grunewald, Simonova, & Creutzfeldt, 1968; Berkhout, Walter, & Adey, 1969; Glass & Kwiatkowski, 1970). The behavioral characteristics of attention, arousal, alerting, and short-term anxiety thus appear to be accompanied by changes in EEG synchronizing activity manifest as desynchronization, alpha blocking, alpha enhancement, or decreased frequency of alpha and/or beta activity. Recent studies suggest that alpha enhancement and alpha blocking are simply different manifestations of the same response continuum to arousal, alerting, and attention (Daniel, 1965; Morrell, 1966; Kreitman & Shaw, 1965; Brown, 1966).

The high alpha frequency of smoker subjects may reflect one or more aspects of the alerting-response continuum. Although alpha blocking occurs more frequently, increased frequency of alpha is often seen during mental work (Giannitrapani, 1966; Morrell, 1966; Kreitman & Shaw, 1965; Berkhout et al., 1969; Glass & Kwiatkowski, 1970). Further, it has been suggested that the shift of the amplitude distribution of the gross EEG toward nongaussian implies an increase in the cooperative activity of cortical neuronal elements during performance of a mental task (Elul, 1969; Walter, Kodo, Rhodes, & Adey, 1967).

High levels of beta activity with a corresponding lowering of content of alpha are generally considered to relate to high levels of arousal. Volavka et al. (1967) conclude that the amount and variability of beta activity are more closely related to the general level of activation than that of other frequency ranges. Similarly Koukkou, Madey, and Yeager (1969) have reported that with the same class of recall, distinctly higher levels of vigilance were associated with learning of unfamiliar material than with relearning of familiar material. High-voltage beta activity may also be associated with the processing of visual information (Clusin, 1969). It seems possible that the high-voltage beta characteristic of smoker subjects may indicate a particular perceptual style related to greater attention to, or enhanced processing of, visual information.

Although only the trend of EEG changes suggests that heavy smokers exhibit a higher and less variable frequency of theta, these differences may be more real than apparent in view of the small frequency range designated for theta and its diversity of behavioral correlates. The relationship of theta to specific levels of vigilance has been indicated by Daniel (1967) and by Legewie et al. (1969). The latters' results indicate that individual EEG differences between mental and motor tasks are reflected especially in the theta range. Dixon and Lear (1964) have further identified theta activity with the awareness threshold.

Relationship of Results to EEG
Correlates of Personality

A number of extensive studies have identified characteristic personality traits of smokers as compared to nonsmokers. For example, Eysenck (1963a) found a direct relationship between degrees of smoking activity and the continuum from introversion to extroversion, but no evidence that such personality configurations could be considered neurotic. Lawton and Phillips (1956) also noted the "nervous" traits of smokers but could not conclude that smokers were necessarily nervous. Heath's (1958) descriptions of personality traits of smokers were confirmed in the present study: "The smokers showed great energy, restlessness, seeking for danger, a kind of independence which kept them actively engaged in some enterprise which appeals . . . the nonsmokers who were found to be characteristically steady, dependable and hard workers, leading quiet, progressive lives . . . although somewhat on the bland uncommunicative side [p. 386]."[2] Heath concluded, very significantly, that "smoking is more than a superficial habit overlayed indiscriminately upon a group of men, but has some origin at least in personality and physiologic characteristics. Such characteristics may have just as much right to a place in the etiology of disease as the tobacco smoke ingestion itself [p. 388]."

Considerable argument exists in the literature on relationships between EEG patterns and personality characteristics. Meaningful relationships are difficult to extract because of the large numbers of EEG aspects which may be involved and because investigators employ different aspects of the EEG or even of alpha activity for evaluations.

Although EEG responses to *short* periods of alerting, attention, or anxiety are well known, EEG responses which tend to characterize *persistent* behavioral states of anxiety, hyperactivity, hyperexcitability, and habitual restlessness are much less well defined. It seems generally assumed that the neurophysiological contributions to alerting responses contribute similarly to the persistent states such as anxiety. EEG responses to mildly alerting or arousal stimuli may, however, undergo habituation and thus may tend not to be sustained, particularly when behavioral responses are not marked. An example of this adaptation is the "first night" anxiety effect commonly found in sleep studies. On the other hand, extreme states of persistent alerting, anxiety, and hyperactivity are generally classified as neurotic or even psychotic. These are accompanied by readily recognizable EEG abnormalities (Doniger, Doniger, Angel-Zillegas, & Angel-Zillegas, 1957; Schneider, 1957; Lester & Edwards, 1966), none of which were seen in the smokers' EEGs. Thus, persistent states lying between the acute and chronic activation, in which the behavioral responses do not interfere with the effective and social functioning of the individual, remain difficult to establish conclusively by electroencephalographic criteria.

In general, extrovert, mentally active, aggressive individuals have been characterized by low levels of alpha activity, higher alpha frequencies, and large amounts of both beta and theta activity (Mundy-Castle, 1958; Saunders, 1960; Sugerman, 1961; Saul, Davis, & Davis, 1949; Broadhurst & Glass, 1969; Giannitrapani, 1969). The EEG characteristics of the smoker subjects across groups correlate well with such data indicating the behavioral characteristic of extroversion. The EEG characteristics for both the heavy and the very heavy smokers were similar to those described by Gray (1964) and by Nebylitsyn (1963), tending toward what Gray described as a "predominance of excitation in dynamism," i.e., to a complex syndrome of neurotic tendencies.

The high incidence of relatively large amplitude, *rhythmic* beta activity in all smoker subjects appears to be a highly specific characteristic of a specific set of personality traits. (A second relationship of this activity, i.e., to drug action, is discussed below.) Rapid cycles of *less* than 25 μV are a component of many normal

[2] It should be noted that these observations of some 15 years ago were made under quite different conditions of stability of social structure, of social interaction, and of social and individual constraints than obtain today. It seems likely that more nonsmokers exhibiting traits noted by Heath for smokers exist today on the basis that there are now more socially acceptable outlets for the energy of hyperactivity, habitual restlessness, aggressive tendencies, etc.

tracings (Lester & Edwards, 1966; Finley, 1944), although not usually reported. Recently Vogel (1966) has defined a special type of normal human EEG in which the alpha waves are replaced by 16 to 19 Hz beta waves which are blocked by eye opening and are optimal in the occipital areas. Data from the families of these subjects suggested a simple autosomal dominant mode of inheritance.

Large amounts of beta activity in the same frequency range as measured here have been reported by Gale, Coles, & Blaydon (1969) as characteristics of extroverts as compared to introverts. A comparison of the integrated outputs of each of the 3 major frequency ranges of the present study to results of Gale et al. show marked similarities between extroverts and smokers and between introverts and nonsmokers. These data also support the claim of (Eysenck, 1963a, 1963b) that smokers tend to be extroverts.

There is thus considerable evidence suggesting that the beta wave characteristics of smoker subjects is of an inherited or constitutional origin. The characteristics of *both* alpha and beta activity in smoker subjects are similar to those reported for extroverts. The relatively high amplitudes of beta in the average- and heavy-smoker groups suggests a condition comparable to the shift toward alpha from a desynchronized pattern, and may indicate that the underlying condition of excitement, anxiety, or arousal was less severe in these subjects and more severe in the heavier smoking groups. If so, it might be deduced that smokers accomplish dosage titration in themselves by means of subjective effects and that these are accompanied by appropriate EEG changes.

The conclusion that smokers evidence quite distinctive EEG patterns which are naturally occurring (genetic or constitutional), rather than of neurotic origin, is further supported by noting two general influences. First, data on beta activity is scarce because of the difficulty of obtaining clean EEG recordings from subjects seemingly deficient in alpha activity. The background of such EEG patterns is usually low amplitude. When conventionally recorded, noise signals predominate. Scalp muscle artifacts also can obscure the tracing. A typical comment is, "50% of the volunteers were not recorded because of inconsistent resting alpha rhythm [Hofer & Hinkle, 1964]." It seems likely that many normal subjects have been ignored in experimental EEG work because of these difficulties. In the present study, four subjects were impossible to record properly, and all four subjects were heavy smokers.

Secondly, it seems doubtful that the increased severity of alerting or arousal patterns occurring with increasing amounts of smoking activity are due to environmentally produced anxiety responses, in view of the fact that smokers comprise some 70 million of the country's population. It is more likely that characteristics such as specific frequencies of alpha and specific amplitudes of beta have not been adequately discriminated to define extremes of the normal ranges as they relate to behavioral traits.

Relationship of Results to Actions of Sedative-Tranquilizer Drugs

A second explanation of the high incidence of large-amplitude beta activity in smoker subjects is that it may result from effects of small doses of certain sedative or tranquilizer agents. The EEG patterns of smokers resemble those described by Gibbs and Gibbs (1962), and by Itil (1968) either for small doses of barbiturates or for the minor tranquilizers. The first phase of the sedative action is production of high-voltage fast activity which may be in the 13 to 28 Hz beta range, but is chiefly manifest in the higher frequency range of 20 to 32 Hz and by amplitudes *above* 25 μV, occasionally reaching 100 μV. Gibbs and Gibbs (1962) note that there apparently is no relationship between this "fast" EEG response to sedatives and the behavioral response as determined clinically.

Only the very heavy smoker group showed EEG characteristics described by Gibbs and Gibbs (1962). They noted that the more intense the normally occurring arousal pattern, the more responsive is the EEG to the production of the fast activity pattern due to the sedative. This lends support to the argument that smokers' EEG patterns tend to be of the intensely alerted type in the absence of smoking activity.

There is growing evidence that nicotine, and/or possibly an integral part of the smoking act, exerts a tranquilizing action on the CNS (Brown, 1967; Geller & Hartmann, 1969; Hauser et al., 1958; Domino and von Baumgarten, 1969). If the effect is mild, one might expect only the earliest indices of drug action, i.e., modest increases of both frequency and amplitude. Such relationships appear to hold in the case of smoking activity and its effect on EEG patterns.

Since the manifestations of arousal, restlessness, anxiety, etc. are increased by an increase in smoking activity, it might be expected that the EEG effect of a mild tranquilizer would be more apparent in average smokers and only weakly apparent in the case of heavy smokers, as judged by both the frequency and the amount of rhythmic activity. The fact that heavy smokers appear only moderately responsive to effects of tranquilization by nicotine (and/or the smoking act) further suggests that the underlying conditions of persistent EEG activation and evidence of behavioral arousal are considerably greater than in either nonsmokers or average smokers. If the drug effect is to favor desynchronization of the EEG, it can be deduced that the usual (nondrug) state of EEG activity in heavy and very heavy smokers tends to be of the alerting type, and would imply a genetic or constitutional origin for both EEG and behavioral characteristics.

These deductions also indicate that the action of smoking or of nicotine is not markedly cumulative. If it were cumulative one would expect that the response of heavy smokers would, over time, approach that of average smokers.

There is suggestive evidence in the present study that long-term effects of withdrawal from heavy smoking are evidenced by disappearance of synchrony, regardless of frequency, and diminution of beta amplitudes. It is most difficult to accumulate former smokers with similar intervals since last smoking. Moreover, subjects who habitually smoke two to three or more packs of cigarettes per day rarely volunteer or will even submit to EEG recording. Further, such EEG records would have to be controlled for changing EEG characteristics occurring with aging. Nonetheless, the trends indicated in the results suggest that the EEG characteristics of former average smokers tend to exhibit EEG patterns similar to those of the nonsmokers, whereas the former heavy smokers appear to have retained several characteristics of the heavy-smoker group. The results imply that either the effect of smoking continues for long periods of time, or that the inherent EEG patterns of individuals who tend to smoke heavily contain the high-voltage beta characteristics. Furthermore, the former heavy smoker group also retained a higher alpha frequency, a tendency for lower abundance of alpha, and a tendency for slightly higher theta frequency, along with less variation of theta frequency also shown by the active smoker.

Hypothesis

The results of the present study, along with the correlation of these results with those cited above from literature; suggest the following explanations of why certain individuals adopt the cigarette-smoking habit.

First, studies of the maturation of the EEG (Pond, 1963) indicate that the slow-frequency EEG patterns of infancy increase progressively to a mean of approximately 10 Hz around the age of 13 and undergo little further change until old age. EEG periods of synchronized activity in the mature subjects (usually at the alpha frequency) alternate with periods of desynchronized activity. In the latter, frequency components tend to be predominantly in the lower portion of the 13 to 28 Hz beta range. The present results suggest that individuals who tend to smoke heavily may continue the EEG "maturation" process, proceeding to the more extreme limits of fast, low-voltage *rhythmic* activity.

Numerous reports have documented the presence of rhythmic, high-frequency (13 to 28 Hz), relatively high-amplitude beta in normal EEG records. This specific EEG activity has received little attention, as the majority of experimental EEG studies emphasizes either alpha activity or responses involving desynchronization.

The high incidence of fast, low-voltage EEG activity found in the present study also suggests a genetic or constitutional origin and is similar to that reported by Vogel (1966). The unusual rhythmicity found for the smokers' beta activity might be accounted for by an analogy to the findings of Gibbs and Gibbs (1962) that such high-frequency rhythmicity occurs with small doses of certain sedative-tranquilizer drugs and that this effect occurs more frequently on a background of desynchronization. If nicotine (and/or smoking) caused stimulation, i.e., alerting, the expected EEG pattern would be that of either desynchronization or attenuation of alpha activity.

Analysis of these various aspects thus suggests that cigarette-smoking activity acts to slow and increase the amount of the rhythmicity of the fast and/or desynchronized activities inherent in the EEG patterns of habitual smokers.

REFERENCES

Armitage, A. K., Hall, G. H., & Morrison, C. F. Pharmacological basis for the tobacco smoking habit. *Nature* (London), 1968, **217**, 331–334.

Barnes, T. C. Cerebral effects of cigarette smoke. (Paper presented at American Society of Pharmacology & Experimental Therapeutics Meeting, Mexico City, July 1966). *The Pharmacologist*, 1966, **8**, 219.

Berkhout, J., & Walter, D. O. Temporal stability and individual differences in the human EEG: An analysis of variance of spectral values. *IEEE Transactions on Bio-Medical Engineering*, 1968, **15**, 165–168.

Berkhout, J., Walter, D. O., & Adey, W. R. Alterations of the human electroencephalogram induced by stressful verbal activity. *Electroencephalography and Clinical Neurophysiology*, 1969, **27**, 457–469.

Berlyne, D. E., & McDonnell, P. Effects of stimulus complexity and incongruity on duration of EEG desynchronization. *Electroencephalography and Clinical Neurophysiology*, 1965, **18**, 156–161.

Broadhurst, A., & Glass, A. Relationship of personality measures to the alpha rhythm of the electroencephalogram. *British Journal of Psychiatry*, 1969, **115**, 199–204.

Brown, B. B. Specificity of EEG photic flicker responses to color as related to visual imagery ability. *Psychophysiology*, 1966, **2**, 197–207.

Brown, B. B. Relationship between evoked response changes and behavior following small doses of nicotine. *Annals of the New York Academy of Science,* 1967, **142**, 190–200.

Brown, B. B. Some characteristic EEG differences between heavy smoker and nonsmoker subjects. *Neuropsychologia*, 1968, **6**, 381–388.

Burch, G. E., & DePasquale, N. P. A study of variables which offer difficulty in the evaluation of the peripheral vascular response to cigarette smoking. *Journal of Laboratory and Clinical Medicine*, 1961, **58**, 694–703.

Clusin, W. EEG and the measurement of visual performance. *Electroencephalography and Clinical Neurophysiology*, 1969, **27**, 707.

Damon, A. Constitution and smoking. *Science*, 1961, **134**, 339–340.

Daniel, R. S. Electroencephalographic pattern quantification and the arousal continuum. *Psychophysiology*, 1965, **2**, 146–160.

Daniel, R. S. Alpha and theta EEG in vigilance. *Perceptual and Motor Skills*, 1967, **25**, 697–703.

Dixon, N. F., & Lear, T. E. Incidence of theta rhythm prior to awareness of a visual stimulus. *Nature*, 1964, **203**, 167–170.

Domino, E. F. Electroencephalographic and behavioral arousal effects of small doses of nicotine: A neuropsychopharmacological study. *Annals of the New York Academy of Science*, 1967, **142**, 216–244.

Domino, E. F., & von Baumgarten, A. M. Tobacco cigarette smoking and patellar reflex depression. *Clinical Pharmacology and Therapeutics*, 1969, **10**, 72–79.

Doniger, M., Doniger, S., Angel-Zillegas, G., & Angel-Zillegas, A. Confrontations des donnees des examens psychologiques et de l'electroencephalogramme chez 100 nevroses. *Electroencephalography and Clinical Neurophysiology*, 1957, **6**, 315–338.

Elul, R. Gaussian behavior of the electroencephalogram: Changes during performance of mental task. *Science*, 1969, **164**, 328–331.

Eysenck, H. J. Personality and cigarette smoking. *Life Sciences*, 1963, **3**, 777–792. (a)

Eysenck, H. J. Smoking, personality and psychosomatic disorders. *Journal of Psychosomatic Research*, 1963, **7**, 107–130. (b)

Eysenck, H. J., Tarrant, M., Woolf, M., & England, L. Smoking and personality. *British Medical Journal*, 1960, **1**, 1456–1460.

Finley, K. H. On the occurrence of rapid frequency potential changes in the human electroencephalogram. *American Journal of Psychiatry*, 1944, **101**, 194–200.

Gale, A., Coles, M., & Blaydon, J. Extraversion-introversion and the EEG. *British Journal of Psychology*, 1969, **60**, 209–223.

Gale, A., Dunkin, N., & Coles, M. Variation in visual input and the occipital EEG. *Psychonomic Science*, 1969, **14**, 262–263.

Geller, I., & Hartmann, R. Tranquilizing action of nicotine: Similarity of effects with meprobamate, a minor tranquilizer. *Proceedings of the 77th Annual Convention of the American Psychological Association*, Washington, D. C., 1969, 867–868.

Giannitrapani, D. Electroencephalographic differences between resting and mental multiplication. *Perceptual and Motor Skills*, 1966, **22**, 399–405.

Giannitrapani, D. EEG average frequency and intelligence. *Electroencephalography and Clinical Neurophysiology*, 1969, **27**, 480–486.

Gibbs, F. A., & Gibbs, E. L. Clinical and pharmacological correlates of fast activity in electroencephalography. *Journal of Neuropsychiatry*, Supplement I, 1962, **3**, S73–S78.

Glass, A. Comparison of the effect of hard and easy mental arithmetic upon blocking of the occipital alpha rhythm. *Quarterly Journal of Experimental Psychology*, 1966, **18**, 142–152.

Glass, A., & Kwiatkowski, A. W. Power spectral density changes in the EEG during mental arithmetic and eye-opening. *Psychologische Forschung*, 1970, **33**, 85–99.

Gray, J. A. Strength of the nervous system as a dimension of personality in man: A review of work from the laboratory of B. M. Teplov. In J. A. Gray, (Ed.), *Pavlov's Topology*. Oxford: Pergamon Press, 1964.

Grunewald, G., Simonova, O., & Creutzfeldt, O. D. Differential EEG changes during visuomotor and cognitive tasks. *Archiv fuer Psychiatrie und Nervenkrankheiten*, 1968, **212**, 46–69.

Hall, G. H. Effects of nicotine and tobacco smoke on the electrical activity of the cerebral cortex and olfactory bulb. *British Journal of Pharmacology*, 1970, **38**, 271–286.

Hauser, H., Schwartz, B. E., Roth, G., & Bickford, R. G. Electroencephalographic changes related to smoking. *Electroencephalography and Clinical Neurophysiology*, 1958, **10**, 576.

Heath, C. W. Differences between smokers and nonsmokers. *Archives of Internal Medicine*, 1958, **101**, 377–388.

Hofer, M. A., & Hinkle, L. E., Jr. Conditioned alpha blocking and arousal: The effects of adrenaline administration. *Electroencephalography and Clinical Neurophysiology*, 1964, **17**, 653–660.

Itil, T. M. Electroencephalography and pharmacopsychiatry: Clinical psychopharmacology. *Modern Problems in Pharmacopsychiatry*, 1968, **1** 163–194.

James, W. H., Woodruff, A. B., & Werner, W. Effect of internal and external control upon changes in smoking behavior. *Journal of Counseling Psychology*, 1965, **29**, 184–186.

Johnson, L., Lubin, A., Naitoh, P., Nute, C., & Austin, M. Spectral analysis of the EEG of dominant and non-dominant alpha subjects during waking and sleeping. *Electroencephalography and Clinical Neurophysiology*, 1969, **26**, 361–370.

Koukkou, M., Madey, J. M., & Yeager, C. L. Memory and vigilance: Spectral EEG analysis during learning in humans. *Electroencephalography and Clinical Neurophysiology*, 1969, **27**, 7.

Kreitman, N., & Shaw, J. C. Experimental enhancement of alpha activity. *Electroencephalography and Clinical Neurophysiology*, 1965, **18**, 147–155.

Lawton, M. P. Psychosocial aspects of cigarette smoking. *Journal of Health and Human Behavior*, 1962, **3**, 163–170.

Lawton, M. P., & Phillips, R. W. The relationship between excessive cigarette smoking and psychological tension. *American Journal of the Medical Sciences*, 1956, **232**, 397–402.

Legewie, H., Simonova, O., & Creutzfeldt, O. D. EEG changes during performance of various tasks under open- and closed-eyed conditions. *Electroencephalography and Clinical Neurophysiology*, 1969, **27**, 470–479.

Lester, B. K., & Edwards, R. J. EEG fast activity in schizophrenic and control subjects. *International Journal of Neuropsychiatry*, 1966, **2**, 143–156.

Lindsley, D. B. Attention, consciousness, sleep and wakefulness. *Handbook of Physiology, Neurophysiology* (Washington, D. C.: American Physiology Society), 1960, **3**.

Lorens, S. A., & Darrow, C. W. Eye movements, EEG, GSR and EKG during mental multiplication. *Electroencephalography and Clinical Neurophysiology*, 1962, **14**, 739–746.

MacNeilage, P. F. Changes in electroencephalogram and other physiological measures during serial mental performance. *Psychophysiology*, 1966, **2**, 344–353.

Matarazzo, J. D., & Saslow, G. Psychology and related characteristics of smokers and non-smokers. *Psychological Bulletin*, 1960, **21**, 552–561.

Morrell, L. K. Some characteristics of stimulus-provoked alpha activity. *Electroencephalography and Clinical Neurophysiology*, 1966, **21**, 552–561.

Mundy-Castle, A. C. Electrophysiological correlates of intelligence. *Journal of Personality*, 1958, **27**, 184–199.

Murphree, H. B., Pfeiffer, C. C., & Price, L. M. Electroencephalographic changes in man following smoking. *Annals of the New York Academy of Science*, 1967, **142**, 245–260.

Nebylitsyn, V. D. An electroencephalographic investigation of the properties of strength of the nervous system and equilibrium of the nervous processes in man using factor analysis. In Teplov, B. M. (Ed.), *Typological Features of Higher Nervous Activity in Man.* Moscow: Academii Pedagogika Nauk Russian Soviet Federative Socialist Republics, 1963, **3**.

Pond, D. A. The development of normal rhythms. In J. D. N. Hill, & G. Parr, (Eds.), *Electroencephalography.* London: MacDonald; 1963.

Saul, L. J., Davis, H., & Davis, P. A. Psychologic correlations with the electroencephalogram. *Psychosomatic Medicine*, 1949, **11**, 361–376.

Saunders, D. R. Further implications of Mundy-Castle's correlations between EEG and Wechsler-Belleview variables. *Journal of the National Institute for Personnel Research* (Johannesburg), 1960, **8**, 91–101.

Schneider, J. Activities rapides de type particulier et troubles du comportment. *Electroencephalography and Clinical Neurophysiology*, 1957, **6**, 271–281.

Schubert, D. S. P. College smoking and personality profiles. (Paper read at American Psychologists Convention, 1958). *American Psychologist*, 1958, **13**, 322.

Seltzer, C. C. Morphologic constitution and smoking. *Journal of the American Medical Association*, 1963, **183**, 639–645.

Seltzer, C. C. Constitution and heredity in relation to tobacco smoking. *Annals of the New York Academy of Science*, 1967, **142**, 322–330.

Seltzer, C. C. Morphological constitution and smoking. *Archives of Environmental Health*, 1968, **17**, 143–147.

Smith, G. M. Personality and smoking. In H. Schievelbein, (Ed.), *Nikotin: Pharmakologie und Toxikolofie des Tabakrauches.* Stuttgart: Georg Thieme Verlag, 1968.

Sugarman, L. Alpha rhythm, perception and intelligence. *Journal of the National Institute for Personnel Research,* 1961, **8**, 170–179.

Ulett, J. A., & Itil, T. M. Quantitative electroencephalogram in smoking and smoking deprivation. *Science*, 1969, **164**, 969–970.

Vogel, F. The genetic origin of slow occipital beta waves in human EEGs. *Humangenetik*, 1966, **2**, 238–245.

Volavka, J., Matousek, M., & Roubicek, J. Mental arithmetic and eye openings: An EEG frequency analysis and GSR study. *Electroencephalography and Clinical Neurophysiology*, 1967, **22**, 174–176.

Walter, D. O., Kado, R. T., Rhodes, J. M., & Adey, W. R. Electroencephalographic base-lines in astronaut candidates estimated by computation and pattern recognition techniques. *Aerospace Medicine,* 1967, **38**, 371–379.

6

SOME RECENT OBSERVATIONS RELATING TO THE ABSORPTION OF NICOTINE FROM TOBACCO SMOKE

A. K. Armitage
Tobacco Research Council Laboratories, Harrogate, England

The common theme of the four preceding chapters has been essentially the role of nicotine in the tobacco-smoking habit, and several interesting hypotheses have been proposed in support of a mass of pharmacological evidence. Domino stated in Chapter 2 that "all tobacco-containing cigarettes which are widely sold in the United States have sufficient nicotine (0.2 to 2.2 mg per cigarette) to produce definite pharmacological effects." I cannot believe that he is correct about this lower figure, and I personally would be surprised if nicotine has anything to do with the smoking habits of those people who smoke such low-nicotine cigarettes. For the main part of my discussion, I propose to concentrate on the important question of nicotine dosage in animal and human experiments. This is a subject which is frequently inadequately considered even by pharmacologists and is usually totally ignored by psychologists. In my opinion, however, it is vitally important to our understanding of the importance of nicotine to the human smoker.

The human smoker can and does adjust the dose of nicotine he takes into his mouth very subtly, by adjusting either the size of his puff or the rate at which he puffs (this was shown very clearly by the elegant experiments of Ashton and Watson [1970], to which Domino [this volume] referred); he can smoke cigarettes which have an acidic smoke or cigars which have an alkaline smoke; and the smoke taken into the mouth can be inhaled very deeply, moderately deeply, slightly, or not at all. Let us consider the experimental evidence relating to these smoking parameters.

A COMPARISON OF THE EFFECTS OF NICOTINE INHALED IN THE FORM OF TOBACCO SMOKE WITH THE EFFECTS WHEN IT IS INJECTED DIRECTLY INTO THE BLOODSTREAM

Figure 1 is a record of femoral blood pressure of a chloralose anesthetized cat artificially ventilated by a smoking machine capable of presenting a portion of a

83

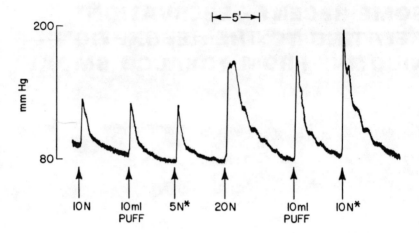

FIG. 1. The tracing shows effects of nicotine on femoral blood pressure of a chloralose anesthetized cat when injected by different routes. 10 N, 20N, etc., indicate the dose of nicotine in μg/kg injected into a femoral vein. Injections marked N* were made into the left atrium. At the second and fifth arrows, a 10-ml portion and a 20-ml portion of a 25-ml puff of cigarette smoke were introduced through a cuffed tracheal tube into the lungs.

human-sized puff of cigarette smoke to the lungs as they are about to inflate. The effects on blood pressure of nicotine, 10 μg/kg and 20 μg/kg, injected intravenously (10N and 20N) were very similar to the effects of 10 ml and 20 ml of cigarette smoke taken into the lungs. The amount of nicotine in the smoke was estimated to be rather less than the 30 μg and 60 μg injected intravenously. These are relatively large doses for a cat, and consequently they cause a large rise in blood pressure. It is, however, clearly apparent that the absorption of nicotine through the lungs and into the pulmonary veins is a highly efficient and exceedingly rapid process. An even more efficient way of giving nicotine is to inject it into the left atrium, as shown in Figure 1 (5N* and 10N*). Only half the amount of nicotine was then required to match the rise in blood pressure caused by 10 μg/kg and 20 μg/kg injected intravenously.

Although these experiments were carried out in cats, I think it is justifiable to conclude that each time a cigarette smoker inhales a puff of tobacco smoke, the dose of nicotine he receives can be mimicked reasonably accurately by a suitable intravenous injection of nicotine. We have calculated that this dose is likely to be between 1 and 2 μg/kg. Clearly it is not feasible to give intermittent injections of nicotine into a pulmonary vein or the left atrium of conscious unrestrained animals, nor is it possible to dose them realistically with tobacco smoke; but what one can do, although it is technically fairly difficult, is to give them a succession of rapid intravenous injections of nicotine into a jugular vein through an indwelling catheter. As far as I know, my colleagues and I at Harrogate are the only group to have given nicotine in this way. I would like now to discuss some of the striking effects of nicotine in both anesthetized and unanesthetized animals when so administered.

EFFECTS ON THE BRAIN OF SMALL MULTIPLE
INTRAVENOUS INJECTIONS OF NICOTINE

Armitage, Hall, and Morrison (1968) studied the effects of intravenous nicotine on the lever-pressing behaviour of thirsty rats which had been trained to press a lever in order to obtain water. Such "rewards" were made available at varying intervals averaging 2 minutes, under which conditions the rats continued to press the lever at a fairly steady rate for 1 to 2 hours. When nicotine was injected intravenously in varying amounts (1 to 4 μg/kg) and at different rates of injection (once every 15, 30, or 60 seconds), the rate of lever pressing was dramatically increased for all rats by at least one of these dose regimes, and it continued at a faster rate for a considerable time after the nicotine injections had stopped. These experiments show that very small doses of nicotine when suitably administered can affect the behavior of normal rats.

Armitage, Hall, and Sellers (1969) showed in cats anaesthetized with "Dial" that nicotine given intravenously in a dose of 2 μg/kg every 30 seconds for 20 minutes (a total of 40 injections) increased the resting output of acetylcholine from the parietal cortex and caused desynchronisation of the electrocorticogram. These findings are supplementary to the classical experiments of Knapp and Domino (1962), to which Domino (this volume) rightly referred in some detail. When the same amount of nicotine was given as a slow continuous infusion over 20 minutes, there was either a much smaller or no pharmacological response. These results are in agreement with the biochemical data of Turner (1971), who determined the levels of nicotine in the blood resulting from multiple injections and continuous infusions of nicotine, and found that higher blood nicotine levels occurred following multiple injections. This series of experiments was made on surgically anesthetized cats, which, although capable of showing electrocortical activation, were clearly unable to show behavioral arousal.

Similar experiments were therefore conducted on the cat *encéphale isolé* preparation (Hall, 1970), which although immobilized, *is* capable of showing behavioral arousal, and has the advantage over a normal conscious unrestrained cat that tobacco smoke can be introduced in a realistic dose into the lungs. Under these conditions the effects of intravenous nicotine in causing activation of the electrocorticogram were even more striking and consistent than in the anesthetized animal. In addition, behavioral arousal also occurred. The similar effects of small amounts of tobacco smoke were mainly due to the nicotine contained in the smoke. The preparation remained in an aroused state so long as the nicotine injections or smoke administration continued. As soon as either treatment stopped, the preparation reverted rapidly to the sleeping-control state.

EFFECTS OF pH ON NICOTINE ABSORPTION
FROM THE MOUTH

What about noninhaling cigarette and cigar smokers who merely take smoke into their mouths and then blow it out? Here the situation is quite different. Figure 2 shows the effects of introducing thirty 25-ml puffs of cigarette smoke and thirty

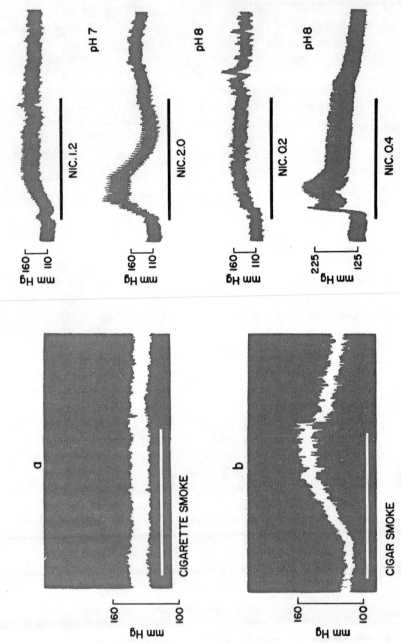

FIG. 2. Records of femoral blood pressure. Thirty puffs of cigarette smoke introduced into the mouth of a chloralose anesthetized cat during 14.5 minutes had no effect on blood pressure (a), whereas a similar quantity of cigar smoke caused a slow steady rise (b). On the right, in another experiment, are shown effects of buffered solutions of nicotine containing 1.2 and 2.0 mg/ml nicotine base at pH 7, and 0.2 and 0.4 mg/ml at pH 8. These solutions were put in the mouth and left there for 10 minutes.

25-ml puffs of cigar smoke into the mouth of a chloralose anesthetized cat. The trachea and esophagus were tied high in the neck, and breathing occurred through a tube inserted in the trachea. Smoke was introduced into the mouth every 30 seconds through a thin rubber dam held firmly in position over the mouth. After 10 seconds the smoke was blown out. Cigarette smoke rarely had any effect on blood pressure. Cigar smoke, on the other hand, caused a rise in blood pressure in each of eight experiments. It should be remembered that for cats under chloralose anesthesia, the threshold intravenous dose of nicotine which causes a rise in blood pressure is usually very small, of the order of 5 μg/kg or less (Armitage, 1965). The preparation is therefore particularly sensitive to the pressor action of nicotine, which provides a convenient index of absorption when nicotine is injected by routes other than intravenous. The first point I wish to stress is that there was only a relatively small rise in blood pressure caused by no less than *thirty* 25-ml puffs of cigar smoke when absorption was only able to occur through the oral mucosa. This is in sharp contrast to the large, more or less instantaneous, rise in blood pressure when only a portion of *one* 25-ml puff of cigarette or cigar smoke was introduced into the lungs.

Absorption through the mouth is therefore a very much slower and less efficient process. Chemical assay of the cigarette and cigar smoke showed that there was more nicotine in a given number of puffs of cigarette smoke than there was in the same number of puffs of cigar smoke. Yet the cigar smoke invariably caused a bigger pharmacological response. The explanation of this apparent anomaly appears to be a simple physiochemical one. Smoke from the cigars used in these experiments, as in all cigars, was alkaline (pH 8.5) compared to the relatively acidic smoke of the cigarettes (pH 5.35). Although tobacco smoke is an aerosol and not an aqueous solution, the percentage nicotine as free base will almost certainly be considerably greater in the alkaline cigar smoke than in the acidic cigarette smoke. It is to be expected that the uncharged nicotine base will diffuse into the bloodstream more readily than the nicotinium ion, as discussed by Travell (1960) in relation to the absorption of nicotine and other alkaloids from various sites in the body. The buccal cavity, however, was not included in her studies. The results from other experiments (Figure 2, on the right) suggest that this explanation is correct. Solutions of nicotine in 0.1 M phosphate buffer in a concentration range of 0.2 to 2.0 mg/ml were put in the mouth for 10 minutes. It can be seen that the concentration of nicotine at pH 7 required to produce a given rise of blood pressure was 5 to 6 times the concentration required at pH 8. The amount of nicotine as free base, however, was similar at the two pH's studied. In agreement with these pharmacological observations, it was found in similar experiments in which radioactive nicotine was put in the mouth, that carotid blood levels of nicotine were very much higher when the solution in the mouth was at pH 8 than when at pH 7 (Armitage & Turner, 1970).

A preliminary study of the effects of cigarette and cigar smoke on the heart rate of human subjects indicates that these observations in cats have some relevance to the human smoking situation. The upper trace in Figure 3 shows the effect on heart rate of a relaxed female subject, sitting in a chair, reading a book, when she smoked her first cigarette of the day. Ten puffs were taken at exactly 1-minute intervals.

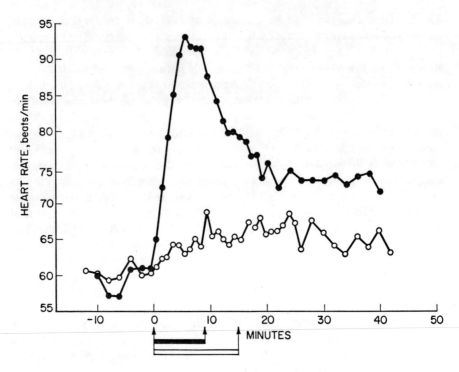

FIG. 3. Effects on the heart rate of two human subjects of smoking a cigarette (●—●) or a cigar (○—○) during the period shown by the arrows on the abscissa.

There was a very rapid increase in heart rate, which reached a peak after the sixth puff. Of ten subjects studied, there was a rapid effect similar to this in six of them (presumed to be inhalers), there was a doubtful effect in three (presumed to be noninhalers), and there was an intermediate effect in one subject. The lower trace shows the effect on heart rate of a male subject smoking his first cigar of the day, during which 16 puffs were taken at 1-minute intervals. The increase in heart rate was less than 10 beats/minutes, and the peak effect occurred about 20 minutes after starting to smoke. This type of response was observed in several subjects who smoked only cigars and had never smoked cigarettes.[1]

There can be no doubt that the cigar smoker gets a dose of nicotine during the smoking of a cigar, even if he does not inhale, but in my opinion it is open to doubt whether he absorbs enough nicotine into his bloodstream quickly enough to produce the pharmacological effects that the inhaling cigarette smoker possibly experiences. Domino (this volume) has given us a very clear and up-to-date statement of what he considers these effects might be. Of particular interest to me were the effects of cigarette smoking and nicotine aerosols on the human patellar reflex and electromyogram of the quadriceps femoris muscle. The nicotine aerosol had considerably less effect than inhaled cigarette smoke, although a similar dose of nicotine in the two different forms was apparently taken by Domino's subjects.

[1] I am grateful to Dr. P. Darby, of Gallaher Ltd., Belfast, for the cigar-smoking data.

This finding can be explained in terms of aerosol particle size: the very much larger mean particle size of the pure nicotine aerosol would presumably lead to deposition in the upper respiratory tract, with certainly less rapid and possibly less complete absorption. It is a pity that Domino and Brown (this volume) have no observations on pipe and cigar smokers, because (a) in Domino's experiments this might indicate whether these smokers are really smoking for the pharmacological effects of nicotine, particularly if some measurement of mood was made concurrently with the pharmacological observations, and (b) it would be of interest to know whether the neurophysiological makeup of pipe and cigar smokers is the same as that of cigarette smokers. Brown found that the basic EEG characteristics of cigarette smokers were different from those of nonsmokers. Could the differences not be a consequence of long-term administration of nicotine as a result of prolonged cigarette smoking? The data for her former-average smokers were in fact very similar to those of the nonsmokers, and some reversal might reasonably be expected when nicotine was "withdrawn."

Domino (this volume) has already made reference to the important experiment of Lucchesi, Schuster, and Emley (1967) who showed clearly that intravenous infusions of nicotine caused a mean reduction of 30% in the number of cigarettes smoked by five subjects during a 6-hour experimental period. If the nicotine had been given as rapid, intermittent intravenous injections, the reduction might well have been greater. The relatively small inhibition of cigarette smoking by nicotine taken orally (Jarvik, Glick, & Nakamura, 1970) was, I suggest, most likely due to inadequate absorption of nicotine. Although secondary conditioning may well be important in the maintenance of a long-standing habit such as cigarette smoking, Jarvik's results do not really provide evidence in support of this hypothesis. In addition to the chewing of nicotine gum and the swallowing of nicotine pills, administration of nicotine in the drinking water is becoming very fashionable (Glick, Zimmerberg, & Jarvik, 1971; Hutchinson & Emley, this volume). The absorption of nicotine from the intestinal tract is therefore clearly relevant to these studies. The only information I personally have on this subject comes from two recent experiments on chloralose anesthetized cats, in both of which it was necessary to inject 1 mg/kg of neutralized nicotine acid tartrate (the dose expressed as base) into the duodenum in order to obtain a rise in blood pressure roughly similar to that caused by 30 puffs of cigar smoke absorbed through the mouth (Figure 2). This is a very large dose taken at one instant; and the same dose taken relatively slowly, as would occur during intermittent drinking, would clearly have much less effect. Jarvik's experiments on rhesus monkeys (which he assures us do not inhale) trained to smoke cigarettes, and the modification of their smoking behavior by giving them nicotine in their drinking water are extremely puzzling because, again, in my opinion it is doubtful whether they absorbed significant amounts of nicotine.

Are we perhaps so obsessed with the absorption of nicotine into the bloodstream that we disregard the effects of nicotine on "taste" and "smell," which are clearly independent of absorption? After all, it is generally considered that the nicotine content of the tobacco is closely associated with "flavor" and "smoking acceptability." Could it be that some smokers, including Jarvik's monkeys, find such effects pleasurable and rewarding? Although Zotterman (1944) reported that nicotine did not produce any stimulating effect on afferent mechanisms of the tongue, a further look at the effects of nicotine on sensory nerve endings to which tobacco smoke has access during the smoking of a cigarette, might provide an explanation of some puzzling observations.

Essman's (this volume) biochemical evidence that nicotine decreased bound and vesicular acetylcholine content without change in the free acetylcholine concentration is consistent with the suggestion made many years ago from pharmacological evidence that nicotine appeared to be acting in the brain by releasing acetylcholine (Knapp & Domino, 1962; Armitage, Milton, & Morrison, 1966; Morrison, 1968). The new observations on the effects of nicotine on 5-hydroxytryptamine metabolism in the brain provide more data for the "neurochemical jungle," but the physiological significance of these biochemical events still awaits discovery. Essman's "bombshell" that relatively small doses of cotinine can exert both behavioral and biochemical effects, which at any rate partially coincide with similar nicotine effects, will no doubt renew interest in the pharmacological properties of cotinine. These have hitherto been considered to be of little importance (Yamamoto & Domino, 1965; Clark, Rand, & Vanov, 1965) so far as effects of nicotine are concerned.

Essman made no reference to brain adrenergic mechanisms, and I would like to conclude by mentioning some additional neurochemical data from the Harrogate Laboratories. Hall and Turner (1972) have recently shown that nicotine injected intravenously (2 μg/kg every 30 seconds for 30 minutes) caused an increased release of ^{3}H-Noradrenaline into the effluent from the perfused third cerebral ventricle of the cat. Similar changes were observed following the administration of cigarette smoke directly into the lungs and after perfusion of the third ventricle with nicotine. An increase in the efflux of ^{3}H-Noradrenaline also occurred when rat hypothalamic tissue slices were incubated with nicotine. These observations suggest that nicotine releases noradrenaline from the diencephalon, in particular the hypothalamus, and they provide an important link for Jarvik's hypothesis that nicotine produces reinforcing effects by stimulating reward mechanisms in the brain by causing or facilitating the release of noradrenaline at these centers (Jarvik, 1970; Stein & Wise, 1969). This hypothesis is certainly an attractive one for explaining the widespread maintenance of the tobacco-smoking habit. It is also one which is extremely difficult to prove or disprove!

Clearly there is no shortage of ideas relating to pharmacological aspects of tobacco-smoking motivation, but since at the most these are only half the story, I suspect that the next real advance will come from a combined pharmacological and psychological approach to the problem. Some quantitative measurement of inhalation and reliable determination of blood levels of nicotine would add substantially to such studies.

REFERENCES

Armitage, A. K. Effects of nicotine and tobacco smoke on blood pressure and release of catecholamines from the adrenal glands. *British Journal of Pharmacology and Chemotherapy,* 1965, **25,** 515-526.

Armitage, A. K., Hall, G. H., & Morrison, C. F. Pharmacological basis for the tobacco smoking habit. *Nature,* 1968, **217,** 331-334.

Armitage, A. K., Hall, G. H., & Sellers, C. M. Effects of nicotine on electrocortical activity and acetylcholine release from the cat cerebral cortex. *British Journal of Pharmacology ana Chemotherapy,* 1969, **35,** 152-160.

Armitage, A. K., Milton, A. S., & Morrison, C. F. Effects of nicotine and some nicotine-like compounds injected into the cerebral ventricles of the cat. *British Journal of Pharmacology and Chemotherapy,* 1966, **27,** 33-45.

Armitage, A. K., & Turner, D. M. Absorption of nicotine in cigarette and cigar smoke through the oral mucosa. *Nature,* 1970, **226,** 1231-1232.

Ashton, H., & Watson, D. W. Puffing frequency and nicotine intake in cigarette smokers. *British Medical Journal,* 1970, ii, 679-681.

Clark, M. S. G., Rand, M. J., & Vanov, S. Comparison of pharmacological activity of nicotine and related compounds occurring in cigarette smoke. *Archives Internationales de Pharmacodynamie et de Therapie,* 1965, **156,** 363-379.

Glick, S. D., Zimmerberg, B., & Jarvik, M. E. Titration of oral nicotine intake with smoking behaviour in monkeys. *Nature,* 1971, **233,** 207-208.

Hall, G. H. Effects of nicotine and tobacco smoke on the electrical activity of the cerebral cortex and olfactory bulb. *British Journal of Pharmacology and Chemotherapy,* 1970, **38,** 271-286.

Hall, G. H., & Turner, D. M. Effects of nicotine on the release of ^{3}H-Noradrenaline from the hypothalamus. *Biochemical Pharmacology,* 1972, **21,** 1829-1838.

Jarvik, M. E. The role of nicotine in the smoking habit. In W. A. Hunt, (Ed.), *Learning mechanisms and smoking.* Chicago: Aldine, 1970.

Jarvik, M. E., Glick, S. D., & Nakamura, R. K. Inhibition of cigarette smoking by orally administered nicotine. *Clinical Pharmacology and Therapeutics,* 1970, **11,** 574-576.

Knapp, D. E., & Domino, E. F. Action of nicotine on the ascending reticular activating system. *International Journal of Neuropharmacology,* 1962, **1,** 333-351.

Lucchesi, B. R., Schuster, C. R., & Emley, G. S. The role of nicotine as a determinant of cigarette smoking frequency in man with observations of certain cardiovascular effects associated with the tobacco alkaloid. *Clinical Pharmacology and Therapeutics,* 1967, **8,** 789 796.

Morrison, C. F. The modification by physostigmine of some effects of nicotine on bar-pressing behaviour of rats. *British Journal of Pharmacology and Chemotherapy,* 1968, **32,** 28-33.

Stein, L., & Wise, C. D. Release of norepinephrine from hypothalamus and amygdala by rewarding stimulation of the medial forebrain bundle. *Journal of Comparative Physiological Psychology,* 1969, **67,** 189-198.

Travell, J. The absorption and fate of nicotine: Absorption from various sites. *Annals of the New York Academy of Science,* 1960, **90,** 13-30.

Turner, D. M. Metabolism of small multiple doses of (^{14}C) nicotine in the cat. *British Journal of Pharmacology and Chemotherapy,* 1971, **41,** 521-529.

Yamamoto, K., & Domino, E. F. Nicotine-induced EEG and behavioral arousal. *International Journal of Neuropharmacology,* 1965, **4,** 359-373.

Zotterman, Y. A. note on the action of lobeline, nicotine and acetylcholine on the afferent nerves of tongue. *Acta Physiologica Scandinavica,* 1944, **8,** 377-379.

7

EXPERIMENTAL METHODS AND CONCEPTUAL MODELS AS APPLIED TO THE STUDY OF MOTIVATION IN CIGARETTE SMOKING[1]

William L. Dunn, Jr.
Philip Morris Research Center

INTRODUCTION

Clark L. Hull (1924) explained his work as a search for "a clue to the charm which tobacco has for those accustomed to its use [p. 53]." Today, almost a half century later, while smokers around the world are smoking cigarettes at the rate of three trillion (3×10^{12}) annually, we still seem a long way from a generally accepted explanation for that charm.

In view of this state of affairs, and after ten years of close-in acquaintance with the problem and its literature, I propose to take a critical look at the methods and models that investigators have been using in search of that clue. The first part of this chapter is a discussion of methods. The second part is a discussion of models.

ON METHODS

Only three experimental designs are to be found among all the studies of the motivation of the cigarette smoker. In fact, the great preponderance of the work has made use of but one design. This is the comparative analysis of smokers and nonsmokers. The direct interrogation approach has been frequently used in surveys, but has not often been reported out in the literature. The third design, the classical experimental approach, has been used hardly at all. I shall discuss each of these three methods in turn.

The Smoker/Nonsmoker Design

If we discount the great volume of post-1965 activity directed toward the development and evaluation of smoking control techniques, the preponderance of

---

[1] The views expressed herein are those of the author and are in no way to be considered as representing the views of The Council for Tobacco Research or of Philip Morris, Inc.

the research on the psychology of smoking has been aimed at differentiating smokers from nonsmokers on measures other than their cigarette-related behavior. The standard procedure has been to sample among self-selected smokers and nonsmokers from an otherwise common population and to obtain "measures" on some personality or behavioral trait or traits, and thereafter to determine whether the difference between the mean measures for the two groups was too great to ascribe to chance.

A great number of differences between groups of smokers and groups of nonsmokers have been identified through the application of the smoker/nonsmoker difference design. I have listed these differences in Table 1, following the Matarazzo and Saslow (1960) precedent of summarizing the reported differences. The references accompanying the traits are not inclusive; they are provided as access references. For example, Smith (1970) is cited for a number of the personality variables because of his systematic summary of all of the empirical work on the relationship between each of these traits and smoking.

Some of the traits or characteristics which appear in Table 1 have been included despite the fact that the evidence for their differentiating power is conflicting. A good example is anxiety level. There have been repeated observations of differences on this measure such that although the difference has not been reproducible under all circumstances, one is led to anticipate some ultimate identification of an isolatable variable that can account for the instances in which differences have been observed. Similarly, not all of the studies reporting on morphological traits have yielded results supporting the existence of the listed traits. As in the case of anxiety, the data are conflicting but provocative.

Even a casual inspection of Table 1 will make evident the redundancy and overlap among the traits. The compilation represents the work of many investigators using diverse conceptual and descriptive frames of reference. Were the communality identifiable and the "pure" traits measurable, our list would be shortened indeed.

This, then, is a summary of our knowledge of the differences between smokers and nonsmokers in the psychological and related spheres. A question arises at this point as to the direct applicability of this knowledge to understanding the motivation of the smoker. It is disturbing to find Hull (1924), long before the proliferation of studies using the smoker/nonsmoker difference design, issuing a warning which has gone unheeded:

> We accordingly find investigators resorting to statistical analysis usually of accidentally available data bearing on the general mental efficiency of habitual smokers and comparing these with simliar data from nonsmokers. The chief interest in these investigations has been the influence of smoking on scholarship in the secondary schools. Accordingly school marks have generally been used as the criterion. A very large number of such studies have been reported . . . . Since Meylan's investigation was reported with more care and insight than the others and illustrates both the weaknesses and possibilities of this method of approach, it alone will be examined , , , , Dr, Meylan investigated 115 smokers and 108 nonsmokers in Columbia University . . . . Over a period of two years the average mark of the nonsmokers was 69% while that of the smokers was 62%. The same tendency was shown by the fact that there were only 4% of failures among the nonsmokers as against 10% among the smokers. It became evident, however, that other factors besides smoking were probably contributing to produce

TABLE 1

Individual Traits and Group Characteristics by Which a Group of Smokers
Can Be Distinguished from a Group of Nonsmokers

Personality Traits

More independent (Pflaum, 1965)
Greater antisocial tendencies (Smith, 1970)
More active, energetic (Schubert, 1959; Straits, 1965)
Higher mean extroversion rating (Smith, 1970)
Happy-go-lucky (Smith, 1969)
Higher mean measure of "orality" (Smith, 1970)
Poorer mental health (Smith, 1970)
Less rigid, less orderly, more impulsive (Smith, 1970)
Greater reliance on "external" than on "internal" controls (Smith, 1970)
More chance-oriented (Straits & Sechrest, 1963)
More emotional (Smith, 1967)
Less agreeable (Smith, 1969)
"Type A" personality (more time-conscious, competitive, etc.) (Rosenman, Friedman, Jenkins,
    Straus, Wurm, & Kositchek, 1966)
Less "strength of character" (Smith, 1969)
Higher anxiety level (Walker, Nicolay, Kluczny, & Reidel, 1969; Srole, 1968; Thomas, 1968)

Life-Style Characteristics

More business-oriented in occupation (Seltzer, 1964)
Poorer academic performance (Veldman & Bown, 1969; Pumroy, 1967; Salber, MacMahon, &
    Welsh, 1962)
More users of alcohol (Higgins, Kjelsberg, & Metzner, 1967; Lilienfeld, 1959)
Religious service attendance less frequent (Cattell & Krug, 1967; Straits & Sechrest, 1963)
Proportionately higher frequence of marriages and job changes (Lilienfeld, 1959)
Higher incidence of prior hospitalizations (Lilienfeld, 1959)
Higher incidence of smoking among parents (Salber & Abelin, 1967)
More active participation in sports (Lilienfeld, 1959)
More auto accidents (Ianni & Boek, 1958)
More users of coffee and tea (Lilienfeld, 1959)

Morphological Traits

Greater body weight (Seltzer, 1963)
Greater height (Seltzer, 1963; Baer, 1966)
Thinner (Higgins & Kjelsberg, 1967)
Taller, relative to cube root of weight (Damon, 1961)
Thinner skin folds (triceps and subscapular) (Higgins & Kjelsberg, 1967)

Demographic Characteristics

More men (U.S. Public Health Service; 1970)
Proportionately more 25- to 45-year-olds (U.S. Public Health Service, 1970)
Lower mean socioeconomic class (Salber & MacMahon, 1961)
Proportionately fewer college men (Higgins, et al., 1967; Lilienfeld, 1959)
More urban residents (Higgins, et al., 1967)

these differences. Investigation showed, for example, that the 66 fraternity men involved in the investigation averaged only 59.1% as against 68.9% for the non-fraternity men, while the non-fraternity men made up the great bulk of the nonsmokers. This raised the question as to whether fraternity life might not be the causal or at least selective factor, rather than tobacco? It was also found that the athletes of the group averaged only 63.2% while the non-athletes averaged 68.3%, and that the athletes were much more apt to be both smokers and fraternity men. This raised the question as to how much of the difference found between the smokers and the nonsmokers was in reality due to engrossment in athletics on the part of the smokers? After tabulating these complex data in various ways, Meylan finally concluded that while bad scholarship is distinctly associated with smoking, it is also distinctly associated with athletics and fraternities and that it is impossible to tell how much, if any, of the bad scholarship associated with tobacco was really caused by it. The effect of smoking on scholarship is thus left undetermined though Meylan deserved much credit for clearly recognizing the extremely complex nature and uncertain meaning of such data. [Hull, 1924, pp. 15–17].

The study of Meylan (1910), cited by Hull (1924), was performed 62 years ago. The pitfalls are still real. Fodor, Glass, and Weiner (1969) collected extensive psychological and physiological data from 200 smoker and 200 nonsmoker healthy young males. They reported higher triglyceride levels (statistically significant) and faster blood-clotting time for smokers. A second study, that of Rosenman, Friedman, Jenkins, Straus, Wurm, and Kositchek (1966), made similar measures over several years on more than 3,000 males between 39 and 60 years of age whom they grouped according to behavioral types (Type A, greater sense of time urgency, etc.; Type B, more complacent). Type A's within the 39-49 year-old group had higher triglyceride levels and shorter blood-clotting time. There was a greater incidence of smoking in the Type A group. But the observed differences in triglyceride levels and blood-clotting time were independent of smoking habits. Could, then, the Fodor-Glass-Weiner findings, interpreted by those authors to be "certain changes in blood chemistry, with detrimental long-range effects [p. 125]" among young smokers, be attributable to a preponderance of Behavior Type A subjects among their smokers? Does the Behavior Type A syndrome cause smoking? Does smoking cause Type A behavior? Does faster blood-clotting time cause smoking? Or do all of these phenomena—Type A behavior, faster blood-clotting time, elevated triglyceride level, and smoking—have some common antecedent?

The 1910 case cited by Hull (1924) and the case involving the two recent studies which I have cited are both illustrations of a very fundamental methodological problem. The investigator of smoking behavior who sets out to determine whether differences exist on some personality or behavioral dimension between smokers and nonsmokers is compelled to allow each of his subjects to self-select his group assignment by becoming, or not becoming, a smoker. This fact automatically commits the investigation to an ex post facto design, whether prospective or retrospective. All of the differentiating traits listed in Table 1 were identified by means of ex post facto investigations.

Kerlinger (1967) defines ex post facto research as "that research in which the independent variable or variables have already occurred and in which the researcher starts with the observation of a dependent variable or variables. He then studies the independent variables in retrospect for their possible relations to, and effects on, the dependent variable or variables". [p. 360] The deficiency in this design rests in the fact that the investigator is unable to control for the effects of extraneous variables. As a consequence, the researcher who, however reluctantly, accepts the ex post facto design must also (but usually does not) accept the limitations imposed upon the interpretation of his results. And the limitations are simply these: Variations in the dependent variable y (smoking vs. nonsmoking) which are observed to be associated with variations in the independent variable x (personality traits, etc.) cannot be interpreted to be attributable to the variations in x. Nor can inferences be made as to the permutative relationships (x then y, y then x), unless it is known that the one predates the other in the chronological history of the subject. Even then, no other than a permutative relationship can be inferred. In this context it is interesting to note that the pre-1924 tendency among investigators of smoking was to assume a y then x relationship and attribute differences in x (academic performance) to differences in y (smoking vs. nonsmoking). Most post-1950 investigators have tended conversely to assume an x then y relationship and attribute differences in y (smoking vs. nonsmoking) to differences in x (personality traits). In neither case are the assumptions about permutation nor the attributions of contingency justified by the data.

Apart from these methodological limitations, how fruitful has the application of this experimental design been? One index of fruitfulness would be the degree to which our power of predicting smoking, or even our power to retrospectively classify smokers vs. nonsmokers, is enhanced.

Smith (1967) writes: "Examination of current literature concerning personality differences of smokers and nonsmokers indicates that accuracy of classification[2] typically ranges from 50% (chance accuracy) to about 60% (.50 SD separation[3]) [p. 310]." Hitting 6 out of 10 rather than at the chance expectation of 5 out of 10 is not great improvement in our power of prediction. Smith's quoted statement referred to data in the literature treated through univariate analytic methods. He expanded his own data collection to include peer ratings and applied more powerful multivariate analytic methods. Under these conditions his median percent correct classification index in a study of some 1,400 college and nursing students was 68% in classifying smokers vs. nonsmokers. When Smith (1969) later applied these multivariate, peer-rating procedures to a preadult group ($N = 562$), cross-validation analyses yielded 66% accuracy of classification of smokers vs. nonsmokers. In his group of junior high school females, the analysis (without cross-validation) yielded a 79% accuracy of classification.

Such findings are encouraging, suggesting that beneath the surface complexity there may well be variables awaiting measurement with even greater discriminatory power. It is also axiomatic that the smoker/nonsmoker design shall continue to be a potential source of leads as to the motivational determinants in smoking. In the final analysis, however, the hypotheses generated from such studies must be corroborated or rejected through controlled experimentation. Sanford (1967), Veldman and Bown (1969), and Hunt and Matarazzo (1970) have called for

---

[2] Accuracy of classification is the percentage of "hits" in classifying subjects into categories with only predictor variable(s) known (in this case, personality "scores").

[3] Where $N = 100$, a 60% classification accuracy is significant at the .05 level. And, of course, as N increases, a correspondingly smaller deviation from 50% (chance accuracy) is required for significance.

the application of more sophisticated approaches to the question of maintenance motivation in smoking.

The Direct Interrogation Approach

Some investigators have accepted the premise that one can find out why a man smokes by asking him. Various techniques have been used: the direct interview (face-to-face, telephone), and the indirect interview (completion of a questionnaire supplied by personal contact, by mail, or through the public media). Schedules for eliciting responses range from loosely structured formats with open-ended questions to multipaged questionnaires with multiple-choice items and rating scales. The information so collected has been treated by techniques ranging from qualitative clinical interpretation to complex multivariate statistical analysis. But whatever form the contact, or the schedule, or the item, or the data analysis may take, the datum unit remains a deliberated-upon, voluntary, retrospective statement about himself by a respondent. The question is raised as to how much credence can be given to the introspective reports of naive smokers? Factors such as the need for social approval of opinions and actions, the need to justify a preference commitment, order of presentation effects, brand imagery effects, halo effects, and the yea-saying tendency are collectively more determinative of a report of a smoke-induced sensory experience than is the sensory experience itself. If such is the equivocal nature of the naive respondent's report of conscious sensory experience associated with smoking, how veridical can a respondent's report be of those far less verbalizable affective experiences associated with smoking?

One of the more sophisticated examples of this approach is the study reported by Ikard, Green, and Horn (1969), in which a 23-item questionnaire was administered to 2,094 smokers. The items in the questionnaire were statements of subjective conditions or affective states associated with smoking—viz. "I smoke cigarettes to stimulate me, to perk myself up"; "When I feel blue, or want to take my mind off cares and worries, I smoke cigarettes"; "When I feel ashamed or embarrassed about something, I light up a cigarette." The respondent indicated how the behavior in each statement was typical of his own by selecting from among five alternatives ranging from "Always" to "Never". The results were subjected to a multiple factor analysis which identified six factors underlying the response patterns to the 23 items. These six factors were labeled "Habitual," "Addictive," "Reduction of Negative Affect," "Pleasurable Relaxation," "Stimulation," and "Sensorimotor Manipulation." The close parallel of these labels to the types of smokers proposed in the Tomkins (1966) model is not surprising; the items of the questionnaire were drafted with the four Tomkins types in mind. It is interesting to note that Tomkins had no sensorimotor manipulation type in his model. Horn, apparently of the opinion that a sensorimotor manipulation dimension also existed, made an ad hoc addition of four sensorimotor manipulation items to the scale which did, of course, "uncover" such a factor. The three factors, "Stimulation," "Pleasurable Relaxation," and "Sensorimotor Manipulation," were then proposed to be three subclassifications of Tomkins' "To increase positive affect" type.

Although we can ill afford not to collect introspective reports from smoking respondents, there is some justification for the contention that the construction of theory solely upon the self-reports of naive respondents as to why they smoke is an overly optimistic enterprise. Not even with a computer can one make a silk purse from a sow's ear.

An Alternative Approach

In the smoker/nonsmoker difference approach we ask the question, "What's different about the smoker?" Not only does this force us into an ex post facto design, but it is also a question tangential to the problem of motivation. In the direct approach we ask the question, "Why does one continue to smoke?" This is the right question, but the investigator is dependent upon the verbalizations of the smoker, a data transmission system known to carry a high level of background noise and extraneous signals which obscure and distort the essential message. We need a design which permits us both to ask the right question and to obtain relevant data. I propose the controlled experiment design. This, of course, is the design of choice always, but in researching human behavior we often cannot use it. Society would not tolerate our taking a hundred youths and randomly selecting fifty to become smokers. Hence, the smoking habit must be studied in situ.

But do we need to study the smoking habit? Perhaps the emphasis upon the recurrence of the behavioral pattern is misguided. If it is an understanding of motivational mechanisms that we seek, it would seem more pertinent were we to focus upon the discrete smoking act and the attendant phenomena.

Investigators of smoking at the biochemical and physiological levels have routinely used the controlled experiment. Typically, measurements are made on the chosen y variable (acetylcholine level, EEG patterns), the independent variable x is introduced (injection of nicotine, inhalation of whole smoke), and y is again measured. Note that in the model physiological study, smoking (or its equivalent) is x, not y as in the psychologist's ex post facto design. Herein lies a profound difference between the typical physiological and the typical psychological study of smoking; the former has been predicting *from* smoking, the latter *to* smoking. Since the basic question in the study of the motivational aspects of smoking is, "Why do people smoke?" it follows that we should be asking at the psychological level what has been asked all along at the physiological level: "What are the immediate effects of smoking?"

Some significant reports of this kind of investigation have already appeared in the literature: Morrison and Armitage (1967) report reduction in free activity level in rats. Increases in lever-pressing activity in rats and cats are reported by Armitage, Hall, and Morrison (1968); and Silverman (1969) concluded that the principal effect upon rats in his experiment was to reduce aggression. In Chapter 11 of this volume, Hutchinson reports a reduction in aggressive responsivity in squirrel monkeys. Bovet, Bovet-Nitti, and Oliverio (1966) describe facilitation in learning effects among rats under their conditions. Inhibition of the extinction of an avoidant response was observed in rats by Driscall and Battig (1970). Battig (1970) interprets the Hebb-Williams test performance of his rats as evidence of a beneficial effect of nicotine on higher integrative functions. Essman, Steinberg, and Colod (1968) report evidence from a study of electrically shocked mice suggestive of a facilitation of memory consolidation. Barlow, Oliverio, Satta, and Thompson (1970) report possible enhanced memory-consolidating processes. EEG activation in animals associated with nicotine administration has been reported by Armitage and Hall (1968), Domino (1967), Schaeppi (1968), and others. B. B. Brown (1968) and Ulett and Itil (1969) have observed EEG activation in humans as a function of smoke inhalation. In other behavioral modalities among humans inhaling smoke: Warwick and Eysenck (1963) report changes in the critical flicker fusion threshold; Clark and Rand (1968) and Domino and von Baumgarten (1969) report patellar reflex reductions.

The list is not inclusive, its purpose being merely to point up the increasing interest in and successful application of the pretreatment and posttreatment design to the study of the immediate behavioral and psychological effects of smoking.

In assessing the trend exemplified by the above studies, I am impressed with the investigators' apparent lack of concern over the motivational relevance of the reported changes induced by nicotine and smoke. Larson, Haag, and Silvette (1961) have pointed rather obliquely to the problem in remarking that there are so many peripheral effects of nicotine that the central effects tend to be obscured. Their frame of reference was clearly neurological rather than motivational, as was Domino's (1967) when he made a similar observation: "This agent [nicotine] has so many pharmacological actions that they easily confound, reinforce, and obscure its direct central actions .... nicotine acts at a variety of sites in the peripheral nervous system. These multiple actions must be considered in any study of nicotine's effects upon the central nervous system. These writers are unquestionably correct in despairing over the confounding plurality of effects induced by nicotine; but I submit that the task is not so much one of separating out central from peripheral effects, but rather one of differentiating the motivationally relevant from the motivationally irrelevant.

On Synergism

Investigators of the behavioral effects of nicotine and smoke are often struck by the markedly wide intraindividual and interindividual variability in response patterns. Armitage and Hall (1968) have observed wide variation suggestive of dichotomous response patterns in the behavioral effects, in the electroencephalographic effects, and in acetylcholine release from the parietal cortex of cats. Silverman (1969), in studying the social behavior of rats, observes, "There seem to be individual differences between rats to which the effects of nicotine are additive [p. 506]." B. B. Brown (1967) reported nicotine effects on the behavior and on the EEG patterns identifiable with specific types of cats classified according to behavior. Bovet (1965) reported the necessity of using split litter techniques in order to reduce variability. Bovet, Bovet-Nitti, and Oliverio (1967) also reported opposite effects of nicotine associated with environmental factors and the strains of the animal genetically classified as "bright" and "dull." Domino (1967) reported differences in the effect of nicotine upon avoidance responses between rats classified as slow and fast in their jump response times. In that same report Domino noted that the observed EEG-activating actions of nicotine, or its behavioral wakeup effect in cats with chronically implanted brain electrodes appeared only when the nicotine was administered during a state of mild central nervous system depression. Pradhan and Bowling (1970) report differential effects from injected nicotine on self-stimulation response patterns between high- and low-response-rate rats.

Wide variability in measurement has also long been reported among investigators using human subjects in smoking studies. McArthur, Waldron, and Dickinson (1958) attempted to extract meaning from the great mass of highly variable data obtained on smoking among Harvard students: "In summary then, we may hypothesize that starting to smoke is largely brought about by one's social environment but that reactions to smoking, once it has started, seem to depend in good part on the personal needs that the newly established habit is able to gratify [p. 272]." Seltzer (1962) paraphrased these observations in biogenetic terms: "Rather than a superficial habit overlaid indiscriminately upon various persons, smoking appears to be a response to a wide variety of personality and behavioral characteristics which have their origin, in part, in the biologic and genetic makeup of the individual [p. 43]."

In view of all this variability, it is likely that we shall ultimately find that the critical mechanisms involved in smoking require the synergistic presence of some other factor, such as anxiety or possibly some constitutionally determined reactivity. The observation that only about half of those who try smoking cigarettes go on to take up the habit certainly suggests some kind of interaction process. Smoking apparently is not sufficiently pleasurable among the disinterested half of the tryers for the aversiveness of smoking to be overridden. Smoke is smoke—whether its inhalation is pleasurable is dependent upon what the individual brings to the situation.

In a sense, this statement brings us full circle, for in proposing a synergism model, I am in fact conceding that smokers are probably different from nonsmokers. Does it not then follow that we should continue to look for smoker/nonsmoker differences? Perhaps the apparent conflict in the position can be clarified schematically. The first-row entry in Table 2 is the simplistic smoker/nonsmoker difference paradigm. In actual practice the sequence is reversed from that shown, which is the aforementioned liability of the ex post facto method; one "measures" y by asking, "Do you smoke?" and then measures x (e.g.,

TABLE 2

A Schematic Representation of Three Research Designs

Type Model	Independent variable	Dependent Variable
Typical Psychological	Trait or state of organism	◄—— Smoker/nonsmoker
Typical Physiological	Smoke inhalation (Nicotine injection)	——► Effect upon organism
Proposed Synergistic	Trait or state ⟍ Smoke inhalation ⟋	——► Differential effect upon organism

personality test scores). In the proposed synergistic experimental model, one manipulates or systematically selects for levels of x_1 (a psychological or physiological trait or state), introduces x_2 (smoke inhalation), and observes for a differential response level y. The significant relationship in such a study would not be between smoking and the measured effect, nor between the trait or state and the measured effect, but between the trait/smoking interaction and the measured effect.

ON MODELS

Having touched upon some of the methodological issues and pitfalls confronting the investigator of smoker motivation, I would like to turn now to a nosological exercise. The first part is an an analysis of the temporal phases of the smoking habit. The second part categorizes the motives which have been proposed by various investigators. Finally, I will perform a cross tabulation of phase and motive.

Phases of the Habit

Jarvik (1970) has proposed that the smoking habit be viewed as consisting of three phases: the initiation phase, including the smoking of those first cigarettes whereby the novice learns of the effects of smoking upon his person; the maintenance phase, wherein the behavior has become repetitive and patterned; and the termination phase, wherein other motive forces counter to those of the maintenance phase become dominant and determine behavior.

I have found it useful to insert a phase between Jarvik's initiation and maintenance phases. This I will call the transitional phase. In this manner we can clearly distinguish between two classes of events—those leading up to trial, and those associated with trial. Preceding trial, awareness is largely extroceptive; the individual's attention is turned upon the interpersonal situation, either real or imaginary. Awareness at the time of trial is largely introceptive as the smoker appraises what is happening to him as a consequence of the novel experience. I am suggesting that we simply limit Jarvik's initiation phase to pretrial events, where clearly the motivational factors are psychosocial in nature, and that we subsume events associated with smoking under the transitional phase. It may well be that a straightforward algebraic summing of the positive and negative experiences occurring in the suggested transitional phase will separate those who will become smokers from those who will remain nonsmokers.

Nearly everyone has at one time experienced the shock of the first inhalation, often accompanied by gagging and nauseousness. On the other hand, nearly everyone who has continued smoking can recall the pleasantness of the light-headedness which followed inhalation, a sensory experience that could be made to recur following a brief time lapse by smoking another cigarette. Whether or not the total experience is judged by the smoker as positive or negative might in time prove to be associated with biochemical, endocrinological, or neurological variables which are either constitutionally fixed (Fisher, 1959) or shaped by experience prior to initial experimentation with tobacco smoke.

There is another justification for the transitional phase. The initial subjective effect, which presumably has a physiological basis, becomes progressively less discernible with continued smoking until most habituated smokers are no longer aware of it. Those habituated smokers who do continue to experience it do so only on occasion and only after periods of extended abstinence. Since the effect is not likely to be sought after by the beginning smoker who has had no occasion to experience it prior to smoking, and since it is no longer supraliminal on the regular smoking regimen for the habituated smoker, the effect and any others that may be peculiar to early trial should be treated independently of both initiation and maintenance events. The possibility remains, however, that we are dealing with a physiological response at its maximum in early trials, diminishing in intensity over time, but continuing on at some subthreshold awareness level of sufficient intensity to alter the affective state of the smoker.

The Motive Classes

So much for the temporal phases of smoking. Consider now the categories of motives imputed to the smoker. The rationale of the categories resides in the locus of the events which have been proposed as having reward value. There are four rather obvious classes.

Physiological. A number of physiological changes occur as transient reactions to the inhalation of smoke. It is not within the scope of this paper to consider the metabolic and biochemical changes which have been reported, nor the myriad of reactions at all physiological levels in animals and in animal tissue upon administration of small to massive doses of nicotine. Table 3 lists several systemic changes which have been observed in humans upon smoke inhalation. They are transient, short-lived changes. The fact that a change does occur upon smoking is sufficient to include it in the list, but as I have stated earlier, the mere occurrence of a given change is not prima facie evidence of its motivational significance. Any physiological or pharmacological reward explanation for smoking must identify the motivationally significant change, either from among those in Table 3 or as identified in subsequent research.

For a critical assessment of the subject, see Jarvik (1970); and for a comprehensive review of the literature on this aspect of smoking, see Larson, Haag, and Silvette (1961) and Larson and Silvette (1968). For our purposes it is best to avoid the many controversies attendant upon this area, e.g., dosage levels, animal vs. human, nicotine vs. whole-smoke, direct vs. indirect action. We shall simply press

TABLE 3

Transient Physiological Responses to
Smoke Inhalation

1. Elevated heart rate
2. Elevated coronary flow
3. Elevated blood sugar level
4. Lowered cutaneous temperature in the extremities
5. Increased blood flow in skeletal musculature
6. A reactive release of adrenalin
7. Alterations in electrical potential patterns of the brain
8. Inhibition of patellar reflex

on with two observations: (*a*) smoke inhalation does produce a host of physiological changes; and (*b*) there is merit in the contention that among these physiological responses are to be found those which are "gratifying," "pleasurable," or "need reducing," and therefore of significance in any discussion of motivational mechanisms sustaining the smoking habit.

Psychosocial. By smoking cigarettes on a more or less regular basis, one takes on the identity of a cigarette smoker, with all the attendant identity connotations. Smoking is a means for informing others as to what kind of person one is, what kind of person one wishes to be, or how one wishes others to relate to him. Numerous writers have described these psychosocial forces in various conceptual terms. Lawton (1962) sums it up by saying, "Initiation of smoking is seen as largely a social and psychological phenomenon mediated by the mechanisms of curiosity, imitation, identification, status striving, and rebellion [p. 170]." Most would accept this statement. Whether the psychosocial factors carry over into the later phases of smoking, and if so, whether they are determinative or merely supportive of continuation, is a matter of considerably less agreement. One point of view is expressed by Matarazzo and Matarazzo (1968): "Once started, however, continuation or discontinuation appears to be, in large part, a function of the socio-psychological characteristics of the individual [p. 339]." This contrasts sharply with Jarvik's statement (1970): "Nevertheless, psychological factors alone cannot be responsible for the maintenance of the smoking habit [p. 18]."

Sensory. Cigarette smoking provides stimuli for the olfactory, gustatory, and visual modalities, as well as for those receptors in the mucosal lining of the respiratory tract which mediate such smoke-related sensations as stinging or low-level pain not unlike that associated with hot food seasonings, and the experience of smoke "presence" in the deeper portion of the respiratory system upon inhalation. The basic taste sensation most characteristic of cigarette smoke is bitterness, presumably ascribable to the nicotine and/or other alkaloids present. There are those who contend that these sensations are the source or sources of primary gratification (J. A. C. Brown, 1963). Such explanations as a "local craving for nicotine scratch" (Ejrup, 1965) and "pulmonary erotism" (Freedman, 1948) imply a primary role for local sensation.

Psychomotor. The sensory and the psychomotor categories overlap to some extent, for there are sensory feedback components to the motor patterns associated with smoking. An arbitrary but clean distinction can be made by conceiving of all the sensorimotor events associated with the cigarette itself under the psychomotor category, and all the sensory events triggered by the smoke under the sensory category. The distinction does not by any means clarify the conceptual difficulties encountered in considering the motivational significance of the psychomotor patterns. We are faced with the question as to whether or not the motor activity of manipulating the cigarette manually and puffing on it orally could, in and of itself, sustain the smoking habit. Such would seem to be the case in gum chewing continued beyond the sugar- and flavor-delivering life of the gum wad. To entertain such an explanation of habitual smoking, we must view the motor activity as being of a class of behavior that has long posed a serious conceptual problem. Most psychologists subscribe to the basic premise that all behavior is motivated. Can motoric behavior generate its own motive force? Can it become autonomous and recycle independently of the dynamics of the host organism? The sudden realization for an inveterate smoker that he is holding a lit cigarette in his hand with no recall as to how it got there, and the lighting of a second cigarette with the first still statically burning in the ash tray, have been pointed out to us as evidence that smoking is functionally autonomous. If such is the case, then smoking must be classed with pencil twirling, foot tapping, tics, and other idiosyncratic behaviors that collectively are referred to as nervous mannerisms, forming that special class of behavior that recurs with seemingly no motive force to make it happen. Discussions pertinent to the general problem and its relatedness to smoking can be found in Larson and Silvette (1968), Jarvik (1970), and Hunt and Matarazzo (1970).

Health Fears

In addition to the four classes of motive forces which have been proposed as implementing the habit, there are also negative motive forces operative. These are collectively labeled here as health fears, since it is the concern for one's physical well-being that is most dominant among them. Moral and aesthetic concerns are present, but their net impact upon smoking behavior is not usually of determinative significance. Health fears are operative to some degree throughout the history of the habit, influencing the selection of the cigarette smoked and often restraining the smoker in his rate of consumption; but they are no more than modulative until the fourth phase of the habit, wherein they become the primary force.

We now have a classification system consisting of the four phases of the habit's history and the five classes of motives that have been proposed as the forces shaping the habit. If we now set up a matrix of the four temporal phases and the five motive classes, as shown in Table 4, we have a handy device for comparing explanatory models. The cell entries are symbols for the hypothesized role of a given class of motive for a given phase of the habit: "P" for primary, "S" for secondary, and "0" for none. By definition, a primary motive is one required for the act to occur. A secondary motive, or any sum of secondary motives, can only

TABLE 4

A Cross Tabulation of Habit Phase and Motive Category, in Which Cell Entries
Are Determined from the Premises of a Representative Psychosocial
Model of Smoker Motivation

Type motive	Habit phase			
	Initiation	Transitional	Maintenance	Termination
Psychosocial	P	P	P	S
Psychophys- iological	0	± S	S	S
Sensory	0	S	S	S
Motor	0	0	S	S
Health	− S	− S	− S	− P

Note.−P = primary, S = secondary, 0 = none.

be augmentive to the primary motive. To what extent secondary motives can prolong the interval to extinction of the habit is a timely and intriguing question.

Consider the case of the typical psychological model wherein the basic premise is that psychosocial motives sustain the habit. Making some arbitrary decisions about the relative roles of the other motivational variables, we arrive at the array in Table 4. The psychosocial motives dominate through the first three phases, being overridden in the fourth phase by health fears. Health fear is present through the habit's history to counter the drives toward smoking, but never determinative until the termination phase. Physiological and sensory gratification are present in all but the first phase, there being also negative physiological experiences in the transitional phase. Gratification arising from the motoric activity has its onset in the maintenance phase.

If we perform this same exercise with the typical physiological model, as shown in Table 5, we find that on the whole there is remarkable similarity. It has been assumed that those who hold the physiological gratification to be primary would concede to the secondary roles ascribed to the sensory, motor, and health motive forces. The difference between the two prototype models lies in the relative significance of the psychosocial and the psychophysiological motives in the transitional and maintenance phases.

The controversy is clearly delineated in the row-to-row transposability of entries for those four cells, and the crucial question is made to stand out in bold relief: Can the habit survive the transitional phase and become established in the maintenance phase in the absence of physiological gratification? If any psychosocial model is to achieve explanatory value, evidence must be provided in the affirmative. If any psychophysiological model is to achieve explanatory value, evidence must be provided in the negative. At present the onus is on the psychosocial model. The task for the psychosocial theorist is conceptually clear but empirically difficult: to dispose of physiological gratification and to demonstrate habit maintenance. As

TABLE 5

A Cross Tabulation of Habit Phase and Motive Category, in which Cell
Entries Are Determined from the Premises of a Representative
Psychophysiological Model of Smoker Motivation

Type motive	Habit phase			
	Initiation	Transitional	Maintenance	Termination
Psychosocial	P	S	S	S
Psychophys- iological	0	P(−S)	P	S
Sensory	0	S	S	S
Motor	0	0	S	S
Health	− S	− S	− S	− P

Note.−P = primary, S = secondary, 0 = none.

Jarvik (1970) has so pointedly remarked, there have been numerous opportunities in the marketplace of psychosocial motives to display their determinacy of smoking behavior. They have not.

A critical study would be one in which smoking patterns are observed during systematic varying of the level of a given smoke constituent. If the smoker is titrating intake, any change in the concentration of the critical component in the smoke should make for compensatory changes in intake behavior. Acceptable manipulation of the critical component, however, must be achieved while holding gustatory, olfactory, and other local-action sensory effects constant, and must be extended over a sufficient period of time to overcome resistance to extinction.

Lucchesi, Schuster, and Emley (1967) injected nicotine intravenously in amounts calculated to be approximately equivalent to the amounts obtained by normal smoking. If only the nicotine were being sought in smoking, then a cessation of smoking would be predicted with injection. Smoking rate declined significantly among the nine subjects, but in no instance to below half the normal number of daily cigarettes. Frith (1971) has recently reported changes in the number of cigarettes smoked as a function of the available nicotine level in the smoke. However, total dependence upon nicotine presence in the smoke for smoking maintenance is yet to be demonstrated.

The task of the proponent of the psychophysiological model would remain unfinished even were he to identify the essential agent or agents in smoke and demonstrate dependency of smoking maintenance upon its presence. The mechanism whereby the agent accomplishes its gratificatory action would remain to be elucidated, as well as the nature of the gratification at the psychological level.

SUMMARY

The Issues

1. Most of the psychological research on the motivational aspects of smoking has been ex post facto, leaving the investigator severely constrained for inferring motivational mechanisms in smoking.

2. By contrast, most of the physiological research related to the subject has been experimental, with good opportunity for controls and inferences. However, by stopping short at the level of pharmacological action and not considering the psychological implications of these actions, the physiologist has not differentiated between the motivationally relevant and irrelevant effects.

3. Speculation about the primary motivational forces in smoking divides investigators into two camps: those who build psychophysiological models hypothesizing primary pharmacological smoking motives, and those who build psychological models hypothesizing primary motivation to reside in the phenomenological sphere.

4. The smoking habit can be best conceptualized as consisting of four stages: initiation, transition, maintenance, and termination. There is general concurrence regarding the dynamics in the initiation and termination phases. The disagreement on the nature of primary motive forces is confined to the transitional and maintenance phases.

5. Smoking motives which impel the smoker to seek stimulation in the sensorial and motoric spheres are operative, but are judged not to be of sufficient force of themselves to sustain the smoking habit.

6. There is mounting evidence of a synergistic relationship between psychological states and the reinforcing nature of the effects of smoking.

Questions for Further Research

1. By what means can the motivational relevancy of a smoke-induced physiological response be ascertained?

2. What are the motivationally critical effects of smoking?

3. Will the habit extinguish in the absence of physiological gratification?

4. How long must observation be continued in the absence of physiological gratification for extinction to occur, or to conclude that extinction will not occur?

5. What is the nature of the motivational mechanism linking the critical elements within the total smoking act to the motivationally critical effects of smoking?

Guidelines for Future Research

1. The experimental approach has not been fully exploited in the study of the motivational mechanisms in smoking. The research design judged to hold the greatest potential is the multivariate study of the interaction between personality/behavioral variables and the transient effects of smoke.

2. The prime objective of any study of the motive forces maintaining the smoking habit should be the evaluation of the motivational significance of the short-lived changes in the smoker attendant upon smoking.

REFERENCES

Armitage, A. K., & Hall, G. H. Nicotine, smoking and cortical activiation. *Nature*, 1968, **219**, 1179–1180.

Armitage, A. K., Hall, G. H., & Morrison, C. F. Pharmacological basis for the tobacco smoking habit. *Nature*, 1968, **217**, 331–334.

Baer, D. J. Height, weight and ponderal index of college male smokers and nonsmokers. *Journal of Psychology*, 1966, **64**, 101–105.

Barlow, R. B., Oliverio, A., Satta, M., & Thompson, G. A. Some central effects in mice of compounds related to nicotine. *British Journal of Pharmacology*, 1970, **39**, 647–652.

Battig, K. The effect of pre- and post-trial application of nicotine on the 12 problems of the Hebbs-Williams Test in the rat. *Psychopharmacologia*, 1970, **18**, 68–76.

Bovet, D. Action of nicotine on conditioned behavior in naive and pretrained rats. In U. S. von Euler, (Ed.), *Symposium on tobacco alkaloids and related compounds*. New York: Pergamon Press, 1965.

Bovet, D., Bovet-Nitti, F., & Oliverio, A. Effects of nicotine on avoidance conditioning of inbred strains of mice. *Psychopharmacologia*, 1966, **10**, 1–5.

Bovet, D., Bovet-Nitti, F., & Oliverio, A. Action of nicotine on spontaneous and acquired behavior in rats and mice. *Annals of the New York Academy of Science*, 1967, **142**, 261–267.

Brown, B. B. Relationship between evoked response changes and behavior following small doses of nicotine. *Annals of the New York Academy of Science*, 1967, **142**, 190–200.

Brown, B. B. Some characteristic EEG differences between heavy smoker and nonsmoker subjects. *Neuropsychologia*, 1968, **6**, 381–388.

Brown, J. A. C. The nature and treatment of smoking. *Medical world*, 1963, **98**, 187–192.

Cattell, R. B., & Krug, S. Personality factor profile peculiar to the student smoker. *Journal of Counseling Psychology*, 1967, 14(2), 116–121.

Clark, M. S. G., & Rand, M. J. Effect of tobacco smoke on the knee-jerk reflex in man. *European Journal of Pharmacology*, 1968, 3, 294–302.

Damon, A. Constitution and smoking. *Science*, 1961, 134, 339–340.

Domino, E. F. The effects of nicotine and smoking on the central nervous system. *Annals of the New York Academy of Science*, 1967, 142(1), 216–244.

Domino, E. F., & von Baumgarten, A. M. Tobacco cigarette smoking and patellar reflex depression. *Clinical Pharmacology and Therapeutics*, 1969, 10(1), 72–79.

Driscall, P., & Battig, K. The effect of nicotine and total alkaloids extracted from cigarette smoke on avoidance behavior in rats under extinction procedure. *Psychopharmacologia*, 1970, 18, 305–313.

Ejrup, B. The role of nicotine in smoking pleasure, nicotinism, treatment. In U. S. von Euler, (Ed.), *Symposium on tobacco alkaloids and related compounds*. New York: Pergamon Press, 1965.

Essman, W. B., Steinberg, M. L., & Colod, M. I. Alterations in the behavioral and biochemical effects of electroconvulsive shock with nicotine. *Psychonomic Science*, 1968, 12(3) 107–108.

Fisher, R. A. *Smoking: The cancer controversy*. Edinburgh: Oliver and Boyd, 1959.

Fodor, T. J., Glass, L. H., & Weiner, J. M. Immediate effects of smoking on healthy young men. *Public Health Reports*, 1969, 84(2), 121–126.

Freedman, B. Conditioned reflex and psychodynamic equivalents in alcohol addiction: An illustration of psychoanalytic neurology, with rudimentary equations. *Quarterly Journal of Studies on Alcohol*, 1948, 9, 53–71.

Frith, C. D. The effect of nicotine content of cigarettes on human smoking behavior. *Psychopharmacologia*, (Berlin) 1971, 19, 188–192.

Higgins, M. W., & Kjelsberg, M. Characteristics of smokers and nonsmokers in Tecumseh, Mighigan. Part II. The distribution of selected physical measurements and physiologic variables and the prevalence of certain diseases in smokers and nonsmokers. *American Journal of Epidemiology*, 1967, 86(1), 60-77.

Higgins, M. W., Kjelsberg, M., & Metzner, H. Characteristics of smokers and nonsmokers in Tecumseh, Michigan. Part I. The distribution of smoking habits in persons and families and their relationship to social characteristics. *American Journal of Epidemiology*, 1967, 86(1), 45–59.

Hull, C. L. The influence of tobacco smoking on mental and motor efficiency. *Psychological Monographs: General and Applied*, 1924, 33 (Whole No. 150).

Hunt, W. A., & Matarazzo, J. D. Habit mechanisms in smoking. In W. A. Hunt, (Ed.), *Learning mechanisms and smoking*. Chicago: Aldine, 1970.

Ianni, F. A., & Boek, W. A study of the relationship between motor vehicle accidents and certain characteristics of drivers. Unpublished masters thesis, Russell Sage College, 1958.

Ikard, F. F., Green, D. E., & Horn, D. A scale to differentiate between types of smoking as related to management of affect. *International Journal of Addictions*, 1969, 4(4), 649–659.

Jarvik, M. E. The role of nicotine in the smoking habit. In W. A. Hunt, (Ed.), *Learning mechanisms and smoking*. Chicago: Aldine, 1970.

Kerlinger, F. N. *Foundations of behavioral research, educational and psychological and sociological inquiry*. New York: Holt, Rinehart & Winston, 1967.

Larson, P. S., Haag, H. B., & Silvette, H. *Tobacco: Experimental and clinical studies*. Baltimore: Williams and Wilkins, 1961.

Larson, P. S., & Silvette, H. *Tobacco: Experimental and clinical studies*. Baltimore: Williams and Wilkins, 1968.

Lawton, M. P. Psychosocial aspects of cigarette smoking. *Journal of Health and Human Behavior*, 1962, 3, 163–170.

Lilienfeld, A. M. Emotional and other selected characteristics of smokers and nonsmokers as related to epidemiological studies of lung cancer and other diseases. *Journal of the National Cancer Institute*, 1959, 22, 259–282.

Lucchesi, B. R., Schuster, C. R., & Emley, G. S. The role of nicotine as a determinant of cigarette smoking frequency in man with observations of certain cardiovascular effects associated with the tobacco alkaloid. *Clinical Pharmacology and Therapeutics*, 1967, **8**, 789–796.

Matarazzo, J. D., & Matarazzo, R. G. Smoking. In D. L. Sills, et al. (Eds.), *International encyclopedia of the social sciences.* New York: Macmillan, 1968.

Matarazzo, J. D., & Saslow, G. Psychological and related characteristics of smokers and nonsmokers. *Psychological Bulletin*, 1960, **57**(6), 493–513.

McArthur, C., Waldron, E., & Dickinson, J. The psychology of smoking. *Journal of Abnormal Psychology*, 1958, **57**(2), 267–275.

Meylan, G. W. *Popular Science Monthly*, 1910, **77**, 170–177. Cited by C. L. Hull, The influence of tobacco smoking on mental and motor efficiency. *Psychological Monographs: General and Applied*, 1924, **33** (Whole No. 150).

Morrison, C. F., & Armitage, A. K. Effects of nicotine upon the free operant behavior of rats and spontaneous motor activity of mice. *Annals of the New York Academy of Science*, 1967, **142**, 268–276.

Pflaum, J. Smoking behavior: A critical review of research. *Journal of Applied Behavioral Sciences*, 1965, **1**, 195–209.

Pradhan, S. N., & Bowling, C. Effects of nicotine on self-stimulation in rats. *Journal of Pharmacology and Experimental Therapeutics*, 1970, **176**(1), 229–243.

Pumroy, D. K. Cigarette smoking and academic achievement. *Journal of General Psychology*, 1967, **77**, 31–34.

Rosenman, R. H., Friedman, M., Jenkins, D., Straus, R., Wurm, M., & Kositchek, R. Coronary heart disease in the Western collaborative group study: A follow-up experience of two years. *Journal of the American Medical Association,* 1966, **195**(2), 87–92.

Salber, E. J., & Abelin, T. Smoking behavior of Newton school children: Five-year followup. *Pediatrics*, 1967, **40**, 363–372.

Salber, E. J., & MacMahon, B. Cigarette smoking among high school students related to social class and parental smoking habits. *American Journal of Public Health and the Nation's Health*, 1961, **51**, 1780–89.

Salber, E. J., MacMahon, B., & Welsh, B. Smoking habits of high school students related to intelligence and achievement. *Pediatrics*, 1962, 780–787.

Sanford, N. Overview I. In S. V. Zagona (Ed.), *Studies and issues in smoking behavior.* Tucson: University of Arizona Press, 1967.

Schaeppi, U. Nicotine treatment of selected areas of the cat brain: Effects upon EEG and autonomic system. *International Journal of Neuropharmacology*, 1968, **7**(3), 207–220.

Schubert, D. Personality implications of cigarette smoking among college students. *Journal of Consulting Psychology*, 1959, **23**, 376–384.

Seltzer, C. C. Why people smoke. *Atlantic Monthly*, 1962, **211**, 41–43.

Seltzer, C. C. Morphologic constitution and smoking. *Journal of the American Medical Association*, 1963, **183**(8), 639–645.

Seltzer, C. C. Occupation and smoking in college graduates. *Psychological Review*, 1964, **71**(1), 1–18.

Silverman, A. P. Behavioral effects of a "smoking dose" of nicotine. *British Journal of Pharmacology*, 1969, **37**(2), 506P-507P.

Smith, G. M. Personality correlates of cigarette smoking in students of college age. *Annals of the New York Academy of Science*, 1967, **142**, 308–321.

Smith, G. M. Relations between personality and smoking behavior in pre-adult subjects. *Journal of Consulting and Clinical Psychology*, 1969, **33**(6), 710–715.

Smith, G. M. Personality and smoking: A review of the empirical literature. In W. A. Hunt, (Ed.), *Learning mechanisms and smoking*. Chicago: Aldine, 1970.

Srole, L. Social and psychological factors in smoking behavior: The midtown Manhattan study. *Bulletin, New York Academy of Medicine*, 1968, **44**(12), 1302–1513.

Straits, B. C. Sociological and psychological correlates of adoption and discontinuation of cigarette smoking. (A report to the Council for Tobacco Research, U.S.A.), Chicago: University of Chicago Press, 1965.

Straits, B. C., & Sechrest, L. Further support of some findings about the characteristics of smokers and nonsmokers. *Journal of Consulting Psychology*, 1963, **27**, 282.

Thomas, C. B. On cigarette smoking, coronary heart disease and the genetic hypothesis. *Johns Hopkins Medical Journal*, 1968, **122**, 69–76.

Tomkins, S. S. Psychological model for smoking behavior. *American Journal of Public Health and the Nation's Health*, 1966, **56**(12), 17–20.

Ulett, J. A., & Itil, T. M. Quantitative electroencephalogram in smoking and smoking deprivation. *Science*, 1969, **164**, 969–970.

U. S. Public Health Service. *Changes in cigarette smoking habits between 1955 and 1966.* (USPHS Publication No. 1000, Series 10, No. 59). Washington, D. C.: U. S. Government Printing Office, 1970.

Veldman, D. J., & Bown, O. H. Personality and performance characteristics associated with cigarette smoking among college freshmen. *Journal of Consulting and Clinical Psychology*, 1969, **33**(1), 109-119.

Walker, R. E., Nicolay, R. C., Kluczny, R., & Riedel, R. G. Psychological correlates of smoking. *Journal of Clinical Psychology*, 1969, **25**(1), 42–44.

Warwick, K. M., & Eysenck, H. J. The effects of smoking on the CFF threshold. *Life Sciences*, 1963, **4**, 219–225.

8

PERSONALITY AND THE MAINTENANCE OF THE SMOKING HABIT[1]

H. J. Eysenck
Institute of Psychiatry, University of London

In their interesting chapter on habit mechanisms in smoking, Hunt and Matarazzo (1970) make some rather scathing comments on the usefulness of studying personality in relation to the maintenance of the smoking habit. "Perhaps because of the superabundance of personality measures and measuring techniques and the relative ease of running significance tests upon differences in group means, plus the ubiquity of simple correlations methods, the personality characteristics of smokers and nonsmokers have been well explored, and to no apparent advantage [p. 82]." To which Coan (1967) adds that "common failings in personality research stem from fixation on haphazardly chosen concepts, preoccupation with particular forms of measurement, and overdependence on available instruments [p. 141]." Hunt and Matarazzo (1970) continue that "where group differences have been found, their statistical significance is inflated by large samples, and the overlapping in the groups renders individual prediction of little value." They doubt "whether the resulting information is pertinent in any immediate sense to the problem of controlling smoking behavior," and conclude that it would be "much better ... to try aversive conditioning [p. 83]." Smith (1970) retorts, "quite contentiously, that a thorough exploration of the personality characteristics of smokers and nonsmokers has *not* yet been accomplished; that what has been learned *is* of some apparent advantage; and that such information *is* pertinent to the problem of controlling smoking behavior [p. 59]." Quot homines, tot sententiae.

The position here taken is in some sense intermediate between these extremes. I would agree with Hunt and Matarazzo that the purely descriptive personality studies so ably summarized by Matarazzo and Saslow (1960), Larson and Silvette

[1] The research on which this chapter is based was supported by a grant from the Tobacco Research Council, England.

(1961), and Smith (1967, 1970) are not, as they stand, of any great explanatory or scientific value, although they do represent a pretty thorough attempt to delineate the personality structure of smokers and nonsmokers. I would argue, however, that when we look at personality not from a descriptive, but rather from a causative point of view, the picture changes dramatically (Eysenck, 1965a); indeed, I would go so far as to say that without bringing personality into the picture, no causative theory stands a chance of receiving proper support from empirical studies, or can be made to reconcile apparently irreconcilable experimental data. In taking this stand, I am simply applying to this particular field a perfectly general theory which I have stated (with some vigor) in *The Biological Basis of Personality* (Eysenck, 1967). As this thesis goes counter to the whole tradition of modern experimental psychology, and is at the same time fundamental to my approach, I would like to state it briefly, with some experimental examples.

The general functional approach of experimental psychologists attempts to reduce all empirical problems to a simple statement of the kind $y = f(x)$, on the assumption that this approach is characteristic of all science. Thus in cryogenics one might say that superconductivity (y) is a function of lowering temperature to within a few degrees of absolute zero (x). So far, so good, but y is also a function of the particular type of metal or alloy used (z); some metals and alloys show superconductivity, others do not. In the same way, psychologists may ask: Is reminiscence (y) a function of length of rest pause (x)? This sounds like a meaningful question, but it is so only if we specify types of persons (z) subjected to the experiment. I predicted that reminiscence would increase with length of rest pause for introverts and decrease for extraverts, and the experiment by Howarth and Eysenck (1968) illustrated in Figure 1 seems to bear out this contention; groups of introverted and extraverted Ss, having learned pairs of nonsense syllables, were asked to reproduce them after varying rest intervals, and produced quite different results. Had we not separated our Ss in this fashion, there would have been no effect of the experimental design at all, but only a huge error variance! The apparently sensible question asked is meaningless unless personality is introduced into the equation, just as the physicist interested in cryogenics must introduce descriptions of materials used into his equation. No wonder that experimental psychologists working with verbal reminiscence have declared it to be a now-you-see-it-now-you-don't phenomenon; in our experiment we find that introverts show reminiscence, extraverts forgetting, while a combination of both groups shows no change over time! Many other examples are given in Eysenck (1967); for the present this one must suffice as a simple illustration of my point. I will return to the theoretical explanation of the empirical finding a little later.

The position here taken is not merely that personality is an important variable in experimental psychology that can be controlled and measured; it is much stronger than that. I would maintain, and I believe that the evidence bears out my contention, that very few, if any, studies in experimental psychology are anything but misleading in their conclusions if they fail to take into account organismic variables (of which personality is the human form, as it were—in animals one would talk about strains or other similar concepts). At the very least, personality variables can throw new light on otherwise dubious or anomalous facts; they can rescue a

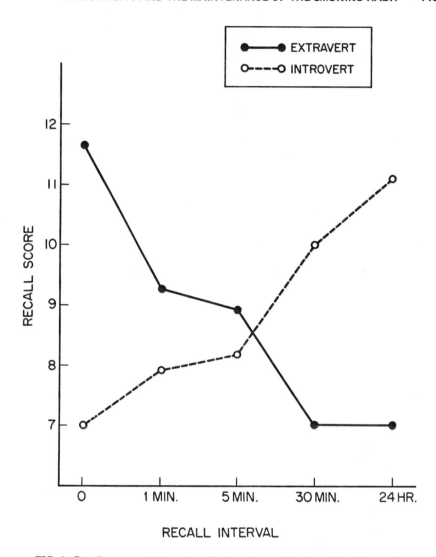

FIG. 1. Recall scores on introverts and extraverts as a function of recall interval.

large proportion of the variance from the error term to which traditional experimentalists have relegated it, thus inflating this term way beyond the main effects and interaction terms concerned with the independent variables. I will not here defend this position in any detail; I will instead try to demonstrate its applicability to the problem of the maintenance of smoking. In doing so I will have to be rather dogmatic on a number of points for the sake of brevity, and simply refer the reader to various publications and summaries; it is of course realized that reality is enormously more complex than is here suggested, and that each statement requires many detailed qualifications. Furthermore, it is not suggested that the variables here dealt with encompass all the factors which maintain smoking; it is merely suggested that further research along the lines here suggested may be fruitful, and that many of the known facts find a ready interpretation along these lines.

The position I am taking is intermediate between two extremes, both of which have many adherents. On the one hand, there are those who deny the importance, relevance, and even the existence of personality in the sense of a semipermanent, enduring set of traits; Skinnerians like Lundin (1969) and theoreticians like Mischel (1968) take this view. It seems that such a view can only be maintained by disregarding a large body of evidence, which I have summarized elsewhere (Eysenck, 1970, 1971b). Quite opposed to this view is that of Allport (1937) and his followers, who adopt an idiographic point of view according to which each person is unique in his reactions, and dissimilar to every other person. Such a view disregards important similarities which obtain between people and which can be graded along certain dimensions (Eysenck, 1947). Type/trait theories lie between these extremes of considering all persons essentially alike, almost like uniovular twins, for experimental purposes, or of considering them all as completely unlike each other, thus making experimental work essentially impossible. Type/trait theories attempt to grade people along certain major dimensions of personality, on the assumption that these dimensions define important areas of similarities and differences, without either exhausting these similarities and differences or limiting the essential uniqueness of all existing objects, both animate and inanimate. The discovery of the major dimensions, their measurement, and the demonstration of their relevance to certain general problems (such as the maintenance of smoking behavior) are empirical problems which should not be preempted on philosophical grounds.

Two major dimensions of personality emerge from almost any large-scale study of human behavior; I have labeled these extraversion-introversion (E) and neuroticism-stability (N), but other terms are also widely used. Cattell prefers exvia-invia and anxiety to denote the same factors (Cattell & Scheier, 1961); Burt (1965) prefers emotionality to both neuroticism and anxiety. Such terminological problems will be disregarded here; there is ample evidence that identical factors in fact emerge from analyses of the items making up the major systems of Cattell, Guilford and Eysenck (Eysenck & Eysenck, 1969). This source will also be useful in demonstrating the widespread support given by the literature for the existence of these two orthogonal factors, not only for adults, but also for children. Choice of these variables may therefore exempt us from the criticisms made by Coan (1967) in the passage quoted in the first paragraph.

Concepts like E and N define a *typology*; this term is anathema to many American psychologists because they associate it with hypotheses about U-shaped or bimodal distributions, or even with categorical separation of the population into groups. No such implications are intended (or have been intended by writers such as Jung, Kretschmer, and Sheldon); for them, as for this writer, *type* is simply a supraordinate concept to *trait*, signifying the fact of observed intercorrelations between different traits. Thus introversion is defined by the intercorrelations between sociability, impulsivity, liveliness, and various other traits. Descriptively, there is no doubt that personality is implicated with smoking; much work has been done to indicate that extraverts smoke cigarettes more frequently than do introverts (Eysenck, 1965a). But such a statement does not link up with experimental and pharmacological studies unless we can find some causal connection between E and N, on the one side, and general physiological and psychological concepts, on the other. I have tried to develop a theory of this kind (Eysenck, 1967) and will now turn to the main tenets of this theory.

The first and most important hypothesis in this theory states that under identical external conditions of low sensory input and low autonomic involvement, extraverts will be characterized by low cortical arousal, introverts by high cortical arousal. Cortical arousal can of course be measured in many different ways, and these different measures do not always (or even usually) correlate very highly together. Nevertheless, a specific hypothesis can be formulated in respect to each type of measurement, and these can then be tested; on the whole, such tests have proved positive in almost every instance. Gale, Coles, and Blaydon (1969) have reviewed the literature on the EEG and have added their own important studies; they conclude that the evidence from the EEG is fairly convincing. Introverts tend to have higher alpha frequencies and lower amplitudes, extraverts lower frequencies and higher amplitudes. In our own laboratories, studies of evoked potentials have shown shorter latencies and greater amplitudes for introverts, longer latencies and lesser amplitudes for extraverts (Hendrickson, unpublished 1972); as predicted, there was an interaction with stimulus intensity, in the sense that these differences were most marked with stimuli of minimum intensity, and decreased with increasing stimulus intensity. Galvanic skin response habituation was found to be quicker in extraverts, and spontaneous fluctuation more apparent in introverts (Crider & Lunn, 1971). Sensory thresholds are lower for introverts in a variety of sense modalities (Eysenck, 1967). Even in the field of learning the hypothetical higher arousal of introverts gives rise to testable hypotheses; my prediction of the reminiscence differential shown in Figure 1 may serve as an example. The theory is based on three assumptions: (a) reminiscence is produced by consolidation of the memory trace (Eysenck, 1965b); (b) consolidation proceeds more strongly, and for a longer period of time, under conditions of high arousal; and (c) while consolidation is active, it interferes with recall/reproduction (Walker, 1958). Given these assumptions, it will be seen that low-arousal extraverts consolidate poorly, have little interference in the early stages of recall, but do not remember well after the passage of 30 minutes or more, due to the poor consolidation of the memory trace. Hence the decline of recall with time for this group. High-arousal introverts consolidate well, have much interference in the early stages of recall, but remember well after the passage of 30 minutes or more, due to the strong consolidation which took place before, but is not interfering any longer. This is but one example of the experimental testing of the arousal hypothesis; many others are given in Eysenck (1967, 1971a). There is thus quite good direct and indirect evidence for some sort of cortical arousal theory of introversion-extraversion; whether this theory takes the precise form suggested by Eysenck (1967), who related it to the ascending reticular formation, or some other form is not crucial for our purpose here.

The causal role of arousal for E is paralleled by that of autonomic activation, controlled by the "visceral brain," for N. Here too there is much evidence for some degree of autonomic specificity, particularly in experiments calling for minimum degrees of activation, and this has sometimes been used as the basis for an argument denying the very existence of a general "emotionality" syndrome. It is interesting to note that the different autonomic systems, although not correlating very highly together, do seem to cooperate in producing what might be called introspective ("verbal report") emotion (Thayer, 1970); verbal report correlates better with each psychophysiological measure than these correlate with each other. Thayer reports combinatorial correlations of autonomic measures with verbal report as high as .62; this does not suggest complete specificity. Autonomic activation and cortical arousal are here regarded as essentially separate causal factors mediating behavior; this separation, however, is only maintained under conditions of low emotional activation. High emotional activation (relatively rare in conditions of civilized living, and particularly in conditions of laboratory experimentation) inevitably produces high cortical arousal, either directly or through the intervention of the ascending reticular activating system. Both E and N are regarded as having a strong genetic basis, and there is much evidence to support this point of view (Eysenck, 1967).

After this somewhat prolonged introduction, we must turn to the theoretical constructs which mediate a link between this theory of personality and the maintenance of smoking behavior. The essential hypothesis providing this link is illustrated in Figure 2. This figure shows on the abscissa the level of stimulation to which the individual is exposed, ranging from low (sensory deprivation) to high (pain). Along the ordinate is plotted hedonic tone, ranging from negative through indifferent to positive. The general relation between these two variables is curvilinear, with a preference for a level of stimulation intermediate between sensory deprivation and pain; this optimum regulation level is denoted OLP. Our theory now states that introverts have an optimum level of stimulation nearer the low-stimulation end of the abscissa, while extraverts have an optimum level of stimulation nearer the high-stimulation end of the abscissa; this displacement is a direct consequence of the degree of cortical stimulation (Eysenck, 1963). The optimal levels of stimulation for extraverts and introverts are graphed in the figure as OL_E and OL_I; the actual distances involved are of course purely notional. Consider now two stimuli, A and B, which are near the low- and high-stimulation ends of the continuum respectively. Stimulus A will be experienced by introverts as having a positive hedonic tone, by extraverts as having a negative hedonic tone, and as relatively indifferent by the average person. Stimulus B, on the other hand, will be experienced as having a negative hedonic tone by introverts, as having a positive hedonic tone by extraverts, and as being indifferent by the average person. If we regard the achievement of positive hedonic tone, and the avoidance of negative hedonic tone, as the fundamental parameters of the law of reinforcement, it can be seen that one and the same stimulus may have positive, negative, or neutral reinforcing properties for different organisms. Conditions of sensory deprivation are more aversive for extraverts than for introverts; conditions of physical pain are more aversive for introverts than for extraverts (Eysenck, 1967).

Just one example must suffice to illustrate the experimental study of this general law.

Weisen (1965) has compared groups of introverted and extraverted subjects, selected on the basis of appropriate Minnesota Multiphase Personality Inventory

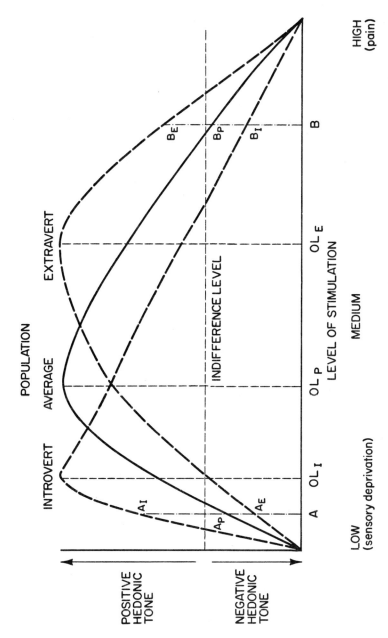

FIG. 2. Relation between level of sensory input and hedonic tone as a function of personality. (Reprinted from Eysenck, 1963.)

(MMPI) scales, in an experiment involving essentially behavior indicative of preference for presence or absence of strong sensory stimulation. Colored lights and loud music constituted the stimulation in question; silence and darkness constituted its absence. The subject pressed a key against a spring, the strength of his push constituting his selected behavior for reinforcement. Under "onset" conditions the room was dark and quiet, and a push of predetermined strength produced noise and light for a 3-second period; unless the button was again pushed with predetermined strength, noise and light would then cease. Subjects could therefore ensure continuance of sensory stimulation by constantly pushing the button strongly, or they could ensure absence of stimulation by pushing the button weakly. Under "offset" conditions the opposite state of affairs prevailed; strong pushing was required to produce periods of silence, weak pushing ensured continuance of light and noise. For the first five minutes of the experiment (operant-level period) no reinforcement was given; this period established the natural strength of button pushing of members of the various groups. This was followed by a 10-minute conditioning period and finally by a 5-minute extinction period.

Figures 3 and 4 show the frequency of correct (reinforced) responses of extraverts and introverts under "onset" and "offset" conditions respectively. It will

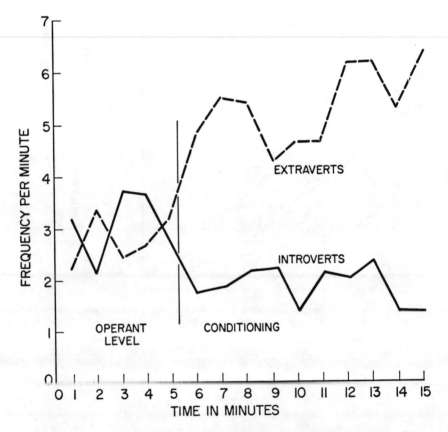

FIG. 3. Response strength of extraverts and introverts under conditions where reinforcement consisted of strong sensory stimulation.

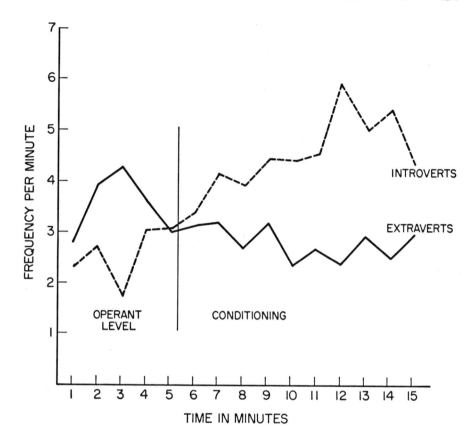

FIG. 4. Response strength of extroverts and introverts under conditions where reinforcement consisted of weak sensory stimulation.

be clear that both groups are similar in their behavior under operant conditions, but that they behave quite differently under experimental conditions. The extraverts increase their rate of correct responses when these are reinforced by stimulation, and decrease their rate when absence of stimulation is the consequence. Introverts increase their rate of correct responses when these are reinforced by absence of stimulation, and decrease their rate when stimulation is the consequence. These results are in good agreement with prediction and may be regarded as replications, as the subjects in the "onset" condition were not the same as those in the "offset" condition. It might be added parenthetically that the choice of personality inventory probably decreased the expected effect; the MMPI was not designed for the measurement of extraversion-introversion in normal groups and is not well adapted for this purpose.

If, as our theory suggests, extraverts are more likely to suffer from underarousal, introverts from overarousal, then the principle of reinforcement suggests that they will adopt quite different life styles, and seek quite different sources of satisfaction. Extraverts will become what has been called "sensation seekers," looking for various sources of thrills, strong sensory stimulation, and generally relief from boredom; this sensation seeking (looking for "arousal jags" is another term which has been used in this connection) may show itself in a variety of ways. The greater sociability of extraverts has been well documented (Eysenck & Eysenck, 1969); other people mediate a great deal of stimulation, both sensory and ideational. Extraverts have been found to seek change in employment, in domicile, in marriage partner; change counteracts habituation and provides arousal. Extraverts have been found much more active sexually; they have intercourse earlier, with more different partners, in more different positions, involving more prolonged love play, and using more "perverted" practices (Eysenck, 1971b). In the laboratory, extraverts have been found to differ from introverts in a large number of experiments based on the hypothesis of lowered cortical arousal of extraverts (Eysenck, 1967, 1971a). There is little doubt that extraverts on the whole behave in a manner not contradictory to our theory.

Drugs provide one method of achieving a change in level of arousal; stimulant drugs like amphetamine have arousing (introverting) effects, while depressant drugs like the barbiturates have the opposite (extraverting) effect (Eysenck, 1963). If nicotine provides the basis for the maintenance of the smoking habit (Jarvik, 1970), then it is not unlikely that this reinforcing effect is mediated by stimulant or depressant action on the CNS. It is clearly desirable to discover whether nicotine, which we shall assume is the crucial chemical constituent of cigarettes, is a stimulant or a depressive drug; depending on the answer to this question, we may be able to link smoking with our provisional personality model, and the arousal-motivation model associated with it.

There is a good deal of evidence suggesting that nicotine has a primarily arousing affect; most of this evidence has come from animal experiments (among the most widely quoted are Armitage, Hall, & Morrison, 1968; Domino, 1967; Ginzel, 1967; Knapp & Domino, 1962; Longo, Berger, & Bovet, 1954; Longo & Bovet, 1952; Longo, Giunta, & Carolis, 1967; Silvestrini, 1958; Stümpf, 1959; and Yamamoto & Domino, 1965; a good summary is given by Herz, 1968). Certain findings enjoin caution on any premature application of these findings to humans, or on taking the generalization too seriously even when animals are concerned. In the first place, problems of dosage have not been solved, or even attacked with any great enthusiasm; it is not well known to what extent dosage curves might depart from the monotonic. There is evidence that while small doses do have a positive effect on arousal, larger ones may have a negative effect; Armitage, Hall, and Sellers (1969) found that doses of 2 mg/kg every 30 seconds for 20 minutes, given intravenously to cats, caused desynchronization of the electrocorticogram, indicating cortical activation, and an increase in the release of cortical acetylcholine. However, a larger dose given less frequently (4 mg/kg every minute for 20 minutes) caused sometimes an increase and sometimes a decrease in cortical activity, such changes being accompanied by an increase or a decrease in cortical acetylcholine output. Apart from dosage effects, there may be sequential effects, a primary arousal phase being followed by a secondary depression phase. Thus Schaeppi (1967) concluded that "EEG desynchronization, retraction of the nicitating membrane, mydriasis and increase in blood pressure, which occur after treatment of the cat's lower brain stem with nicotine, indicate an increase in the animal's level of vigilance. Conversely, the secondary phase, consisting of synchronization, relaxation of the nicitating membrane, miosis and decrease in blood pressure indicates a low level of vigilance [p. 47]." Similarly, Goldstein, Beck, and Mundschenk (1967) comment that "the electroencaphalographic effects of nicotine start with an arousal reaction. By conventional methods of examination of cortical EEG and of behavior, this arousal per se is not different, at least in animals, from the arousal elicited by a variety of other stimulant agents such as amphetamine, caffeine, LSD, deanol, etc., or from that due to sensory stimulation alone. However, contrary to what is observed with a number of agents, the arousal in animals treated with very small doses of nicotine is of short duration and is followed by three distinct phases: a period of EEG alternation between sedation and excitation, a period of behavioral and EEG sedation and sleep, and, finally, a frequent occurrence of 'paradoxical' or 'activated' sleep [p. 170]." It thus seems that even with identical doses, different affects may be obtained at different times after administration.

Behavioral studies (e.g. Bignami, Robustelli, Janku, & Bovet, 1965; Bovet, Bovet-Nitti, & Oliverio, 1967; Bovet & Gatti, 1965; Michelson, 1961; Morrison & Armitage, 1967; Morrison, Goodyear, & Sellers, 1969; Morrison & Lee, 1968; Morrison & Stephenson, 1969; Robustelli, 1963) have also been interpreted as giving support to the view that nicotine acts as a stimulant drug; no secondary phase has been reported in this work. However, it is not easy to accept the majority of the reported studies as having much bearing on the question at issue, largely because pharmacologists are prone to interpret behavior in a rather common-sense manner which pays little attention to theoretical niceties. Apparently "aroused" and "uninhibited" behavior may often be interpreted as evidence of cortical arousal, but this is incorrect. As I have often pointed out, one of the main functions of the cortex is precisely the inhibition of behavior functionally related to the lower centers (Eysenck, 1967); extraverts behave in an uninhibited fashion because of the low arousal of the higher cortical centers, whose low level of function fails to exert sufficient control. Even if this hypothesis should not prove acceptable, it must be clear that a firm theoretical link must be forged between cortical arousal and any particular item of behavior before this item of behavior can be accepted as evidence of differential degree of arousal.

To give one worked-out example from our own studies in this field, consider the application of the arousal-consolidation theory of learning briefly mentioned previously in our discussion of the reminiscence effect. McGaugh (1965) has shown that, very much as required by our theory, stimulant drugs when administered *after* the learning phase improve performance, presumably through facilitating consolidation, while depressant drugs have the opposite effect. In three of our studies we have used nicotine, as well as other drugs, to test the hypothesis that nicotine is indeed a stimulant drug. The general setup of the experiment is as follows. After some experience with the Hebb-Williams type of maze, the animal is given one run through Problem 4, under timed conditions, and with the number of errors noted; he is then fed for 2 minutes at the end of the maze, injected with the drug or the placebo, and returned to his cage. Another trial is given after 24 hours, followed by further trials in an identical manner, until 10 trials have been run. Note that the effect of the drug must be on consolidation because (*a*) it is administered *after* the learning trial, and (*b*) its effects are certain to have worn off after 24 hours, when the next trial is scheduled. A typical result is shown in Figure 5, which

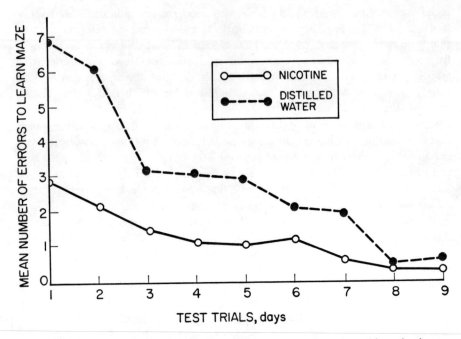

FIG. 5. Scores on nine trials succeeding original learning trial, when either nicotine or placebo was injected after each run.

is taken from Garg and Holland (1968). Test trial 1 (which is of course the second learning trial) already shows a marked superiority of the nicotine-injected animals over the placebo-injected animals, and this superiority is maintained throughout the course of the experiment, at least until hardly any errors are made by either group of animals. The effect is similar to that of other stimulant drugs, like picrotoxin, and the opposite to that of depressant drugs, like pentobarbital sodium; Figure 6, taken from another paper by Garg and Holland (1967), shows the effect clearly. It is interesting that the noninjected control group does less well than the water-injected and the dry-needle control groups; this may be due to cortical arousal produced by the injection process, and the sensory stimulation produced thereby.

The drug effects are not only replicable and consistent with our hypothesis; they are different in degree for different strains (Garg and Holland, 1969). Special strains of high and low avoidance conditioning rats, and of high and low emotionally reactive rats, were submitted to this test, and it was found that the facilitative effect of nicotine was greater in the high avoiders than in the low avoiders; this is of interest, as in terms of our theory it might be suggested that high-avoidance conditioning is more likely to occur in animals having high cortical arousal. Replication of this study would be necessary before this isolated finding can be taken very seriously, and it would indeed be preferable if other behavioral measures of high and low arousal could be used to breed suitable strains; one such effort is going on in our laboratory at the moment. It is also of interest to note that the emotionally reactive strain surpasses the nonreactive strain on the test at all stages, and with or without drug administration; it seems likely that the stressful testing situation produces greater arousal in emotional than in nonemotional animals. These experiments illustrate some of the requirements which one should demand of any test purporting to demonstrate the alleged arousal-producing properties of nicotine, or of any other drug; the link with theory will be apparent.

In addition to the problem of dosage, a further problem is provided by the existence of individual differences between animals (or humans) in their reactions (Motulsky, 1965). Brief reference has already been made to this. Brown (1967) has documented this in animals, Murphree, Pfeiffer, and Price (1967) in humans; and although these studies are not altogether convincing, they are in agreement with many other experiments on a variety of drugs suggesting great individual differences among people (Eysenck, 1963). Of particular interest in this connection is the so-called sedation threshold (Shagass, 1954, 1956, 1957; Shagass & Jones, 1958; Shagass & Naiman, 1965, 1956; Claridge & Herrington, 1960). According to our theory, introverts are located further away from the sedation (inhibition, disarousal) end of the arousal continuum than are extraverts; consequently they would require *more* of a depressant drug to reach the same degree or state of

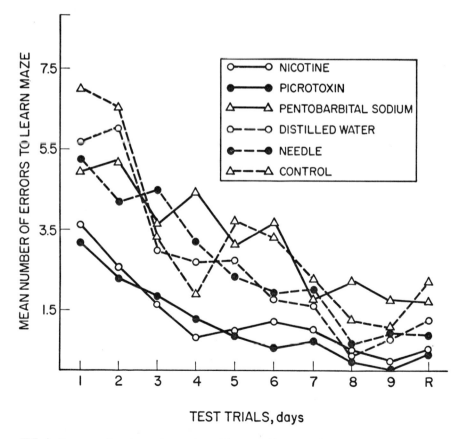

FIG. 6. Scores on learning and retention trials succeeding original learning trial, when different drugs were injected after each run.

disarousal. The experiments quoted, and many others cited by Eysenck (1967), demonstrate that this is indeed so; there are marked differences in the amount of sodium amytal required by extraverts and introverts (both normal and neurotic subjects have been used in these studies) to reach an identical point of disarousal defined either behaviorally or by EEG recording. No similar experiments seem to have been done in the animal field, although there should be no difficulty in doing so. Nor has there been any similar work in relation to a hypothetical "arousal threshold," where one would expect extraverts to require greater doses of a stimulant drug than introverts.

When we turn to the electrophysiological and behavioral effects of nicotine on humans, we find that very little concentrated work has in fact been done in this important field; in fact, most of the studies to be reviewed have been done in our own laboratory. Even where tentative conclusions have been advanced, the experiment often cannot be accepted without criticism. Thus the EEG studies of Hauser, Schwartz, Roth, and Bickford (1958), Lambiase and Serra (1957), and Wechsler (1958) were all entirely qualitative. On the whole most results would probably not be contradictory to the conclusions arrived at by Murphree et al. (1967): "The effects of smoking, as reflected in the electroencephalogram, appear to be stimulant rather than tranquilizing, although subjects may exhibit individual differences [p. 260]." It is interesting to note that this conclusion was counter to the original thinking of this group; as they say, "Initially we were thinking of smoking as having mild tranquilizing or antianxiety effects. Our view was that smokers absorb enough nicotine chronically to go past the point of ganglionic stimulation to the point of blockade. We reasoned that if there are neurophysiological mechanisms in the brain analogous to those in ganglia, we should see, in the quantitative electroencephalogram, some evidence of depressant effects from smoking. This now appears to be incorrect [p. 246]."

Our own data, using a somewhat more satisfactory technique of analysis, bear out this general conclusion (Philips, 1971). This study was designed, as none of the others mentioned had been, to study the immediate and subsequent effects of smoking. "The present aim of this study was to examine EEG changes following smoking one cigarette to see if there was any support for the claim that it produces EEG signs of increasing CNS activation [p. 72]." Computer methods—using a Power Spectral Analysis—were used to delineate reliably the form and duration of the changes. The data were examined under both resting and working conditions, up to 20 minutes following smoking; the visual task consisted of critical flicker fusion (CFF). Subjects were tested under experimental (smoking) and control (nonsmoking) conditions; no order effects became apparent. The major finding of the experiment was that smoking a cigarette produced a significant change in the amount of predominant frequency present in the EEG during and immediately after visual stimulation. A minimal effect was present as long after as 20 minutes, in terms of failure to return to the level of activity of the control. "If the initial alpha desynchrony is indicative of a facilitatory effect of smoking on EEG responsivity to visual stimuli, this still appears to be present since adaptation has not occurred after 20 minutes [p. 69]. Altogether, Philips concludes that her findings "support the view that small amounts of nicotine absorbed in cigarette smoke act as a stimulant or activator [p. 72].

In an earlier experiment, Warwick and Eysenck (1963) had used the CFF directly as a measure of cortical efficiency, their hypothesis being that nicotine (either absorbed during smoking, or orally administered) would raise the CFF threshold, such an increase being a recognized sign of cortical arousal. Two experiments were carried out, and the predicted rise was found under both conditions of administration. Figure 7 shows the results of the oral administration of a small dose of nicotine; it is clear that a marked effect is produced by the drug, as compared with placebo and no-drug control groups. In a later report, Warwick and Eysenck (1968) reported on the effects of nicotine on a variety of experimental measures, including serial reaction time, reminiscence, motor tremor, spiral rotation after-effects, visual masking, a modified version of the CFF test, and two-flash threshold. These experiments are too voluminous to report in detail, but the conclusion reached was that "on the whole the results substantiated the hypothesis (that nicotine had an arousing effect), although of course the proof is indirect and requires to be supplemented by more direct physiological methods [p. 168]." Warwick and Eysenck (1969) also investigated the occurrence of sex differences in reaction to nicotine on these tests, and the differences between smokers and nonsmokers; they concluded that both these variables required to be controlled in experimental studies of the effects of nicotine.

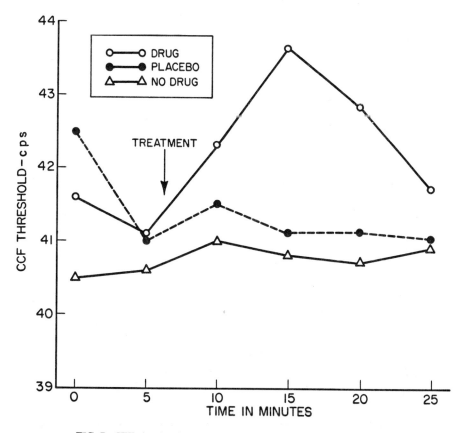

FIG. 7. CFF thresholds under drug, placebo, and no-drug conditions.

A further series of studies from our laboratory was reported by Frith (1967a, 1967b, 1967c), who used the finger-tapping test whose relevance to the concept of arousal and introversion-extraversion had been demonstrated by Spielman (1963) and Eysenck (1964). It was hypothesized and demonstrated that involuntary rest pauses (IRPs) occur more frequently in extraverts than in introverts; these IRPs are indexed in terms of gaps between successive taps which are unduly long ("unduly long" is of course precisely defined in mathematical terms). The theory predicting this effect is based on the assumption that reactive inhibition will accumulate more quickly in individuals having low cortical arousal, and that reactive inhibition will show itself in the form of IRPs. A detailed discussion of theory and results is given by Eysenck (1967).

Frith carried out a whole series of experiments on the effects of nicotine on tapping. He found that subjects tended to adopt different strategies to cope with the buildup of inhibition, so that analyses had to be carried out on different subgroups of the total sample. Thus while some Ss followed the theoretical pattern of dissipating reactive inhibition by producing IRPs, others rather slowed down the production of taps. Controls were instituted to make this difficult, e.g., by having Ss tap to the sound of a metronome, or by having them keep a pointer in a given place, which could only be accomplished by keeping up a given rate of tapping. Other controls included isolating the tapping finger so that it became impossible to vary the actual movement made, e.g., by shifting from finger movement to hand or arm movement. Analysis of three different types of scores (rate of tapping, occurrence of IRPs, and change in average gap length) revealed that "on all three measures nicotine decreased the change in performance over time [Frith, 1967c, p. 1547]." It was also found that "only those subjects who performed poorly under placebo were affected by nicotine [p. 1547]"; this is not an isolated finding, and it suggests that sometimes failure to find drug effects may be due to failure to break down the group of subjects into good and poor performers. For good performers, the task may have to be made longer, or harder, or more productive of reactive inhibition in some other way. All in all, these studies support the view that nicotine is a stimulant drug in the small doses used.

In another study, Frith (1968a) used a measure of salivation increment following upon placing four drops of lemon juice on the tongues; it had been shown by S. B. H. Eysenck and H. J. Eysenck (1967) that, as hypothesized, introverts show a much greater increment than do extraverts. The hypothesis in the case of nicotine administration was, of course that administration of this drug would shift the reactions of the subjects in an introverted (high arousal) direction, and thus increase the difference between lemon-juice and control conditions. This was indeed found: "Nicotine significantly increased the difference between response and resting level [Frith, 1968a, p. 81]." Unlike the Eysenck studies, the investigation under discussion used a special saliometer in which the saliva was collected via a disc held by negative pressure over Stensen's duct; the saliva displaced alcohol, which then fell past a photocell in discrete drops of constant size, each drop producing a deflection of a polygraph record from which the quantity of saliva and the rate of secretion could easily be measured. The stimulus liquid was injected along a tube attached to that collecting the saliva, and entered the mouth from several points around the disc covering Stensen's duct. In spite of the greater sophistication of this device, as compared with the simple manual method used by Eysenck, the method proved less effective and had several disadvantages which probably reduced the size of the effect, although this was still fully significant statistically.

In yet another study, Frith (1968b) took up the hypothesis, already considered several times, that arousal increases consolidation. Using the pursuit rotor, he administered practice on a variable-pattern polar tracking device, with a centrally placed equilateral triangle as the path to be followed. The subject tracked the target with a rigid L-shaped stylus containing a photoelectric cell at its tip; the target to be followed was a pattern of light produced by a rotating gap in an opaque cover over a light source. Subjects were instructed to keep the stylus in contact with the glass covering the track and target. Number of hits for each 10-second period, and total time on target for each period, were recorded. The experiment was arranged in rather a complex pattern, but the conclusion was quite clear: "Nicotine, acting during a programmed rest pause, significantly facilitated the consolidation of pursuit rotor learning [p. 1155]." This effect appeared in scores based on mean hit lengths, but not in scores based on total time on target, probably because of the greater variability of the later scores resulting from the inclusion of rest pauses (IRPs) in this index of performance.

Taking all the data reviewed here together, it is apparent that the hypothesis of nicotine producing a positive effect on arousal is strongly supported. There are of course inevitable anomalies in the data, but these are perhaps less obvious than in most generalizations in this field, and many of them may find an easy explanation in terms of composition of the samples tested, of dosage used, of personality-type differences from one study to another, or even of time of day when testing took place—Eysenck (1967) has reviewed some of the evidence showing superior performance by introverts in the morning and by extraverts in the afternoon; and Blake (1967a, 1967b) has shown that this pattern is replicated in changing body temperature of introverts and extraverts. Agué (1971) has shown in a very careful experiment that the very act of smoking (number of puffs, nicotine uptake, etc.) is different at different times of day, as are the physiological effects produced. But overall the pattern is sufficiently homogeneous to make this conclusion a reasonable one to hold at the present time.

We may now try to integrate this evidence with a general theory of smoking maintenance, to the effect that persons who on the hedonic tone/stimulation curve (Figure 2) are to the left of the point of optimum arousal (i.e., who are below their optimal level) will attempt to raise their level of arousal either by change of environment, activity, etc., or by pharmacological means, e.g., by the intake of nicotine. The choice between these two different types of reaction is presumably governed by such factors as environmental constraints, availability of cigarettes or arousal-producing activities, preexisting habits, knowledge of the arousal-producing effects of nicotine, etc. This hypothesis would integrate into our model the fact that extraverts smoke more cigarettes than introverts because according to Figure 2 the optimum level of arousal for extraverts is displaced to the right; in other words, ceteris paribus, they will be more likely to be in a state of underarousal than will introverts. It would follow that they would have recourse to pharmacological methods of raising their level of arousal more frequently than would introverts; i.e., they would smoke more cigarettes. We have already noted that extraverts are also characterized by behavioral methods of increasing arousal level, i.e., through increase in sensory stimulation, environmental change, sexual adventures, etc.; smoking thus takes its natural place as one of many ways to achieve this end.

One testable deduction from this hypothesis would be that under controlled laboratory conditions (i.e., when recourse to arousal-producing activity is made difficult or impossible) there should exist for each individual a preferred intake of nicotine, such that it brings him up to, or at least near, his optimum level of arousal; less intake of nicotine would make him fall short (underarousal), more intake of nicotine would make him exceed this point (overarousal). Quite generally, then, it is postulated that the tobacco habit is maintained because it is an artificial aid in producing a preferred level of arousal; it is the change from a less preferred to a more preferred level which constitutes the positive reinforcement which the smoker derives from this habit. There is some evidence from animal work (monkeys) that nicotine by itself can become a reinforcement (Deneau & Inoki, 1967; Jarvik, 1967). As Jarvik says, "We conclude that it is possible to elicit and maintain smoking behavior in monkeys with no other incentive and on a free choice basis, but it is relatively weak compared to other ingestive behavior, such as drinking, which satisfies an obvious physiological need [p. 294]." Such results are reassuring, but they cannot of course take the place of human experiment, where much finer grading of responses can be expected.

Perhaps the early work of Johnston (1942) is relevant here; he showed that the craving of habituated smokers could be successfully appeased by nicotine injections instead of smoking. Similarly, Proosdij (1960) reports that during World War II, chewing tobacco and snuff became popular among workers in munition factories where smoking was prohibited. Studies such as these indicate fairly clearly that it is the nicotine in the cigarette which plays the crucial role in the reinforcement process; apparently it is the ability of the nicotine to change the arousal level in the desired direction, and to the desired extent, which is responsible for the maintenance of the smoking habit.

A crucial experiment along these lines was performed in our laboratory by Frith (1971a). He discounts the negative results of Goldfarb, Jarvik, and Glick (1970), who failed to find that altering the nicotine content of the smoker's cigarette altered his smoking behavior, for two reasons. (a) The experimental cigarettes contained lettuce to which varying amounts of nicotine were added. The nasty taste of the lettuce appears to have swamped all other effects, causing the subjects to smoke fewer experimental cigarettes than their normal brand, whatever the nicotine content. (b) Only the number of cigarettes smoked was studied, which provides a rather crude measure of smoking behavior. Frith's method overcame these difficulties:

9 male subjects (unpaid student volunteers) were given three kinds of cigarettes to smoke on three days, in a balanced order for days by cigarette type. The different kinds of cigarette were given on three successive days. Normally the subjects smoked at least 15 cigarettes per day. On the days of testing no cigarette was smoked before 9.0 a.m, when the first experimental cigarette was offered. The different nicotine deliveries in the cigarettes were achieved by appropriate leaf blending and choice of suitable filters. The cigarettes were made entirely from flue-cured leaf and no nicotine was added artificially at any stage of manufacture. The actual deliveries in the smoke, after passage through the filter, of Particulate Matter (Water and Nicotine Free "Tar") and of nicotine are

shown in Table 1.

It can be seen that the nature of the experimental cigarettes is not entirely satisfactory for the aims of the experiment since the "tar" content tends to be confounded with the nicotine content, when cigarette 3 is compared with cigarettes 1 and 2. However these cigarettes probably have the most controlled levels of nicotine possible while still remaining indistinguishable from commercially available cigarettes. Indeed there are commercially available cigarettes containing such extreme amounts of nicotine, although in The U.S. Department of Health Education and Welfare's chart 70% of the standard sized cigarettes listed contain between 1.2 and 1.6 mg/cig of nicotine.

The following measures of smoking behaviour were taken: the number of cigarettes smoked in an 8-h period (9.0 a.m. to 5.0 p.m.), the desire for a cigarette on a 7 point scale immediately before and after smoking a single cigarette, the time taken to smoke a single cigarette, the rate of puffing and the volume per puff. To obtain these last measures the subjects had to smoke one cigarette (the last of the 8-h period) through a special holder down to 1 cm from the tip.

This holder consisted of a perspex orifice plate mounted in a tube with pressure tappings. A sharp edged hole of 1 mm diameter provided a sufficient pressure drop to be measured without interfering with the smoker's puffing. Each cigarette was cut so that the tip could be placed in one end of the holder and the rest of the cigarette in the other end. The differential pressure across the orifice was measured with a Grass PT5 transducer. The resulting DC current was directly proportional to the volume of air passing through the transducer. This technique was developed by P.I. Adams of the Imperial Tobacco Co. This method gives an indirect measure of the amount of smoke drawn through the cigarette. It cannot, of course, give any indication as to how much of this smoke was actually inhaled.

RESULTS

The subjects could reliably distinguish cigarette type 3 from the other two kinds (Friedman analysis of variance by ranks; $\chi^2 = 7.72$, $p < 0.05$). They could not distinguish between types 1 and 2. They reported that cigarette 3 was stronger than the others and some subjects reported physiological changes while smoking this cigarette such as a racing heart.

Table 2 shows the relationship between cigarette type and the number of cigarettes smoked during the 8-h period.

A trend χ^2 test showed a significant linear relationship between these variables ($\chi^2 = 8.01$, $p < 0.01$). Cigarettes of all types produced a decrease in the desire for a cigarette immediately after they had been smoked. Table 3 shows the relationship between the size of this decrease in desire and cigarette type. Here again the trend χ^2 test was significant ($\chi^2 = 5.75$, $p < 0.05$).

TABLE 1

Contents of Cigarette Smoke

Cigarette type	Particulate matter[a] mg/cigarette	Nicotine mg/cigarette
1	14.6	1.02
2	17.1	1.37
3	30.8	2.11

Note.—Adapted from Frith (1971).
[a]Water- and nicotine-free.

TABLE 2

Consumption and Cigarette Type

Group	Cigarette type			
	1	2	3	Total
Subjects smoking more than their experimental mean	7	5	1	13
Subjects smoking less than their experimental mean	2	4	8	14
Total	9	9	9	

Note.–Adapted from Frith (1971).

TABLE 3

Change in Desire and Cigarette Type

Group	Cigarette type			
	1	2	3	Total
Subjects showing more than their mean change in desire	1	4	6	11
Subjects showing less than their mean change in desire	8	5	3	16
Total	9	9	9	

Note.–Adapted from Frith (1971).

TABLE 4

Means and Standard Deviations of Smoking Variables

Cigarette type		Time (sec)	Puffs/sec	Volume/puff (arbitrary units)
1	M	333.7	0.54	12.1
	sd	88.5	0.28	4.7
2	M	345.8	0.53	14.7
	sd	81.6	0.19	5.3
3	M	402.9	0.43	12.7
	sd	68.8	0.19	4.1

Note.–Adapted from Frith (1971).

Results from the detailed study of smoking behaviour showed similar effects. Means and standard deviations for the three variables are shown in Table 4.

There was a very high correlation between the total time taken to smoke a cigarette and the average rate of puffing ($r = -0.86$) regardless of cigarette type and puff volume. This indicated that any cigarette required a more or less constant number of puffs to be smoked. Both these correlated measures showed the same effect of cigarette type. This took the form of a significant linear relationship between cigarette type and these measures such that the more nicotine there was in a cigarette the longer the subject took to smoke it ($F = 7.29; df = 1,16; p < 0.01$).

There was also a significant relationship between puff volume and cigarette type such that subjects had larger puff volumes for type 2 than for type 1 or 3 ($F = 10.28$; $df = 1,16; p < 0.01$). It is difficult to find any plausible explanation of this result. Perhaps it arose because cigarette type 2 contained the same amount of nicotine as commonly available brands. During the smoking of a single cigarette there was a marked decrease in puff volume and puff rate, but this effect was not related to cigarette type [Frith, 1971a, pp. 189-191].

Frith concluded that "this experiment has provided some data in support of the hypothesis that smokers can alter their behaviour to suit the nicotine content of their cigarettes. In particular the smokers in this experiment took longer to smoke a cigarette with more nicotine in it. Presumably this change in behaviour enabled the smoker to obtain the physiological and psychological effects he desired of the nicotine whatever the nicotine content of his cigarettes [p. 191]." Frith also argued that this might constitute a useful experimental technique because, "if the nicotine content of the cigarettes remained constant and yet the smoker changed his behaviour, then it could be assumed that the amount of nicotine he desired had changed, for example as a result of a stressful situation. It might thus be possible to measure rapid fluctuation in a person's desire for nicotine by measuring how long he took to smoke a standard cigarette [p. 191]."

Confirmation comes from the work of Ashton and Watson (1970), who used different filters to produce high-nicotine and low-nicotine cigarettes. They tested their subjects under three conditions: resting, easy simulated driving task, and stressful driving task. They found that "during both of the driving tasks and during the resting period after the tasks the subjects smoking the low-nicotine cigarettes took more frequent puffs than those smoking the high nicotine cigarettes.... As would be expected from the increased puff frequency, the average time taken to finish a cigarette was less in the groups smoking the low-nicotine cigarettes. Records of respiration made during the smoking showed no differences in overall rate or in the depth of respiration at or after each puff between the two groups of smokers. Hence these results suggest that the subjects smoking the low-nicotine cigarettes were attempting to compensate for the high filter retention of nicotine by a faster puffing rate. The puff volume appeared to be relatively constant, though small differences may not have been detected." It was also found that the resting puff rate was significantly greater during rest than during the easy task, and the nicotine obtained from the cigarettes per unit time was also significantly greater than during the task; this was true for both the "high-nicotine" and the "low-nicotine" group. "This finding suggests the possibility that the subjects were striving for a higher nicotine dose during the resting period. There was also a tendency in both the high- and low-nicotine cigarette groups to take more puffs and obtain more nicotine during the level 2 [stressful] than during the level 1 [easy] task [p. 680]."

Ashton and Watson go on to say that "in the absence of suitable methods for determining blood levels of nicotine there is unfortunately no way of measuring how much of the nicotine taken into the mouth was absorbed into the body; but all subjects inhaled when smoking and there was no detectable difference in the mean depth of respiration between the groups smoking different cigarettes. These findings are thus consistent with the possibility that there exists an 'optimum' nicotine dose for a given activity and that smokers unconsciously modify their smoking patterns in an attempt to obtain this dose [p. 681]." It is necessary to add that this hypothesis contains certain inconsistencies which require sorting out. Thus the fact that under resting conditions subjects take in more nicotine (produce more arousal) than when working on the easy task (which itself presumably produces some cortical arousal, thus leaving less to be produced by pharmacological action) makes good sense in terms of our theory. But how is it that when working on the stressful task (which presumably produces more arousal than the easy task) subjects yet take in more nicotine than when working on the easy task? (Admittedly this difference was not quite significant statistically; but as it goes in the wrong direction, it should not be dismissed too cavalierly.) It would be necessary to postulate that in the one case the effect of nicotine was to increase arousal, while in the other it was to decrease arousal. Now we have already seen that such contradictory effects are indeed encountered in the case of nicotine, and Ashton and Watson refer to some of this work; however, these opposing effects were due to different dosages, low dosages producing arousal, high dosages producing sedation. Here we find that higher dosages produce (presumably) greater arousal in the rest group, but lower arousal in the stressful task group! It is clearly necessary to invoke some sort of interaction effect.

We may begin by noting the well-known fact that nicotine injection is accompanied by cortical arousal and also by an increased production of acetylcholine, a transmitter substance for the propagation of nerve impulses in the cerebral cortex. Armitage et al. (1968) have shown, as already mentioned, that with small doses of nicotine, arousal and increased production of acetylcholine were observed; but with slightly larger doses there occurred a similar pattern in some experiments, while in others the result was a lowering of arousal and a decrease in the production of acetylcholine. "It appears, therefore, that nicotine can have two effects, it can either cause an increase or a decrease in the acetylcholine release from the parietal cortex and can cause changes in the EEG consistent either with increased or decreased cortical activity. It seems likely that the effect varies from cat to cat, and even with the small changes in the dose of nicotine and the rate of injection." And finally Armitage, Hall, and Morrison conclude: "We suggest that the effect of nicotine in man probably depends critically on the dose and rate of self-administration and also on whether he is excited or depressed [p. 334]."

Possibly a general solution to the problem raised can be found in the application of principles familiar from the work on the sedation threshold, already referred to, and from Pavlov's principles of the "law of strength" and that of "paradoxical reactions." Work on the sedation threshold has shown us that less of a depressant drug is needed to bring an extraverted subject to the sedation threshold; presumably this rule can be reversed to state that less of a stimulant drug is needed to bring an introverted subject to the arousal threshold. Such a law would tell us that under quiet laboratory conditions, the amount of nicotine required to reach this threshold differs from person to person according to his introversion/extraversion score. How can we define such a threshold? Pavlov (1927) suggested that an increase in what we would now call cortical arousal was accompanied by an increase in "output"; this is the law of strength. He also suggested, however, that this law only applied up to a certain point; beyond this point "protective inhibition" set in the produced paradoxical effects, such that with increasing arousal, "output" was in fact decreased. It is difficult to deal with Pavlov's physiology in modern terms, and we may with advantage drop reference to it and restate our suggestion in somewhat different terms. We would suggest that the effects of nicotine depend on the degree of arousal in the cortex; when arousal is high, the effects are depressing, whereas when arousal is low, the effects are stimulating. The degree of arousal is primarily a function of two factors: (*a*) the personality of the subject (primarily his position on the extraversion-introversion continuum); and (*b*) the conditions obtaining at the time, i.e., external determinants of arousal such as degree of sensory stimulation, etc. Certain minor factors may have to be added to this list (we have already mentioned time of day, for instance) and these minor factors—as well as the major ones mentioned under (*b*)—may interact with personality; we have seen that extraverts have relatively low arousal in the morning, relatively high arousal in the evening. However, the final common pathway of these various factors must be the state of arousal, as indexed by the EEG or some other suitable measure, and the theory suggests that depending on this state the effects of nicotine will be positive or negative, arousing or depressing. This would mean that nicotine would be uniquely reinforcing, tending under all conditions (in suitable doses) to produce a shift in arousal directed towards the optimum degree shown in Figure 1. Possibly this is the reason why this habit is so difficult to give up, and so strongly reinforcing for so many people. (A similar slight ambiguity has sometimes been observed in relation to alcohol also, where small and large doses may appear to have antagonistic properties.)

Note the phrase "in suitable doses", inserted in the sentence above, suggesting that the shift produced by nicotine in the arousal level could always be reinforcing. As Armitage et al. (1968) have suggested, the smoker has "finger-tip control" over the actual uptake of nicotine; he can vary the interpuff interval, the strength and length of puff, the total number of puffs taken; he can inhale or not, as he pleases, and he can select cigarettes having a nicotine content most suitable for his habitual requirements. Thus we can combine our two sets of hypotheses and state that the selection and manner of smoking a cigarette interact with the personality type of the smoker, and with the situation, to produce the final end effect—the change in arousal level which will be most reinforcing. None of these elements can fruitfully be studied by itself, as all interact in complex ways to produce the final result. (Possibly another point should be emphasized here; the effects of nicotine are likely to be profoundly different depending on the previous exposure of the smoker to the drug. This factor in turn can be split up into two quite different factors: short-term exposure, i.e., length of time since smoking the last cigarette; and long-term exposure, i.e., habitual intake of nicotine over the last few years. For the sake of simplifying our exposition, these factors have been kept implicit rather than made explicit; for serious experimental work they must always be borne in mind, however.)

It is interesting to note that in quite a different context (the study of "flooding" as a therapeutic method in behavior therapy), Rachman (1969) came to conclusions rather similar to ours; he suggested that arousal is an inverted-U-shaped function of arousal-producing conditions. Watts (1971) also furnished data to support this suggestion, in a clinical context; and Straits (1965) came near to making the same suggestion in his analysis of smoking behavior. A direct experimental study of this hypothesis would seem overdue.

Armitage et al. (1968) remark that "tobacco smokers have frequently stated that they are either 'tranquilized' or 'stimulated' as a result of smoking a cigarette and although this evidence is purely subjective it cannot be dismissed [p. 334]." In terms of our theory, it would seem to follow that: (*a*) introverts should more frequently use nicotine for tranquilizing purposes, extraverts for stimulating purposes; and (*b*) people smoking under conditions of "boredom" should use nicotine for stimulating purposes, people smoking under conditions of "stress"

TABLE 5

Questionnaire Items Used by Frith (1971b) to Obtain Data
Upon Which Figure 8 is Based

Item Number	Situational Statement
1	You are having an important interview for a job.
2	You have to fill in a complicated tax form.
3	You have to look through several hundred coins to see if there are any rare and valuable ones.
4	You are having a quiet evening with friends.
5	You are witnessing a violent and horrifying film.
6	You have to drive at speed in heavy traffic.
7	You have to wait for your train home, which is very late.
8	You are having a restful evening alone reading a magazine.
9	You are sitting in a dentist's waiting room knowing that you are to have a particularly difficult filling.
10	You are trying to hold a conversation at a large and very noisy party.
11	You are very tired and need to keep awake.
12	You have to ask your boss for a raise at a time when he is known to be in a bad mood.
13	You are trying to account for the discrepancy between your spending for the month and your bank statement.
14	You are looking through a long list of names to see if you can find anyone you know.
15	You are chatting with friends during a tea-break.
16	You have just been informed of the death of a close friend.
17	You have to do some rapid mental arithmetic for an intelligence test.
18	You are traveling on a train for several hours.
19	You go for a solitary walk in quiet countryside.
20	You have just heard the announcement of a plane crash, and you think a friend may have been involved.
21	You are having an important telephone conversation in a very noisy office.
22	You have just had a very big meal.

should use nicotine for tranquilizing purposes. An experiment relevant to these hypotheses has been performed in our laboratory by Frith (1971b). In his own words:

> If nicotine acts as a stimulant, then a person is most likely to smoke when he has an undesirable low level of arousal. Such a low level of arousal would probably result from a combination of circumstances. The person would be particularly prone to low levels of arousal by his very nature and would also be in a situation inducive of a particularly low level of arousal (tiring, boring, etc.). Another person might smoke because he was particularly prone to high levels of arousal and found himself in a highly arousing situation. It seems very likely that these two would be different people. Thus it should be possible to isolate two extremes of smoking behaviour. There should be one group of people who smoke mostly in situations inducing low levels of arousal in order to increase their arousal level, and there should be another group of people who smoke in situations which induce high levels of arousal in order to reduce their arousal level [p. 73].

As a test of this hypothesis, Frith (1971b) constructed a questionnaire listing 22 situations which might make it likely that a person would be tempted to light a cigarette; 12 of these were high-arousal and 10 were low-arousal situations. The actual list used is given in Table 5. The subjects had to imagine themselves in each of these situations and indicate what their desire for a cigarette would be on a seven-point scale. Ninety-eight subjects, of both sexes, took part in the experiment; ages ranged from 18 to 50. All were cigarette smokers. The 25 variables (including sex, age, and number of cigarettes smoked per day) were intercorrelated and factor analyzed; two main factors were extracted. These are presented in graphic form in Figure 8. It will be seen that all questionnaire items have loadings with identical sign on the first factor; this suggests that a person who is tempted to light up in one situation is also likely to light up in another. The highest loading is for number of cigarettes smoked per day. The second factor opposes the low-arousal situations to the high-arousal situations, in conformity with expectation. It is interesting to note that sex has the highest loading on this factor; "the men tended to have the highest desire for a cigarette in situations inducing boredom and tiredness, while the women had their highest desire in stress inducing situations [p. 74]." It is relevant to note that men have always been found to have higher extraversion scores than women (Eysenck & Eysenck, 1969), as well as lower neuroticism scores; this suggests that a repetition of the experiment using personality questionnaires might indicate that extraverts smoke to increase arousal, introverts to reduce it.

Frith's factor contrasting different occasions for smoking finds some support in a study by McKennell (1970), where a factor analysis of occasions to smoke brought to light several factors, of which two relevant ones were "relaxation smoking" and "nervous irritation smoking"; he too, unfortunately, failed to administer personality questionnaires. However, sex comparisons gave results similar to Frith's. The data are a little difficult to disentangle because they are confounded by differential smoking habits of men and women (sex is not included in the factor analysis, but percentage figures for males and females are given in his Table 7); nevertheless it is clear that for his adults, men exceed women for relaxation smoking, and women exceed men for nervous irritation smoking, when allowance is made for the fact that men are heavier smokers than women.

There is also some support for Frith's finding from a study by Ikard, Green, and Horn (1969). As a small part of his survey, Horn asked people how much they

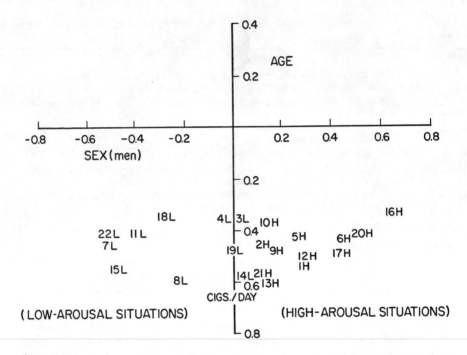

FIG. 8. Graphical representations of 22 situations, age, sex and cigarettes per day, showing their loadings on the first two factors of a principal component analysis. From Frith (1971).

agreed with statements like, "When I feel uncomfortable or upset about something, I light up a cigarette." There were five such statements with which women agreed significantly more often than men. All described situations of stress and high arousal (e.g., feeling worried, angry, upset, etc.). Unfortunately there were no questions describing low-arousal states. However, with one statement, "I smoke cigarettes to stimulate me," more men than women agreed, although not significantly so.

The distinction here drawn is similar in many ways to Tomkins' (1966) typology of smokers, particularly his two main types classified according to the distinction between positive-affect and negative-affect smoking. In the latter, "the individual smokes primarily to reduce his feelings of distress, or his fear, or his shame, or his disgust, or any combination of these. He is trying to sedate himself rather than to stimulate . . . himself [p. 19]." In contrast, positive-affect smoking occurs in those individuals who characteristically smoke under pleasant circumstances which are relaxing—possibly so relaxing as to require some measure of arousal! The third type recognized by Tomkins is a mixture of the other two, resulting in addiction, and the fourth is a "pure habit" smoker; McKennell failed to discover any smokers corresponding to this type in his large-scale study.

Frith draws attention to one possible difficulty in the interpretation here offered. People who do not inhale, absorb virtually no nicotine (Kuhn, 1965), and thus the pharmacological effects of nicotine would be irrelevant to their smoking behavior. Therefore if the people who reported wishing to smoke under stress tended not to inhale their cigarettes, then their behavior requires an explanation quite different from that here proposed. For example, the ritual of lighting and holding a cigarette might be important in reducing the effect of the stressful situation; Freeman (1948) has shown that even irrelevant muscular activity reduces anxiety. Now Todd (1969) has reported that of over 4,000 cigarette smokers, 77.7% of the men inhaled the smoke, whereas only 53.0% of the women did so. Future studies along these lines should certainly include questions about inhaling, as well as questionnaires of extraversion and neuroticism in their purview.

It is possibly relevant to this discussion that while nearly all studies on the relation between smoking and personality have found positive correlations with extraversion, the expected correlation with neuroticism has usually failed to materialize. One possible reason for this might be the fact that most studies (certainly this is true of the large-scale ones) have been confined to men; if men smoke in order to stimulate themselves, then "sedation smoking," which has relevance to neuroticism, would not be found among them. If this type of smoking is more frequent among women, however, then we might expect to find a positive correlation between smoking and neuroticism in women. Waters (1971) has carried out such a study; a standard questionnaire, which was completed by 1,718 individuals (83.5% of the available sample) selected at random from the electoral roll, asked about smoking habits and included questions from which a grade for neuroticism was obtained. The results suggested that, in women, smokers are more neurotic than nonsmokers, and there was a statistically significant correlation between the number of cigarettes smoked per day and the neurotic grade. No such relations were found for the men. Here too no questions were asked about inhaling, so that while the results are in line with expectations set up by our theory, alternative explanations are still possible.

One alternative, or possibly rather extension, of our general theory should at least be mentioned here, in spite of the rather speculative nature of the hypotheses involved. The theory in question may serve to explain the facts depicted in Figure 2, and consequently may serve as a basis for the predictions we have made rather freely from the generalized relationship basic to that figure. Delgado, Roberts, and Miller (1954) and Olds and Milner (1954) have opened up a series of investigations demonstrating the existence of several pain and pleasure centers; Olds and Olds (1965) describe three such centers. First of all we have the primary reward and aversion systems, which are believed to counteract each other; certainly the aversion system appears to inhibit the primary reward system upon activation, and diminishes the effects on behavior attributed to that system. No evidence has been found of reciprocal action of the primary reward system on the aversion system (Brady & Conrad, 1960; Olds & Olds, 1965). Now, as Berlyne (1971) points out, "the primary reward and aversion system are . . . closely connected, and at least partially identifiable, with the brain structures controlling the manifestations of heightened arousal. Powerful and virtually insatiable rewarding effects can be obtained by stimulating the lateral hypothalamus and the medial forebrain bundle, and important tracts of nerves that pass along the sides of the hypothalamus. This is what Olds calls the 'positive reinforcement focus' [p. 75]." However, it has been shown that even the elimination of large amounts of tissue from this area leaves strong primary rewarding effects intact (Valenstein & Campbell, 1966), suggesting that the essential focus of the system lies in the reticular formation, which is of course the area primarily concerned with arousal. The aversion system (Old's "periventricular system") consists of fibers passing through the medial hypothalamus into the midbrain tegmentum, which is largely occupied by parts of the reticular formation. "A substantial body of experiments shows that stimulation within either the primary reward system or the aversion system produces familiar signs of increased arousal, including changes in heart rate, high frequency EEG waves, and increased bodily movement [Berlyne, 1971, p. 78]."

The secondary reward system, on the other hand, appears to be more closely related to the trophotropic or dearousal system. "Olds's experiments point to the existence of what he calls a 'positive-reinforcement-field', which has a much larger extent than the positive reinforcement 'focus' or primary reward system and is generally to be found rather higher up, toward the top of the brain-stem and in the limbic system, which occupies the lowest and most primitive parts of the cerebrum." Activation of this system results in dearousal; its stimulation leads to slow heart beats, the appearance of low-frequency EEG waves, and reduced motor activity. It is suggested that the secondary reward system produces rewarding effects indirectly, i.e., by inhibiting the aversion system, which in turn inhibits the primary rewarding system. "Activation of the secondary rewarding system thus produces reward by releasing the primary rewarding system from inhibition [Berlyne, 1971, p. 79]."

Berlyne thus distinguishes between two mechanisms of reward, involving these three systems. One mechanism produces reward when arousal is lowered after rising to an uncomfortably high level; this he supposes to depend on the secondary reward system. "When food is presented to a hungry animal or when fear is alleviated through the appearance of a reassuring stimulus, the secondary reward system becomes active. This, we have seen, reduces the activity of the aversion system, which means a lowering of arousal and an alleviation of unpleasantness [p. 79]." The other mechanism works through arousal increase rather than arousal reduction and comes into play when arousal is raised to a moderate extent. It will be clear that the arousal-increasing properties of small amounts of nicotine, administerd in low-arousal situations, and to extraverts in particular, would activate the primary rewarding system, through the second mechanism postulated. On the other hand, the arousal-decreasing properties of somewhat larger amounts of nicotine, administered in anxiety-producing situations, and to introverts in particular, would activate the secondary reward system, and through it deactivate the aversion system. This theory has been presented in very abbreviated form; but although it is clearly very speculative, it may nevertheless lend itself to experimental falsification, though perhaps only in animals. In any case, it seems to fit in well with the general theory outlined in the earlier part of this paper, and may anchor it more firmly in biological reality.

The model of smoking behavior and its maintenance here sketched out has some obvious relevance to attempts to reduce or eliminate the habit. The growing importance and success of behavior therapy (Eysenck & Beech, 1971) has brought about a flood of attempts to use techniques such as aversion therapy and desensitization for the purpose of smoking behavior modification. The outcome of all this work has not been commensurate with the effort (Keutzer, Lichtenstein, &

Mees, 1968, Bernstein, 1969); this is not surprising when we consider the methods used in terms of our model. We have postulated that (a) different people smoke for different reasons, primarily to either increase or decrease cortical arousal, and that (b) they do so in different situations that are producing either too little or too much arousal. This suggests immediately that no general method of treatment would be likely to be effective for all subjects; indeed, a method which might help some individuals might have the opposite effect on others! A person using smoking as a tranquilizer might benefit from desensitization, but might in fact get worse under aversion therapy, where the electric shocks and other strong stimuli used might increase his already too high degree of arousal. It seems clear that most of the attempts to modify smoking behavior have suffered from a lack of theoretical sophistication. In most cases an existing method has been adapted to the problem without careful prior theoretical analysis, and without any attempt to take into account important variables relevant to the situation. An attempt to "cure" people of the smoking habit should incorporate an investigation of their personality structures, their reasons for smoking (along the lines of the study by Frith, 1971b), their methods of smoking (number of cigarettes, number and spacing of puffs, inhalation or not, etc.). On the basis of this knowledge it might then be possible to prescribe *for that particular person* a course of treatment which should of course be based on a detailed analysis of the problem presented, as well as on thorough knowledge of the methods available and of their theoretical justification and background. Studies which are treatment-centered, i.e., which start out with the notion of testing a given type of treatment by administering it to every member of a randomly constituted experimental group, for comparison with an equally randomly constituted control group, are doomed to failure; they resemble a hypothetical attempt in the medical field to bring together a random sample of ill people and to administer to them a particular type of treatment irrespective of the particular ills with which they happened to be afflicted. Such attempts are motivated by the belief that all smoking is caused and reinforced by a single, uniform factor common to all smokers; as we have seen, such a belief is hardly tenable any longer. Such undirected activity can have no other result than to bring into disrepute the methods of behavior therapy which, like all methods of behavior modification, require careful analysis and theoretical insight before they can be applied with success; they are not to be regarded as foolproof panaceas to be dispensed at random (Eysenck & Rachman, 1965).

This brings us to the end of a rather far-ranging discussion of what is undoubtedly a rather complex model of smoking behavior and maintenance. In part the complexity is perhaps due to imperfect understanding, but not, I believe, altogether. There is no doubt that smoking presents a very complex problem, and that many different parameters are involved in its understanding and control. I have tried to indicate some of the reasons why I believe that personality variables are crucial to such an understanding, and why I cannot agree that neglect of these variables can lead to anything but one-sided understanding and failure to encompass the fullness of the phenomena in question. The importance of different situations leading to smoking is widely recognized; it is equally important to realize that different people experience these situations in different ways. Such a remark is scientifically meaningful only if we can independently identify and classify people according to their reactions to relevant situations; this I have tried to do in terms of a general theory which has received a great deal of support in recent years. The model finally put forward here also has some claims to be supported by relevant research, but I would be the first to agree that much further research is needed to make it acceptable. Fortunately the model has one great advantage, from the scientific point of view: it is easily falsifiable, and the predictions made from it are fairly clear-cut and testable. It is my hope that research over the next few years will succeed in supporting or falsifying the model in a fairly definitive fashion.

REFERENCES

Agué, C. Smoking and nicotine: An evaluation of its psychological, physiological, and behavioural effects upon habitual users. Unpublished doctoral dissertation, University of London, 1971.

Allport, G. *Personality*. London: Constable, 1937.

Armitage, A. K., Hall, G. H., & Morrison, C. F. Pharmacological basis for the tobacco smoking habit. *Nature*, 1968, **217**, 331-334.

Armitage, A. K., Hall, G. H., & Sellers, C. M. Effects of nicotine on electrocortical activity and acetylcholine release from the rat cerebral cortex. *British Journal of Pharmacology*, 1969, **35**, 157-160.

Ashton, H., & Watson, D. W. Puffing frequency and nicotine intake in cigarette smokers. *British Medical Journal*, 1970, **3**, 679-681.

Berlyne, D. E. *Aesthetics and psychobiology*. New York: Appleton, 1971.

Bernstein, D. A. Modification of smoking behaviour: An Evaluation Review. *Psychological Bulletin*, 1969, **71**, 418-440.

Bignami, G., Robustelli, F., Janku, I., & Bovet, D. Action de l'amphétamine et de quelques agents psychotropes sur l'acquisition d'un conditionnement de fuite et d'évictement chez des rats selectionnés en fonction du niveau particulièrement bas de leur performances. *Comptes Rendue des Séances de l'Académie des Sciences* (Pairs), 1965, **260**, 4273-4278.

Blake, M. J. F. Relation between circadian rhythm of body temperature and introversion-extroversion. *Nature*, 1967, **215**, 896-987. (a)

Blake, M. J. F. Time of day effects on performance in a range of tasks. *Psychonomic Science*, 1967, **9**, 349-350. (b)

Bovet, D., Bovet-Nitti, F., & Oliverio, A. Action of nicotine on spontaneous and acquired behavior in rats and mice. In H. B. Murphree (Ed.), The effects of nicotine and smoking in the central nervous system. *Annals of the New York Academy of Science*, 1967, **142**, 261-267.

Bovet, D., & Gatti, G. L. Pharmacology of instrumental avoidance under training. *Proceedings of the 2nd International Pharmacologists Meeting*, Prague, 1963. Oxford: Pergamon Press, 1965.

Brady, J. V., & Conrad, R. G. Some effects of limbic system self-stimulation upon unconditioned emotional behaviour. *Journal of Comparative and Physiological Psychology*, 1960, **53**, 128-137.

Brown, B. B. Relationship between evoked response changes and behaviour following small doses of nicotine. In H. B. Murphree (Ed.), The effects of nicotine and smoking in the central nervous system. *Annals of the New York Academy of Science*, 1967, **142**, 190-200.

Burt, C. Factorial studies of personality and their bearing on the work of the teacher. *British Journal of Educational Psychology*, 1965, **35**, 368-370.

Cattell, R. B., & Scheier, I. H. *The meaning and measurement of neuroticism and anxiety*. New York: Ronald Press, 1961.

Claridge, G. S., & Herrington, R. N. Sedation threshold, personality, and the theory of neurosis. *Journal of Mental Science* (London), 1960, **106**, 1568-1583.

Coan, R. V. Research strategy in the investigation of personality correlates. In S. V. Zajona (Ed.), *Studies and issues in smoking behaviour*. Tuscon: University of Arizona Press, 1967.

Crider, A., & Lunn, R. Electrodermal lability as a personality diversion. *Journal of Experimental Research in Personality*, 1971, **5**, 145-150.

Delgado, M. M. R., Roberts, W. W., & Miller, N. E. Learning by electrical stimulation of the brain. *American Journal of Physiology*, 1954, **179**, 587-593.

Deneau, G. A., & Inoki, R. Nicotine self-administration in monkeys. In H. B. Murphree (Ed.), The effects of nicotine and smoking in the central nervous system. *Annals of the New York Academy of Science*, 1967, **142**, 277-279.

Domino, E. F. Electroencephalographic and behavioural arousal effects of small doses of nicotine: A neuropharmacological study. In H. B. Murphree (Ed.), The effects of nicotine and smoking in the central nervous system. *Annals of the New York Academy of Science*, 1967, **142**, 216-244.

Eysenck, H. J. *Dimensions of personality.* London: Routledge & Kegan Paul, 1947.

Eysenck, H. J. (Ed.) *Experiments with drugs.* Oxford: Pergamon Press, 1963.

Eysenck, H. J. Involuntary rest pauses in tapping as a function of drive and personality. *Perceptual and Motor Skills*, 1964, **18**, 173-174.

Eysenck, H. J. *Smoking, health and personality.* New York: Basic Books, 1965. (a)

Eysenck, H. J. A three-factor theory of reminisience. *British Journal of Psychology*, 1965, **56**, 163-181. (b)

Eysenck, H. J. *The biological basis of personality.* Springfield, Ill.: Charles C. Thomas, 1967.

Eysenck, H. J. *The structure of human personality.* (3rd ed.) London: Methuen, 1970.

Eysenck, H. J. Personality and sexual adjustment. *British Journal of Psychiatry*, 1971, **188**, 593-608. (a)

Eysenck, H. J. (Ed.) *Readings in extroversion-introversion.* London: Staples, 1971. 3 vols. (b)

Eysenck, H. J., & Beech, R. Counter conditioning and related methods. In A. E. Bergin & S. L. Garfield (Eds.), *Handbook of psychotherapy and behaviour change: An empirical analysis.* London: Wiley, 1971.

Eysenck, H. J., & Eysenck, S. B. G. *Personality structure and measurement.* London: Routledge & Kegan Paul, 1969.

Eysenck, H. J., & Rachman, S. *The causes and cures of neurosis.* San Diego: R. R. Knapp, 1965.

Eysenck, S. B. G., & Eysenck, H. J. Salivary response to lemon juice as a measure of introversion. *Perceptual and Motor Skills*, 1967, **24**, 1047-1053.

Freeman, G. L. *The energetics of human behavior.* Ithaca, N.Y.: Cornell University Press, 1948.

Frith, C. D. The effects of nicotine on tapping: I. *Life Sciences*, 1967, **6**, 313-319. (a)

Frith, C. D. The effects of nicotine on tapping: II. *Life Sciences*, 1967, **6**, 321-326. (b)

Frith, C. D. The effects of nicotine on tapping: III. *Life Sciences*, 1967, **6**, 1541-1548. (c)

Frith, C. D. The effects of nicotine on the consolidation of pursuit rotor learning. *Life Sciences*, 1968, **7**, 77-84. (a)

Frith, C. D. Personality, nicotine and the salivation response. *Life Sciences*, 1968, **7**, 1151-1156. (b)

Frith, C. D. The effect of varying the nicotine content of the cigarettes on human smoking behaviour. *Psychopharmacologia*, 1971, **19**, 188-192. (a)

Frith, C. D. Smoking behaviour and its relation to the smoker's immediate experience. *British Journal of Social and Clinical Psychology*, 1971, **10**, 73-78. (b)

Gale, S., Coles, M., & Blaydon, J. Extroversion-introversion and the EEG. *British Journal of Psychology*, 1969, **60**, 209-223.

Garg, M., & Holland, H, C. Consolidation and maze learning: A comparison of several post-trial treatments. *Life Sciences*, 1967, **6**, 1987-1997.

Garg, M., & Holland, H. C. Consolidation and maze learning: A further study of post-trial injections of the stimulant drug (nicotine). *International Journal of Neuropharmacology*, 1968, **7**, 755-759.

Garg, M., & Holland, H. C. Consolidation and maze learning: A study of some strain/drug interactions. *Psychopharmacologia*, 1969, **14**, 426-431.

Ginzel, K. H. Introduction to the effects of nicotine and the central nervous system. In H. B. Murphree (Ed.), The effects of nicotine and smoking on the central nervous system. *Annals of the New York Academy of Science*, 1967, **142**, 101-120.

Goldfarb, T. L., Jarvik, M. E., & Glick, S. D. Cigarette nicotine content as a determinant of human smoking behaviour. *Psychopharmacologia*, 1970, **17**, 89-93.

Goldstein, L., Beck, R. A., & Mundschenk, D. L. Affects of nicotine upon cortical and subcortical electrical activity of the rabbit brain: Quantitative analysis. *Annals of the New York Academy of Science*, 1967, **142**, 130-180.

Hauser, H., Schwartz, B. E., Roth, G., & Bickford, R. G. Electroencephalographic changes related to smoking. *Electroencephalography and Clinical Neurophysiology*, 1958, **10**, 576.

Hendrickson, E. An examination of individual differences in cortical evoked response. Unpublished doctoral dissertation, University of London, 1972.

Herz, A. Neuropharmakologie und psychopharmakologie des nikotins. In H. Schievelbein (Ed.), *Nikotin pharmakologie und toxikologie des tabakrauches*. Stuttgart: Thieme, 1968.

Howarth, E., & Eysenck, H. J. Extroversion, arousal and paired-associates recall. *Journal of Experimental Research in Personality*, 1968, **3**, 114-155.

Hunt, W. A., & Matarazzo, J. D. Habit mechanisms in smoking. In W. A. Hunt (Ed.), *Learning mechanisms and smoking*. Chicago: Aldine, 1970.

Ikard, F. F., Green, D. E., & Horn, D. A. scale to differentiate between types of smoking as related to the management of affect. *The International Journal of Addictions*, 1969, **4**, 649-659.

Jarvik, M. E. Tobacco smoking in monkeys. In H. B. Murphree (Ed.), The effects of nicotine and smoking on the central nervous system. *Annals of the New York Acacemy of Science*, 1967, **142**, 280-294.

Jarvik, M. E. The role of nicotine in the smoking habit. In W. A. Hunt (Ed.), *Learning mechanisms and smoking*. Chicago: Aldine, 1970.

Johnston, L. M. Tobacco smoking and nicotine. *Lancet*, 1942, Oct.–Dec., 742.

Keutzer, C. S., Lichtenstein, E., & Mees, H. C. Modification of smoking behaviour: A review. *Psychological Bulletin*, 1968, **70**, 520-533.

Knapp, D. E., & Domino, E. F. Action of nicotine on the ascending reticular activating system. *International Journal of Neuropharmacology*, 1962, **1**, 333-338.

Kuhn, H. Tobacco alkaloids and their pyrolisis products in the smoke. In U. S. von Euler (Ed.), *Tobacco alkaloids and related compounds*. Oxford: Pergamon Press, 1965.

Lambiase, M., & Serra, C. Fume e sistema nervosa. *Acta Neurologica* (Napoli), 1957, **12**, 475-493.

Larson, P. S., & Silvette, H. *Tobacco: Experimental and clinical studies*. Baltimore: Williams & Wilkins, 1961.

Longo, V. G., Berger, G. P., & Bovet, D. Action of nicotine and of the "gangliopleégiques centraux" on the electrical activity of the brain. *Journal of Pharmacology*, 1954, **111**, 349-359.

Longo, V. G., & Bovet, D. Studio electroencephalographico dell antagonismo svolto dai farmiaci antiparkinsoniani sui tremori provocati dalla nicotina. *Bollettino della Societa Italiana di Biologia Sperimentale*, 1952, **28**, 612-615.

Longo, V. G., Giunta, F., & Carolis, A. D. de. Effects of nicotine on the electroencephalograph of the rabbit. In H. B. Murphree (Ed.), The effects of nicotine and smoking on the central nervous system. Annals of the New York Academy of Science, 1967, **142**, 159-169.

Lundin, R. V. *Personality: An experimental approach*. (2nd ed.) London: Macmillan, 1969.

Matarazzo, J. D., & Saslow, G. Psychological and related characteristics of smokers and non-smokers. *Psychological Bulletin*, 1960, **57**, 493-513.

McGaugh, J. L. Effects of drugs on learning and memory. *International Review of Neurobiology*, 1965, **8**, 139-196.

McKennell, A. C. Smoking motivation factors. *British Journal of Social and Clinical Psychology*, 1970, **9**, 8-22.

Michelson, M. J. Pharmacological evidence of the role of acetylcholine in the higher nervous activity of man and animals. *Acta Neurologica Scandinavica*, Supplement, 1961, **3**, 140-147.

Mischel, V. *Personality and assessment*. New York: Wiley, 1968.

Morrison, C. F., & Armitage, A. K. Affects of nicotine upon the free operant behaviour of rats and spontaneous motor activity of mice. In H. B. Murphree (Ed.), The effects of nicotine and smoking on the central nervous system. *Annals of the New York Academy of Science*, 1967, **142**, 268-276.

Morrison, C. F., Goodyear, J. M., & Sellers, C. M. Antagonism by antimuscarinic and ganglion-blocking drugs of some of the behavioural effects of nicotine. *Psychopharmacologia*, 1969, **15**, 341-350.

Morrison, C. F., & Lee, B. N. A comparison of the effects of nicotine and physostigmine on a measured activity in the rat. *Psychopharmacologia*, 1968, **13**, 210-221.

Morrison, C. F., & Stephenson, J. A. Nicotine injections as the conditioned stimulus in discrimination learning. *Psychopharmacologia*, 1969, **15**, 351-360.

Motulsky, A. G. The genetics of abnormal drug responses. *Annals of the New York Academy of Science*, 1965, **123**, 167-177.

Murphree, H. B., Pfeiffer, S., & Price, L. M. Electroencephalographic changes in man following smoking. In H. B. Murphree (Ed.), The effects of nicotine and smoking on the central nervous system. *Annals of the New York Academy of Science*, 1967, **142**, 245-260.

Olds, J., & Milner, P. Positive reinforcement produced by electrical stimulation of septal area and other regions of rat brain. *Journal of Comparative and Physiological Psychology*, 1954, **47**, 419-427.

Olds, J., & Olds, M. Drives, rewards and the brain. In F. Barron (Ed.), *New directions in psychology*. Vol. 2. New York: Holt, Rinehart & Winston, 1965.

Pavlov, I. P. *Conditioned reflexes.* Translated by G. V. Anrep. London: Oxford, 1927.

Philips, C. The E.E.G. changes associated with smoking. *Psychophysiology*, 1971, **8**, 64-74.

Proosdij, C. van. *Smoking, its influence on the individual & its role in social medicine.* New York: Elsevier, 1960.

Rachman, S. Treatment by prolonged exposure to high intensity stimulation. *Behavior Research and Therapy*, 1969, **7**, 295-302.

Robustelli, F. Azione della nicotina sull'apprendimento del ratto nel labirinto. *Accademia Nazionale Lincei, Serie 8*, 1963, **34**, 703-709.

Schaeppi, V. Effects of nicotine administration to the cat's lower brain stem upon electroencephalogram and autonomic system. In H. B. Murphree (Ed.), The effects of nicotine and smoking on the central nervous system. *Annals of the New York Academy of Science*, 1967, **142**, 40-49.

Shagass, C. The sedation threshold. *Electroencephalography and Clinical Neurophysiology*, 1954, **6**, 221-233.

Shagass, C. Sedation threshold. *Psychosomatic Medicine*, 1956, **18**, 410-419.

Shagass, C. A measurable neurophysiological factor of psychiatric significance. *Electroencephalography and Clinical Neurophysiology*, 1957, **9**, 101-108.

Shagass, C., & Jones, A. L. A neurophysiological test for psychiatric diagnosis: Results in 750 patients. *American Journal of Psychiatry*, 1958, **114**, 1002-1009.

Shagass, U., & Naiman, J. The sedation threshold, manifest anxiety, and some aspects of ego function. *American Medical Association Archives of Neurology and Psychiatry*, 1965, **74**, 397-406.

Shagass, C., & Naiman, J. The sedation threshold as an objection index of manifest anxiety in psychoneurosis. *Journal of Psychosomatic Research*, 1956, **1**, 49-57.

Silvestrini, B. Neuropharmacological study of the central effects of henacytzine and hydroxyzine. *Archives Internationales de Pharmacodynamic et de Therapie*, 1958, **110**, 71-85.

Smith, G. M. Personality correlates of cigarette smoking in students of college age. In H. B. Murphree (Ed.), The effects of nicotine and smoking on the central nervous system. *Annals of the New York Academy of Science*, 1967, **142**, 308-321.

Smith, G. M. Personality and smoking: A review of the empirical literature. In W. G. Hunt (Ed.), *Learning mechanisms and smoking*, Chicago: Aldine, 1970.

Spielman, J. The relation between personality and the frequency and duration of involuntary rest pauses during massed practice. Unpublished doctoral dissertation, University of London, 1963.

Straits, B. C. Sociological and psychological correlates of adoption and discontinuation of cigarette smoking. Report submitted to the Council for Tobacco Research, U.S.A., 1965.

Stümpf, C. Die wirkung von nikotin auf die hippocampustatigkeit des kaninchens. *Archiv fuer Experimentelle Logie und Pharmakologie*, 1959, **235**, 421-436.

Thayer, R. Activation states as assessed by verbal report and four psychophysiological variables. *Psychophysiology*, 1970, **7**, 86-94.

Todd, G. F. (Ed.), *Statistics of smoking in the United Kingdom.* (5th ed.) (Research Paper I) London: Tobacco Research Council, 1969.

Tomkins, S. S. Psychological model for smoking behavior. *American Journal of Public Health and the Nation's Health,* 1966, **56,** Supplement 56, 17-20.

Valenstein, E. S., & Campbell, J. F. Medial forebrain bundle: Lateral hypothalamic area and reinforcing brain stimulation. *American Journal of Physiology,* 1966, **210,** 270-274.

Walker, E. L. Action decrement and its relation to learning. *Psychological Research,* 1958, **65,** 128-142.

Warwick, K. M, & Eysenck, H. J. The effects of smoking on the CFF threshold. *Life Sciences,* 1963, **4,** 219-225.

Warwick, K. M., & Eysenck, H. J. Experimental studies of the behavioural effects of nicotine. *Pharmakopsychiatrie Neuro-Psychopharmakologie,* 1968, **1,** 145-169.

Warwick, K. M., & Eysenck, H. J. Experimental studies of the behavioural effects of nicotine. Part II. Interaction of smoking habits. *Pharmakopsychiatrie Neuro-Psychopharmakologie,* 1969, **2,** 217-222.

Waters, W. E. Smoking and neuroticism. *British Journal of Social Medicine,* 1971, **25,** 162-164.

Watts, F. Desensitization as an habituation phenomenon. Part I. Stimulus intensity as determinant of the effects of stimulus lengths. *Behaviour Research and Therapy,* 1971, **9,** 209-217.

Wechsler, R. L. Effects of cigarette smoking and intravenous nicotine on the human brain. *Federation Proceedings,* Baltimore, 1958, **17,** 169.

Weisen, A. Differential reinforcing effects of onset and offset of stimulation on the operant behavior or normals, neurotics, and psychopaths. Unpublished doctoral dissertation, University of Florida, 1965.

Yamamoto, K. I., & Domino, E. F. Nicotine-induced E.E.G. and behavioural arousal. *International Journal of Neuropharmacology,* 1965, **4,** 359-373.

9
NESBITT'S PARADOX

Stanley Schachter
Columbia University

I suppose that all of us cherish a pet paradox—some perverse concatenation of data that simply doesn't make sense—some set of facts, each well established, each on the surface incompatible with the others. My own favorite is "Nesbitt's Paradox," a perversity that I've picked at for years with all of the therapeutic success of a small boy torturing the scab on his knee.

Probably the least equivocal, best established fact about the physiological consequences of smoking is that it leads to sympathomimetic symptoms. Summarizing a wealth of happily replicating studies, the Surgeon General's Report notes, "Smoking 1 to 2 cigarettes causes in most persons, both smokers and nonsmokers, an increase in resting heart rate of 15 to 25 beats per minute, a rise in blood pressure of 10 to 20 mm Hg systolic and 5 to 15 mm Hg diastolic, and an increase in cardiac output of about 0.5 l/min/sq.m. [U.S. Public Health Service, 1964, p. 318] ." It is presumed that nicotine stimulates the sympathetic ganglia and causes the discharge of epinephrine and norepinephrine. In addition to these consistent indications of peripheral activation, there are indications that nicotine is a CNS activator as well. Murphree, Pfeiffer, and Price (1967), for example, conclude from their EEG studies that "the effects of smoking, as reflected in the electroencephalogram appear to be stimulant rather than tranquilizing [p. 260] ." In short, smoking a cigarette leads to a set of physiological consequences, peripheral and central, that we customarily associate with states of arousal or activation or emotionality.

On the other hand, if you ask smokers why they smoke, overwhelmingly they respond in sedational terms. In the Meyer, Friedman, and Lazarsfeld (this volume) interview study, smokers were asked, "Why do you smoke?" The question could be interpreted historically (How did you get started smoking?) or instrumentally (What do you get out of smoking?). Of 126 respondents, 76 interpreted the question instrumentally. Of this group, 64% answered in sedational terms, that is, with such replies as, "It relaxes me," "It calms me down," and so on. Not a single respondent answered in terms that could be coded as indicating arousal, such as, "It stimulates me," or "It bucks me up." And these are typical results; other studies concerned with similar matters (Ikard, Green, & Horn, 1968) have also indicated that smokers describe the effects of smoking in predominantly sedational, not activational, terms.

There, then, is Nesbitt's Paradox. The known physiological effects of smoking a cigarette are those that we consider as indicating states of activation or arousal. The psychological effects of smoking, at least as far as smokers describe them, are sedational. Before picking at this particular paradox, however, let us be sure that it is one and that the facts are straight. Though I'm fairly sure that as a confirmed smoker, I, too, would say, "It relaxes me," I suspect I would mean that if I don't smoke I get upset, or that the budding withdrawal symptoms some time after I've put out my last cigarette make me just uneasy enough to induce me to light up my next one which, indeed, does then relax me. Perhaps, then, it's a paradox and perhaps it's not.

Since these instances where there is an apparent discrepancy between a behavioral or psychological event and the physiological machinery presumed to account for or to accompany this event have been of particular fascination to my colleagues and to me in our work on emotion and on eating behavior, we seized upon this potential paradox, and Paul Nesbitt (1969) designed an experiment to determine whether or not the behavioral arm of this presumed paradox was, indeed, fact. As a measure of anxiety, Nesbitt employed the willingness of his subjects to expose themselves to electric shocks of varying intensities. Presumably, the greater his anxiety, the less willing will a subject be to be shocked.

Nesbitt's experiment was conducted within the guise of a study of the evoked GSR—the series of changes in potential that follow electrical stimulation. Subjects were told that in order to get the "true wave form" it was "necessary to average over a number of repetitions of the stimuli (electrical stimulation), and over a number of intensities of the stimuli [p. 14]." The line of patter continued:

"The averaged GSR does change with drugs and various chemicals. Our particular interest is in nicotine. Nicotine is the principal pharmaceutical component in tobacco smoke. The GSR for cigarette, cigar, and pipe smokers seems to be affected differently by nicotine than is the GSR for non-smokers . This may be related to why some people smoke and others do not. That is, there may be a difference in biological reactivity to nicotine. These are differences that can't be felt by smokers of course, but they still can be important in determining dependence on cigarette smoking. And this is of course why it is so important to us, why we really need nonsmokers to smoke for us as well as smokers [p. 14]."

This scientific-sounding gibberish was designed, first, to explain to the subjects why it was necessary that they be shocked and, second, to convince nonsmokers that for the sake of science it was necessary that they smoke during the experiment.

There were three smoking conditions:

1. High nicotine, in which the subjects smoked a Belair cigarette containing, according to the U.S. Federal Trade Commission (1970), 19 mg tar and 1.6 mg nicotine.

2. Low nicotine, in which subjects smoked a Cascade cigarette containing 8 mg tar and 0.3 mg nicotine.

3. No nicotine, during which the subject simply puffed on an unlighted cigarette.

Electrodes had been fastened to the subject's arm, and immediately after the subject had taken his first puff, the experimenter said, "I'll want you to tell me three things. First, when you first feel the shock (sensitivity threshold). Second, when it first feels painful (pain threshold). Third, when it is too painful for you to bear anymore (endurance threshold) [Nesbitt, 1969, p. 17]." The subject was asked to inhale again, and the shocks began. These were constant current shocks of 0.11 second-duration delivered every 15 seconds. There were a total of 28 shocks, starting with a subthreshold 40 microamperes and increasing, if the subject still hadn't reached his endurance threshold, to a jarring 5 milliamperes. Throughout the shock period, the subjects were instructed to inhale once every 30 seconds.

There were a total of 60 subjects—half of them smokers and half nonsmokers. Smokers were defined by Nesbitt as anyone who had smoked at least 7,000 cigarettes during his lifetime (about a pack a day for a year) and was still smoking. Since almost everyone has experimentally tried a cigarette or two, nonsmokers were defined as anyone who had smoked a total of 50 cigarettes or less during his lifetime.[1] All subjects were Columbia University male undergraduates ranging in age from 18 to 26.

Before turning to Nesbitt's main results, let us first examine, within this experiment, whether or not the pharmacologist's arm of this paradox is a fact. As an indicator of autonomic arousal, the subject's pulse was taken before he started puffing and again a few seconds after he had put out his cigarette. As can be seen in the table, there is no question but that smoking works just as the pharmacologists tell us it should. When the subject is puffing at an unlighted cigarette, his pulse rate goes down from one measure to the next. When the subject is actually smoking, his pulse rate goes up, and the magnitude of the increase is a direct function of the nicotine content of the cigarette. By this indicator, then, smoking has had autonomic, arousing effects.

Turning to the behavioral arm of the paradox, Figure 1 presents the relevant data. Along the ordinate is plotted the mean endurance threshold,[2] that is, the average number of increasingly intense shocks that subjects were willing to take before calling it quits. If, as seems reasonable, concern and anxiety are determinors of how much shock a subject will take, if cigarette smoking is calming, then smoking subjects should take more shock than nonsmoking subjects. As can be seen in the figure, this is very much the case for chronic smokers and not at all the case for chronic nonsmokers ($F = 8.33$, interaction $p < .01$). Chronic smokers take considerably more shock when they are smoking a low-nicotine cigarette than when

[1] In order to insure that nonsmokers inhaled during the experiment, all subjects were, prior to smoking, instructed on the "proper" way to inhale. It was an unnecessary precaution, and I hold it a tribute to the pot generation that few of the nonsmokers appeared to have difficulty inhaling.
[2] There are no between-condition differences of any consequence for sensitivity thresholds. Pain thresholds vary in the same fashion as do endurance thresholds.

TABLE

The Effect of Nicotine on Pulse Rate

Subject	Base rate	Mean change from base rate, in beats per minute		
		No nicotine	Low nicotine	High nicotine
Smokers	79.2	−2.75	+1.26	+8.06
Nonsmokers	76.2	−3.14	+3.06	+10.66

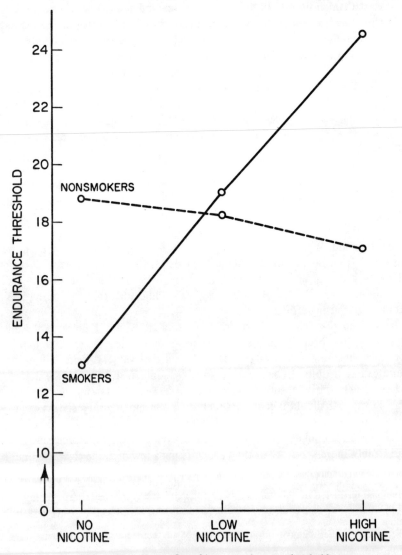

FIG. 1. The effects of smoking on endurance threshold.

they are not smoking, and take by far the greatest amount of shock when they are smoking high-nicotine cigarettes. These are, I should add, differences of major magnitude, for, in amperage terms, the endurance thresholds of smokers in high-nicotine and in no-nicotine conditions differed by an average of 2,450 microamperes.

In distinct contrast, the manipulations have had little effect on nonsmokers, though there is a trend, nonsignificant, in a direction opposite to that manifested by chronic smokers. For nonsmokers, endurance thresholds tend to decrease as nicotine content increases.

So Nesbitt's Paradox is, for chronic smokers, a fact. When a smoker says that smoking keeps him calm, he appears to mean just that. How are we to explain this perverse pair of facts? Before struggling with possible explanations, let us delimit what it is that we are trying to explain. From Nesbitt's experiment we know the following basic facts about the phenomenon:

1. The paradox holds true for chronic smokers, but not at all for nonsmokers, upon whom smoking a cigarette has little effect. Any explanation, then, cannot be in terms of the cigarette or nicotine proper, but must cope with the interaction of habitual smoking and the acute effects of a single cigarette.

2. For chronic smokers, the "calming" effect appears to be a direct function of the nicotine concentration of the cigarette. This finding, I must admit, is something of a relief, for it permits us to ignore that world of explanations constructed around oral and manipulative gratifications. Subjects in the high- and low-nicotine conditions go through precisely the same set of oral and manipulative activities while in the process of smoking their single cigarette.

Now I'm not going to suggest that I have the explanation for this phenomenon or, indeed, that we're even close to understanding it. I would, however, like to outline the two suggestions that Nesbitt and I considered most seriously.

The first of these explanations is based on the assumption that the intensity of an emotional state is a positively increasing function of deviation from baseline level of autonomic activity. Numerous studies have supported such a proposition. Studies that have manipulated emotional states and measured consequent sympathetic activity have consistently demonstrated that a general pattern of sympathetic arousal accompanies a successfully manipulated emotional state such as fear, anxiety, joy, etc. Similarly, studies that have directly manipulated sympathetic activation by use of sympathomimetic and sympatholytic agents (cf. Schachter, 1971) have with fair consistency demonstrated that, in the appropriate situations, the degree of emotionality varies with the degree of manipulated sympathetic activity. Though the evidence is consistent, it is for present purposes also unfortunately crude, for almost all of these studies manipulated only two points on a continuum (e.g., placebo vs. one dose level of epinephrine). For the sake of my argument, however, do be good enough to assume that we are talking about a continuously increasing function.

Let us assume that in Nesbitt's study, the cigarette that is actually smoked establishes the "ground" level of sympathetic activity and that the additional activation caused by being shocked and by worrying about being shocked is superimposed on this ground level. We know that this ground level of activation varies directly, in Nesbitt's experiment, with the nicotine content of the cigarette.

If we accept the "law of initial values," it follows that the additional arousal induced by being shocked and by worrying about being shocked will be least in the high-nicotine condition and greatest in the no-nicotine condition. From our basic assumption, then, it would have to follow that emotionality would also correspond to this ordering. Although the work of Wilder (1950) and of Lacey (1956) indicates that "the magnitude of response is related to prestimulation level" in such a way that "high autonomic excitation preceding stimulation is correlated with low autonomic reactivity upon stimulation [Lacey, 1956, p. 156]," it does not follow that this is necessarily so in Nesbitt's experiment. There is no directly relevant evidence in this study proper, but fortunately some of my colleagues are working on a related experiment which, so far, indicates that it is the case. In this experiment, subjects, all smokers, work for about an hour making a series of perceptual judgments. After each judgment, they are rated "right" or "wrong," and the situation is so rigged that all subjects must be wrong at least several times during the experimental session. There are two sets of conditions: in one pair of conditions, the subject is shocked whenever he makes an error; in the other, he is not shocked when he makes an error. In addition, subjects smoke two cigarettes in one pair of these conditions, and do not smoke at all in the other two conditions. There are, then, four conditions schematized as follows:

1. Subjects smoke; errors shocked.
2. Subjects smoke; errors not shocked.
3. Subjects don't smoke; errors shocked.
4. Subjects don't smoke; errors not shocked.

Subjects serve as their own controls and all of the 16 subjects run so far have been represented in all four conditions.

Heart rate is monitored continuously throughout the experimental session, and the effect of these two manipulated variables on this indicator of sympathetic arousal is presented in Figure 2, where heart rate readings are plotted against several chronologically ordered events in the course of the experiment. The two bottom curves in the figure represent mean heart rate readings in those conditions where the subjects did not smoke. As can be seen, the shock manipulation is having an effect, for consistently shocked subjects have a higher heart rate than no-shock subjects. The effect is strongest in the early stages of the experiment, when tension is undoubtedly highest. The upper two curves plot heart rate readings in those conditions in which the subjects smoked. The effects of the shock manipulation on heart rate are noticeably smaller than in the no-smoking conditions, particularly in the early stages of the experimental hour. These differences aren't dramatic, but they are consistent, and they do provide a first tentative indication that smoking a cigarette may mask the cardiovascular effects normally triggered by disturbing events.

This, then, is a possible explanation for Nesbitt's Paradox. It does, however, have one disturbing flaw the whole line of reasoning should apply to nonsmokers as well as to smokers, and in Nesbitt's experiment, of course, smoking has no effect on the endurance thresholds of nonsmokers. This should, of course, disqualify this explanation; but I'm afraid that there is just enough plausibility to this whole line of reasoning so that I'm unwilling just yet to dismiss it out of hand. There is evidence in Nesbitt's study that cigarettes made several of his nonsmoker subjects

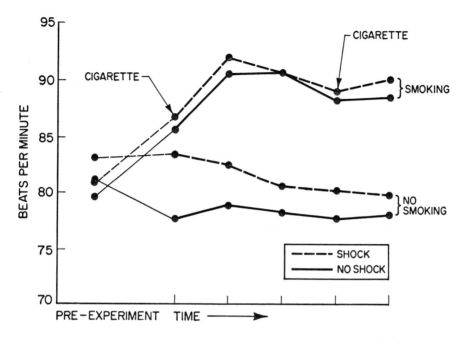

FIG. 2. The effects of electric shock and smoking on heart rate.

somewhat queasy and uncomfortable. It is conceivable that such subjects felt biologically uneasy enough so that they were unwilling to increase their discomfort by exposing themselves to more and more painful shocks. I hate to use this particular excuse to sneak out of this difficulty, for by doing so I open up a Pandora's Box of possible alternative explanations; but there is no way out of it short of discarding this explanation.

Our other pet explanation has little to do with physiology proper, but is essentially a cognitive hypothesis concerned with how the individual interprets and labels the set of internal physiological events that are set in motion by disturbing or frightening events. As we all know, such events are presumed to throw the autonomic nervous system into action, epinephrine is released, heart rate goes up, blood pressure goes up, blood sugar increases, and so on. Now notice that many of these physiological changes are precisely those changes that we're told are produced by smoking a cigarette. What happens, then, to the smoking smoker in a frightening situation? He feels the way he usually does when he's frightened, but he also feels the way he usually does when he's smoking a cigarette. Does he label his feelings as fright or as smoking a cigarette? I would suggest, of course, that to the extent that he attributes these physiological changes to smoking, he will not be frightened. And this, I propose, is a possible explanation for the strikingly calming effect that smoking a cigarette had on the chronic smokers in Nesbitt's experiments.[3]

---

[3] Though both this cognitive hypothesis and the explanation based on the law of initial values are designed to explain the fear-reducing effects of smoking, it should be specifically noted that either interpretation is applicable not only to fear but also to any emotional state that involves some degree of autonomic activation. Thus it should be expected that smoking a cigarette will, for heavy smokers, attenuate the intensity of emotional states such as euphoria, anger, sexual arousal, and so on.

Now all of this may seem farfetched, but I suspect that if I describe the results of some of the experiments in which we have directly manipulated attribution, this view of matters will become somewhat more plausible. In one of these studies (Nisbett & Schachter, 1966), the subjects believed that we were studying the effects of a drug called Suproxin on skin sensitivity. The test of skin sensitivity was similar to that used by Nesbitt in his work on the evoked GSR—that is, a series of electric shocks progressively increasing in intensity, with the subject's job being the identification of sensitivity, pain, and endurance thresholds. Ten minutes before testing, the subjects took a Suproxin pill, of course a placebo. There were essentially two conditions. In one of these, before they took the pill they were told the following about its side effects: "What will happen is that you may have some tremor, that is your hand will start to shake; you will have some palpitation, that is your heart will start to pound; your rate of breathing may increase. Also, you will probably get a sinking feeling in the pit of your stomach, like butterflies." All of these are symptoms which were widely reported by pretest subjects who introspected about their physiological reactions to shock. To the extent that this manipulation is effective, subjects should attribute their shock-produced symptoms to Suproxin and not to shock.

In the other conditions, subjects were told the following about Suproxin's side effects: "What will probably happen is that your feet will feel numb, you may have an itching sensation over parts of your body, and you may get a slight headache." None of these symptoms, of course, is produced either by the shock or by the placebo. Subjects in this condition, then, will experience the physiological symptoms produced by shock and by anticipation of shock and, since no plausible alternative exists, will perforce attribute these symptoms to the shock experience.

If this attribution line of thought is correct, we should expect that when subjects attribute their shock-produced symptoms to the pill, they should take more shock than when they attribute these symptoms to the shock itself. And this indeed was the case, with results that are just as striking as those of the smoking study. When subjects attributed their symptoms to Suproxin, they tolerated an average of 1,450 microamperes before reaching their endurance threshold. When they did not attribute their symptoms to the pill, they chickened out at 350 microamperes. Obviously, this manipulation of attribution had profound effects.

Aside from the fact that we have absolutely no direct evidence supporting this view as the explanation of the smoking paradox, I have one clear discomfort with this interpretation of the smoking data. This set of ideas about the "labeling" or "attribution" process has been formulated (Schachter, 1971) in language that implies that the subject is making a conscious, rational decision—as if in the Suproxin experiment, the subject were to say to himself, "Aha, I feel this way because of that pill, not because of these shocks. Therefore, I deduce that I am not afraid, and hence I will take more shocks." I think it unlikely that any subject in the Suproxin experiment conducted such a monologue; I think it inconceivable that any subject in the smoking experiment did so. This is discomforting, but I don't believe that it is a mortal blow to an attribution explanation, for I'm pretty sure that by shifting my language I can make this a more palatable hypothesis.

For now, though, enough. Nesbitt's Paradox appears to be fact, and I trust it is clear that I do not yet understand this fact. I have a sentimental attachment to the interpretive suggestions that I have made, but at the moment there is probably no compelling reason to prefer either of these interpretations to hypotheses that may please you more.

REFERENCES

Ikard, F. F., Green, D. E., & Horn, D. The development of a scale to differentiate between types of smoking as related to the management of affect. Paper presented at the meeting of the Eastern Psychological Association, Washington, D. C., April, 1968.

Lacey, J. The evaluation of autonomic responses: Toward a general solution. *Annals of the New York Academy of Sciences,* 1956, **67,** 123-164.

Murphree, H. B., Pfeiffer, C. C., & Price, L. M. Electeoencephalographic changes in man following smoking. *Annals of the New York Academy of Sciences,* 1967, **142,** 245-260.

Nesbitt, P. Smoking, physiological arousal, and emotional response. Unpublished doctoral dissertation, Columbia University, 1969.

Nisbett, R., & Schachter, S. The cognitive manipulation of pain. *Journal of Experimental Social Psychology,* 1966, **2,** 227-236.

Schachter, S. *Emotion, obesity, and crime.* New York: Academic Press, 1971.

U.S. Federal Trade Commission. *Tar and nicotine content of cigarettes.* Washington, D.C.: U.S. Government Printing Office, November, 1970.

U.S. Public Health Service. *Smoking and health: Report of the Advisory Committee to the Surgeon General of the Public Health Service.* (USPHS Publication No. 1103) Washington, D.C.: U.S. Government Printing Office, 1964.

Wilder, J. The law of initial values. *Psychosomatic Medicine,* 1950, **12,** 392.

10
THE RELATIONSHIP OF SMOKING AND HABITS OF NERVOUS TENSION[1]

Caroline Bedell Thomas
The Johns Hopkins University School of Medicine

I shall present in this chapter some findings on the smoking behavior of a defined population observed up to 25 years, and shall relate this smoking behavior to habits of nervous tension, several habits of daily life, and other psychobiological characteristics. The data were obtained in a long-term study of the precursors of hypertension and coronary disease. Seventeen consecutive classes of Johns Hopkins medical students, graduating in 1948 through 1964, were measured and tested from many points of view. As part of the protocol, each student completed a Habit Survey, a Family Attitude Questionnaire, and a battery of physiological tests. All of these data were recorded early in medical school, the median age at the time being 22 years. Now physicians, the subjects are between 30 and 60 years old. Their health and habits are being carefully followed by mail. All subjects were questioned in detail about their smoking habits in 1968-1969.

The psychological variables to be considered came from the Habit Survey and the Family Attitude Questionnaire completed while in medical school. The Habit Survey included questions about smoking, drinking, sleeping, and other habits of daily life, as well as about reactions to stress. Reactions to stress were obtained by having the subject check off, from among a list of 25, those habits of nervous tension (HNT) characteristic of him. This checklist, shown in Table 1, was designed to give indirect evidence about the individual's neurohumoral response to stress (Thomas & Ross, 1963). Scales for anxiety, anger, and depression were derived from those HNT items showing the highest degrees of association with each other (Thomas, Ross, & Higinbothom, 1964). Sixteen of the 25 HNT items were incorporated in the three scales as shown in Table 2. Linear scales for alcohol frequency, tiredness on awakening, and insomnia were based on distributions already reported (Thomas & Ross, 1968b). The Family Attitude Questionnaire,

[1] This work was supported by The Council for Tobacco Research, U.S.A., and the Clayton Fund of the Johns Hopkins University.

which was primarily concerned with the relationships between the medical student and his parents, formed the basis for three family attitude scales: matriarchal dominance, demonstrativity within the family, and closeness to parents (Thomas & Ross, 1968a). The physiological variables selected for use here from among those recorded in the examination are familiar ones that have been previously defined (Thomas, Ross, & Higinbothom, 1964).

Discriminant function analysis is the study of two or more groups of subjects with respect to a number of variables, permitting the determination of how the groups are different, how they are similar, and which of the variables are of most value in distinguishing between or among the groups. The computational methods utilized in the early analyses have been described previously (Thomas, Ross, & Higinbothom, 1964). Recently, a discriminant function analysis of two criterion groups has been carried out by means of a computer program originating in the Biometric Laboratory of the University of Miami (Clyde, Cramer, & Sherin, 1966).

TABLE 1

Habits of Nervous Tension Checklist: Part of the Habit Survey
Administered to 1168 Medical Students

Whenever you find yourself in situations of undue pressure or stress, how do you usually react? (Underline all reactions which are characteristic of you.)

1. Exhaustion or excessive fatigue
2. Exhilaration
3. Depressed feelings
4. Uneasy or anxious feelings (sighing, tight feelings in throat or chest, dry mouth, clammy hands, etc.)
5. General tension ("keyed up" feelings—difficulty in becoming relaxed)
6. Increased activity
7. Decreased activity
8. An increased urge to sleep
9. Increased difficulty in sleeping
10. Increased urge to eat
11. Loss of appetite
12. Nausea
13. Vomiting
14. Diarrhea
15. Constipation
16. Urinary frequency
17. Tremulousness or shakiness
18. Anger (expressed)
          (concealed)
19. Gripe sessions
20. Concern about your physical health
21. A tendency to check and recheck your work to assure yourself of accuracy
22. An urge to confide and seek advice or reassurance
23. An urge to be by yourself and get away from it all
24. Irritability with concern as to who is to blame
25. Philosophic effort with no reactions out of the ordinary

Briefly describe your chief reactions to pressure or stress and the situations in which they most commonly occur (competitions, examinations, family situations, etc.).

TABLE 2

The Three Derived Scales and the HNT Items
Comprising the Scales

Depression scale	Anxiety scale	Anger scale
Exhaustion	Anxious feelings	Anger
Depressed feelings	General tension	Gripe sessions
Decreased activity	Difficulty sleeping	Irritability
Urge to sleep	Loss of appetite	
Concern about health	Tremulousness	
Urge to be alone	Urge to confide	
	Urge to eat (−)[a]	
Score range: 0 to +6	−1 to +6	0 to +3

Note.–The scales are based on a phi correlation matrix. A scale score is equal to the number of items checked on that scale.

[a]*Urge to eat* is the only item which counts negatively.

When a stepwise discriminant analysis is performed, the power of each variable to achieve maximum separation between the groups is computed mathematically, and the variables are then entered in the analysis in the order of their importance. For this purpose, we used the BMD07M computer program, which calls for at least three criterion groups (Dixon, 1968).

We initially compared the characteristics of subjects grouped by their smoking habits at the time of entry into the longitudinal study (Thomas, Ross, & Higinbothom, 1964). In these and subsequent analyses, the study population was limited to white males, the largest group, for the sake of homogeneity.

The first analysis we reported concerned three smoking-habit groups:

1. Nonsmokers, including 386 nonsmokers and occasional smokers.

2. Heavy cigarette smokers, consisting of 141 smokers of 20 or more cigarettes a day.

3. Intermediate cigarette smokers, including 165 subjects who either smoked 1 to 19 cigarettes a day or smoked cigarettes mixed with pipes.

The somatic variables included in the analysis were body weight, blood pressure, heart rate, and cholesterol level. The psychological variables included were scale scores for anxiety, depression, and anger. The overall discrimination between the three groups in this study was highly significant ($p < .005$). The main differentiating power resided in the *heart rate* and the *anxiety score*, both of which increased with the quantity of cigarettes smoked daily. The *anger score* rose in similar fashion, but did not quite reach significance in this particular comparison. *Cholesterol* and *pulse pressure* made contributions at the 5% level of significance, while *relative body weight* and the *depression score* failed to show any differentiating power.

In a similar discriminant analysis of eight smoking groups, the overall differences were again significant at the $p < .005$ level, but only one dimension was statistically significant. The greatest difference was found between the nonsmokers and the heavy cigarette smokers, with the other six classifications (occasional, pipe, former, mixed, light, and moderate) arrayed between in near predictable order.

This year we have turned our attention to smoking habits over time, and have grouped the subjects in various ways to determine how their longitudinal smoking habits are related to the various measures obtained on them while in medical school. In this series of studies, pipe and cigar smokers have been excluded to simplify the analyses. We first compared the characteristics of lifetime nonsmokers (who never smoked anything regularly) with two groups of regular cigarette smokers: continuing smokers (pure cigarette smokers who were never regular smokers of pipes or cigars), and former smokers (formerly pure cigarette smokers who now do not smoke at all). Later we compared heavy and light cigarette smokers, regardless of whether or not they eventually stopped smoking, defining heavy smokers as those who had smoked 20 or more cigarettes a day at some time before age 30, and light smokers as those who had never smoked 20 a day up to age 30. By using age 30 as the cutting point, differences in age on entering medical school were evened up, and theoretically every subject had been exposed to the smoking milieu for the same number of years.

The proportion of positive HNT responses for the three lifetime smoking groups is shown in Table 3. It will be seen that the continuing smokers more frequently gave positive responses to all items in the anxiety scale.[2] The difference between the nonsmoker and continuing-smoker groups exceeds the 5% level of significance on two of the HNT items in the anxiety scale, namely, *urge to confide* and *tremulousness.* For most of the anxiety scale items, the proportion of positive responses by the former-smoker group was intermediate between the nonsmokers and continuing smokers. None of the items in the anger or depression scales reached significance.

We then carried out a stepwise discriminant analysis, using lifetime nonsmokers, former cigarette smokers, and continuing cigarette smokers as our criterion groups. Twenty-one continuous psychobiological variables were entered, including the three HNT scales, four habits closely associated with nervous tension (frequency of drinking coffee and alcohol, insomnia, tiredness on awakening), three Family Attitude scales, the total number of responses to the HNT questionnaire, seven well-studied physiological variables, and three age variables. Only subjects with complete data were used, so that the criterion groups were reduced in size. It should be kept in mind that the *variables* were *cross-sectional,* characterizing the subjects in youth, while the *smoking habits* upon which the criterion groups were based were *longitudinal,* representing lifetime smoking habits up to middle age.

Table 4 shows the results of the 21-variable stepwise analysis, with the variables listed in the order in which they entered. It is noteworthy that lifetime nonsmokers showed the lowest scale scores for *anxiety* (step 5), *anger* (step 8), and *depression* (step 21), when compared with former cigarette smokers and continuing cigarette smokers. They were not the most important variables, however. *Number of cups of coffee a day* had the most discriminating power and so entered at the first step,

[2] Because *urge to eat* was found to be negatively correlated with *anxiety* in a phi correlation matrix, this is a reversal of what would be expected for this item.

TABLE 3

Percentage of Subjects in Three Lifetime Smoking Habit Groups
Giving a Positive Response to Single HNT Items

Scale	Habit of nervous tension (HNT item)	Lifetime nonsmokers (N = 437) %	Former cigarette smokers (N = 144) %	Continuing cigarette smokers (N = 251) %
Anxiety scale	Urge to confide	23.3***	23.6**	33.9***/**
	Tremulousness	12.1**	17.4	17.5**
	Anxious feelings	48.3	43.7*	53.4*
	Loss of appetite	33.6	38.2	39.8
	Difficulty sleeping	43.7	45.8	49.8
	General tension	79.4	80.6	82.5
	Urge to eat (-)[a]	16.5	18.1	18.5
Anger scale	Anger	17.8	22.2	21.9
	Irritability	8.5	9.7	9.6
	Gripe sessions	15.8	16.7	13.9
Depression scale	Exhaustion	14.0	9.7	15.1
	Depression	19.5	16.7	22.7
	Decreased activity	5.3	2.1	4.4
	Urge to be alone	18.5	16.0	19.1
	Urge to sleep	14.6	17.4	12.7
	Concern about health	4.8	4.9	4.8
Unscaled items	Exhilaration	17.8**	25.7**	21.1
	Diarrhea	15.8*	13.9	11.2*
	Constipation	3.4	4.9	5.6
	Vomiting	0.5	0.7	1.2
	Philosophic effort	22.2	24.3	21.5
	Nausea	5.3	4.9	6.4
	Check and recheck	24.7	24.3	24.7
	Urinary frequency	30.4	30.6	31.5
	Increased activity	65.0	66.7	66.5
Mean number of positive responses		5.6**	5.8	6.1**

Note.—Differences within a row are evaluated by t test, two groups at a time.

[a]*Urge to eat* is negatively correlated with *anxiety*.

 *.10 > p > .05.

**p < .05.

***p < .01.

with continuing smokers drinking nearly three cups a day on the average, in contrast to less than two for nonsmokers. *Alcohol frequency* came next in importance. Again continuing smokers had the highest mean scale score (close to 2, which means a few drinks regularly) and nonsmokers the lowest (close to 1, which means drinks occasionally).

TABLE 4

The Results of a Stepwise Discriminant Analysis of Smoking Habits Over Time, as Related to Other Characteristics of Medical Students: The Psychobiological Variables Listed in Descending Order of Significance

Step no.	Variable	Range[a]	Lifetime nonsmokers ($N = 321$)	Former cigt. smokers ($N = 101$)	Continuing cigt. smokers ($N = 178$)	F value to enter or remove
			Mean values			
1	Coffee, cups a day	0 to 9+	1.69	2.43	2.96	32.04***
2	Alcohol frequency	0 to 5	1.26	1.74	1.82	7.42***
3	Systolic change: cold pressor test	−12 to +58	+13.38	+11.94	+11.29	4.61**
4	Resting heart rate	39 to 114	68.89	71.80	70.37	4.01**
5	Anxiety	−1 to +6	2.23	2.33	2.59	3.45*
6	Cholesterol	108 to 420	223.98	213.03	223.25	3.23*
7	Resting diastolic pressure	42 to 105	69.37	68.55	68.09	2.53
8	Anger	0 to 3	0.43	0.56	0.49	1.28
9	Matriarchal dominance	−8 to +11	−1.34	−1.75	−1.56	1.48
10	Age of subject at tests	19 to 35(49)	22.89	23.04	22.78	0.77
11	Ponderal index	11.01 to 14.84	13.02	13.01	12.98	0.55
12	Closeness scale	−8 to +11	8.86	8.92	8.70	0.63
13	Resting systolic pressure	80 to 154	113.82	113.34	113.47	0.42
14	Relative body weight[b]	72 to 163	102.91	103.30	103.60	0.44
15	Demonstrativity	0 to 18	3.82	3.85	4.21	0.41
16	Tired on awakening	0 to 2	0.78	0.85	0.96	0.32
17	Mother's age at subject's birth	17 to 46	28.59	28.24	28.68	0.31
18	Father's age at subject's birth	19 to 61	32.49	32.88	32.94	0.42
19	Total HNT responses	0 to 21	5.61	6.08	6.18	0.29
20	Insomnia	0 to 4	0.67	0.61	0.76	0.29
21	Depression	0 to 6	0.75	0.84	0.84	0.13

Note.—Nonsmokers–continuing smokers: $df = 21,477$, $F = 5.02$, $p < 0.0001$.
Nonsmokers–former smokers: $df = 21,400$, $F = 2.32$, $p < 0.001$.
Continuing smokers–former smokers: $df = 21,257$, $F = 1.09$, $p < 0.36$.
[a]Ranges are for the total white male sample with data ($N = 913$ to 1130).
[b]For relative body weight, 100% equals the mean for each subject's sex-age-height group in the 1912 standard tables.

162

The *anxiety* scale was the only HNT or Family Attitude scale to reach significance. The mean *number of positive HNT responses,* which almost reaches the 5% level of significance as a single variable, entered at the nineteenth step because most of its power had already been expressed by the HNT scales which entered ahead of it.

Of the physiological variables, *systolic pressure change* during the cold pressor test and *resting heart rate* reached significance, while *resting systolic* and *diastolic pressure* did not. *Cholesterol* entered at step 6; the low mean cholesterol for former smokers on which its significance depends was an unexpected finding which will only have meaning if it is replicated elsewhere. *Ponderal index* entered before relative body weight, but neither was significant. The remaining variables, including *age* and *family attitudes,* contributed little to the differentiation.

To determine the overall significance of the differences between the criterion groups, three 2-group discriminant function analyses were performed using these 21 variables. The results are shown in the footnote to Table 4. There is a highly significant difference between the lifetime nonsmokers and the continuing cigarette smokers, a less significant difference between lifetime nonsmokers and former cigarette smokers, and no significant difference between continuing and former cigarette smokers.

The efficacy of the discriminant functions in differentiating between criterion groups may be judged by the number of persons classified correctly. In the most significant two-group comparison, 70.7% of the lifetime nonsmokers and 64.3% of the continuing smokers were classified correctly. While this is somewhat better than would be expected by chance, there is still considerable overlap.

So far, then, we have found that lifetime nonsmokers differ significantly from cigarette smokers, whether or not they have stopped smoking. Nevertheless, while continuing smokers and former smokers do have similar psychobiological characteristics, former smokers differ from nonsmokers to a lesser degree. In order to better understand this subtle difference, we next compared continuing smokers with former smokers in respect to particular aspects of their smoking history: age at starting and quantity of cigarettes smoked per day. Table 5 shows that while there was little or no difference between the two groups with respect to age at starting to smoke, there was a difference in the amount of cigarettes smoked. Both in medical school and at some time before age 30, a greater proportion of continuing smokers smoked a pack or more of cigarettes a day. It seemed worthwhile, therefore, to make comparisons based on the quantity of cigarettes smoked. Because our interest here centers on the psychological aspects of nervous tension, physiological and age variables are not considered further.

When smokers are dichotomized into *heavy* and *light* on the basis of the maximum number of cigarettes smoked daily before age 30, (regardless of whether the subject continued or stopped smoking), strikingly different psychological profiles for the two groups emerge. Heavy smokers have higher mean values for all of the 10 psychological variables as shown in Table 6. When taken singly, the first five variables listed showed highly significant differences by t tests. In two-group discriminant analysis the overall significance was extremely high ($p < .0001$). The classification again showed considerable overlap. While 70.7% of the light smokers

TABLE 5

Comparison of Continuing and Former Smokers
as to Age of Starting and Quantity Smoked
as Reported in Medical School Between
1947 and 1961 and at Follow-Up

Age started smoking	Continuing cigarette smokers ($N=178$) %	Former cigarette smokers ($N=101$) %	Significance (x^2)
<15	11.8	11.9	
15–18	55.6	59.4	
19–22	28.6	21.8	N.S.[c]
<22	0.6	1.0	
Unknown	3.4	5.9	
Heavy smoker[a] in medical school	44.4	30.7	$p<.05$
Heavy smoker before age 30[b]	56.2	45.5	$p<.10$

[a]Heavy smoker–20 or more cigarettes a day.
[b]The youngest subjects in the Precursors Study attained the age of 30 in 1971.
[c]N.S. = not significant.

TABLE 6

Psychological Profiles of Heavy versus Light
Cigarette Smokers

Variable	Heavy smokers[a] Mean ($N=146$)	Light smokers[b] Mean ($N=133$)	p
Alcohol frequency	2.06	1.50	<0.001
Anger	0.67	0.35	<0.001
Coffee, cups per day	3.14	2.35	<0.001
Depression	1.03	0.63	<0.005
Tired on awakening	1.06	0.76	<0.005
Demonstrativity	4.33	3.81	<0.10
Matriarchal dominance	−1.44	−1.84	N.S.[c]
Insomnia	0.78	0.62	N.S.
Anxiety	2.56	2.43	N.S.
Closeness	8.82	8.74	N.S.

Note.—$F(10,268) = 4.39; p < .0001$.
[a]Smoked a maximum of 20 or more cigarettes a day before age 30, regardless of whether they continued or stopped.
[b]Smoked a maximum of less than 20 cigarettes a day before age 30, regardless of whether they continued or stopped.
[c]N.S = not significant.

were classified correctly, only 56.2% of the heavy smokers were, suggesting that many who smoke over a pack a day for a period of time are not, in fact, different from light smokers.

We next compared lifetime nonsmokers with two groups of heavy smokers, and then with two groups of light smokers (Table 7). When nonsmokers and two groups of heavy smokers are compared, *coffee intake, alcohol frequency,* and *anger* contributed most heavily to the discrimination (Run A). When nonsmokers are compared with two groups of light smokers, on the other hand, *coffee intake* again enters first, but *anxiety* enters second, while *anger* and *alcohol frequency* do not enter until the seventh and eighth steps (Run B). This emphasizes once more the importance of the higher *coffee intake* of cigarette smokers in general, of the higher *alcohol frequency* and greater *anger* under stress of heavy smokers, and the greater *anxiety* under stress of light smokers, while Table 6 shows that heavy smokers also react to stress with more *depression* and are more *tired on awakening* than light smokers.

The correlation coefficients between the smoking habit (as measured by the maximum number of cigarettes smoked daily before age 30) and eleven psychological variables are given in Table 8. The highest values of r are found between *total HNT responses* and the three HNT scales: *anxiety, anger,* and *depression.* The other correlations of any importance tend to be intercorrelations

TABLE 7

Stepwise Discriminant Analysis Using
10 Psychological Variables

Run A			Run B		
Criterion groups		N	Criterion groups		N
Lifetime nonsmokers		321	Lifetime nonsmokers		321
Former heavy cigarette smokers		46	Former light cigarette smokers		55
Continuing heavy cigarette smokers		100	Continuing light cigarette smokers		78
Step no.	Variable entering	F value to enter or remove	Step no.	Variable entering	F value to enter or remove
1	Coffee, cups a day	38.79***	1	Coffee, cups a day	8.80**
2	Alcohol frequency	12.05***	2	Anxiety	5.05**
3	Anger	4.63*	3	Matriarchal dominance	1.93
4	Tired on awakening	1.63	4	Depression	1.11
5	Matriarchal dominance	0.68	5	Demonstrativity	0.91
6	Anxiety scale	0.45	6	Closeness	0.86
7	Insomnia	0.43	7	Anger	0.87
8	Depression	0.30	8	Alcohol frequency	0.82
9	Demonstrativity	0.20	9	Tired on awakening	0.62
10	Closeness	0.17	10	Insomnia	0.19

*$p < .05$.
**$p < .01$.
***$p < .001$.

TABLE 8

Correlation Matrix for Amount of Smoking[a] and 11 Psychological Variables on 600 Subjects
(321 Nonsmokers, 101 Former Smokers and 178 Continuing Smokers)

	1 Smoking[a]	2 Coffee	3 Alcohol	4 Anxiety	5 Anger	6 Depression	7 Tired	8 Insomnia	9 Demonstrativity	10 Matriarchal Dominance	11 Closeness
2 Coffee	.18*										
3 Alcohol	.18*	.17*									
4 Anxiety	.05	-.05	.05								
5 Anger	.12	.00	.10	.16*							
6 Depression	.10	.00	.08	.22**	.29***						
7 Tired on awakening	.17*	.00	.15	.18*	.10	.16*					
8 Insomnia	.09	.01	.08	.12	.13	.14	.17*				
9 Demonstrativity	.07	.03	.02	.23**	.21**	.19**	.14	.11			
10 Matriarchal dominance	.08	-.01	-.01	.06	.11	.02	.08	.05	.10		
11 Closeness	.04	.04	-.05	.06	-.08	-.08	-.06	-.06	.20**	-.22**	
12 Mean number of HNT responses	.13	.00	.12	.61***	.52***	.64***	.20**	.19**	.34***	.12	-.07

[a]Maximum cigarettes smoked daily before age 30.

*$p < .10$; **$p < .05$; ***$p < .01$.

within categories of variables: social habits of smoking and drinking, habits of nervous tension, sleep habits, and family attitudes.

What do these findings contribute to the growing body of knowledge concerning smoking behavior? They not only confirm previous reports (Heath, 1958; McArthur, Waldron, & Dickinson, 1958; Lilienfeld, 1959; Matarazzo & Saslow, 1960; Straits & Sechrest, 1963; Walker, Nicolay, Kluczny, & Riedel, 1969) that smokers are more anxious and consume more coffee and alcohol than nonsmokers, but add several new perspectives. Within the broad range of psychobiological characteristics studied, increased coffee consumption was the most important hallmark in youth of the cigarette smoker, whether he later continued to smoke or stopped, compared with the lifetime nonsmoker. Early in medical school, the mean values for *coffee consumption, alcohol frequency,* and *anxiety* for smokers who ultimately stopped were intermediate between those of continuing smokers and nonsmokers, although closer to those of the continuing-smoker group. This trend may have been due largely to the fact that, as a group, the former smokers were lighter smokers. Although former smokers closely resembled continuing smokers as to age at starting to smoke, fewer smoked heavily before the age of 30.

For this reason, cigarette smokers were dichotomized on the basis of the maximum quantity of cigarettes smoked daily before age 30, regardless of whether or not they continued to smoke heavily or at all. In this comparison, increased *alcohol frequency* and *anger* surpassed higher *coffee consumption* in distinguishing heavy smokers from light smokers, whereas heightened *anxiety* characterized heavy and light smokers almost equally. When the means for *coffee* and *alcohol consumption, anxiety,* and *anger* are examined across four smoking groups, light smokers who stopped smoking tended to have the lowest values, but there was no consistent difference between those who stopped smoking and those who continued (Table 9). It would seem, therefore, that heavy smokers and light smokers face somewhat different problems in attempting to stop smoking, and that increased *alcohol consumption* and *anger* superimposed on increased *coffee intake* and *anxiety* may be major factors in making it harder for heavy smokers to stop.

These findings appear to fit well with Tomkins' (1966) model for smoking behavior, in which he defines three types of smokers: the positive-affect smoker,

TABLE 9

Means for Important Psychological Variables across Four Cigarette-Smoking Groups

Variable	Light Smokers		Heavy Smokers	
	Former ($N = 55$)	Continuing ($N = 78$)	Former ($N = 46$)	Continuing ($N = 100$)
Coffee, cups per day	2.2	2.4	2.6	3.4
Alcohol frequency	1.4	1.6	2.2	2.0
Anxiety	2.1	2.7	2.6	2.5
Anger	0.4	0.3	0.8	0.6

who smokes primarily for enjoyment; the negative-affect smoker, who smokes to alleviate primary types of distress such as anger, fear, shame, and contempt; and the addictive smoker, a negative-affect smoker for whom lacking a cigarette becomes an important additional form of distress (Tomkins, 1966; Tomkins, 1968). If, as Tomkins (1966) believes, it is easiest for positive-affect smokers to stop smoking, then we can postulate that light smokers tend to be positive-affect smokers, while there is a preponderance of negative and addictive smokers in the heavy-smoker group. The fact that, in their youth, heavy smokers had reported experiencing nearly twice as much *anger* under stress as light smokers indicates that they were, in fact, more aware of one of Tomkins' primary negative affects.

What can be said about the time sequence in which the distinctive characteristics of the cigarette smoker develop? Do they precede, accompany, or follow the appearance of the smoking habit? Since around 70% of cigarette smokers had started smoking by age 18, while many were much younger, it seems reasonable to assume that drinking coffee and alcohol were not important precursors of smoking, but rather accompanied or followed the smoking habit. It is more difficult to document the time relationship between feelings of anxiety and anger and the beginning of the smoking habit. In a factor analysis of the main occasions for smoking (McKennell, 1970), the first factor, "nervous irritation smoking," contained items related to habits of nervous tension: smokes when irritable, smokes when anxious or worried, smokes when angry, and smokes when nervous (McKennell, 1970). McKennell found the same factors, with very similar reliability coefficients, both for 564 adolescents and for 775 adults, which suggests that "nervous irritation" as an occasion for smoking begins early. Among adolescents, the highest proportion of those reporting "nervous irritation" as an occasion for smoking was found in the group which had smoked for 5 or more years, starting before age 16. For both adolescents and adults, the "nervous irritation" factor showed the highest correlation with addiction .High scores on the "nervous irritation" factor were thought by McKennell to characterize Tomkins' negative-affect and addictive types of smoking behavior. These findings strongly suggest that inner needs related to "nervous irritation" lead to negative-affect and addictive smoking, rather than the contrary.

Another of McKennell's factors, "social smoking," combines the items "smokes when drinking tea and coffee" and "smokes when drinking alcohol" with "smokes in company" and "smokes in a party," indicating the strong social implications of smoking and drinking coffee and alcohol. Another factor, "social confidence smoking," was of particular interest in that the item "smokes in order to be grown up," which loaded on this factor, "was one of the most powerful discriminators between adolescent smokers and ex-smokers (McKennell, 1970, p. 12)."

In a review of the literature on personality and smoking (Smith 1970), the anger in response to stress reported by us was included under "anti-social tendencies" together with measures of rebelliousness, belligerence, psychopathic deviance, misconduct, and disagreeableness (Smith, 1970; Thomas, 1960). Twenty-seven of 32 analyses from 19 published reports indicated that smokers were more "antisocial" than nonsmokers. This characteristic seems to stand in contrast to another finding on which there is almost total agreement, that smokers are more extraverted than nonsmokers (McArthur et al., 1958; Schubert, 1959; McArthur, Waldron & Dickinson, 1958; Matarazzo & Saslow, 1960; Schubert, 1959; Eysenck, Tarrant, Woolf & England, 1960; Eysenck, 1963; Schubert, 1965; Thomas, Fargo & Enslein, 1970). Taken together, extraversion and "antisocial" tendencies seem to imply that smokers interact with others more readily than nonsmokers, but that in doing so they often encounter frustrations and disappointments that arouse feelings of anger, rebelliousness, and so on. In this setting, smokers use cigarettes as a way of alleviating their distress.

It therefore seems not unreasonable to conclude that adolescents who are outgoing and desire to obtain social acceptance are often aware of anxiety and anger in situations of stress, and that cigarette smoking, particularly heavy cigarette smoking, stems in large part from the inner need to cope with their negative affect. As they are drawn into social situations and gain acceptance, coffee and alcohol intake tend to rise. The constellation of increased cigarette smoking, coffee consumption, and alcohol frequency becomes the outward mark of inner conflict between warm, outgoing, positive feelings and frustrated, angry, rebellious feelings which need to be repressed to gain social acceptance.

SUMMARY

Comparison of the psychological profiles, in youth, of 321 lifetime nonsmokers and 279 continuing and former cigarette smokers showed highly significant differences. The psychological profiles were based on detailed questionnaires completed when the subjects were medical students at a mean age of 23 years. Smoking habits have been reported periodically over the 10- to 24-year time span since the former medical students, now physicians, entered the study. In a stepwise comparison of nonsmokers, former smokers, and continuing smokers, highly significant differences were found in levels of coffee drinking and alcohol drinking in medical school. Continuing smokers had the highest levels, nonsmokers the lowest. In several comparisons of smokers and nonsmokers, both anxiety and anger, as measured in youth, were significantly higher among cigarette smokers. Anxiety was a significant differentiating variable in two 3-group comparisons: nonsmokers, former smokers, and continuing smokers; and nonsmokers, former light smokers, and continuing light smokers. Anger was significant in differentiating heavy smokers from light smokers (regardless of continuing or stopping) and in comparing nonsmokers, former heavy smokers, and continuing heavy smokers. Anger was associated with heavy smoking. Feelings related to depression and tiredness on awakening were reported in youth more frequently by heavy smokers than by light smokers. Insomnia and scales for family attitudes did not prove to be significant as single variables, although they made minor contributions to the overall discriminatory analyses. Heightened awareness of nervous tension, particularly feelings of anger and anxiety, appears to lead to increased use of cigarettes, coffee, and alcohol.

REFERENCES

Clyde, D. J., Cramer, E. C., & Sherin, R. J. Multiple statistical program. Coral Gables, Fla.: Biometric Laboratory of the University of Miami, 1966. (Soft-bound)

Dixon, W. J. (Ed.) *BMD: Biomedical computer programs.* Los Angeles: University of California Press, 1968.

Eysenck, H. J. Smoking, personality and psychosomatic disorders. *Journal of Psychosomatic Research,* 1963, **7,** 107.

Eysenck, H. J., Tarrant, M., Woolf, M., & England, L. Smoking and personality. *British Medical Journal,* 1960, 5184, 1456.

Heath, C. W. Differences between smokers and nonsmokers. *Archives of Internal Medicine,* 1958, **101,** 377.

Lilienfeld, A. M. Emotional and other selected characteristics of cigarette smokers and nonsmokers as related to epidemiological studies of lung cancer and other diseases. *Journal of the National Cancer Institute,* 1959, **22,** 259.

Matarazzo, J. D., & Saslow, G. Psychological and related characteristics of smokers and nonsmokers. *Psychological Bulletin,* 1960, **57,** 493.

McArthur, C., Waldron, E., & Dickinson, J. The psychology of smoking. *Journal of Abnormal Psychology,* 1958, **56,** 267.

McKennell, A. C. Smoking motivation factors. *Journal of Social and Clinical Psychology,* 1970, **9,** 8.

Schubert, D. S. P. Personality implications of cigarette smoking among college students. *Journal of Consulting Psychology,* 1959, **23,** 376.

Schubert, D. S. P. Arousal seeking as a central factor in tobacco smoking among college students. *International Journal of Social Psychiatry,* 1965, **11,** 221.

Smith, G. M. Personality and smoking: A review of the empirical literature. In W. A. Hunt (Ed.), *Learning mechanisms in smoking.* Chicago: Aldine, 1970.

Straits, B. C., & Sechrest, L. Further support of some findings about the characteristics of smokers and nonsmokers. *Journal of Consulting Psychology,* 1963, **27,** 282.

Thomas, C. B. Characteristics of smokers compared with nonsmokers in a population of healthy, young adults, including observations on family history, blood pressure, heart rate, body weight, cholesterol and certain psychologic traits. *Annals of Internal Medicine,* 1960, **53,** 697.

Thomas, C. B., Fargo, R., & Enslein, K. Personality characteristics of medical students as reflected by the Strong Vocational Interest Test with special reference to smoking habits. *Johns Hopkins Medical Journal,* 1970, **127,** 323.

Thomas, C. B., & Ross, D. C. Observations on some possible precursors of essential hypertension and coronary artery disease. VIII. Relationship of cholesterol level to certain habit patterns under stress. *Bulletin of the Johns Hopkins Hospital,* 1963, **113,** 225.

Thomas, C. B., & Ross, D. C. Precursors of hypertention and coronary disease among healthy medical students: Discriminant function analysis. V. Family attitudes. *Johns Hopkins Medical Journal,* 1968, **123,** 283. (a)

Thomas, C. B., & Ross, D. C. Precursors of hypertension and coronary disease among healthy medical students: Discriminant function analysis, IV. Using certain habits of daily life (sleeping, eating, drinking, studying and exercise) as the criteria. *Johns Hopkins Medical Journal,* 1968, **122,** 196. (b)

Thomas, C. B., Ross, D. C., & Higinbothom, C. Q. Precursors of hypertension and coronary disease among healthy medical students: Discriminant function analysis. I. Using smoking habits as the criterion. *Bulletin of the Johns Hopkins Hospital,* 1964, **115,** 174.

Tomkins, S. S. Psychological model for smoking behavior. *American Journal of Public Health and the Nation's Health,* 1966, **56,** 17.

Tomkins, S. S. A modified model of smoking behavior. In E. F. Borgatta & R. R. Evans (Eds.), *Smoking, health and behavior.* Chicago: Aldine, 1968.

Walker, R. E., Nicolay, R. C., Kluczny, R., & Riedel, R. G. Psychological correlates of smoking. *Journal of Clinical Psychology,* 1969, **25,** 42.

11

EFFECTS OF NICOTINE ON AVOIDANCE, CONDITIONED SUPPRESSION AND AGGRESSION RESPONSE MEASURES IN ANIMALS AND MAN[1]

Ronald R. Hutchinson and Grace S. Emley[2]
Fort Custer State Home, Augusta, Michigan

INTRODUCTION

It is the position of this discussion that tobacco usage involves a powerful chemical reinforcement process and that the chemical reinforcer is nicotine. We come to this conclusion because the experiments that we have conducted demonstrate that for both animals and man the administration of minute doses of nicotine (*a*) produces rapid and pronounced decreases in the effects of stressful and unpleasant stimulation through the reduction of the reflex behavioral processes normally generated thereby, while (*b*) simultaneously enhancing reactions which allow the reduction or termination of such stressors. There is widespread agreement that a reduction in the impact of aversive events constitutes powerful reinforcement for the behaviors producing such reduction, and similarly, that the behaviors producing such reduction, and similarly, that the behaviors producing enhancement of responses which lead to escape from or avoidance of aversive events are powerfully reinforced by such response enhancement. These ideas will be discussed in greater detail in later sections of this chapter.

AN EXPLANATION OF METHODS

The methods which are employed in this work were developed during the last 10 years in the course of our studies of aggressive and other emotional reactions. The

[1] Preparation of these materials was supported in part by Office of Naval Research Contract N 00014-70-A-0183-0001, National Aeronautics and Space Administration Grant NGR-23-010-004, National Science Foundation Grant GB-18413, the Michigan Department of Mental Health, Western Michigan University, and Philip Morris, U.S.A.

[2] Our thanks go to Dr. J. M. Louisell of the Fort Custer State Home staff, and to E. R. Hallin, N. J. Murray, N. A. Hunter, V. V. Pufpaff, R. Sauer, S. Hunt, S. Carpenter, G. Hamilton, B. Snowden, and K. Pisor of the Research Department of the Home, for their assistance.

basic animal paradigm which we have found suitable for behavioral, physiological, and pharmacological work is depicted in Figure 1. A squirrel monkey subject is seated in a restraint chair. For studies involving noxious stimulation, the tail may be shaved and restrained in a stockade device, and electrodes may be attached.

FIG. 1. A schematic illustration of the basic squirrel monkey paradigm used in our studies of behavioral, physiological and pharmacological processes relating to emotional behavior.

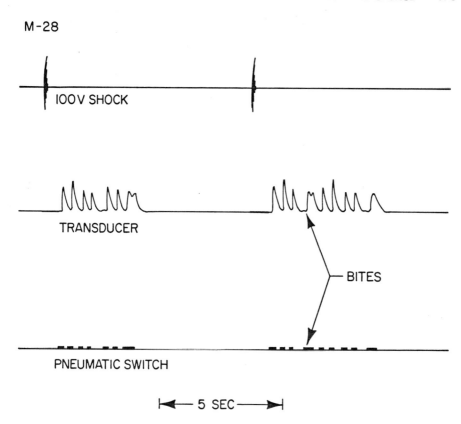

FIG. 2. An example of the effect of individual 100 msec shock deliveries upon the biting attack reaction for one squirrel monkey subject. The center tracing illustrates the polygraph records obtained from a Statham P23AC pressure transducer, while the lower tracing illustrates the duration of pneumatic switch closure. Intensity, frequency, or duration measures may be thus obtained.

Depending upon the experiment, a variety of stimuli may be presented via lights, speakers, etc., on the intelligence panel in front of the animal. In studies of aggression a gum rubber hose is suspended in front of the animal at approximately shoulder level, several inches from the panel extending from the right to left walls. The hose is connected via a pneumatic switch system to recording and programming devices located elsewhere. For studies involving manipulative manual behaviors, a pull chain connected to a switch may be suspended from the ceiling, or a response lever may be placed on the intelligence panel several inches above the waist lock. In studies involving food reinforcement, a small pellet tray is mounted on the intelligence panel on the opposite side from the lever, several inches above the waist lock. Subjects typically are studied for 1-hour periods either 5 or 7 days a week, depending upon the nature of the experiment. At all other times subjects live in individual cages in our animal colony quarters.

Figure 2 illustrates the typical behavior observed in experiments involving delivery of response-independent electric tail-shock. It can be seen that after shock delivery, with a delay of several hundred milliseconds, subjects bite repetitively upon the rubber hose. The center section of Figure 2 indicates a polygraph tracing provided by a pressure transducer, while the lower record shows the information available at the output of a pneumatic switch. This biting attack behavior has been shown to be a reliable and valid correlate of aggression in natural environments in this and other species (Azrin, Hutchinson, & Hake, 1963; Azrin, Hutchinson, & Sallery, 1964; Hutchinson, Azrin, & Hake, 1966; Hutchinson, 1972; Ulrich & Azrin, 1962; Azrin, Rubin, & Hutchinson, 1968). The behavior can be produced by a variety of nociceptive conditions, including electric shock (Hutchinson et al., 1966; Hutchinson, Azrin, & Renfrew, 1968; Hutchinson, Renfrew, & Young, 1971), a physical blow (Azrin, Hake, & Hutchinson, 1965), physical restraint (DeFrance & Hutchinson, in press), termination of food reinforcement programs (Hutchinson, Azrin, & Hunt, 1968), termination of reinforcing chemical stimulation (Emley, Hutchinson, & Brannan, 1970), and shifts to more stringent work requirement programs (Hutchinson, Azrin, & Hunt, 1968).

Figure 3 illustrates the biting attack typically observed when a monkey is subjected to intermittent programs of positive reinforcement. Attacks occur predominantly during the latter portion of the postreinforcement pause or in early portions of the fixed-ratio run.

The recurrent presentation of noxious events in a predictable sequence leads rapidly to the classical conditioning of the biting performance. There is one interesting variation. Figure 4 shows a record from an individual session for one subject receiving 400-volt shocks each 4 minutes. The behavior is characterized by the burst of responses immediately after each shock. Biting also develops

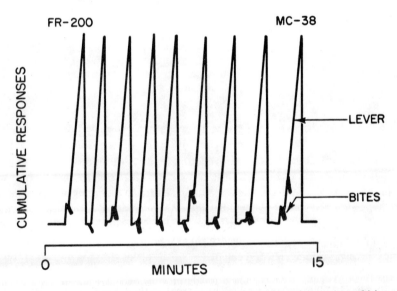

FIG. 3. The record of one squirrel monkey subject, showing the consistent biting attack responses produced during intermittent reinforcement on fixed-ratio 200. Biting attack tends to occur in the latter portions of the fixed-ratio pause or in early portions of the ratio run. This subject was at 80% of his free feeding weight and received 190 mg banana-flavored Noyes pellets.

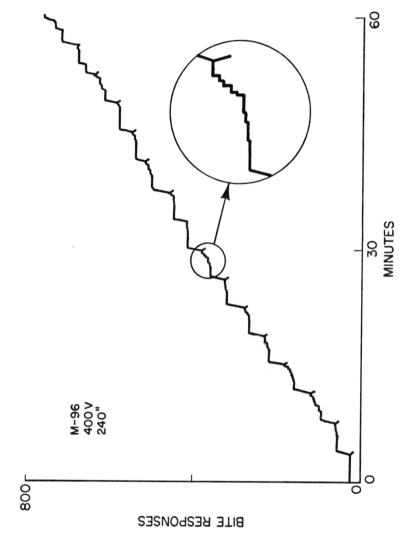

FIG. 4. The record of a single squirrel monkey subject during fixed, periodic response-independent 100-msec electric shocks. Note that subsequent to an individual shock, a rapid flurry of biting attacks occurs. Following this, no behavior is seen until later in the interval, when there is a progressive increase in biting responses as the next shock approaches, immediately before shock delivery behavior is again suppressed.

175

progressively toward the period of the next shock *except* that the behavior ceases entirely for the last few seconds before shock delivery. A stylized portion of the record is enlarged in the lower right-hand corner of the figure. In later studies it was discovered that this anticipatory biting occurred most typically when no other response alternative was available. When allowed the opportunity both to bite upon the rubber hose and to engage in a manual manipulative response, such as pressing a lever or pulling a chain, the post-shock and pre-shock behaviors became highly differentiated upon the two manipulanda. Figure 5 illustrates this consistent dual pattern of responding by four different subjects. The left portion of the figure shows pairs of cumulative records from individual sessions for each subject. All subjects showed a pattern of immediate post-shock biting followed by a pattern of pre-shock lever pressing or chain pulling. Typical also is that although lever pressing is elevated as shock approaches, this performance ceases completely a few seconds before shock delivery. Some animals continue to show some biting also prior to

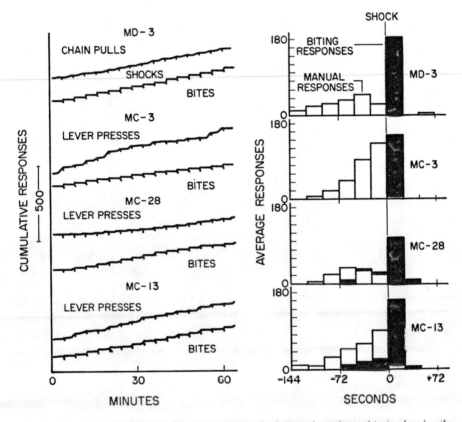

FIG. 5. Pairs of cumulative records from four individual squirrel monkey subjects, showing the pattern of responding of post-shock biting attacks and pre-shock manual manipulations which develop when two response sensors are present. Note that all subjects illustrate a suppression of lever presses and biting attacks during the period immediately prior to an ensuing shock. The pattern of interresponse times for both biting and manual responses relative to the moment of shock delivery are displayed in the right portion of the figure.

shock, but as the right-hand portion of Figure 5 illustrates, all subjects show a shift in relative and absolute frequencies of behavior from manual behavior before shock to biting after shock. These three separate processes of (*a*) post-noxious event biting, (*b*) pre-noxious event manual manipulative and motor reactions, and (*c*) immediate pre-noxious stimulus suppression of all behaviors, have previously been discussed and interpreted by us as valid indicants of aggression (fighting), escape (fleeing), and suppression (freezing) (Hutchinson, Renfrew, & Young, 1971; Hutchinson & Emley, 1972; Emley & Hutchinson, 1972; Hutchinson, 1971-1972). These reaction patterns have served as a complex behavioral baseline for the study of a variety of pharmacological and physiological interventions (Hutchinson & Emley, 1972; Emley, Hutchinson, & Hunter, 1971; Emley & Hutchinson, 1972; Renfrew, 1969; DeFrance & Hutchinson, 1971, in press).

RESULTS

The Effects of Certain Drugs on Aggression, Flight, and Freezing

As we became more confident that these three measures reflected respectively upon three basic emotional processes typically found in the context of noxiousness, pain, aversion, unpleasantness, or demanding tasks, we decided to test a variety of pharmcological agents often used through prescription or personal decision in such contexts. It was gratifying to discover that the three behavioral indices were differentially sensitive to different pharmacological compounds. Some drugs tended to produce general elevations in all response measures, while some drugs tended to reduce all behaviors, Most significant to us, however, was the observation that certain drugs would differentially influence the three response patterns, i.e., one might be raised while another was lowered. Such effects are summarized for seven different drugs in Figure 6. Portions of these data have been reported earlier (Hutchinson & Emley, 1971, 1972; Emley, Hutchinson, & Hunter, 1971; Emley & Hutchinson, 1971, 1972). It can be seen that *d*-amphetamine and caffeine tend generally throughout their range of effect to increase both the responses of post-shock biting and pre-shock lever pressing. A significant difference between the two drugs is that amphetamine in general tends to increase post-shock biting attack behaviors more than it raises pre-shock manual behaviors, and at a lower dosage. Two other drugs, phenobarbital and morphine, appear highly similar also by these tests. Both the responses of pre-shock lever pressing or chain pulling and post-shock biting attacks are progressively decreased throughout the range of effective doses.

For the drugs chlorpromazine, chlordiazepoxide, and nicotine, however, a different pattern of actions was discovered. These three drugs as a class tend throughout a major portion of their effective dose range to differentially affect the pre-shock and post-shock behaviors. Attack behaviors are decreased, while the pre-shock anticipatory motor behaviors are simultaneously increased. This ability of a compound to simultaneously reduce postevent irritability and aggressiveness while increasing anticipatory manual and motor reactions of a type necessary for reinforcement interactions (Azrin, Hutchinson, & Hake, 1967; Mowrer, 1939; Brogden, Lipman, & Culler, 1938; Skinner, 1938) is considered by us to be a basic characteristic of the tranquilizer-type compound (Emley & Hutchinson, 1972). It

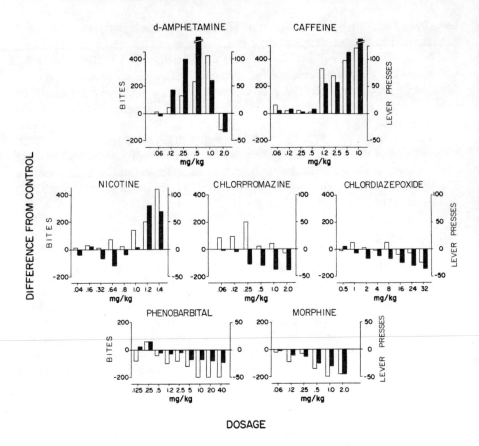

FIG. 6. The changes in biting attacks and lever presses which occur from saline control tests during administration of several doses of the drugs d-amphetamine, caffeine, nicotine, chlorpromazine, chlordiazepoxide, phenobarbital, and morphine.

was a bit surprising to us to discover that nicotine by our tests clearly fell within this unique class of agents which could (at least at low and intermediate doses) differentially affect the post-shock and pre-shock behaviors. Nicotine does differ from both chlorpromazine and chlordiazepoxide in one aspect: higher doses of these major and minor tranquilizers produce major depressions in all behaviors, while at higher doses of nicotine just the opposite is true; general elevations in both response classes are noted. The effects of nicotine are shown over a range of dosage in Figure 7. This is the record of an individual subject cumulated by sessions. The column of records on the left is of hose biting, while the column of records on the right is of manual responding recorded during the same sessions as the biting record on the opposite side. As the drug dose increases, biting is progressively reduced while manual behaviors are elevated until approximately 1 mg/kg body weight. From this dose level, biting and manual behaviors are elevated together in a general stimulation effect.

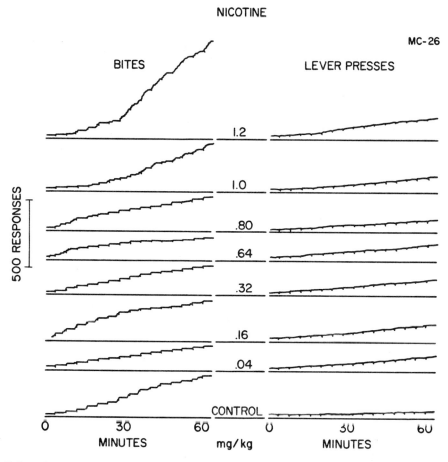

FIG. 7. Pairs of cumulative records from a single squirrel monkey subject over the range of acute doses of nicotine and of the saline control session. Records on the left column are of biting attacks; those in the right column are of lever presses. The intershock interval is 4 minutes.

Effects of Chronic Nicotine Intake upon Attack and Anticipatory Motor Reactions

The effects of acute drug administration during individual sessions as described above were highly intriguing. We set out next on a program of studying the effects of chronic drug administration using several different compounds. For our purpose here I will be discussing only the results with nicotine. Ten squirrel monkey subjects were studied in an ascending and descending series of doses of periods of up to 8 weeks. We discovered in early tests that nicotine could be administered chronically in drinking water and would produce no effect on water intake throughout the dose range of interest. Figure 8 illustrates that nine of the ten subjects in that study showed a progressive decrease in post-shock responding at progressively higher doses of chronic drug intake. For five of these subjects some tendency to show initial elevations in biting were observed, but post-shock responses were reduced at immediately higher doses. For eight of these nine

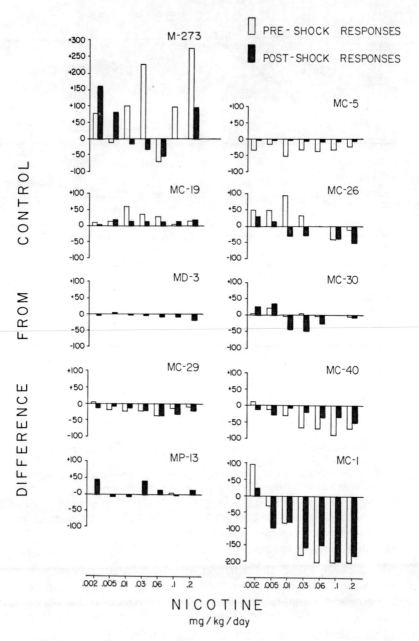

FIG. 8. Changes from distilled water control baseline conditions produced in 10 subjects over a period of weeks during chronic administration of several doses of nicotine.

subjects the behavioral reductions were differential. Pre-shock responding was reduced less than was the post-shock biting attack, or was actually elevated throughout a portion of a range where post-shock attack behavior was reduced. For nine of the ten subjects studied, there was at least one separate drug dose, and

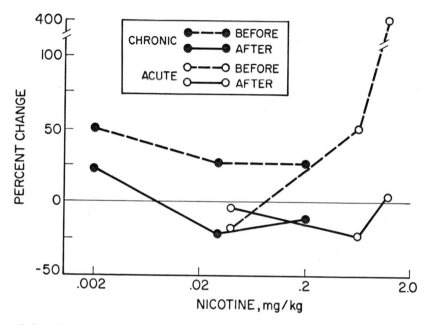

FIG. 9. Percent changes in responding during drug tests as compared with saline control baseline conditions for three subjects on acute injections and three subjects on chronic oral nicotine intake at the total absolute daily intake doses listed. Two subjects were listed by each method.

typically there were three separate drug doses, at which this differential effect of an elevation in pre-shock responses with simultaneous reduction in post-shock responses was observed. The single exception to this differential effect (Subject 10) was seen with MC-5 and is portrayed in the upper-right-hand corner of Figure 8. It is notable that MC-5 was also the only animal which did not have any hose-biting responses whatever. In fact, it is one of but five subjects of the several hundred previously studied by this laboratory which has displayed this absence of biting attack. There appear to be no noticeable dentition problems or other observable reasons why this subject should have shown this pattern. It seens highly significant to us that this baseline behavioral discrepancy coincides with a highly unusual effect of the drug. It may be noted that for MC-5, nicotine throughout the range of doses tested produced a greater reduction in pre-shock manual behaviors than in the post-shock manual behaviors.

There are great individual differences in effect of chronic nicotine intake on magnitude of response changes, pattern of relative shifts in performance, and doses at which these various effects are produced. Nevertheless the consistency of post-shock response decreases with differential influence between post- and pre-shock behaviors remains consistent. Another discovery of our studies was that the range of effective doses during chronic drug administration was much below that required to produce equivalent effects from acute drug injections. In Figure 9 a comparison of the chronic and acute drug doses necessary to produce these differential effects upon the pre-shock and post-shock responses are shown for six subjects. Consistent drug effects during chronic administration were produced at as low an absolute total daily drug dose as .002 mg/kg. This was approximately one one-hundredth of the total daily drug intake necessary when given in a single acute pretest injection.

Effect of Abrupt Termination of Nicotine Intake

When drug doses were progressively reduced, the effects originally observed at the previous similar doses prior to the ascending series were not immediately recovered; rather, time was necessary for the dissipation of major effects of drug termination. When the drug was withdrawn after chronic administration, subjects showed temporary large increases in post-shock biting attack behavior. Figure 10 presents cumulative records for one subject, MC-30, during the twentieth day of drug intake and the first and third days subsequent to drug withdrawal. Biting

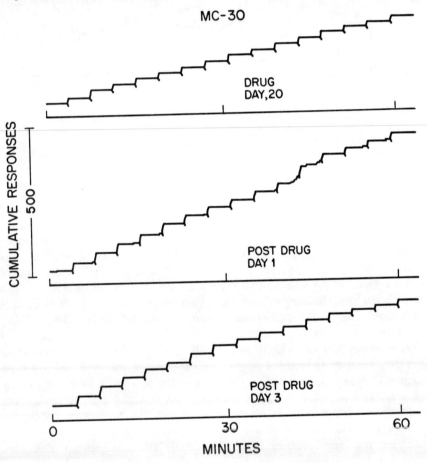

FIG. 10. Sample records from one squirrel monkey subject showing session records for the last day of drug, the first day subsequent to drug termination, and the third day subsequent to drug termination. Note both the increased number of bites subsequent to each shock on day 1, as well as the occurrence of pre-shock biting attacks prior to ensuing shocks. By postdrug day 3, behavior is reduced to control levels, though not to the level produced by drug administration.

attack was initially elevated subsequent to drug withdrawal. By the third postdrug session, attacks were back to the predrug biting level, though not as low as during drug intake.

Effects of Nicotine Upon Conditioned Suppression in the Estes-Skinner Procedure

Though it seemed clear from both our acute and our chronic administration studies that nicotine had the ability to increase responding during periods prior to the delivery of a noxious event such as an electric shock, we decided to test further a similar effect in a more traditional procedure—that of the conditioned suppression paradigm developed by W. K. Estes and B. F. Skinner (Estes & Skinner, 1941).

Four monkeys and 12 albino rats were food-deprived and conditioned to lever-press for 190-mg banana pellets and 45-mg Noyes sugar sweetened pellets, respectively, on a variable-interval reinforcement schedule. Subsequent to the establishment of consistent responding, tone-shock stimulus pairs were delivered on an unpredictable 7-minute variable-interval, response-independent schedule. The tone was 30 seconds in length and was coterminous with a 200-millisecond shock. Shocks were delivered to the tail in the case of the monkeys, and via a scrambled floor grid program in the case of the rats. Shock voltages were adjusted to produce marginal responding during the tone stimulus. When responding was stable during saline control injections, all subjects of both species were injected with several different doses of nicotine in a counterbalanced dose series, and the effect upon the suppression of responding during the tone stimulus, relative to responding during the absence of tone, was assessed.

Figure 11 shows the suppression ratio differences from saline control tests obtained at several different doses for both species. For monkey subjects, responding previously suppressed during the tone stimulus was enhanced at lower nicotine doses but reduced at higher doses of nicotine. This reduction at higher doses was associated with major disruptions in the ongoing food-acquisition response baseline where baseline rates often were very much lower. For the rat subjects (Sprague-Dawley strain), administration of nicotine reduced suppression during the tone stimulus at low and intermediate doses also. The baseline performance for food acquisition was disrupted by higher drug doses for this species also. These data confirm the "antianxiety" effects of nicotine during a positive reinforcement schedule for both rats and monkeys.

Extension of Basic Findings to Humans

Our interest in aggression and emotional reactions is fundamentally directed to understanding human behavior. As our findings with animals have accrued, we have made extensions to studying human subjects under similar though less stressful conditions. The basic paradigm which we have developed involves recording both behavioral and physiological measures from subjects during the introduction of nociceptive or frustrating events. The basic test chamber and subject format is seen in Figure 12. Volunteer normal human adults come daily to the experimental laboratory at the same hour each day and are tested for between 15 and 45 minutes. The test chamber is air-conditioned and electrostatically and acoustically shielded. Subjects typically are prepared for recordings of heart rate

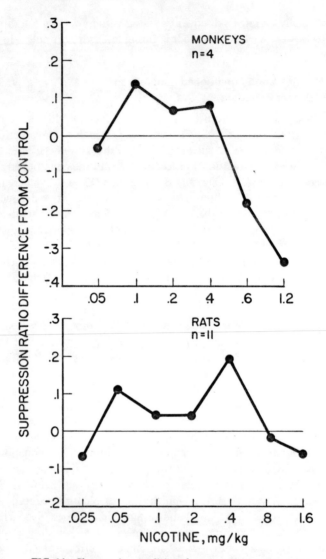

FIG. 11. Changes in conditioned suppression ratios upon drug administration compared to saline control suppression ratio values. Ratio differences are for four squirrel monkey subjects and 11 of 12 albino laboratory rats at the range of dosages shown.

and for EMG recordings from several different muscle groups. Initial studies were conducted to discover whether jaw clenching and teeth grinding would occur in humans subsequent to instatement of conditions of a type similar to those that in animals produce overt biting attack upon a rubber hose. To record from temporalis and masseter muscle groups, electrodes are placed on the scalp and face area of subjects, as shown in Figure 13. Basically the procedure involves the recording in both integrated and unintegrated fashion from both sides of the head, as fully described elsewhere (Hutchinson & Pierce, 1971; Hutchinson, Emley, & Sauer,

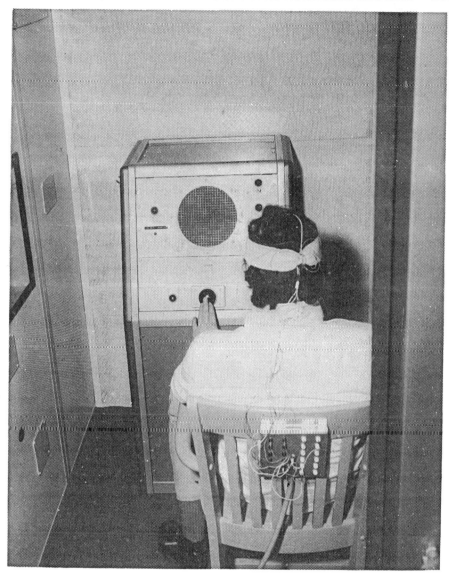

FIG. 12. A photograph of the experimental chamber, test console, subject seating arrangement, and electrode-attachment procedure used in the studies with humans.

1971). Two separate patterns of biting, eccentric and concentric, may be recorded in this manner and are recorded electromyographically as differential temporalis and masseter contraction patterns. We have found that masseter contractions are a sensitive and reliable index of irritability as evidenced by correlative verbal behavior, response force, and attendance at subsequent test sessions (Pierce, 1971). Subjects are informed that the electrodes attached on the head are for the recording of brain waves. This is believed a necessary deception, since focus on mouth process, partly under volitional control, might severely jeopardize the recording of spontaneous activity. At the conclusion of testing, all subjects are informed of the

ELECTRODE PLACEMENTS

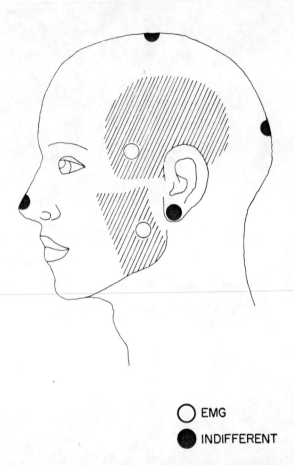

○ EMG

● INDIFFERENT

FIG. 13. A schematic illustration of the anatomic placement of electrodes for recording temporalis and masseter muscle potentials. The upper muscle group is the temporalis muscle, while the muscle shaded area on the jaw stylizes the underlying masseter muscle. The indifferent electrodes are connected in parallel to cancel local noise.

nature of the recordings. Figure 14 illustrates samples of masseter EMG recordings taken from two subjects during periodic delivery of fixed-interval, response-independent 3,000-Hertz tones of 110-decibel amplitude. Each subject shows a pattern of posttone jaw clenching and, subsequent to several sessions of such tone deliveries each 3 minutes, anticipatory bites shortly before the next tone stimulus.

In other studies, subjects were exposed to various programs of intermittent monetary reinforcement for a button-pressing task. As the work requirement was increased to significant fixed-ratio values, patterns of jaw clenching developed during the postreinforcement pause or in early portions of the fixed-ratio run.

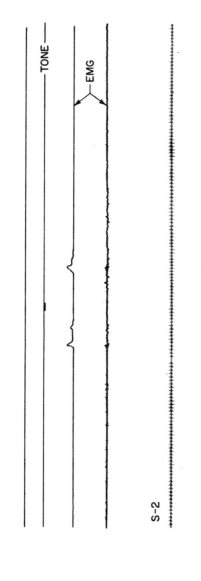
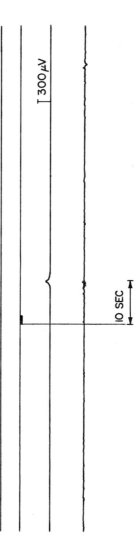

FIG. 14. Sample records for two human subjects, showing jaw clenching immediately following delivery of a 100-decibel tone stimulus and (for Subject 1) preceding the tone stimulus. The upper line of the two EMG tracings has been integrated, while the lower is the direct unintegrated record.

187

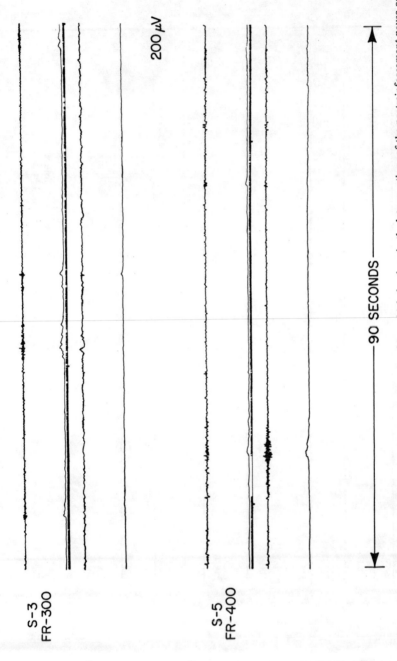

200 μV

|← 90 SECONDS →|

S-3
FR-300

S-5
FR-400

FIG. 15. Session records for two subjects, showing the jaw clenching which develops in the later portions of the postreinforcement pause or in early portions of the fixed-ratio run during fixed-ratio reinforcement of button pressing for money (25 cents). The upper tracing for each subject is the unintegrated record of masseter muscle potential, while the second tracing is the integrated record of masseter potential. The third record shows individual button presses (upward deflection) and reinforcements (downward deflection). The fourth tracing is the unintegrated record of temporalis muscle potential. The fifth tracing is the integrated record of temporalis muscle potential.

These effects are illustrated in Figure 15 for two subjects. Subsequent tests demonstrated that instatement of extinction would produce extended periods of jaw clenching also (Hutchinson & Pierce, 1971; Hutchinson, Emley, & Sauer, 1971). Thus both major classes of noxious stimulation shown previously in animal work to be the causes of aggressivity—(a) the instatement or onset of noxious or painful events, and (b) the offset of reinforcing events—produced responses in humans which manifest temporal and topographic patterns that are highly similar or actually identical to those seen in earlier work with animals.

Effects of Cessation of Cigarette Smoking on Jaw Clenching in Humans

As a variety of studies have shown that cigarettes and the opportunity to smoke constitute powerful positive reinforcers for smokers (Lindsley, 1962; Hutchinson & Azrin, 1961), it seemed of interest to determine what effects would be observed on the jaw clenching subsequent to the termination of the smoking practice by smokers. Accordingly eight subjects were selected from a volunteer group of persons scheduled to participate in a smoking withdrawal clinic. The subjects agreed to alternate participation in our research program at the laboratory. Subjects came each day at the same time, 1 day a week, for the week prior to quitting smoking and for the 4 weeks subsequent to cessation of smoking. Upon entering the laboratory, the subjects' heart rate and blood pressure were checked. They were next prepared for masseter and EMG recordings and conducted to the experimental

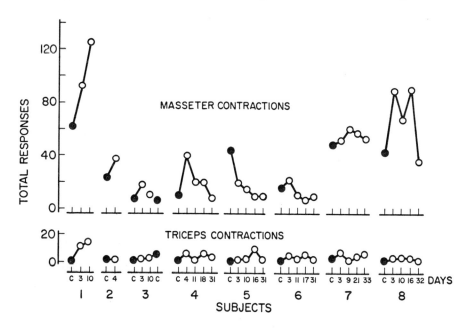

FIG. 16. The effect of cessation of cigarette smoking upon masseter and triceps contractions for eight human subjects. The filled circles are for the test prior to smoking cessation. The open circles indicate subsequent weekly tests. Subjects 1 and 2 terminated the experiment after 1 and 2 weeks respectively, Subject 3 after one week. All resumed smoking immediately.

test space. Their only task was to sit relaxed for 30 minutes while the experimenter collected polygraph records. Seven of the eight subjects showed an increase in the frequency of spontaneous jaw contractions during the weeks subsequent to terminating cigarette usage. Figure 16 shows masseter muscle contractions and a control recording of triceps muscle contractions before and after smoking cessation. All subjects except Subject 5 showed an increase in jaw contraction subsequent to

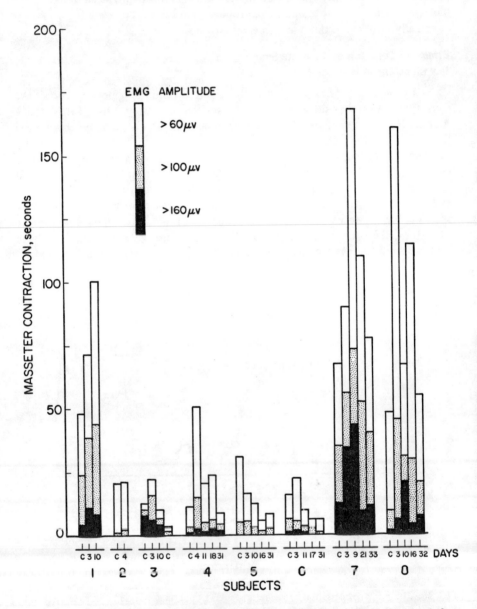

FIG. 17. The duration of masseter contractions of three different intensities in a session before cessation of smoking and for four weekly sessions after termination of tobacco usage for eight subjects

quitting smoking. Subjects 1 and 2 terminated the experimental program and resumed smoking almost immediately. Subject 3 resumed smoking in the fourth week. The other five subjects all completed the month-long observation period. Each of these five subjects also showed a progressive reduction in masseter contractions recorded on subsequent weekly test sessions. Triceps muscle contraction recordings showed no consistent pattern of change.

Subjects not only showed an increase in the frequency of jaw clenching following cessation of smoking, but they also showed a rise in the duration of high-force jaw contractions. Figure 17 illustrates this pattern for all eight subjects. The light bars illustrate the duration of biting at a low force (voltage of 60 microvolts or greater), shaded bars indicate moderate-force contractions (100 microvolts), and solid bars the duration of high-force contractions (160 microvolts or greater). All force durations of contraction increase progressively and then decrease in later postsmoking sessions. Subject 5 is again an exception to the general pattern.

It may be interesting to note that all three of the subjects who did not complete the study were females, and those that did complete the study were all males. It has been reported by others that termination of cigarette usage is a more formidable process for females (Horn, 1971). These data then provide additional evidence that the chronic intake of nicotine or the smoking habit constitutes a major reinforcement episode, and that the termination of such participation results in a marked increase in measures of jaw contraction shown by other studies to be a sensitive index of current noxiousness.

Effects of Nicotine Upon Stress-Produced
Jaw Contractions in Humans

The purpose of our next study was to determine directly the effects of nicotine administration in human subjects upon bite contraction during stressful episodes. Nicotine was administered to nonsmoking subjects without their immediate awareness; thus any effect could be attributed to the direct action of the nicotine.

Four volunteer adult males were tested during 30-minute daily sessions in an environment where they were exposed to a 110-decibel 3,000-hertz tone for 2 seconds each 3 minutes. As shown previously in Figure 14, this program of stimulation causes a pattern of jaw contraction immediately after the tone and also tends to produce bite contractions prior to subsequent tone deliveries.

Subjects were required to drink 5 ounces (147 ml) of distilled water each day, 15 minutes prior to testing. When performance was considered stable, 5 mg of nicotine were added to the 5-ounce volume of water. This quantity was found to be below threshold for detection in earlier experiments here in the laboratory, but was known to be sufficient to produce reliable physiological changes in a majority of subjects (Johnston, 1942; Silvette, Hoff, Larson, & Haag, 1962). The drug was administered for two days, and on a subsequent day control observations were again taken under distilled water control conditions.

All subjects showed reduced masseter muscle contractions during those sessions when they received nicotine. Figure 18 presents these results, showing frequency of masseter contractions on days before, during, and after nicotine administration. Biting contractions were less frequent, and those that occurred were of reduced

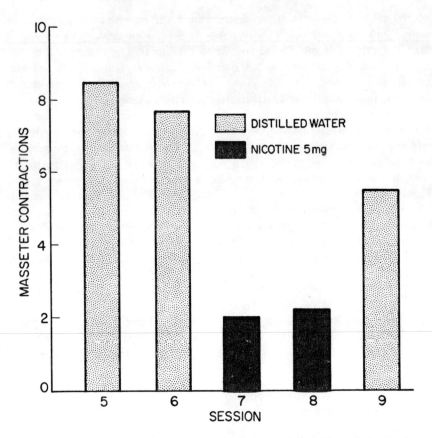

FIG. 18. Average number of masseter contractions for four subjects during the last two predrug sessions, during two sessions in which each received 5 mg of nicotine, and for one postdrug session.

amplitude. Figure 19 shows the average bite contraction force on the two predrug days, the two drug days, and the postdrug day.

Nicotine reduced the frequency and intensity of jaw contractions, and in addition produced a disproportionate reduction in those jaw contractions occurring immediately after the tone. Figure 20 illustrates this ratio of responses occurring before the tone relative to those occurring after the tone for all four subjects on the same 5-day ABA sequence. Thus in all ways tested in this experiment, nicotine produced changes in human responses which were identical to those produced during both acute and chronic administration in monkeys in similar testing paradigms.

DISCUSSION

The present results have demonstrated that for both squirrel monkeys and humans, the intake of small quantities of nicotine produces a differential reduction in behavioral patterns associated with aggressiveness, hostility, and irritability. It

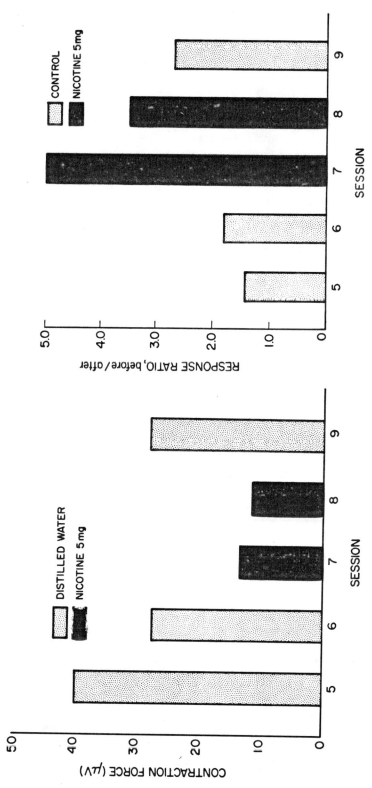

FIG. 19. The average force of jaw contractions for all four human subjects during two predrug sessions, two drug sessions, and one postdrug session.

FIG. 20. The ratio of bite responses occurring in the last two-thirds of the intertone interval relative to bites occurring in the first third of the intertone interval for the two predrug sessions, two drug tests, and one postdrug session.

193

was shown that this effect was similar to that produced by chemical agents of both the major and minor tranquilizer groups. Additionally it was shown for both monkeys and man that these same doses of nicotine which would reduce aggressiveness would simultaneously elevate orienting and anticipatory reactions, an effect characteristic also of compounds in both the major and minor tranquilizer groups. It was also shown that for both rats and monkeys, nicotine reduced the suppression caused by contact with a fear or anxiety-producing stimulus. Finally, it was shown that termination of nicotine intake after extended periods of ingestion caused temporary increases in hostility, aggressiveness, and irritability in both monkeys and man. The findings reviewed here seem to support strongly the proposition that the intake of nicotine in a stressful or noxious environment will constitute a reinforcing event, and the termination of such a practice will constitute a punishing or negatively reinforcing event.

If the foregoing analysis is correct, what has prevented its general detection and acknowledgment from earlier studies? Several factors seem important in this regard. One confusion probably regards the apparently "nicotine-free" basis of the smoking habit which has been reported by several workers (Goldfarb, Jarvik, & Glick, 1970; Finnegan, Larson, & Haag, 1945). Modification of nicotine levels in cigarettes often did little to alter the smoking practice. Unfortunately, most of these studies were of short duration, despite the well known fact that stimuli previously associated with powerful reinforcers can produce and sustain response sequences independent of primary reinforcement for long periods of time, particularly under conditions of intermittent reinforcement (Kelleher & Gollub, 1962; Hendry, 1969). The degree of reinforcement through reduced noxiousness and enhanced anticipatory process associated with the use of cigarettes or other tobacco agents has undoubtedly been intermittent and variable for all users. Temporary tests of nicotine-free, i.e., primary reinforcement-free, product could therefore be expected to produce very little effect during a short period of time. Fortunately such misunderstandings are being cleared up, as it now seems established that a predictable relationship between nicotine ingestion and the frequency of cigarette usage does exist (Lucchesi, Schuster, & Emley, 1967; Frith, 1971).

A second confusion which has confronted investigators has been the great difficulty of inducing significant tobacco or nicotine usage in animal subjects. Usage of other chemical agents which spontaneously reinforce their acquisition and intake behaviors, such as oxygen, sugars, carbohydrates, water, and the opiates, has been far more readily established in animals (Deneau & Inoki, 1967; Glick, Jarvik, & Makamura, 1971). The difficulty with tobacco usage may derive from an incomplete consideration of the dual nature of the reinforcement process in practically all organisms. Two major and separate classes of environmental stimulus events support behavior. One class involves the onset or the maintenance of certain energy levels, while the other class involves the reduction or termination of certain energy levels. The former we call positive reinforcers, and these in general involve the intake of or contact with substances which are nutritive or essential for life and health, or the mimics of such agents. The other class of reinforcement process involves the reduction of noxiousness, aversiveness, pain, irritation, or stress.

The present studies suggest that the agent nicotine achieves its behavioral effect by reducing reactions and affects caused by noxious or painful agents in a manner similar to major and minor tranquilizers and sedatives. It is not surprising, therefore, that animal models which have involved the stress-free opportunity to ingest nicotine have not produced significant nicotine ingestion. The present findings further suggest that we now need to provide the reinforcement opportunity for nicotine ingestion (as well as the other compounds mentioned) while systematically manipulating the environmental level of noxiousness and stress. It seems certain to us that such studies would yield positive results.

REFERENCES

Azrin, N. H., Hake, D. F., & Hutchinson, R. R. Elicitation of aggression by a physical blow. *Journal of Experimental Analysis of Behavior,* 1965, **8,** 55-57.

Azrin, N. H., Hutchinson, R. R., & Hake, D. F. Attack avoidance and escape reactions to aversive shock. *Journal of the Experimental Analysis of Behavior,* 1967, **10,** 131-148.

Azrin, N. H., Hutchinson, R. R., & Sallery, R. D. Pain-aggression toward inanimate objects. *Journal of the Experimental Analysis of Behavior,* 1964, **7,** 223-228.

Azrin, N. H., Rubin, H. B., & Hutchinson, R. R. Biting attack by rats in response to aversive shock. *Journal of the Experimental Analysis of Behavior,* 1968, **11,** 633-639.

Brogden, W. J., Lipman, E. A., & Culler, E. The role of incentive in conditioning and extinction. *American Journal of Psychology,* 1938, **51,** 109-117.

DeFrance, J., & Hutchinson, R. R. Epileptiform activity in the basolateral amygdala related to aggression. *Michigan Mental Health Research Bulletin,* (Winter) 1971, **5,** 36-38.

DeFrance, J. F., & Hutchinson, R. R. Electrographic changes in the amygdala and hippocampus associated with biting attack. *Physiology and Behavior,* in press.

Deneau, G. A., & Inoki, R. Nicotine self-administration in monkeys. *Annals of the New York Academy of Sciences,* 1967, **142,** 277-279.

Emley, G. S., & Hutchinson, R. R. Similar and selective actions of chlorpromazine, chlordiazepoxide, and nicotine on shock-produced aggressive and anticipatory motor responses in the squirrel monkey. *American Psychological Association Proceedings,* 79th Annual Convention, 1971, 759-760.

Emley, G. S., & Hutchinson, R. R. Basis of behavioral influence of chlorpromazine. *Life Sciences,* 1972, **11,** 43-47.

Emley, G. S., Hutchinson, R. R., & Brannan, I. B. Aggression: Effects of acute and chronic morphine. *Michigan Mental Health Research Bulletin,* (Fall) 1970, **4,** 23-26.

Emley, G. S., Hutchinson, R. R., & Hunter, N. A. Selective actions of morphine, chlorpromazine, chlordiazepoxide, nicotine and d-amphetamine on shock-produced aggressive and other motor responses in the squirrel monkey. *Federation Proceedings,* Federation of American Societies for Experimental Biology, 1971, **30,** 390.

Estes, W. K., & Skinner, B. F. Some quantitative properties of anxiety. *Journal of Experimental Psychology,* 1941, **29,** 390-400.

Finnegan, J. K., Larson, P. S., & Haag, H. B. The role of nicotine in the cigarette habit. *Science,* 1945, **102,** 94-96.

Frith, C. D. The effect of varying the nicotine content of cigarettes on human smoking behaviour. *Psychopharmacologia,* 1971, **19,** 188-192.

Glick, S., Jarvik, M., & Makamura, R. Dot & Randi & Phoebe & Frieda. *The Sciences,* 1971, **11,** 22-23.

Goldfarb, T. L., Jarvik, M. E., & Glick, S. D. Cigarette nicotine content as a determinant of human smoking behavior. *Psychopharmacologia,* 1970, **17,** 89-93.

Hendry, D. P. *Conditioned reinforcement.* Homewood, Ill.: Dorsey Press, 1969.

Horn, D. What's happening to smoking behavior. *A Summary of the Proceedings of the 1st National Conference on Smoking and Health,* Sept. 9-11, 1970. Washington, D.C.: National Interagency Council on Smoking and Health, 1971. Pp. 15-20.

Hutchinson, R. R. Environmental causes of aggression. *Nebraska Symposium* 1971. Lincoln: University of Nebraska Press, 1972.

Hutchinson, R. R., & Azrin, N. H. Conditioning of mental-hospital patients to fixed-ratio schedules of reinforcement. *Journal of the Experimental Analysis of Behavior*, 1961, **4,** 87-95.

Hutchinson, R. R., Azrin, N. H., & Hake, D. F. An automatic method for the study of aggression in squirrel monkeys. *Journal of the Experimental Analysis of Behavior*, 1966, 9, 233-237.

Hutchinson, R. R., Azrin, N. H., & Hunt, G. M. Attack produced by intermittent reinforcement of a concurrent operant response. *Journal of the Experimental Analysis of Behavior*, 1968, **11,** 489-495.

Hutchinson, R. R., Azrin, N. H., & Renfrew, J. W. Effects of shock intensity and duration on the frequency of biting attack by squirrel monkeys. *Journal of the Experimental Analysis of Behavior*, 1968, **11,** 83-88.

Hutchinson, R. R., & Emley, G. S. The behavioral basis of action of tranquilizers. *Michigan Mental Health Research Bulletin*, (Spring) 1971, **5,** 19-22.

Hutchinson, R. R., & Emley, G. S. Schedule-independent factors contributing to schedule-induced phenomena. In R. M. Gilbert & J. D. Keehn (Eds.), *Schedule effects: Drugs, drinking and aggression.* Toronto: University of Toronto Press, 1972.

Hutchinson, R. R., Emley, G. S., & Sauer, R. A. Effects of cessation of cigarette smoking on jaw clenching. Paper presented at the American Psychological Association, Washington, D.C., September, 1971.

Hutchinson, R. R., & Pierce, G. E. Jaw clenching in humans: Its measurement, and effects produced by conditions of reinforcement and extinction. Paper presented at the American Psychological Association, Washington, D.C., September, 1971.

Hutchinson, R. R., Renfrew, J. W., & Young, G. A. Effects of long-term shock and associated stimuli on aggressive and manual responses. *Journal of the Experimental Analysis of Behavior*, 1971, **15,** 141-166.

Johnston, L. Tobacco smoking and nicotine. *Lancet* (London), 1942, **2,** 747.

Kelleher, R. T., & Gollub, L. R. A review of positive conditioned reinforcement. *Journal of the Experimental Analysis of Behavior*, 1962, **5,** 543-597.

Lindsley, O. R. Operant conditioning methods in diagnosis. In J. H. Nodine & J. H. Moyer (Eds.), *The First Hahnemann Symposium on Psychosomatic Medicine.* Philadelphia: Lea and Febiger, 1962, 41-54.

Lucchesi, B. R., Schuster, C. R., & Emley, G. S. The role of nicotine as a determinant of cigarette smoking frequency in man with observations of certain cardiovascular effects associated with the tobacco alkaloid. *Clinical Pharmacology and Therapeutics*, 1967, **8,** 789-796.

Mowrer, O. H. A stimulus response analysis of anxiety and its role as a reinforcing agent. *Psychological Review*, 1939, 8, 125-131.

Pierce, G. E. Effects of several fixed-ratio schedules of reinforcement and of extinction upon temporalis and masseter muscle contractions in humans. Unpublished masters thesis, Western Michigan University, 1971.

Renfrew, J. W. The intensity function and reinforcing properties of brain stimulation that elicits attack. *Physiology and Behavior*, 1969, 4, 509-515.

Silvette, H., Hoff, E. C., Larson, P. S., & Haag, H. B. The actions of nicotine on central nervous functions. *Pharmacological Review*, 1962, **14,** 137-173.

Skinner, B. F. *The behavior of organisms: An experimental analysis.* New York: Appleton-Century-Crofts, 1938.

Ulrich, R. E., & Azrin, N. H. Reflexive fighting in response to aversive stimulation. *Journal of the Experimental Analysis of Behavior*, 1962, **5,** 511-520.

12

THE EFFECTS OF SMOKING ON MOOD CHANGE

Norman W. Heimstra
University of South Dakota

When considering the motivational mechanisms of smoking we are, of course, dealing with a complex topic that can be approached from several points of view. Typically, research in this area has been aimed at defining the motivational factors which cause a person to begin to smoke and to continue smoking. Thus, Logan (1970) suggests that "initially smoking must be motivated extrinsically; youth learns to smoke to be accepted, to rebel, to reduce their feelings of inferiority, from curiosity, or the like.... In time smoking generates its own intrinsic motivation, which may make it functionally autonomous even after the initiating drives are no longer present [p. 142]." A number of different motives have been suggested as being responsible for the onset of smoking behavior and for its continuation, often in spite of sustained efforts to extinguish the behavior.

It is also possible to deal with the motivational aspects of cigarette smoking from a somewhat different point of view. Instead of being primarily concerned with the motives that bring about and sustain smoking behavior, the possible effects of smoking on maintaining or modifying motivational mechanisms, other than those underlying the smoking behavior itself, should also be considered. Thus, when smoking is viewed as a consummatory response which reduces a drive, it is thought to modify some physiological need to smoke. However, as a behavioral act it may also modify or maintain some other motivational mechanisms which are not, as such, generally considered as motives for smoking. Take, as an example, the affective state of an individual.

Some consider the affect system as the primary motivational system (Tomkins, 1962; Izard, 1965). While the scope and complexity of the discussions of these writers concerning the role that affect plays in behavior does not lend itself to summary, in brief, it is viewed as a major subsystem of personality. It is thought

[1] With the exception of Experiment IV, all research reported was supported by grants from the Council for Tobacco Research, U.S.A.

that positive affect leads to integrative behavior and effective functioning, while "negative affect leads to discordance among personality subsystems, nonintegrated behavior, less effective functioning [Izard, 1965, p. 20]." It would appear, then, that any act an individual can take to counteract negative affect would, in most cases, be desirable. Under certain conditions, smoking may accomplish this objective.

As Izard (1965) points out, in this area there is an abundance of terms, e.g., affect, emotion, feeling, mood, sentiment, etc., which are sometimes used interchangeably and sometimes as distinct and separate concepts. In our studies we have been concerned with the affective state labeled *mood* and with the effects that smoking has on mood change under a variety of experimental conditions. Typically in the literature on mood the term is applied to the same aspects of experience and behavior to which it is applied by the layman in everyday use. Nowlis (1965) suggests a general definition of mood that encompasses these applications. According to Nowlis mood is defined as the effect on a person of his own configurations of activity. "These configurations may be conceptualized as fundamental patterns of general functioning and orientation, such as level of activation, level of control, level of concentration, direction of social orientation, and positive (pleasant) or negative (unpleasant) general appraisal [p. 353]."

In several of the investigations which are discussed in this paper, the effects of smoking on mood change were not of primary interest when the study was conducted. These investigations were typically designed to study the effects of smoking on various aspects of psychomotor performance, and measurement of mood was usually incidental. However, these measures, which were obtained from several studies under quite different conditions, suggest some interesting relationships between smoking and mood. Experiment V, however, was designed to evaluate the effects of smoking on mood change when subjects were exposed to a highly stressful film.

GENERAL METHODS

Mood Measurement

In each of the studies that are reported, details as to the particular experimental conditions which were involved will be given. In each case, however, mood measures were obtained immediately before and after a subject participated in the task that was required in the experiment. The Mood Adjective Check List (MACL), because of its ease of administration and scoring and its broad coverage of mood states, was used to measure the subjects' mood in all cases. Steps in the development of this instrument and research utilizing it are discussed in detail by Nowlis (1965).

As Nowlis points out, the MACL is based on a limited but easily accessible form of behavior, the tendency of a person to apply to mood certain adjectives which complete the sentence "I feel _____." Much of the research of Nowlis and his co-workers has been concerned with developing a population of adjectives which best describe a number of dimensions of mood.

The MACL consists of a list of adjectives which describe an individual's mood. The subject rates himself on a four-point scale for an adjective, each adjective being descriptive of a particular mood factor or dimension. For example, the subject is confronted with an adjective such as "relaxed." Following the adjective are four symbols as shown below:

relaxed   VV   V   ?   No

The subject is instructed to circle "VV" if he definitely feels relaxed *at the moment,* "V" if he feels slightly relaxed, "?" if he cannot decide whether he feels relaxed at the moment, and "No" if he definitely does not feel relaxed. The MACL that was used contained adjectives describing the mood factors of aggression, anxiety, surgency, concentration, fatigue, social affection, sadness, and egotism.

A factor score for each of the eight mood factors was determined by adding the total ratings for all the mood adjectives representing a given factor. In summing the ratings, "VV" was assigned a score of 4, "V" was 3, "?" was 2, and "No" was 1. The sum, then, of the ratings on all the adjectives describing a given mood factor was considered as the subject's score for that particular factor and was used for purposes of analysis. While various statistical analyses can be performed on these data, in the studies reported here the primary interest was in whether or not smoking tended to reduce mood fluctuation or change. Consequently, *t* tests were conducted between the scores subjects in the various experimental conditions received on the before and after mood measures in order to determine whether the changes, if any, were significant.

Subjects

Subjects in all the studies consisted of college students who were recruited from the student body at the University of South Dakota. In most cases subjects were paid to participate in the investigations. Typically, on the basis of a questionnaire that a subject completed upon reporting to the laboratory, he was categorized as either a smoker or a nonsmoker. A nonsmoker was defined as an individual who had not used tobacco in any form for at least one year. A smoker was defined as one who regularly smoked a pack or more of cigarettes per 12-hour working day, who used this form of tobacco exclusively or primarily, who consistently inhaled, and who had smoked for at least a year.

Subjects in the nonsmoker group served as controls, while subjects categorized as smokers were randomly assigned to groups designated as "Smoker" or "Smoker-deprived."

RESULTS

Experiment I

In this study (Heimstra, Bancroft, & DeKock, 1967), 60 male subjects were assigned to one of three groups of 20 subjects each. One group consisted of nonsmokers, another of smokers who were allowed to smoke during the experiment, and a third group of smokers who were not allowed to smoke.

TABLE 1

Direction and Significance of Change Between Pretest and
Posttest Mood Factor Scores

Mood factor	Group		
	Nonsmoker	Smoker	Smoker-deprived
Aggression	increase*	–	increase**
Anxiety	–	–	–
Surgency	decrease*	–	–
Concentration	decrease*	decrease*	decrease*
Fatigue	increase**	increase**	increase**
Social affection	decrease*	–	decrease*
Sadness	–	–	–

*p = .05.
**p = .01.

All subjects were required to operate a driving simulator for a 6-hour period without a rest pause. Basically, this task required a subject to continually track a moving target and, in addition, to respond to several subsidiary tasks. A number of performance measures were obtained during the test session, including measures of tracking performance, reaction time, and vigilance. Mood measures were taken before and after the 6-hour test session. The primary objective of the study was to determine whether smoking had any effect on performance in the simulator.

In terms of the performance measures obtained, the results showed no significant differences between smokers and nonsmokers. However, deprived smokers showed significantly more errors on the tracking and vigilance tasks than subjects in the other groups.

The results of the mood analysis are shown in Table 1. It can be seen from this table that, in the case of the smokers, there was a significant change between pretest and posttest mood scores on only two factors—those of concentration and fatigue. In the case of the nonsmokers, significant changes took place in five of the factors and, with the deprived smokers, significant changes occurred in four mood factors.

Experiment II

Subjects were again assigned to nonsmoker, smoker-deprived, and smoker groups. In this investigation (Bancroft, Heimstra, & Warner, 1967), subjects were tested on a pursuit rotary tracking apparatus for 3 consecutive hours without rest. They were also required to respond to a reaction time subsidiary task. In additon to the performance measures, several psychophysiological measures were also obtained, and the MACL was administered before and after the test session. The primary purpose of this study was to determine the effects of smoking deprivation on psychomotor performance.

Twenty subjects were assigned to each of the three groups. However, subjects in each group were further divided into two subgroups, with one subgroup performing on a difficult version of the tracking task and the other subgroup on an easier version. All subjects in the smoker group smoked cigarettes as instructed by the experimenter. They smoked a total of nine cigarettes at 20-minute intervals.

Results of the analysis of performance-measure data showed that tracking performance of the smoker-deprived group was significantly inferior to that of the smokers and the nonsmokers and, during the less difficult task condition, they also had slower reaction times. The physiological measures (skin conductance, blood pressure, and eosinophil count) showed no significant differences between groups.

Analysis of the pretest and posttest mood factor scores for subjects who were tested on the easier of the two tracking tasks revealed a significant change in only the mood dimension of sadness for the nonsmoker group and in concentration for the smoker group. Mood change was much more apparent for subjects who were tested under the more difficult condition. As can be seen from Table 2, only one mood factor (fatigue) showed a significant change in the smoker group, four factors in the nonsmoker group showed significant changes, while five mood factors showed a significant change between the pretest and posttest measures in the case of the smoker-deprived group.

TABLE 2

Direction and Significance of Change Between Pretest and Posttest Mood Factor Scores

Mood factor	Group		
	Nonsmoker	Smoker	Smoker-deprived
Aggression	—	—	—
Anxiety	—	—	—
Surgency	increase**	—	decrease**
Concentration	decrease**	—	decrease**
Fatigue	increase**	increase**	increase**
Social affection	decrease**	—	decrease**
Sadness	—	—	—
Egotism	—	—	decrease**

*p = .05.
**p = .01.

Experiment III

In this study, 45 male subjects were assigned to each of the three groups, i.e., smoker, nonsmoker, and smoker-deprived (15 subjects per group). Subjects performed on a target detection task which required that they attempt to detect an odd letter among a background array of 32 similar letters which were projected on a screen. For example, the target letter might be an R among a background array of B's, or a C among O's and so forth. On half the slides, no target letter was present. A slide was presented every 10 seconds during a test session that lasted 90 minutes. The MACL was administered before and after each test session. This study was aimed at determining whether smoking affected target detection performance. Analysis of the performance measures showed no significant differences between the three groups.

Analysis of the mood change scores is shown in Table 3. In this situation, the only significant changes in mood factors for the smoker group were in the concentration and fatigue factors. There were significant changes in five mood factors in the nonsmoker group and in six mood factors in the smoker-deprived group.

TABLE 3

Direction and Significance of Change Between Pretest and Posttest Mood Factor Scores

Mood factor	Group		
	Nonsmoker	Smoker	Smoker-deprived
Aggression	increase*	–	increase**
Anxiety	–	–	increase*
Surgency	decrease*	–	decrease*
Concentration	decrease**	decrease*	decrease**
Fatigue	increase*	increase*	increase**
Social affection	decrease*	–	decrease*
Sadness	–	–	–
Egotism	–	–	–

*p = .05.
**p = .01.

Experiment IV

The subjects were 50 male and 50 female college students, unpaid volunteers, who were tested for a 1-hour period in a device which involved two types of tracking tasks and a reaction time task. The purpose of the study was to determine if sex differences in psychomotor performance existed; and at the time the study was conducted, smoking was not considered as a variable. However, subjects were

TABLE 4

Direction and Significance of Change Between Pretest and
Posttest Mood Factor Scores

Mood factor	Females group		Males group	
	Smokers	Nonsmokers	Smokers	Nonsmokers
Aggression	–	increase*	–	increase*
Anxiety	–	–	–	–
Surgency	decrease*	decrease*	–	–
Concentration	–	decrease*	–	decrease*
Fatigue	increase*	increase**	increase*	increase*
Social affection	–	decrease*	–	increase**
Sadness	–	–	–	–
Egotism	–	–	–	–

*$p = .05$.
**$p = .01$.

allowed to smoke during the test if they so desired, and all that was recorded on the data sheet was whether or not they had smoked. This was done because it was thought that the physical act of smoking might interfere with operation of the device. The MACL was administered to each subject before and after the test session. At the time of the investigation, the MACL data were not analyzed.

These data were recently analyzed in order to determine if differences in mood change were shown for subjects who smoked during the test session and for those who did not. While there was no smoker-deprived group in this case, it was possible to separate both the male and female subjects into two groups based on whether or not they smoked while being tested in the device. Data sheets for 14 of the female subjects and 20 of the male subjects indicated that they had smoked. On the basis of this classification, the before and after mood factor scores were compared to determine whether significant mood changes had taken place. The results of this analysis are shown in Table 4. In the group of females, there were significant changes in two mood factors in the case of the smokers and in five mood factors with the nonsmokers. With the male subjects, in the smoker group there was one significant change (fatigue) and four significant changes in the nonsmokers.

Experiment V

A total of 231 subjects (all college students) were involved in this investigation—118 women and 113 men. The subjects, as in previous studies, were assigned to groups of nonsmokers, smokers, and deprived smokers. In the case of the women, there were 27 subjects in the nonsmoker group, 46 in the smoker-deprived group, and 45 in the smoker group; while in the case of the males, there were 33

TABLE 5

Direction and Significance of Change Between Pretest and Posttest Mood Factor Scores

Mood factor	Females			Males		
	Nonsmoker	Smoker	Smoker-dep.	Nonsmoker	Smoker	Smoker-dep.
Aggression	increase**	increase**	increase**	increase**	—	increase**
Anxiety	increase*	increase**	increase**	increase**	increase**	increase**
Surgency	decrease**	decrease**	decrease**	decrease**	decrease**	decrease**
Concentration	increase**	increase**	increase**	increase**	increase**	increase**
Fatigue	decrease*	—	decrease**	decrease**	—	decrease**
Social affection	decrease**	decrease**	decrease**	decrease**	decrease**	decrease**
Sadness	increase**	increase**	increase**	increase**	increase**	increase**
Egotism	decrease*	decrease**	decrease**	decrease*	decrease**	decrease**

*$p = .05$.
**$p = .01$.

nonsmokers, 48 smoker-deprived, and 32 smokers. All subjects were paid to participate in the study.

Subjects, who were tested in groups of four or five, completed the MACL and then viewed a film which, based on previous work with a number of films, had been shown to be stressful and would drastically alter all of the mood factors measured by the MACL. The film, entitled *Hiroshima-Nagasaki, August 1945,* is 16 minutes long, black and white, and with sound. It is available from the Center for Mass Communication of the Columbia University Press. Subjects in the smoker groups were required to smoke cigarettes continuously during the showing of the film, while smokers in the deprived group were not permitted to smoke. Immediately after the film, subjects again completed the MACL.

Analysis of the mood change data revealed that significant change occurred in virtually all mood factors for all groups, regardless of whether they smoked, were nonsmokers, or were deprived of cigarettes during the showing of the film. In only three instances did no change take place. In each of these cases, however, smokers were involved. The results of the analysis are shown in Table 5.

In a second phase of this experiment, male subjects were administered the MACL and then were exposed to the film for three showings during which the only "break" was during the two short periods when the film was being rewound. During this period, which lasted approximately 55 minutes, subjects in the smoker group smoked at least three cigarettes, while those in the nonsmoker and smoker-deprived group smoked no cigarettes. After the completion of the session, all subjects again completed the MACL.

In the nonsmoker and smoker-deprived groups, all mood factors showed significant changes between the pretest and posttest administration, with changes being in the direction of those shown in Table 5. However, in the smoker group no significant changes took place in the mood factors of aggression, anxiety, and surgency.

DISCUSSION

In the studies reported here, measures of subjects' mood were obtained before and after subjects were exposed to complex psychomotor or perceptual tasks or to a highly stressful film. During the performance tasks or during the film, some groups of subjects smoked, and other smokers were not permitted to smoke, while still other groups consisted of nonsmokers.

The data obtained from these studies strongly suggests that smoking will modify mood states or, more specifically, will tend to reduce fluctuation or change in mood. Typically, subjects who smoked during the various experimental conditions involving psychomotor or perceptual tasks showed significant mood changes in, at most, two mood factors (fatigue and concentration), while subjects in the smoker-deprived and nonsmoker groups showed change in five or six of the mood factors. Thus, if one compares the number of occurrences of significant mood changes of smokers and nonsmokers in Tables 1 to 4, it can be seen that only eight significant changes took place among the smokers, while 23 changes occurred among the nonsmokers.

It should be emphasized that these studies were not specifically designed to investigate the relationships between smoking and mood, and consequently the designs were such that a number of interesting questions remain unanswered. For example, the question of the relationship between the task itself, smoking, and mood change is not clear. It is probable that there is an optimal lever of difficulty and task-induced stress that will most clearly illustrate the effects that smoking will have on mood change. Thus, when a task is too simple, such as was the case with the "easy" task in Experiment II, there are practically no mood changes shown by subjects in any of the groups. Similarly, when a task or situation is too demanding or too stressful, it is likely that mood change will occur regardless of whether or not an individual smokes. This is demonstrated in Experiment V, where subjects were exposed to a short but highly stressful film dealing with the atomic bombing of Hiroshima and Nagasaki. In this case, virtually all mood factors in all groups showed a significant change. Of some interest, however, is the fact that when the duration of the stressful situation was increased by showing the film several times, the trend of fewer mood changes being demonstrated by the smoker group, in contrast to the nonsmoker and smoker-deprived groups, once again became more obvious. Certainly there are a number of questions concerning situational variables that will have to be answered before we can, with any degree of certainty, draw firm conclusions about effects of smoking on mood change.

Assuming that smoking does indeed modify mood, what practical significance does this have? Admittedly it is interesting to demonstrate that this sort of effect is found, since one of the justifications that many people give for smoking is that it "relaxes" or "calms" them. We have not been able to show, however, that there is any real relationship between mood change, or lack of mood change, and the various psychomotor performance measures that have been obtained in the studies reported. Thus, when correlations were run between change scores of various mood factors and scores on the performance measures, very low correlations were found. While the highest correlations were shown between the fatigue and concentration mood factor change scores and performance, these were still low. It would appear that, for individual subjects, whether or not their mood changed during the test session was not an important determinant of their performance on the psychomotor tasks.

Possibly, mood change, and the effects that smoking may have in modifying or eliminating this change, can be meaningfully considered within the broad and unwieldy concept of "mental health." While any discussion of smoking and mental health rapidly bogs down because of the lack of a definition of mental health, it is often assumed that smoking does play a beneficial role in maintaining this particular condition. If one further assumes that the affective state of the individual has some relationship to mental health and that smoking has some influence on the affective state, then an admittedly tenuous link between smoking and mental health can be hypothesized. If, as Izard (1965) assumes, positive affect leads to integrative behavior and effective functioning, and negative affect leads to nonintegrated behavior and less effective functioning, then an individual who can reduce or minimize negative affect may be "healthier" than an individual who cannot. Smoking may help accomplish this reduction of negative affect. Obviously, we do not have the data available which would permit making a statement of this type with any degree of certainty, but it is an interesting speculation.

REFERENCES

Bancroft, N. R., Heimstra, N. W., & Warner, H. D. Relationship between smoking, psychomotor performance and stress. Report submitted to the Council for Tobacco Research, U.S.A., December 1967.

Heimstra, N. W., Bancroft, N. R., & DeKock, A. R. Effects of smoking upon sustained performance in a simulated driving task. *Annals of the New York Academy of Science,* 1967, **142**, 295-307.

Izard, C. E., Wehmer, G. M., Livsey, W. J., & Jennings, J. R. Affect, awareness, and performance. In S. S. Tomkins & C. E. Izard (Eds.), *Affect, cognition and personality.* New York: Springer, 1965.

Logan, F. A. The smoking habit. In W. A. Hunt (Ed.), *Learning mechanisms in smoking.* Chicago: Aldine, 1970.

Nowlis, V. Research with the mood adjective check list. In S. S. Tomkins & C. E. Izard (Eds.), *Affect, cognition and personality.* New York: Springer, 1965.

Tomkins, S. S. *Affect, imagery, consciousness.* Vol. 1. *The positive affects.* New York: Springer, 1962.

13

GENERAL COMMENTS ON PROBLEMS OF MOTIVATION RELEVANT TO SMOKING[1]

Neal E. Miller
Rockefeller University

Evidence (Damon, this volume) demonstrates the rapidity and universality with which smoking and other uses of tobacco have been adopted, sometimes despite strong cultural resistance, by people in virtually all of the societies in the world who have been exposed. We also have had ample evidence on the extreme difficulty which many people have in stopping smoking. These two types of evidence indicate that some strong form of basic biological motivation probably is involved.

Although I am not an expert on smoking, I would like to direct your attention to some general points about psychological research that I hope will be useful in evaluating and planning investigations of the motivational variables influencing this particular category of behavior.

NEEDS VERSUS DRIVES

In order to survive, organisms must be motivated to approach common things in the environment that are good for them and to avoid those that are bad. But this is not the best of all possible worlds; there is the problem of evil. Thus there are some exceptions to the proposition that organisms are built in such a way that they are motivated to do things that are good for them. Quite understandably, these exceptions must involve events that are either rare or of recent orgin, so that they have not had a long time to exert a strong evolutionary pressure.

Because of the exceptions, psychological theory must distinguish between *needs*, which are something that the organism requires to be healthy, and *drives*, which motivate the subject to seek out the goal objects or activities that serve as a reward for those drives. For example, somebody exposed to carbon monoxide may have a desperate need to escape it but no strong drive to motivate him to do anything about that vital need. Similarly, patients with pernicious anemia may need to eat

[1] Supported by U.S. Public Health Service research grant MH 13189.

raw liver to live, but very few of them find this rewarding; in fact, most of them hate it. On the other side of the picture, some of us who are getting a little heavy may not need any more fattening food but still are motivated strongly to continue to eat it, and find it extremely hard to resist such food when it is on the table. Similarly, an intravenous injection of cocaine or amphetamine may produce such a great rewarding sensation of ecstasy that the person is driven to desperate efforts to secure the drug that will allow him to repeat that experience, but such an injection may satisfy no biological need and may actually be harmful.

DELAY WEAKENS REINFORCEMENT

The problem of the relationship between motivation and what is good for the individual is further complicated by the fact that an immediate reward or punishment is much more effective than a delayed one. Thus it is all too easy for an animal or person to learn to do something that has good consequences in the short run but bad ones in the long run.

By bringing up the foregoing points I do not mean to rule out the possibility, which certainly merits further rigorous investigation, that smoking has beneficial effects; I merely mean to emphasize certain alternatives that must be considered before coming to that conclusion.

THREE MECHANISMS MOTIVATING SELF-ADMINISTRATION

I have distinguished between drives and needs, immediate rewards and delayed ones. Next I would like to describe three different mechanisms for motivating self-administration or addiction.

The first is illustrated by an experiment by Davis, Lulenski, and Miller (1968). Rats were injected automatically with a small dose of a fairly quick-acting barbiturate via a chronic catheter into the jugular vein every time that they pressed a bar. With this dose they did not learn to press the bar under comfortable circumstances. But it is known that fast-acting barbiturates can produce a prompt reduction in the strength of fear, and that a reduction in the strength of fear can serve as a reward (Miller, 1964). Therefore it is not surprising that when the rats were made fearful by being given occasional electric shocks which they could do nothing to escape, they learned to press the bar to give themselves the injection of the barbiturate that reduced their fear. Because of the evidence presented in this volume that cigarettes do have a calming effect and also apparently reduce anger which, in turn, also can be an occasion for fear and conflict, it seems plausible that a reduction in fear and other tensions may be one of the rewards for smoking cigarettes; and, since fear and conflict can be harmful, even producing psychosomatic damage, such as lesions in the stomach (Miller, 1969), such a reduction in fear could be beneficial. In this case, one would expect people to smoke more when they are tense and anxious, something that seems to be true. But if this first mechanism were the only factor, one would not expect people to smoke at all when they are calm, a prediction that certainly is false.

As an illustration of the second mechanism, I would like to present some data that Dr. Jack Davis and I collected but never carried quite to the point of publication before an epidemic of Pseudomonas infection wiped out the experiment and he left for a position elsewhere. We found that if rats were given a very small injection of morphine through a chronic intravenous catheter every time they pressed a bar, vitually none of them would spontaneously learn to press the bar for this small dose. But if we had previously given them increasingly large doses of morphine and then stopped these, so that the rats were suffering from withdrawal symptoms, virtually every one of them would learn to press the bar for morphine. This illustrates, of course, what is well known, that at least part of the addictive quality of morphine and other opiates derives from the fact that withdrawal creates very unpleasant symptoms that the drug temporarily alleviates. Anecdotal evidence suggests that nicotine can function in this same way. But in unpublished work in my laboratory, Dr. Ronald Paolino has joined that group of other investigators who have failed to secure clear-cut evidence on rats for addiction based on withdrawal from nicotine. Nevertheless, this problem certainly seems to be worthy of further investigation.

Finally, general clinical evidence, as well as a certain amount of experimental evidence, strongly suggests the third mechanism, namely, that certain drugs such as cocaine and amphetamine may produce a direct pleasant or even ecstatic experience that serves as a reward without the necessity for any clear-cut previous drive of tension, anxiety, or withdrawal symptoms.

The foregoing three types of effects or mechanisms are not necessarily mutually exclusive. For example, morphine almost certainly has the first, anxiety-reducing effect along with its ability to produce noxious withdrawal symptoms which, in turn, are corrected by a further dose of the drug. Furthermore, there is some evidence that a sufficient dose of it can produce a pleasant high on the first occasion without the necessity for a background of strong fear and tension (Schuster & Thompson, 1969). This absence of need for fear and tension, however, could stand further investigation.

WHY ARE ANIMALS LESS STRONGLY MOTIVATED THAN PEOPLE?

An important problem is the extent to which the motivation for cigarettes and other forms of tobacco involves one or more of the three foregoing mechanisms. To date, the use of experimental animals to secure rigorously controlled answers to such questions has not been uniformly successful. The rapidity with which people all over the world have adopted the use of tobacco contrasts sharply with the difficulty that most experimenters seem to have had to date in producing similarly strong motivations in experiments on animals. If indeed the proneness quickly to become strongly motivated to consume tobacco is a peculiarly human trait, this phenomenon might have interesting psychological and pharmacological implications and might provide a clue to crucial features of its mode of action.

The difficulties of animal experiments on self-administration raise some interesting questions: (a) Is the difficulty because nicotine is not the motivationally active principle? (b) Is it because the rewarding effects of nicotine are peculiar to the species of man and are not exhibited by lower animals? (c) Is it because the exact circumstances of smoking and other uses of tobacco are not mimicked closely enough by the animal experiments?

I presume that the first of these questions can and will be answered by more ingenious techniques for forcing animals to inhale cigarette smoke during a habituation period and allowing them to do so during subsequent tests for self-administration. But the other uses of tobacco seem to indicate that the vaporization and combustion involved in cigarettes are not an essential element of administering the active agent.

We might be tempted to take advantage of the fact that tobacco is used in a number of different forms to design an experiment to see the degree to which one form can be substituted for another. But in interpreting such experiments, we should bear in mind the fact that drives can be *channeled* (Miller, 1959, pp. 263-266), so that, for example, hunger may become an appetite for a specific kind of food prepared in a specific way. Thus, certain people in our own Midwest may consider sweet corn a delicacy but be revolted at the thought of eating snails, while those in France may have exactly the opposite reaction. Even rats may have to become habituated to a particular type and form of food before it serves as an effective reward for them. This is a phenomenon that merits much further experimental study in general. Evidence also suggests that it can apply to the consumption of tobacco.

To turn to the second and third questions above, one of the ways in which people seem to differ from primates and primates from rats is in the ability to respond to somewhat more delayed rewards and to use various cues as a basis for secondary reinforcement to bridge a gap between a response and a reward. This suggests studying the speed of onset of the rewarding action of a dose of nicotine or cigarette smoke. The onset of the rewarding action could be similar to the time of onset of a physiological symptom such as a change in heart rate or blood pressure, or it could be somewhat different. One would expect that there should be some relationship between the rewarding, and possibly the satiating, effects of smoking and the pattern of puffs and also the optimal length of a cigarette. Similarly, it could be that holding the cigarette in the hand or the tobacco in the cheek could provide cues to bridge any appreciable gap, if indeed there is one, between the initial act and the rewarding effect. If it should be that a delayed-reward factor is important, the results of animal experiments might be improved by providing extremely perspicuous cues that come on immediately when the act of self-administration, pressing a bar or taking a puff, is initiated and persist for some time thereafter. If we can produce an animal model that involves strong motivation comparable to that observed in many people, the ability to intervene in a rigorously controlled way should accelerate our analysis of the motivational factors involved in smoking.

TEST FOR JOYFUL AS WELL AS STRESSFUL AROUSAL

To turn to another topic, I have mentioned briefly the possible role of stress, and it has come up in a number of other places in this volume. But it may be that the key variable is arousal, whether it be from aversive stimuli as in stress or, quite the opposite, from an exciting, joyous occasion. We need more investigation of the effects of happy arousal.

MUSCARINIC VERSUS NICOTINIC CODING IN THE BRAIN?

Finally, I want to mention a type of work going on in my laboratory that may lead us into research that is somewhat more relevant to the subject of this volume. For some time, various students in my laboratory have been studying the effects of injecting, via a chronic cannula directly into the brain, minute quantities of presumptive transmitter substances or drugs that affect the action of such substances (Grossman, 1960; Miller, 1965; Slangen & Miller, 1969). We have found that in the perifornical area of the rat's brain, minute injections of cholinergic substances such as acetylcholine or carbachol will cause completely satiated rats to drink water and to be motivated to work to get water; while in the same area via the same cannula, minute injections of adrenergic substances such as norepinephrine or epinephrine will cause satiated rats to eat food and to work to get it.

Carrying this work further, one of my associates, Dr. Sarah Leibowitz (1970, 1972) has shown that the adrenergic effects may be separated into two mutually antagonistic alpha and beta components. Alpha receptors are concentrated in the perifornical area and in the ventromedial nucleus. Stimulation of them inhibits the stop-eating action of the ventromedial nucleus and hence releases eating and hunger-motivated behavior. Beta receptors are concentrated in the perifornical area and in the lateral hypothalamus. Stimulation of them inhibits the hunger-inducing action of the lateral hypothalamus and hence has the opposite effect of functioning to stop eating.

At present a postdoctoral student in my laboratory is investigating the possibility that some central cholinergic systems may be organized into muscarinic and nicotinic effects that are antagonistic like the alpha and beta adrenergic ones. He is Dr. Gary Berntson, and he has been studying (1971) aggression, the so-called "cold" prey-stalking reactions, and defensive threat reactions that can be elicited by electrical stimulation of certain points in the hypothalamus and other related areas in the brain of the cat. He is extending these studies to the effects of chemostimulation. His preliminary findings indicate that, in certain locations of the cat's brain, aggression and prey stalking can be elicited by minute injections of a cholinergic agonist, and that this effect is muscarinic. He is now starting to try to find out whether or not there is a central nicotinic system that may be antagonistic to the muscarinic one. If such a system should exist, it might be at least part of the explanation for the effects of smoking on aggression. The irritability of habitual smokers who are deprived of cigarettes is well known; in fact, years ago a group of us (Sears, Hovland, & Miller, 1940) made successful use of it, along with some other diabolical frustrations, in experimentally arousing human aggression. The present volume contains evidence from both human and animal studies indicating that smoking can have the opposite effect of calming aggression. Dr. Berntson may be able to find a central mechanism mediating such an effect.

REFERENCES

Berntson, G. G. Blockade and release of hypothalamically and naturally elicited aggressive behaviors in cats following midbrain lesions. Unpublished doctoral dissertation, University of Minnesota, 1971.

Davis, J. D., Lulenski, G. C., & Miller, N. E. Comparative studies of barbiturate self-administration. *International Journal of Addictions,* 1968, 3, 207-214.

Grossman, S. P. Eating or drinking in satiated rats elicited by adrenergic or cholinergic stimulation, respectively, of the lateral hypothalamus. *Science,* 1960, **132**, 301-302.

Leibowitz, S. F. Hypothalamic β-adrenergic "satiety" system antagonizes an α-adrenergic "hunger" system in the rat. *Nature,* 1970, **226**, 963-964.

Leibowitz, S. F. *Central adrenergic receptors and the regulation of hunger and thirst.* New York: Association for Research in Nervous and Mental Diseases, 1972.

Miller N. E. Liberalization of basic S-R concepts: Extensions to conflict behavior, motivation and social learning. In S. Koch (Ed.), *Psychology: A study of a science.* Vol. 2. New York: McGraw-Hill, 1959.

Miller N. E. The analysis of motivational effects illustrated by experiments on amylobarbitone sodium. In H. Steinberg, A. V. S. de Reuck, & J. Knight (Eds.), *Animal behaviour and drug action.* London: Churchill, 1964.

Miller, N. E. Chemical coding of behavior in the brain. *Science,* 1965, **148**, 328-338.

Miller, N. E. Psychosomatic effects of specific types of training. *Annals of the New York Academy of Sciences,* 1969, **159**, 1025-1040.

Schuster, C. R., & Thompson, T. Self-administration of and behavioral dependence on drugs. *Annual Review of Pharmacology,* 1969, **10**, 483-502.

Sears, R. R., Hovland, C. I., & Miller, N. E. Minor studies of aggression. I. Measurement of aggressive behavior. *Journal of Psychology,* 1940, **9**, 275-295.

Slangen, J. L., & Miller, N. E. Pharmacological tests for the function of hypothalamic norepinephrine in eating behavior. *Physiology and Behavior,* 1969, **4**, 543-552.

14

SOME COMMONALITIES AMONG THE PRECEDING REPORTS OF STUDIES ON THE PSYCHOLOGY OF SMOKING

Joseph D. Matarazzo
University of Oregon Medical School

This discussion is addressed primarily to the four chapters in this section which are reports of original investigations, namely, those by Schachter, by Thomas, by Hutchinson and Emley, and by Heimstra.

Although the approaches and the experimental methodologies of these four research teams have differed markedly, the results of several of them have shown an interesting degree of apparent similarity. For example, the human Ss in the Hutchinson & Emley study showed a decrease in aggressiveness (as measured by degree of masseter contractions) when given small doses of nicotine. Apparently consistent with this is the finding by Heimstra that only his smoker group (those allowed to smoke) showed *no* increase in aggressive mood during each of four stress-producing, monotonous tasks. Nonsmokers showed the most increase in aggressive mood under the same conditions in four out of four tasks. The deprived smoker (i.e., the smoker not allowed to smoke) also showed an increase in aggressive mood, but only in two of the four stress situations. Heimstra's smokers, on the other hand, quite probably found themselves in a boring and therefore stress-producing trap under these conditions of experimenter-induced monotony. Possibly reasoning from prior experience with similar situations in which they had no cigarettes available and in which their anger mounted accordingly, these smokers lighted up a cigarette to *equalize* for this expected increase in aggression in order to *maintain* their initial mood without change. This possibility is suggested by the fact that only the smokers who were allowed to smoke maintained themselves with almost no mood change on all the mood dimensions sampled, even though the four monotonous tasks produced verbalizations of roughly equal feelings of fatigue in *all three* groups, and the three groups did *not* differ in their error scores. The nonsmokers and deprived-smokers, under the same four stress conditions, had changes in such mood dimensions as aggression (increase), surgency (decrease), concentration (decrease), and social affection (decrease). Possibly smoking maintains one's psychological "steady state" in an otherwise stressful situation.

Inasmuch as it takes only a minute or two for a subject to fill it out, Hutchinson & Emley might wish to use Heimstra's *Mood Adjective Check List* with their human subjects in future research. Would their *S*s have shown a *decrease* in aggressive mood when nicotine was given (even subthreshold to taste in water), or an *increase* in aggressive mood when a placebo was given instead? Also, it would be very interesting for Hutchinson & Emley to see what correlation they might get between the degree of aggressive mood reported by a subject on the *Mood Adjective Check List* and the magnitude of the masseter contraction at the same time. In other words, do mood and muscle tone covary in a positive and linear relationship? Such an analysis would provide concurrent validation for their masseter contraction measure as an index of aggressive feelings.

There is a potential overlap between Schachter's reported results and those of Heimstra and also those of Hutchinson & Emley. Importantly, the relationship is seen from just the opposite perspective. When in a shock-stress situation, Schachter's smokers showed a provocative linear increase in the amount of shocks (pain) they could endure as a function of the amount of nicotine they were simultaneously ingesting. That is, when they were "smoking" an unlit cigarette (*no* nicotine), their mean endurance threshold was a mere 13 shocks accepted. When smoking the *low*-nicotine cigarette, this mean endurance threshold increased to 19 shocks accepted. And when smoking the cigarette with the *highest* nicotine content, the endurance threshold reached a mean of 24.5 shocks accepted. Although the methodologies among these studies certainly differ enough to make such reasoning highly speculative, it would appear that under the condition of highest nicotine intake, Schachter's *S*s are figuratively if not literally gritting their teeth less (in the Hutchinson and Emley sense) and concurrently are *not* experiencing an increase in their feelings of aggressiveness toward the world.

Hollywood movies during the 1930–1960 era always seemed to show Humphrey Bogart, John Wayne, and similar heroes lighting up a cigarette before the showdown scene. Schachter's research suggests this common Hollywood portrayal of the tranquilizing effect of nicotine was correct insofar as it allowed the hero to "take more on the chin" than he otherwise could be expected to endure. The linear increase in heart rate of Schachter's *S*s also fits in with this Cannon-type of "fight-flight" or homeostatic model—or alternately, Selye's more modern stress model, which he briefly reviews in the introductory chapter of this volume. Schachter's nonsmokers under the same conditions failed to parallel those of his smokers, in the sense that smoking did not increase their shock threshold; and this, too, is not at all unlike the *mood* data that Heimstra has reported for his nonsmokers. Heimstra's nonsmokers differed markedly in mood change relative to his smokers under the same four conditions. The smoker-deprived group experienced mood changes similar to those of the nonsmokers, again suggesting that Heimstra's experienced smokers are aware of their own endurance thresholds in Schachter's sense and use nicotine to maintain a steady state (or even an *increase* in tonus) when their current life situation changes to one of increased stress. Schachter's other results, showing an increase in heart rate under shock stress, are also consistent with the type of theorizing which he, Hutchinson and Emley, and Heimstra have been doing. There are differences, of course, among the findings of these three studies which eventually will have to be understood.

I turn now to Thomas' results of her 25-year longitudinal study of Johns Hopkins medical students who are now well into their careers. Among other things, she has shown us a positive relationship between the quantity of cigarettes smoked daily and such measures as heart rate, anxiety score, anger score (although this latter fell short of statistical significance), and consumption rates for coffee and alcohol.

At first blush it would appear that Thomas' finding of a trend toward a higher chronic anger score in her continuing-smoker group is just the opposite of those one would expect from the Hutchinson and Emley and the Heimstra data. According to the results from these two other laboratories, the smoker smokes to *reduce* anger. This suggests that a group of *continuing* smokers should have a *lower* lever of anger than nonsmokers. However, this reasoning is not altogether necessary. Rather, using Thomas' data we might reason alternatively as follows: Smokers as a group tend to have a very *high* level of anger relative to nonsmokers. However, these individuals have learned over time that cigarette smoking reduces this high anger level, although never quite to the same low level of anger as that which characterizes the level found in the nonsmokers. Modest support for this reasoning can be seen in Thomas' Table 1. Her continuing smokers have a higher anger score (21.9) than her nonsmokers (17.8); but her former smokers have an even higher score (22.2) than her smokers (21.9).

Thomas' personality-temperament results, showing that smokers drink more coffee and more alcohol, and have higher heart rates, more anxiety, more anger, etc., are consistent with the hypothesis that her smokers are physiologically in a much greater state of *reactivity* relative to the nonsmoker. This is also not inconsistent with Schachter's results and those of the other panelists.

The studies included in this section also can be viewed in terms of two of the three models into which Dunn (this volume) has conceptualized the studies to date on psychology and smoking. The study by Thomas fits Dunn's first model, namely, *a comparative analysis of smokers and nonsmokers.* This is not surprising inasmuch as Dr. Thomas began this study several decades ago when such comparative studies represented the most frequent methodological model or approach employed by investigators in this area. The theoretical chapter by Eysenck follows quite nicely on the heels of Dunn's critique. In it Eysenck has reviewed the strengths and limitations of these early descriptive and comparative studies as a lead-in to his view that the development of a scientific field must depend, ultimately, on the capacity of that area to generate a miniature theoretical model. This latter, as we know, would both encompass the empirical findings from Dunn's two more primitive classes (the comparative-analysis and direct-interrogation approach), and also would have the power to identify new directions for research not otherwise obvious from these two other approaches. Dunn has said of this third approach that it generates questions such as: If X then Y (see third row of his Table 2). In Eysenck's scholarly discussion, he has reviewed both his still-developing miniature theoretical personality system *and* numerous examples of Dunn's Type 3 studies which his miniature theory has generated in the area of smoking behavior. The other three investigative chapters in this section (those by Hutchinson and Emley, Heimstra, and Schachter), in common with Eysenck's work, more closely fit this type of research in the language of Dunn than they do his first two research strategies. These three research teams were less interested in how smokers differed from nonsmokers than they were in the scientifically more heuristic or robust approach of utilizing the smoking behavior, per se, as a mirror of more general psychological states or traits— and in designing new experiments therefrom.

As I mentioned earlier, all four studies seem to agree that smoking is a response somehow related to an individual's maintenance of a "steady state," whether this requires a *decrease* in the external stimulation or stress or an *increase* in it; and also that ups and downs in feelings of aggression may be one of the mood states that are critical in the life space of the smoker.

Several years ago such a personality state (aggressive mood) would have been difficult to assimilate for personality and smoking investigators who, in those days, employed the comparative-analysis approach. Anxiety and extroversion were two highly ubiquitous states or traits found in the majority of these early comparative studies. Aggression failed to loom prominently as a personality characteristic of smokers a decade ago (Matarazzo & Saslow, 1960). Yet in a recent review, Smith (1970) found that such an aggressive personality dimension was studied in 32 analyses in 19 studies, and smokers were found to show more of it than nonsmokers in 27 of these 32 analyses. The studies discussed here are good examples of how this trait of aggressivity, found in almost all of these comparative analyses, can now be used as the *independent* variable in future researches. Thus, following Dunn's synergistic design, investigators can now reason as follows: Given the postulate that the smoker uses smoking to moderate his covert response of "hostility" or "aggression" ("rebelliousness," in Smith's terminology), then if we place the smoker in a situation of stress which elicits such response, we should expect a reduction in that response under a smoking condition relative to a no-smoking condition. The miniature theoretical model proposed by Schachter involving "attribution" may be an even more powerful framework within which to generate new research leads than the anxiety-stress model of Cannon which I have used for expository purposes above.

I am aware that I have made a number of speculative leaps in this brief review of potential similarities across the four investigations reported in this section. My excuse is that it is the function of a discussant to behave like a honeybee and to aid in the process of crossfertilization. I am aware that I have dealt too lightly with "Nesbitt's Paradox" in my suggestion that smoking may help to produce a psychological "steady state"; but this confusion and "noise" which I undoubtedly have left in the system hopefully will be frustrating enough to motivate our four investigators to further pursue the development of their own conceptual models.

REFERENCES

Matarazzo, J. D., & Saslow, G. Psychological and related characteristics of smokers and nonsmokers. *Psychological Bulletin*, 1960, 57, 493-513.

Smith, G. M. Personality and smoking: A review of the empirical literature. In W. A. Hunt (Ed.) *Learning mechanisms in smoking.* Chicago: Aldine, 1970.

15

SMOKING ATTITUDES AND PRACTICES IN SEVEN PRELITERATE SOCIETIES[1]

Albert Damon
With the collaboration of P. Maranda, E. K. Maranda, J. F. Gehan,
M. J. Konner, M. S. Konner, D. D. Mitchell, J. N. Mitchell,
R. B. Pollnac, M. C. Robbins, H. M. Ross, and J. Rutherford

The purpose of this study is to determine whether there are social reasons for smoking, apart from individual motives such as personal psychodynamics, gratification, habit, or addiction. Tobacco's firm hold on its users is shown by its worldwide adoption wherever it is not specifically forbidden, as by Islam or Seventh-Day Adventists, and by the difficulty of reducing consumption in countries like Britain and the United States, where its hazards have been widely advertised. The hypothesis is that part of tobacco's appeal may reflect strong social stimulus or support, whether overt or covert.

To this end, surveys were conducted according to a standardized format in seven preliterate or "primitive" societies (as defined by the World Health Organization, 1968) as opportunity arose, four in Melanesia (Solomon Islands) and three in sub-Saharan Africa. The Solomon Island societies were investigated in connection with a Harvard-Peabody Museum long-range research project on cultural and biomedical relationships (Damon, in press). Two Solomon Islands groups were on Malaita Island: namely, the Lau, fisherman living in a saltwater lagoon (P. Maranda and E. K. Maranda, ethnographers), and the Baegu, a neighboring group of inland shifting cultivators (H. M. Ross). The two other Solomon societies were from Bougainville Island: the Nagovisi, living inland from the southwest coast (D. D. Mitchell and J. N. Mitchell), and the Aita, living at altitudes of about 3,200 feet in the Emperor Range in the north (J. Rutherford). In extent of acculturation to Western or

[1] Supported by the National Institute of General Medical Sciences, the National Science Foundation, the National Clearinghouse for Smoking and Health, and the Council for Tobacco Research, U.S.A. The Solomons research, part of the Human Adaptability Section of the International Biological Program, was conducted with the permission and kind assistance of the Administrations of the British Solomon Islands Protectorate and the Territory of Papua and New Guinea, Commonwealth of Australia.

cosmopolitan ways of life, the order was Nagovisi, Lau, Baegu, and Aita, from most to least.

The three African groups were the Buganda, a rural population near Masaka, 80 miles from Kampala, in southeastern Uganda (Robbins & Pollnac, 1969) and the Zhun/twa (!Kung) Bushmen and Herero of northwestern Botswana (M. J. Konner and M. S. Konner). The Bushmen were nomadic hunters and gatherers, living in flexible bands, whereas the Herero were more sedentary cattle-keepers, living in small villages at widely separated cattle posts. In state of acculturation, the Buganda would rank first among the seven groups, having been under British administration for about 100 years. The Herero would be equivalent to the Nagovisi, while the Bushmen followed the most traditional and least acculturated way of life.

In addition to the seven surveys, a detailed search was made (by J. F. Gehan) through data on 26 Oceanian societies in the Human Relations Area Files at Harvard, for the social settings and roles of tobacco usage.

SUBJECTS AND METHODS

In each society the ethnographers, who were well acquainted with their respondents and fluent in their languages, selected a small sample of 14 to 38 subjects, covering both sexes, a wide range of adult ages, and a range of religious affiliation. The latter was important because Moslems (29% of the Buganda) and Seventh-Day Adventists (23% of the Baegu and 17% of the Aita) forbid smoking. All of the Lau and Bushmen, 38% of the Baegu, and 7 to 10% of the Nagovisi, Aita, and Buganda were pagan. All of the Herero were German Protestants, who are permitted to smoke.

Contact with tobacco, to an extent sufficient for the habit to become prevalent, dates to about 1900 for the Lau and Baegu, to whom it was introduced by native workmen returning from European-managed plantations. Although the Nagovisi were aware that tobacco was grown by their neighbors to the south on Bougainville, the Siuai and Buin, in the early years of the twentieth century, smoking really began with the introduction of pipes and tobacco by Catholic missionaries in the 1930s. The Aita have been in regular contact with Western culture only since 1965, but so rapid has been the pace of acculturation that only 7.2% of the representative present sample were pagan. The Buganda have been exposed to tobacco for roughly a century; the Herero and Bushmen, since before 1900. All seven groups smoked locally grown tobacco, as well as cured tobacco of Western origin; six groups cultivated their own, and the Bushmen obtained it from the Herero.

A questionnaire originally devised and completed among the Lau by P. Maranda was modified as required for the other groups. It contained questions concerning the fact of smoking, amount and type of tobacco smoked, context of smoking, attitudes toward smoking, its effect on appetite, and the number of days one could abstain.

RESULTS

Results for the seven groups are summarized in the table. No easy generalization is possible, but a few trends can be discerned. All adults smoked as much as possible, unless forbidden by religion. The Herero and Bushmen, particularly the latter, had a much more positive attitude toward smoking than the other five groups and were the least able to abstain for more than 3 days. The Aita tended to respond idiosyncratically, their answers to "closed" questions ("Is tobacco a food?") being usually affirmative or conforming to what they believed the ethnographer wanted them to say. To "open" questions ("What is tobacco like?"), they rarely volunteered information. Their responses therefore appear frequently at the extremes of the rank order for the seven groups. For the Bushmen and Herero most items, particularly the "virtues of smoking" and "social and psychological effects," were administered as "closed" questions. This, together with their minimal acculturation, may account for the occasional appearance of the Bushmen at the extremes of the rank order.

The several groups had been exposed to varying amounts of health information or religious antismoking propaganda—by Seventh-Day Adventists in the Solomon Islands and by Muslims in Uganda, as already stated. Such exposure or indoctrination of course influenced their responses—for example, about 45% of all respondents were aware of a health hazard in moderate and heavy smoking. This held true even among the Herero and Bushmen, who had had very little antismoking exposure. One wonders why so many of them felt that smoking might be hazardous.

Except for the Herero, and even more the Bushmen, the social benefits of smoking were minor and incidental. In the other five groups the great preponderance of satisfactions from smoking were personal and individual. Few respondents could identify any specific advantage derived from smoking, though 47% felt it improved one's public appearance. Nevertheless, a substantial proportion, 41% over the five groups, felt unable to abstain for even one day. There was general agreement (68%) that tobacco decreases appetite. The Herero and Bushmen, however, attributed social as well as personal advantages to tobacco. For example, 47% of the other five groups, but 71% of the Herero and 80% of the Bushmen, felt that smoking improves one's public appearance. Similarly, they felt to a much greater degree that smoking increases social rapport and kindness toward others. The Herero and Bushmen felt, to a greater extent than the others, that tobacco increases appetite.

It is of considerable interest that even in these seven societies, where smoking begins in childhood, 48% of all respondents stated that children are forbidden to smoke, and another 33% considered smoking "bad" for children. The ethnographers for the Baegu and Bushmen suspected that their disapproval was for selfish rather than altruistic or health reasons—that is, tobacco being scarce and highly prized, adults preferred to keep it for themselves. In any case, the discrepancy between prescribed and actual behavior seems to be widespread among mankind.

About half (44%) of the smokers in all seven groups had been initiated into smoking by family members, and another 27% by friends; but apart from general sociability and its occasional use in trade, tobacco did not enter into formal transactions or relationships among kin.

Among the Solomon Islanders there was little incorporation of tobacco into their myths, unlike betel nut. The pagan Lau forbade smoking during ritual

TABLE

Smoking in Seven "Primitive" Societies

	Lau[a]	Baegu[a]	Nagovisi[b]	Aita (Sample 1)[b]	Aita (Sample 2)[b]	Buganda[c]	Zhun/twa Bushmen[d]	Herero[d]	Range%
	1	1	2	2	2	3	4	4	
No. of respondents	14 (100)	26 (100)	18 (100)	86 (100)	17 (100)	45 (100)	14 (100)	14 (100)	
Smokers	14 (100)	20 (77)	18 (100)	51 (59)	9 (53)	38 (84)	14 (100)	12 (85)	
Male	7	10	10	28	—	29	7	6	
Female	7	10	8	23	—	9	7	6	
Nonsmokers	0 (0)	6 (23)	0 (0)	35 (41)	8 (47)	7[f] (16)	0 (0)	2[h] (15)	
Age range	23–94	20–87	17–65	21–50	21–50	10–81	16–70	18–65	
Religion:									
R. Cath.		10 (38)	16 (89)	38 (44)		13 (34)			
Anglican									
Methodist				28 (33)					
7th-Day Adv.		6 (23)		14 (16)					
Other Prot.						12 (32)	14 (100)	14 (100)	
Muslim						11 (29)			
Pagan	14 (100)	10 (38)	2 (11)	6 (7)		3 (8)			
Total	14 (100)	26 (99)	18 (100)	86 (100)		38 (100)	14 (100)	14 (100)	
Amount smoked per day	1/7 to 2 oz.	1/7 to 2 oz.	1/14 to 1 oz.	1/28 to 1 oz.		0 to 10 cigarettes	2–35 pipes	0–35 pipes	
Context:									
Anytime/anywhere	13 (93)	26 (100)	18 (100)		9 (100)	0 (0)	14 (100)	12 (86)	0–100
Alone only	1 (7)					8 (21)			7–21
At home						10 (26)			

In public only						13 (34)		1 (7)	7-34
No answer			18 (100)			7 (18) non-smokers		1 (7)	7-100
Attitude toward others' smoking:									
Object to it					7 (41)[e]				
It's bad	1 (7)	6 (23)				9 (24)		1 (7)	7-24
It's good	4 (29)	4 (15)				26 (68)	8 (57)	11 (79)	15-79
Their own business	5 (36)	10 (38)	18 (100)			2 (5)			5-100
Stimulates own smoking	3 (21)	6 (23)					14 (100)[i]	12 (86)[i]	21-100
No answer	1 (7)				10 (59)	1 (3)	6 (43)	2 (14)	7-59
Awareness of health hazard:									
Not hazardous			1[illegible] (56)		7 (41)	14 (37)	7 (50)	6 (43)	37-56
No opinion	5 (36)	12 (46)					1 (7)	2 (14)	7-46
Surprised at question	5 (36)	6 (23)							23-36
Is hazardous	4 (29)	8 (31)[e]	[illegible] (44)		7 (41)	24 (63)	6 (43)	5 (36)	29-63
Possibly hazardous					3 (18)			1 (7)	7-18
Children's smoking:									
Permitted		10 (38)	2 (11)		1 (6)	10 (27)	2 (14)	2 (14)	6-38
Forbidden	13 (93)	8 (31)	16 (89)		16 (94)		9 (64)	5 (36)	31-94
Bad for them	1 (7)	8 (31)				28 (73)	3 (21)	7 (50)	7-73
Age when started to smoke:									
Below 10		g	6 (33)			3 (8)		1 (7)	7-100

TABLE (continued)

	Lau[a]	Baegu[a]	Nagovisi[b]	Aita (Sample 1)[b]	Aita (Sample 2)[b]	Buganda[c]	Zhun/twa Bushmen[d]	Herero[d]	Range%
	1	1		2	2	3	4	4	
10-14			12 (67)				3 (21)	4 (29)	21-67
15-19	14 (100)	26 (100)			1 (11)	28 (74)	5 (36)	4 (29)	11-100
20-24					2 (22)		6 (43)	4 (29)	22-43
25-29					6 (67)				
No answer						7 (18)		1 (7)	7-18
Smoking initiated by:									
Family	8 (57)	16 (62)	5 (28)		6 (67)	8 (27)	5 (36)	7 (50)	27-67
Friends	2 (14)	8 (31)	10 (56)		7 (0)	13 (43)		1 (7)	0-56
Others	4 (29)	2 (8)	3 (17)		3 (33)	9 (30)	9 (64)	6 (43)	8-64
Virtues of smoking—strength:									
Decreases						14 (37)	2 (14)	2 (14)	14-37
No effect	10 (71)	16 (62)	14 (78)		16 (94)	12 (32)		7 (50)	32-94
Increases	4 (29)	10(38)	4 (22)		1 (6)	10 (26)	12 (86)	5 (36)	6-86
No answer						2 (5)			
Virtues of smoking—wisdom:									
Decreases	11 (79)	16 (62)	9 (50)		16 (94)	5 (13)	1 (7)	3 (21)	7-94
No effect	3 (21)	10 (38)	9 (50)		1 (6)	24 (63)	13 (93)	11 (79)	6-93
Increases						6 (16)			
No answer						3 (18)			
Friendliness, cleverness, agility:									
Decreases						4 (10)	1 (7)	1 (7)	7-10

	(1)	(2)	(3)	(4)	(5)	(6)	(7)	Range
No effect	12 (86)	16 (62)	5 (28)	15 (88)	5 (13)	13 (93)	13 (93)	13-88
Increases	2 (14)	10 (38)	13 (72)	2 (12)	27 (72)	13 (93)	13 (93)	12-93
No answer					2 (5)			
Working capacity:								
Decreases					10 (26)	1 (7)	1 (7)	7-26
No effect	9 (64)	16 (62)	8 (44)		12 (32)			32-64
Increases	5 (36)	10 (38)	10 (56)		15 (40)	13 (93)	13 (93)	36-93
No answer				17 (100)	1 (3)			3-100
Planning ability:								
Decreases					9 (24)			
No effect	14 (100)	25 (96)	5 (28)		12 (32)	1 (7)	2 (14)	7-100
Increases		1 (4)	13 (72)		5 (40)	13 (93)	12 (86)	4-93
No answer				17 (100)	2 (5)			5-100
Cures illness:								
No effect	12 (86)	26 (100)	16 (89)	9 (53)	23 (61)	5 (36)	8 (57)	36-100
Any illness (chest, heart head, stomach, & other)						7 (50)		
Minor complaints	2 (14)		2 (11)	8 (47)	15 (39)	1 (7)	4 (29)	11-50
No answer						1 (7)	2 (14)	7-14
Effect of heavy smoking:								
Bad	4 (29)	11 (42)	11 (61)	8 (47)	11 (29)	1 (7)	4 (29)	7-61
None	10 (71)	15 (58)	7 (39)			2 (14)	3 (21)	14-71
Good				7 (41)	27 (71)j	11 (79)	6 (43)	41-79
No answer				2 (12)			1 (7)	
Social & psychological effects—rapport:								
No effect	8 (57)	15 (58)			23 (60)		1 (7)	7-60

225

TABLE (continued)

	Lau[a] 1	Baegu[a] 1	Nagovisi[b] 2	Aita (Sample 1)[b] 2	Aita (Sample 2)[b] 3	Buganda[c] 4	Zhun/twa Bushmen[d] 4	Herero[d] 4	Range%
Increases	6 (43)	11 (42)	18 (100)			15 (40)	14 (100)	13 (93)	40-100
No answer									
Problem solving:									
No effect	8 (57)	16 (61)	2 (11)			21 (55)	1 (7)	1 (7)	7-61
Improves	6 (43)	9 (35)	16 (89)			17 (45)	12 (86)	13 (93)	35-93
No answer							1 (7)		
Generosity, kindness:									
No effect	8 (57)	17 (65)	17 (94)			23 (60)		4 (29)	29-94
Increases	6 (43)	9 (35)	1 (6)		2 (12)	15 (40)	14 (100)	10 (71)	6-100
No answer									
Self-expression:									
No effect	8 (57)	16 (62)	18 (100)			21 (55)	1 (7)	2 (14)	7-100
Improves	6 (43)	10 (38)				17 (45)	13 (93)	12 (86)	38-93
No answer									
Public appearance:									
No effect	7 (50)	14 (54)	7 (39)			26 (68)	2 (14)	4 (29)	14-68
Improves	7 (50)	12 (46)	11 (61)			12 (32)	12 (86)	10 (71)	32-86
No answer									
Method of smoking:									
Pipe only	8 (57)	12 (46)	12 (67)		4 (8)	14 (37)	4 (29)	7 (50)	8-67
Cigarettes only	4 (29)	5 (19)	3 (17)		22 (43)	24 (63)		3 (21)	17-63
Both	2 (14)	9 (35)	3 (17)		25 (49)	(not asked)	9 (64)	4 (29)	14-64

Snuff

								Range
Definition of tobacco—a food?								
Yes	1 (7)	23 (88)			17 (45)	13 (93)	6 (43)	7-93
No	13 (93)	3 (12)	18 (100)		21 (55)	1 (7)	7 (50)	7-100
No answer						1 (7)	1 (7)	
What is tobacco like?								
Food	3 (21)	2 (8)			1 (3)	5 (26)		3-26
Food but better						3 (21)	3 (21)	
Less than food							1 (7)	
Milk, water							1 (7)	
Beer							1 (7)	
Sugar						1 (7)		
Betelnut			13 (73)		24 (63)			21-63
Just tobacco	3 (21)	11 (42)	5 (28)		8 (21)			14-21
Pleasure	2 (14)	4 (15)			3 (8)			8-15
Warmth	2 (14)	4 (15)						
Worthless							1 (7)	
Not like anything						2 (14)		
No opinion	4 (29)	5 (9)			2 (5)			5-29
No answer					3 (21)	3 (21)	7 (50)	21-50
Effect on appetite:								
Decreases	11 (79)	18 (70)	12 (67)	17 (100)	9 (24)	4 (29)	4 (29)	24-100
No effect	3 (21)	8 (30)	6 (33)		15 (40)	4 (29)		29-40
Increases					9 (24)	6 (43)	10 (71)	21-71
No opinion					5 (13)			
Days one can abstain:								
None	2 (14)	2 (8)	15 (83)	1 (11)	27 (87)	8 (57)	9 (64)	8-87
1-3			2 (11)	3 (33)	3 (10)	6 (43)	4 (29)	10-43
4+	12 (86)	24 (92)	1 (6)	5 (55)	1 (3)		1 (7)	3-92

TABLE (continued)

	Lau[a] 1	Baegu[a] 1	Nagovisi[b] 2	Aita (Sample 1)[b] 2	Aita (Sample 2)[b] 2	Buganda[c] 3	Zhun/twa Bushmen[d] 4	Herero[d] 4	Range%
Type of tobacco usually smoked:									
Local	7 (50)	11 (55)	1 (6)		7 (14)	11 (35)	1 (7)	1 (7)	6-55
Other	7 (50)	9 (45)	1 (6)			20 (65)	3 (21)	1 (7)	6-65
Both			16 (89)		44 (86)		10 (71)	12 (86)	71-89
No response						7 non-smokers			

Note.—Where no entry occurs, either the question was not asked, or the data were elicited or recorded in such fashion as to be judged too unreliable for inclusion. The parenthetic entries are percentages.

[a]Malaita, Solomon Islands.
[b]Bougainville, Solomon Islands.
[c]Uganda, Africa.
[d]Botswana, Africa.
[e]Seventh-Day Adventists.
[f]Muslim.
[g]Currently, all, before World War II; i.e., for all respondents, age 16 and above.
[h]Former smokers.
[i]Question presented differently.
[j]Question did not distinguish between good and bad effect.

ceremonies, whereas the pagan Bushmen, on the contrary, had made smoking an integral part of theirs.

The Bushmen are in fact exceptional among the present seven societies. They are the least acculturated, the most favorably disposed toward tobacco, and the only group where tobacco smoking serves a strong social as well as individual function. In an "open" question not tabulated, 50% of the Bushmen said they preferred smoking with other people, or that they usually did, whereas only 29% of the Herero responded in this way, 64% preferring or mostly smoking alone. This difference corresponded to the ethnographers' observation of the social nature of tobacco smoking among the Bushmen, who often passed the same pipe around from person to person during intense, prolonged group discussion.

Not only does tobacco serve a useful social function in everyday Bushman life, but they alone, of the seven societies, have incorporated tobacco into their rituals. (Apparently myths take a long time to become established, since none of the seven societies had myths about tobacco.) While not essential, tobacco is considered a very important adjunct to the medicine-trance dance, their central ritual event. Tobacco is smoked in a rapid succession of deep inhalations, and some Bushmen respondents believed that tobacco could induce trance states. The altered state of consciousness which certainly occurs during the trance dance may be facilitated by smoking in this fashion, a use of tobacco which would be pharmacological rather than symbolic.

DISCUSSION

The absence of ritual or myths involving tobacco in six of these seven societies contrasts with the frequency of such association in North and South America (Mogey, 1969). Among 26 Oceanian societies—not including the present Solomon Islanders—in Harvard's Human Relations Area Files, smoking was customary in 22 (85%), but only two societies had incorporated tobacco into their rituals (J. F. Gehan, personal communication, 1971). Tobacco smoking in Oceania and among the African Herero and Buganda is possibly too recent, only two or at most three generations having smoked, for myths or rituals to have sprung up about tobacco. The Bushmen are exceptional in having incorporated tobacco into their key ritual after a similar exposure.

The prevalence of smoking need not, however, parallel the length of a group's exposure to tobacco. Virtually all of the Solomon Islanders and the Africans in the present study smoked, unless smoking was forbidden by their religion, whereas the percentage of cigarette smokers among southwestern American Indians, who have of course been exposed to tobacco for centuries, has been reported (Sievers, 1968) as only half that of the general population of the United States. Most of the Lau women were addicted and, as noted in the table, 51% of all persons queried in the seven present societies could not abstain for a whole day. This sounds like the situation reported by a Yanomamö Indian informant of southern Venezuela and northern Brazil, who told the enthnographers: "When we are out of tobacco we crave it intensely, and we say we are ... in utter poverty [Chagnon, LeQuesne, &

Cook, 1971, p. 73]." These ethnographers confirmed the Yanomamös' inability to refrain from tobacco (chewing) for several hours.

The Herero and Bushmen, particularly the latter, attributed more virtues, social as well as personal, to tobacco than did the Solomon Islanders or the Buganda, who smoked mainly for personal rather than social reasons.

CONCLUSION AND SUMMARY

People of four Solomon Island tribes and one tribe in Uganda, queried as to tobacco usage, did not report or recognize social factors as a major stimulus or support for smoking. Personal gratification was their dominant motive. Within this "personal" (as contrasted to "social") category, psychological needs or satisfactions were reported but also played a minor role. By exclusion, physiological satisfaction is the dominant factor. Further evidence for this view is provided, among these tribes, by the rapid adoption of tobacco smoking once it is introduced, its pervasive use except when forbidden by religion, and the frequent inability of smokers to abstain for even a few days, despite knowledge of the health hazard.

Although the pastoral Herero and the hunting-gathering Bushmen of southern Africa were likewise aware of tobacco's health hazard, all adults smoked. These two groups attributed to tobacco more virtues, both personal and social, than did the other five. For the Bushmen, tobacco served important social and ritual functions, having been incorporated into their central ritual event, the medicine-trance dance. But even here, tobacco was used pharmacologically rather than symbolically. The low frequency of ritual use and the absence of myths concerning tobacco in these seven societies, as well as among 26 additional Oceanian societies surveyed in the Harvard Human Relations Area File, contrasts with the frequent involvement of tobacco in rituals and myths among North and South American Indians.

On the whole, among these seven societies personal gratification is much stronger than social influence in maintaining the smoking habit.

REFERENCES

Chagnon, N. A., LeQuesne, P., & Cook, J. M. Yanomamö hallucinogens: Anthropological, botanical, and chemical findings. *Current Anthropology*, 1971, **12**, 72-74.

Damon, A. Human ecology in the Solomon Islands. *Journal of Human Ecology*, 1973, in press.

Mogey, J. The sociology of smoking. Unpublished report prepared for National Clearinghouse on Smoking and Health, 1969.

Robbins, M. C., & Pollnac, R. B. Drinking patterns and acculturation in rural Buganda. *American Anthropologist*, 1969, **71**, 276-284.

Sievers, M. C. Cigarette and alcohol usage by southwestern American Indians. *American Journal of Public Health and the Nation's Health*, 1968, **58**, 71-82.

World Health Organization. Research on Human Population Genetics. (WHO Tech. Rep. No. 387) Geneva: World Health Organization, 1968.

16

COLD TURKEY IN GREENFIELD, IOWA: A FOLLOW-UP STUDY

Francis J. Ryan[1]
Philip Morris Research Center

This report is based on the study of an occasion on which an "entire community" attempted to stop smoking at the same time. Although thousands of people quit and resume smoking every year in this country, theirs are usually individual decisions made in the privacy of the home. Seldom are more than a few friends or members of their families aware that they are attempting to quit smoking. When an entire community quits en masse, however, everyone is aware of the community decision, and all are able to support the attempts of would-be quitters while applying general social prohibitions on public smoking by noncon-formists. Such community action campaigns should maximize the number and success rate of would-be quitters while minimizing the number of recidivists.

One community-wide effort in Greenfield, Iowa, occurred during August 1969. It was in part an attempt by the town's City Council to publicize Greenfield as a site for new industry and new residents, and in part a public relations stunt suggested by United Artists on behalf of the motion picture, *Cold Turkey*, then being photographed on location in Greenfield. The plot of this film involved the efforts of a small town to quit smoking for 30 days and thus earn a $25 million prize. For undertaking the real-life campaign paralleling the plot, United Artists paid the town treasury a more modest $6,000.

From this rather unusual genesis many people in Greenfield made a serious attempt to give up smoking. All smokers in town were urged to quit, and many signed pledges to abstain. The "evils" of smoking were well publicized, together with the contrasting "benefits" of not smoking. August 8, the date the town quit, was a local holiday advertised as Cold Turkey Day. It was a carnival occasion, with

[1] Acknowledgments are due to Raymond Fagan, who initially proposed the study; to William L. Dunn, Jr., for implementing its early stages; to the other staff members of the Philip Morris Research Center who aided in the collection and analysis of data; and particularly to David Raybin, who supervised their activities.

speeches, pretty girls, free balloons, sidewalk sales by merchants, and a bonfire into which cigars, cigarettes, and pipes were thrown. During the month of abstinence, movie-making activities and antismoking attitudes dominated the lives of the townsfolk. Hundreds worked as film extras; the fall opening of school was postponed; a huge sign on the outskirts of town welcomed visitors and requested, "No Smoking, Please." Most merchants cooperated by removing tobacco from sale or sight, and, in fact, few people smoked in public. There was general agreement that the campaign appeared to be quite successful.

After the 30 days, the successful quitters were honored in a public ceremony, and the enforcement of the former smoking taboo was relaxed, although the antismoking attitudes lingered. The sign remained, cigarettes were either not on sale or not on display in downtown shops, and most citizens found pride in their mutual accomplishments.

Here, then, was a rare opportunity to study the influence of demographic and personality variables upon response to a high-saturation antismoking campaign and to observe for behavioral changes in a large sample of in situ smoking quitters.

Seven months after Cold Turkey Day, we queried the inhabitants on the long-term effects of the antismoking campaign. We wanted to know how many had quit, whether the short-term annoyances of quitting had persisted, and whtther the quitters and nonquitters could be differentiated by socioeconomic or personality variables.

PROCEDURES

Local Girl Scouts distributed questionnaire packets to every person within the city limits who had been at least 14 years old on Cold Turkey Day, smokers and nonsmokers alike. Each packet held a questionnaire covering demographic data, a smoking history, and a copy of Cattell's (1970) personality inventory, the 16 PF Form A. The decennial census tallied 2,212 residents of all ages a week after 1,592 people accepted our packets, so it appears that we contacted most of the eligibles.

After the questions were answered in private, the returns were mailed to a Richmond, Virginia, consumer research firm. Respondents were guaranteed local anonymity and were paid $5 for completing the questionnaires. They were given no advice by the Scouts, and they did not know the identity of the sponsor, although it was known in town that a tobacco company supported the research.

Returns were accepted during the next 5 weeks and, with the help of advertisements in the local paper, totaled 1,435, or 90.1% of the handout. Usable data came from 1,385 respondents, the discards being mostly from elderly nonsmokers who had not filled out the questionnaires properly. Two returns were arbitrarily voided because they appeared to have been filled out by the same person.

The high return rate had been expected because of the town's identification with the film and its topical plot. For all practical purposes it would be impossible to duplicate the extent of community and individual involvement in this antismoking effort. If ever there was a people, a place, and a time for an antismoking campaign to have succeeded brilliantly, it was among the people of Greenfield in the late summer of 1969. The impact of the campaign on this community could not be equaled by any conceivable effort anywhere in America today.

RESULTS

The extent of participation and relative success in quitting is shown in Table 1. There had been 444 active smokers in town before the idea of quitting had been raised. "Active smokers" were those people who reported in April 1970 that they had been active smokers in May 1969 and that in their lifetime they had smoked more than 2 packages of pipe tobacco or 5 packs of cigarettes or 50 cigars.

Stripped of the publicity, and secure in their anonymity, a large number of smokers (62.6%) reported that they had not quit "cold turkey" with the town. About 23% of these nonquitters had cut back their consumption, however, and almost all claimed they had not smoked in public out of respect for those who were trying to quit. Part of the campaign's apparent success stemmed from this nonquitter switch from both public and private smoking to only private smoking.

Of the would-be quitters, the men were more successful than the women. Compared to men as a group, the women of Greenfield were less likely to have been smokers, less likely to have participated in the antismoking campaign, less likely to have succeeded in staying off for 30 days, and once off their cigarettes they were less likely to have stayed off for 7 months. Only 3.9% of the female active smokers and 14.2% of the male active smokers were able to stay off for 7 months. These long-term quitters represented about 10.6% of the original smoking population.

Hunt and Matarazzo (1970), in summarizing many reports of long-term quitting using various techniques, show that the percentage of nonrecidivists decreases as a function of time since original success in a negatively accelerated fashion. The percentage of Greenfield's original 30-day quitters who lasted at least 7 months falls almost exactly on their curve: 51.1%.

TABLE 1
Number of Successful and Unsuccessful Participants

Group	Total		Men		Women	
Respondents	1,385		604		781	
Nonsmoker (May)	941		315		626	
Smoker (May)	444 (100.0%)		289 (100.0%)		155 (100.0%)	
No try to quit	278 (62.6%)		172 (59.5%)		106 (68.4%)	
Tried to quit	166 (37.4%)	(100.0%)	117 (40.5%)	(100.0%)	49 (31.6%)	(100.0%)
Failed, resumed within month	74	(44.6%)	48	(41.0%)	26	(53.0%)
Lasted Month	92	(55.4%)	69	(59.0%)	23	(47.0%)
Lasted 7 months +	47	(28.3%)	41	(35.0%)	6	(12.2%)

These numbers suggest that there is no long-term advantage to community quitting compared to individual quitting, but the data on quitting success in general is so variable that it is difficult to interpret this observation. Bernstein (1970) has summarized the short-term effects of a number of clinical attempts to stop smoking. They range from complete failure to complete success (via hypnosis) in such chaotic fashion that it is difficult to make any generalization about the relative efficiency of the community effort versus the alternative techniques. A fair generalization might be that the atypical Greenfield effort under atypical conditions produced only typical success.

Mannerisms and Complaints

Those who tried to quit noticed changes in their nervous mannerisms and increases in a number of physical symptoms. Most attempted to replace smoking by ingestion of snack food and drinks. Even after 7 months the successful long-term quitters continued to eat more nuts, mints, candy, ice cream, etc., than before. Those who reported that they had mannerisms such as tapping their feet or fingers, biting their lips, twiddling their thumbs, or chewing on matches were asked whether they did this more frequently than before. Depending on the mannerism, from 2 to 10% of the nonsmokers or nonquitting smokers said they did it more frequently than before, while 23 to 50% of the long-term quitters had increased the frequency of these habits.

Similarly, when asked whether they were ever troubled by a list of minor complaints, such as being restless and tense, blue or depressed, ill-tempered, apt to doze off, constipated, bothered by loss of energy, and gaining weight, from 5 to 15% of the nonsmokers with the symptoms said they were worse than before, but 25 to 65% of the long-term quitters said they were more troubled than before. The short-term consequences of quitting, as evidenced by the mann...sms and the complaints, were still annoying the former smokers months later.

Age, Income, and Socioeconomic Status

The number of long-term quitters is so small that when broken into age and sex subgroups only a few cells have any meaningful data. What is available suggests that the campaign's long-term success was greatest among the middle-aged men and was least among the young. The remainder of this paper therefore concentrates upon a single age and sex subgroup, the nonstudent males under the age of 60. They are employed, healthy, active, mostly longtime smokers, and they include two-thirds of the long-term quitters in their ranks.

Approximate personal income and socioeconomic status of the quitters, nonquitters, etc., are shown in Table 2. Respondents had checked a range within which their incomes lay. For convenience in data treatment, all scores within a range were considered at the range midpoint, except that incomes "over $20,000" were arbitrarily[2] counted as $22,000. Tabled entries represent resultant means.

Men who did not try to quit, or who tried to quit but then resumed smoking, had lower incomes than those who tried or who quit successfully. A number of

---

[2] Use of any estimate over $20,000 does not affect conclusions, but exaggerates scores of quitters, successful quitters, etc.

TABLE 2

Income and Socioeconomic Status of Nonstudent
Males Under Age 60 ($N = 206$)

Category	Average personal income	Average socioeconomic score
Didn't try to quit ($N = 117$)	$7,620	55.7
Quit on Cold Turkey Day ($N = 74$)	8,750	63.2
Quit prior to Cold Turkey Day ($N = 15$)	9,560	80.0
Lasted 30 days ($N = 52$)	9,450	70.8
Lasted 7 months+ ($N = 31$)	9,640	74.7
Quit but resumed before 30 Days ($N = 37$)	7,970	59.3
Resumed over Winter ($N = 21$)	9,170	65.5

these men quit before Cold Turkey Day, in anticipation of the campaign. They had high incomes, and they also had high success.

Socioeconomic level was determined by applying the procedures of the U.S. Bureau of Census (1967), which has scaled occupational status by assigning high numbers to well-paid, highly respected occupations which require considerable education, talent, or skill, and low numbers to poorly paid, less respected jobs which require little education or ability. Thus a surgeon rates 99, a machinist is 68, a barber is 37, a laundress is 9, etc. Averaging these occupation ratings for the entire town, using head-of-household rating for the dependents, the respondents' mean was 56.4, typical of a small white community in the north central census district. The mean score for the nonstudent males under 60 was 60.7. Among the latter group we have arbitrarily referred to those with scores above group average as an "Upper Class" and to those with scores below group average as a "Lower Class." Among the nonstudent males under age 60, the early quitters had much higher socioeconomic scores than the Cold Turkey Day quitters, who were in turn higher than the nonquitters. Those who quit for 30 days had higher socioeconomic scores than those who quit but resumed before a month. Among those who lasted a month, those who were still off after 7 months had higher socioeconomic scores than those who had resumed over the winter.

It is clear that the upper class was much more successful in quitting than the lower class. The quit rates were different in the two class groups: 64/117 (or 54.7%) of the upper-class nonstudent males under age 60 tried to quit, but only 25/85 (or 29.5%) of the lower-class nonstudent males under age 60 made an effort to quit. No one from the lower class tried to quit before Cold Turkey Day, but 15 of the upper class did. The success rates were different: among the upper-class early quitters, 93.4% lasted 30 days and 66.7% lasted 7 months; among upper-class Cold Turkey Day quitters, 55.2% lasted 30 days and 36.8% lasted 7 months; among lower-class quitters, 44% lasted 30 days and 12% lasted 7 months.

Even in Greenfield, where conditions for mass participation were optimal, the antismoking campaign affected the base of the socioeconomic pyramid very little. It was the town's power structure which quit, not the man in the street.

The quitters were joiners, and examination of the organizations to which they belonged was illuminating: they not only joined, but they led. The list of quitters is studded with former presidents, treasurers, secretaries, etc., of the local veterans' organizations, service clubs, social organizations, church trustees, charity drives, and political parties. They were the power structure in a very real sense.

Personality Characteristics

The 16 PF was chosen to evaluate personalities in Greenfield because it is suitable for self-administration to a large group of normal people. It asks no questions which overtly deal with sex, religious beliefs, or body functions, and it can be administered to young and old without arousing any public indignation. It measures 16 primary personality factors, from which several secondary factors can be derived. The factors are described by adjectives and nouns describing extremely high or low scorers, and by alphanumeric codes A through Q4.

Because quitting was related to social class, we examined the personality differences among the upper- and lower-class nonstudent men under 60, including smokers and nonsmokers, before examining the smoking groups (see Table 3). Applying the t-test to the mean raw scores of these factors, uncorrected for age, we found eight factors in which the classes were *not* statistically different. These factors measure affectothymia (outgoing or reserved, Factor A); ego strength (C); dominance (E); premsia (tender-mindedness, I); protension (suspicion and jealousy, L); guilt proneness (0); self-control (Q3); and state of tension (Q4).

Combining both social classes together, on these factors, (see Table 4), we found that only two factors differentiated the successful 30-day quitters and those who hadn't tried to quit: ego strength (C) and self-control (Q3). The quitters scored high on ego strength. They might be described as calm, mature, even phlegmatic compared to the nonquitters. The latter might be described as easily upset, lacking in frustration tolerance, generally dissatisfied, and easily annoyed. The difference in means, treated as if we were dealing with two random samples from an infinite population, was significant ($t = 2.47$, $df = 163$).

The successful 30-day quitters had high scores on the self-control factor. They might be described as socially precise, showing persistence and willpower. The nonquitters had lower self-control scores and might be described as undisciplined people who follow their own urges and are careless of protocol ($t = 2.90$, $df =$

TABLE 3

The Personality Scores of Nonstudent Men under 60 Years Old
in the Upper and in the Lower Classes

Factor	Upper class $(N = 199)$			Lower class $(N = 130)$		National norms adult males	
	Mean	σ		Mean	σ	Mean	σ
A	9.32	3.12		8.92	2.73	9.67	3.35
B	7.50	2.11	***	6.88	1.81	5.92	2.06
C	15.25	3.48		14.93	3.17	16.08	3.75
E	11.27	3.91		11.15	3.33	13.51	3.90
F	13.13	3.94	***	12.10	3.85	13.38	4.43
G	13.96	2.97	***	12.88	3.39	13.84	3.60
H	12.00	4.81	***	10.70	4.41	13.76	5.61
I	7.45	2.99		7.89	2.77	8.39	3.50
L	9.18	3.33		9.53	3.11	8.83	3.20
M	10.82	2.97	***	11.48	2.77	12.15	3.43
N	10.89	2.40	***	10.28	2.57	11.70	2.62
O	10.40	3.63		11.15	3.47	9.33	3.67
Q1	9.35	2.66	***	8.56	2.48	10.36	2.83
Q2	11.31	3.24	***	12.59	3.05	10.12	3.46
Q3	11.13	3.05		10.82	2.91	11.13	3.11
Q4	12.90	4.49		13.20	4.22	10.98	4.86
Anxiety	6.30		***	6.68		5.50	
Extra	4.66		***	4.02		5.50	

***Asterisks have been placed between means described as significantly different in
the accompanying text.

163.). The adjectives used in describing these groups are those which the test
constructors and others have applied to high and lower scores on the traits
in question. The relationship of these characteristics to giving up smoking is
obvious.

The two social classes differed in eight of the primary factors and two important
derived factors (see Table 3). The higher-class group was more abstract in its
thinking (B), more surgent (F), had higher superego strength (G), was more
adventurous and socially bold (H), more concerned with practical matters (M),
more worldly and shrewd (N), more experimenting (Q1), and more group-
dependent (Q2) than the lower class. Conversely, the lower class might be described
on these same factors as being less intelligent (B), more prudent and serious (F),
more apt to evade rules or feel few obligations to society (G), more restrained and
diffident (H), more imaginative and Bohemian (M), more forthright and artless (N),
more conservative (Q1) in the sense of being uninterested in change, and more
self-sufficient and resourceful (Q2) in the sense of not being interested in group
activity. In the two most important derived factors, the upper class was also more
extraverted and less anxious than the lower class.

TABLE 4

The Personality Scores of the Nonstudent Men Under 60 Years Old
among Nonquitters and 30-Day Quitters, Listed by Each Class
Separately Where Classes Differed, or for the Two Classes
Combined Where Classes Failed to Differ

Factor	Upper class		Combined		Lower class	
	Didn't try to quit (N=53)	Lasted 30 days (N=41)	Didn't try to quit (N=113)	Lasted 30 days (N=52)	Didn't try to quit (N=60)	Lasted 30 days (N=11)
A			9.07	9.71		
B	7.47	7.56			6.70	7.27
C			14.74	*** 16.08		
E			11.53	11.35		
F	12.77	13.90			12.48	11.09
G	13.02	*** 14.51			12.82	12.36
H	11.53	13.41			10.63	8.55
I			7.82	7.38		
L			9.85	8.94		
M	10.92	10.73			11.28	*** 13.18
N	11.32	11.32(ok)			10.33	10.27
O			11.05	10.58		
Q1	9.19	9.51			8.38	8.18
Q2	12.04	*** 9.85			12.73	12.36
Q3			10.42	*** 11.92		
Q4			13.36	12.60		
Anxiety	6.74	*** 5.75			6.72	7.16
Extra	4.46	*** 5.27			4.15	*** 3.20

***Asterisks have been placed between means described as significantly different in the text. Discussion of the differences and description of the factors is covered in the text. Where there are no differences in personality scores between the upper and lower classes, the data have been combined.

We had not expected to find so many social class personality differences in this small community, particularly in light of our rather unsophisticated division of the population into only two classes. It seems that each generation of social scientists and novelists must rediscover anew and wide variety of personalities to be found in middle America.

These social class differences became confounded with smoking behavior differences because of the lower class's general lack of interest or lack of ability to quit. Not all of the social class differences were reflected in smoking behavior, however. Intelligence (B), surgency (F), social boldness (H), worldliness (N), and conservatism (Q1) appeared unrelated to smoking behavior whether class differences were taken into account or not.

Six factors did reveal differences in smoking behavior among one or both classes. In the upper class the successful 30-day quitters and nonquitting nonparticipators differed in superego strength (G), group dependency (Q2), anxiety, and extraversion. In the lower class they differed in Bohemianism (M) and extraversion.

The upper class quitters had higher superego scores, and might be described as more conscientious, persevering, staid, and rule-bound. The nonquitters scored lower, indicating people who were more impatient, rule-evading, less apt to follow through with a task, and casual and lacking in effort for group undertakings ($t = 2.45$, $df = 92$). Among the generally more impatient lower class, there was no significant effect of this factor on smoking behavior.

The upper-class quitters were much more strongly group-dependent (Q2) than their peer nonparticipators, whose high score on this factor indicated that they were very self-sufficient. "Group dependence" is characterized by a tendency to go along with group decisions, a lack of individual resolution, even a real need for group support. The upper-class nonquitters were more like the lower class in general: strongly independent people who are accustomed to going their own way ($t = 3.01$, $df = 92$).

In the important derived measure of anxiety, the upper-class quitters had anxiety scores significantly lower than their nonquitters. This is what would be expected if smoking serves some tranquilizing and anxiety-reducing function. Only those who do not need the tranquilizing effect would be able to quit ($t = 2.77$, $df = 92$). There was no anxiety difference in the scores of the lower-class quitters or nonquitters, however, possibly because the lower class as a group contained relatively few nonanxious people.

Among the upper class, the quitters had higher extraversion scores than the nonquitters ($t = 1.92$, $df = 92$), but among the lower class the finding was reversed, the quitters were more introverted. ($t = 1.72$, $df = 69$). All these scores were really on the introverted side of the national norms, and the reason for the interaction of social class and extraversion may be somehow related to this generally introverted character of the townspeople. It is not clear why there should be a difference in the personality characteristics of quitters in the two social classes, but it should not be astonishing to consider that the same personality characteristics which lead to one behavior in one group might lead to the opposite behavior in another group.

The only remaining difference was in a tendency for the lower-class quitters to score higher on Factor M than their nonquitters. High scores on M represent the more imaginative, Bohemian personality, compared to the nonquitting group, which is characterized as practical and unimaginative, of sound, realistic, and dependable judgment ($t = 2.27$, $df = 73$). Continuing to smoke is more conventional behavior than quitting, of course.

Smokers and Nonsmokers

It is often suggested that there are differences in personality betweeen smokers and nonsmokers. Among the nonstudent men under 60, when the average personality scores of dedicated smokers (nonquitters) were compared to those of men who had never been smokers, the only differences were that upper-class nonsmokers were more rule-bound (G) and more conventional (M) than their nonquitter peers ($t = 3.57$, $df = 96$; $t = 1.88$, $df = 96$).

SOME FINAL COMMENTS

One of the hopes of a man who joins an antismoking campaign probably is that in the unity of the group he will find a strength to counteract his own weaknesses. The Greenfield data suggest that this may in fact be true, that the more group-oriented a man is, the better the chance he has of quitting during a group effort. But similarly it suggests that for non-group-oriented people with strongly independent ways, a group effort is a waste of time. Willingness to undertake new projects, strong self-control, and a general freedom from anxiety are important factors in quitting smoking. These are far from novel observations, but it is reassuring to have data to support the folklore's emphasis on willpower as a principal determinant of success.

The ability of the personality test to describe what some might think to be obvious deserves further comment. It is not being used here to indicate that there is some underlying constitutional difference between smokers and nonsmokers, a position criticized recently by both Smith (1970) and Hunt and Matarazzo (1970), but instead to show that personality factors are related to changes in the observable behaviors of the smokers. It stresses not the fact that smokers differ greatly from nonsmokers—and indeed, we are not impressed that they do differ—but the fact that among smokers, smoking behavior is highly dependent upon personality characteristics, so that one type of person may be expected to have one consumption rate or pattern, and another person may have a different rate or pattern. In the present study the pattern of interest is the ability to quit.

The implications of the socioeconomic differences in quit rate are manifold. If it is the power structure, the establishment, which is most apt to quit, then what will happen when today's large numbers of anti-establishment youth mature? Will smoking become in time a predominantly blue-collar behavior? Should the national antismoking effort be concentrated on television commercials, which are watched by the lower class, which doesn't intend to quit, or concentrated on some other target group by some other media?

The observation that successful quitting is most apt to occur only among people in the top of the social structure explains why many professional people, basing their observations on the observed behavior of colleagues who no longer smoke, have found it hard to believe that tobacco sales have held rather constant over recent years despite the "apparent" success of antismoking campaigns. Certainly it explains why the Greenfield power structure was so deceived.

The data showing different personality factors dominant in the different social classes scream for explanation. Does belonging to the class help create the personality, or is it the personality characteristic which affects ability to remain in or progress to a higher class?

As pointed out elsewhere in this volume, any attempt to explain smoking behavior which ignores demographic variables (such as sex, age, income, social class) and personality types can only be a deceptive oversimplification. In Greenfield we can see that all these factors were acting at once, and that each had a contributory effect on rate of participation in the campaign and on ability to give up smoking.

REFERENCES

Bernstein, D. A. The modification of smoking behavior: An evaluative review. In W. A. Hunt (Ed.), *Learning mechanisms in smoking*. Chicago: Aldine, 1970.

Cattell, R. B., Eber, H. W., & Tatsuoka, M. M. *Handbook for the Sixteen Personality Factor Questionnaire*. Champaign, Ill.: Institute for Personality and Ability Testing, 1970.

Hunt, W. A., & Matarazzo, J. D. Habit mechanisms in smoking. In W. A. Hunt (Ed.), *Learning mechanisms in smoking*. Chicago: Aldine, 1970.

Smith, G. M. Personality and smoking: A review of the empirical literature. In W. A. Hunt (Ed.), *Learning mechanisms in smoking*. Chicago: Aldine, 1970.

U.S. Bureau of Census. *U.S. Census of Population, 1960: Subject Reports. Socio Economic Status*. (Final Rep. PC (2), Pt. 5C.) Washington, D.C.: U.S. Government Printing Office, 1967.

17

MOTIVATIONAL CONFLICTS ENGENDERED BY THE ON-GOING DISCUSSION OF CIGARETTE SMOKING

Alan S. Meyer, Lucy N. Friedman, and
Paul F. Lazarsfeld
Columbia University

INTRODUCTION

This paper summarizes a study of the responses of a variety of Americans to the continuing campaign against smoking. Whatever the outcome of the antismoking campaign and the discussion around it, future historians will want to understand it. The present study was aimed at adding to their supply of data in a specific way. It provides information on the manner in which a small but diversified group experienced the increase of antismoking materials and how they reacted to them.

We would emphasize that our sample of just over 200 individuals was neither randomly selected nor representative of any defined universe. They included, however, a continuum of smokers going from those who smoked with no efforts to quit, to those who had stopped long enough to reasonably be considered quitters. In between, there was an obvious middle group, which we call "oscillators": they had made numerous unsuccessful efforts to stop smoking. Within each group, we questioned at least a few cases of men and women, married and single, young and old, and white-collar and blue-collar workers. We interviewed in four settings on the east coast: New York City; suburban Westchester County in New York State; Bridgeport, Connecticut; and rural areas in New Jersey.

Our posture towards these respondents was neutral but inquiring. We developed a flexible but focused interview guide with a sprinkling of standardized questions: Why has the campaign been relatively ineffective in getting large proportions of smokers to quit? Why do adolescents continue to take up smoking at reportedly increased rates? How do smokers who believe that smoking is hazardous manage their conflicts? How do persons in close contact—such as married couples—react to the controversy about cigarettes and health, particularly if one partner smokes and the other doesn't? These are among the many questions that we raised about the effects of the campaign.

Multiple copies of each interview were made, cut up and filed according to a variety of topics. We then analyzed these excerpts and the interviews as a whole to describe types of responses to the campaign and to identify themes and mechanisms which would help explain the persistence of these responses. As a preliminary check on selected qualitative results we ran cross tabulations using 177 cases whose responses and other data were punched on IBM cards.

A final methodological note: our study is basically qualitative. We were more interested in hypothesis finding than in hypothesis-testing. We would like to think that the hypotheses that have been generated might be put to rigorous testing under more systematically controlled conditions.

RESPONSES TO THE CAMPAIGN

We have distinguished several types of smokers who differ with respect to the regularity of their smoking or nonsmoking and/or with respect to the conflicts or difficulties they experience in maintaining their smoking pattern.

Within the continuous-smoker group, for example, we found two contrasting types: those with no regrets and those in great conflict. In order to obtain enough cases of the continuous smokers with conflict, we defined as continuous smokers those who had quit only once together with those who had never quit. While this dilutes the pureness of these types, we still found interesting differences between them.

Other response types found within the "oscillators" and the current abstainers are also discussed below.

Continuous Smokers With No Regrets

Continuous smokers with no regrets comprised 23% of the continuous-smoker group. The remainder of the continuous-smoker group included, according to our ratings, 23% with minimal conflict, 44% with moderate conflict, and 10% with great conflict. Most of the "no-conflict" group were aware of reported health risks of cigarettes. They rely on their own experience and on their present time perspective to counter the reports and thus avoid feeling any conflict about their habit. They have developed two major mechanisms for effectively resisting the antismoking campaign. These can generally be described as rejecting the cautionary statements and discounting their importance.

The latter can be done by attaching more importance to present pleasures than to possible dangers in an uncertain future, by citing a variety of perceived risks like pollution, and by citing continued good health.

A most ingenious way of denying alleged dangers is for the smoker to take over the language of correlation which he has learned from the health educators, and then to use it to "disprove" the latter's medical reports of a positive relationship between cigarettes and specific diseases.

If one knows of smokers who did not die from cancer and also knows of nonsmokers who did die of cancer, one can create a homemade correlation table based on real experiences. This is just what many of our unconflicted smokers do. For these smokers, none of whom were college graduates, firsthand observations override impersonal statistics reported in the media.

A man with a seventh grade education who owns and operates a country store and admits to a slight case of emphysema, put it all together:

> ... now I've known a couple of different men that had emphysema pretty bad but I've known men 90 years old smoking cigarettes, rolled their own when they was boys and continued on and they seem to work until they die. It maybe cuts their wind, it doesn't give them cancer. There's young people in their 40's dying from heart attacks, cancer. Some of them never smoked. There's a man comes in here, he's a school teacher, he said he used to go around in a crowd with a fella who every time he see'd anyone light a cigarette, he'd knock it out of their mouth. He'd never smoked. A couple of years later he died of cancer, so there's the story.

And there we have the *"smoker's own cancer correlation table."* Although this man said, perhaps glibly, that the antismoking commercials were true, he was easily able to pick and choose those cases in his experience which support the view that smoking is safe.

Smokers with more education apparently find it more difficult to ignore the antismoking campaign. A young lawyer who had been smoking for a little more than a year without apparent conflict developed an amazingly diversified repertoire of resistances in depth. Here is a list of his armamentaria:

1. He rejects the relevance of impersonal statistics ("... doesn't mean anything about me....").

2. He pushes away or blocks out unpleasant thoughts ("... I've blocked it to a point where I don't think about it....").

3. He invokes the right to privacy ("... I think it's not a proper public issue....").

4. He finds fault with the way the reports are communicated (he says the statistics are not sufficiently focused and the reports are probably exaggerated).

5. He softens the warning ("... I can't imagine that smoking can be good for you....").

6. He cites other risks ("Breathing other pollutants is bad for you....").

7. He invokes humor ("... when they changed the warning on the pack I was more amused than anything.").

8. He invokes medical authority ("One thing I've observed, nurses smoke.").

While this lawyer may be a candidate for increasing conflict if he becomes more exposed to social pressures against smoking, he appears to combine the determination of a new habitué with the varied skills of a professional defender of causes which are under attack.

Continuous Smokers With Great Conflict

Smokers who continue to smoke in spite of great conflict comprised, as we have noted, 10% of the continuous-smoker group. They expend a great deal of energy in defending their habit. They often reveal their conflicts over whether to smoke or to quit by frequent expressions of self-doubt and self-blame. They are more likely than the unconflicted group to smoke at least a pack a day and to have smoked for less than 20 years.

Unlike the contented smoker, the conflicted, continuous smoker tends to believe the reported hazards and to agree, with reservations, that the hazards apply to himself. These beliefs plus pressures from others to stop give rise to a variety of mechanisms by which continuous smokers manage their conflicted feelings. The major problem for such a smoker is how to manage the guilt which commonly accompanies conspicuous continuation of a habit felt to be unhealthy and unwanted.

Short of trying to quit, persons who are convinced by the claims made in the antismoking campaign appear to take one or more of the following options borrowed from a legal model: some claim exemption from the "law" (i.e., the reported hazards) by cutting down, etc.; or plead innocent of the "crime" (i.e., of "real" smoking); some plead "incompetence" by stressing their lack of will or powerlessness to control their inclinations.

Such smokers sometimes weigh the costs and benefits of smoking against those of quitting and conclude that it is better to continue; and finally, some smokers compensate for any feeling of conflict by engaging in minor acts or vague promises which make it psychologically more comfortable for them to continue. For example, they plan to quit sometime in the future.

These techniques suggest a constant struggle among smokers with conflicts to achieve some sense of control over their particular dependency or to justify the absence of control. Thus, some mechanisms feature active efforts, however brief, to achieve a modicum of control, while others deny the possibility or desirability of action.

A few salient examples of such processes will serve to indicate the variety and imaginativeness of the mechanisms used to manage the conflict.

Magnifying the Costs of Quitting. Quitting can be quite legitimately seen as costly in terms of the loss of certain benefits derived from smoking. These include: pleasure, ease of social interaction, relaxation, a routine for structuring and spending time, and a source of psychic income. These deprivations can produce other costs disturbingly familiar to many smokers: psychological distress, reduced interpersonal competence, and increased physical symptoms.

Our respondents provide a variety of data describing both the benefits of smoking and the difficulties of quitting experienced by themselves or by others.

Drawing on numerous reports of anticipated difficulties of quitting and on reports of gains from smoking, we discerned a new mechanism: the *smoker's own cost/benefit balance sheet.* Its main theme is: "to quit is to suffer, to smoke is to benefit." Among women especially, it is liable to take the form of "to quit is to gain unwanted weight, to smoke is to stay slim." Here quitting is seen as losing control, smoking as a means of diet control. Men appear more likely to magnify the costs of quitting by more directly juxtaposing them against the costs of diseases reported to be cigarette-related.

The Self-Perpetuating Cycle of Delayed Gratification. One smoker "quit" smoking in the middle of his interview. He had expressed regret about smoking, in relation to his young children, when he announced to the interviewer his intention to quit. During the remainder of the visit, he kept saying, "See, I almost lit one, but didn't."

This suggested that we use the interview situation as a kind of magnifying glass with which to examine the decision to delay a wanted cigarette—regardless of the length of the delay. We found, as have others, that talking or thinking about smoking can trigger either "postponing" or "lighting up." Even those who exhibited or reported a tendency to light up in such situations, however, assured the interviewer that they could postpone others.

On the basis of a number of relevant interviews, we tentatively identified what looks like a *self-perpetuating cycle of delayed gratification.*

This minicycle, which we call "postponement and plunge," consists of a series of feelings and actions which serve to mutually reinforce each other by triggering off the next behavior in the sequence. The variables appear to interact in the following order:

1. A feeling of being out of control, dependent.
2. Guilt or shame over being too weak to act.
3. Delaying a cigarette.
4. A feeling of some control and pride.
5. Increasing tension or distress from denial of immediate gratification.
6. Relapse into smoking.
7. Release and relief through gratification.
8. Enjoyment because of knowledge of new delays ahead.
9. Renewed regularity of smoking.
10. Recurrence of a feeling of dependency and loss of control.

In the broader spectrum of mechanisms, "delaying a cigarette in order to enjoy it more" should be seen as a very brief cycle of abstinence and relapse in which there is no serious intention to quit even temporarily. Yet such delayed gratification may well be a major mechanism for the management of conflict.

Types of Oscillators

We then turned to longer cycles of abstinence and relapse in which there is greater likelihood of intent or action to quit. We defined an "oscillator" as a current smoker who has been through at least three waves of this relapse cycle. Summarizing some findings briefly, we found two rather distinct patterns.

One we called *symptomatic oscillators* because they quit and resumed along with the onset and remission of such recurrent ailments as colds, chest pains, and coughing. These oscillators experience little or no difficulty when they quit, they abstain for short time periods of several days, and they feel no disappointment or shame on their resumption. Quitting is for this group a form of self-medication.

A second group of relapsers we call the *self-management oscillators.* Characteristically, they have quit for vague reasons of health or a desire for self-control, have some difficulty when they quit, abstain for longer periods (weeks or months), return to cigarettes because of external stimuli, and are unhappy with themselves when they relapse.

These contrasting types suggest unique combinations of three sets of variables:

1. *Conditions around stopping:* why and how difficult.
2. *Length of abstinence.*
3. *Conditions around resumption:* why and with what feelings.

Since the way these variables interact appears to correspond to meaningful distinctions between chronic relapsers, we believe this would be a worthwhile line to pursue in large-scale statistical studies.

Current Abstainers

In examining our sample of current quitters of at least 6 months' duration, we found it useful to view them within the context of our analysis of oscillators. We couldn't help but wonder which of these abstainers were possibly "oscillators in the temporary disguise of quitters" and which were on their way to termination of smoking.

When we compared *first-time quitters* with those *abstainers who had quit one or more times before,* we found differences which suggested that the "experienced quitters" were more like the "self-management" quitters. The fact that they appeared to suffer more and to have abstained for longer periods than the self-management group supports the view that the length of abstinence is associated with degree of difficulty in quitting.

The first-time quitters were more likely to have quit in response to external authority. They quit relatively easily, as did the symptomatic oscillators, but more out of concern for the future. They didn't mention relapse as a possibility. It would be of interest to see whether these first-time quitters are more successful in avoiding relapse than those who have relapsed before.

Oscillation as a Mechanism to Reduce Conflict

The three types of oscillators outlined above—symptomatic oscillators, self-management oscillators, and oscillators possibly in disguise as quitters—all suggest that oscillation, by giving at least an illusion of self-management, often becomes a mechanism for reducing conflict. The fact that oscillators in our sample are less likely to have conflict about smoking than non-oscillators supports the contention that oscillating reduces regret.

The actual processes by which oscillation diminishes conflict appear to include one or more of the following: (a) some smokers feel that periodic quitting lowers overall nicotine intake; (b) multiple relapses may support the notion that successful quitting is rare; (c) proof that one can stop for a while may nourish the notion that relapsing is all right because one can quit again; (d) secret quitting can help protect one's dignity on relapsing and keep conflict about smoking low; or (e) one can resume again at a lower daily dosage and consider the effort successful.

Institutionalized Oscillation

Not smoking in church, in buses, or in other official no-smoking areas is institutionalized and produces regularized, if short-lived, oscillation. Outside authority, plus diversionary activities, plus the short period of abstinence, seem to account for the relative ease of abstaining. These facilitating factors combine with internal commitment to a cultural norm in the case of Orthodox Jews. This group provides an interesting example of institutionalized abstinence for a 24-hour Sabbath period each week. Some of our Orthodox respondents, however, experience greater difficulty just prior to the end of the Sabbath. For some the difficulty is heightened as the days grow longer. The group raises interesting questions about the factors that may account for hard and easy quitting.

SPECIAL SETTINGS

Our sample was selected so that we could examine more closely the responses of smokers and others to the antismoking campaign within the context of three different interpersonal and sociocultural settings. These included the intimacy of couplehood, the parent-child relationship, and socioeconomic class.

Marriage: A Natural Laboratory for Observing Smoking

When smokers live in close and continuous contact with their spouses who may themselves be smokers or nonsmokers, very different patterns of interaction are found to emerge in response to the antismoking campaign.

We observed these patterns separately for *united houses*—marriages in which both spouses smoked—and *divided houses* in which only one spouse smoked. In 23 out of 78 couples studied, we had interviewed both husband and wife. In this paper, we shall describe the nature of intervention and its consequences in both divided and united houses.

We were surprised to find that over half of the houses united in smoking revealed intervention to reduce the smoking of at least one spouse. Since the initiator is vulnerable to counterattack, the attack is usually imaginative and complicated. It generally takes one of two forms or a combination of both: blaming the other for their common habit or appealing for joint efforts at regulation.

Responses are usually simple and direct. Some recipients respond positively with expressions of mutual concern or joint plans for cutting down. Others react defensively by invoking autonomy, by smoking more, or by throwing the charges back at the attacker. Because of the latter's vulnerability, intervention rarely leads to serious conflict.

Efforts to get the smoking spouse to stop was common in divided houses. The attack by the nonsmoker was generally routine and featured health risks as the reason to stop.

The responses of the smoker spouse were more imaginative. Some responded by overtly or covertly smoking more, some charged that the attack was part of a general nag, and still others claimed their nonsmoking spouse couldn't know or understand the habit. All of these reactions share in common an effort to shift the focus from smoking to that of personal autonomy and the right to manage one's own life.

Since intervention in divided houses was more likely to produce strong conflict than in united houses, we expected that smoking would be a more unstable state in divided houses. A comparison did, in fact, reveal that smokers in divided houses were more likely to have tried to quit, and were more likely to want to quit and to think it was important to do so. Smokers in divided houses were also more likely to believe the reported health hazards.

This led us to consider the possible analogies between the interaction in divided couples and the interaction between smokers and nonsmokers in the society at large. The pattern in society has so far been predominantly that of peaceful coexistence. Continuation of the antismoking campaign with a growing emphasis on antipollution arguments, however, may lead to greater conflict in the future. More smokers might then react as those in some divided houses do by trying to quit or to resist such pressures by invoking privacy and autonomy.

How Parents Encourage Their Children to Smoke

Our interviews with parents and children revealed the details of a new and dramatic children's crusade. Most children of smoking parents at some point "bug" their parents to stop smoking. By and large they fail. Yet a recent study reports an increase in new smokers from 12 to 18 years of age between 1968 and 1970.

Although additional data collected from a sample of high school students shows that those who bugged their parents are less likely to smoke themselves than those who didn't bug their parents, the unabated rate of teenage smoking warrants explanation.

We discern a learning process by which youngsters are primed to take up smoking, which includes at least the four following steps: (a) Children learn that their smoking parents don't immediately get sick and die as implied by the antismoking messages on television and in school. Each year that such parents live undermines the creditability of the campaign. (b) They learn the mechanisms which these parents use to reject or neutralize the antismoking arguments. (c) They learn from their smoking parents that smoking is a prerogative of adulthood. And (4) they learn from older siblings and peers that smoking is still an effective way to gain status during adolescence.

Parents' Reactions to the Children's Crusade. This process is often facilitated by parents' reactions to their children's efforts to get them to give up cigarettes. Some parents try to reassure their children by explaining why cigarettes are not a danger in their case. Others reject the children's right to intervene, thus further establishing smoking as an adult right. Finally, some parents engage in role reversal in which they respond childishly to their own children as if the latter were authorities.

Role reversal sometimes takes the form of rebellion in which the parent self-righteously smokes more than before their children protested. Other parents react to the protests with feelings of extreme guilt. A young lawyer, in a humorous vein, explained why he cut down:

> I did it because the kids got to me. Playing on my love and guilt. That's a terrible way to make people behave, for a 3-year-old to act like a Jewish mother.

Humor in this case points up the striking reversal of roles which may follow from even very small children pointing out to their parents the reported dangers of cigarettes.

Loss of Parental Authority and Reactions to Outside Influences. Some parents, often those with less education, see smoking as natural. They tell their children to wait until they reach a certain age or are old enough to "buy their own." The more educated smokers are more likely to express dismay at the "hypocrisy" of "do as I say, not as I do." To regain some semblance of control, such parents sometimes say, "If you must smoke, do it in front of me."

Parents who smoke often feel a loss of authority over their children's smoking behavior and may sense a loss of their children's respect for parental judgment. These feelings may be accompanied by ambivalent attitudes toward antismoking authorities. Parents frequently described their children as having been "brainwashed" by teachers and television. This negative term suggests that their children have been railroaded or sold a bill of goods. One parent showed her negative feelings toward outside authorities by expressing great amusement when her child's antismoking teacher was caught smoking.

Adolescent Rebellion, Emulation, and Autonomy. Traditional motives for youthful experimentation with smoking have included rebellion against authority, assertion of individual autonomy and independence, and emulation of adults, peers, and older siblings.

The new antismoking environment is likely to have changed the meaning of these forces. One effect of the campaign against smoking may well be to make smoking an even more adult behavior. Smoking now can mean one is old enough to judge the health reports for oneself and take risks. Cigarettes may have become more useful to adolescents for autonomy and as a weapon of rebellion.

Some parents appear to adjust to the threat of their children's smoking as a weapon against them by subtly or not so subtly encouraging them to choose cigarettes. By such encouragement, parents may help to reduce the potency of smoking as a weapon of rebellion or to prevent the use of other weapons like narcotics.

Finally, it is possible that some conflicted smoking parents unconsciously welcome their children's conversion from opponents or neutrals to fellow participants and allies. After all, if their own children feel it's all right to smoke after the "brainwashing" they've been through, cigarettes can't really be as bad as they say. Anyway, one can always quit!

Socioeconomic Differences

Although our respondents did not constitute a random sample and our main concern was not with statistical differences, we could not help but be struck by consistent class distinctions. Smokers with blue-collar backgrounds did not share the same attitudes and behaviors in reference to cigarettes as did smokers with white-collar backgrounds.

Most of the differences we observed between the classes are derivable from well-established sociological findings concerning class differences. For instance, it has been found that white-collar persons tend to have a future orientation, compared to a present orientation among the lower classes. Since the white-collar smoker is probably more concerned about what he can do to live a long, healthy life, the alleged health hazards—which he is initially more likely to accept—also make him experience greater regret about his smoking.

There were two findings, however, which did not fit readily into class distinctions noted in sociological literature. The first of these surprising results is plotted in Figure 1, which shows that the daily cigarette consumption of our blue-collar smokers dropped precipitously with an increase in years smoked, whereas there was an increase for our white-collar smokers. The second unexpected

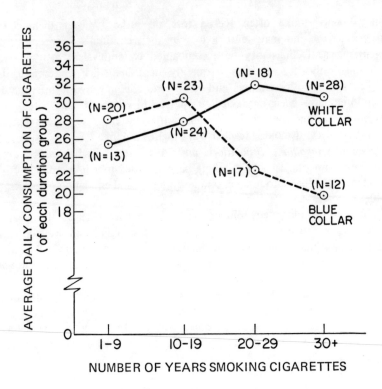

FIG. 1. Interaction of class, number of cigarettes smoked daily, and years smoked.

finding was the greater tendency among our white-collar smokers, compared to our blue-collar smokers, to report nervousness, anxiety, and a craving for cigarettes when they "quit" smoking (i.e., gave it up at least temporarily). Conversely, the blue-collar smokers were more likely to report they felt nothing or even positive effects when they gave up cigarettes.

In studying these two leads which we found particularly curious—the interaction of amount smoked and years smoked, and the suggestion of a bimodal distribution of quitting ease according to class—we pursued two lines of analysis. In the first instance we looked at the variables which triggered our smokers to continue to smoke; and in the second, we explored how these variables differentially entered the lives of our blue- and white-collar groups. Our descriptions of the two life styles were derived from the typical occupational roles of the two classes. Support for the following view of how the variables interacted with the life styles of each group was gleaned from our interview data.

The Interaction of Class, Years Smoked, and Cigarettes Smoked. In searching for an explanation, we considered the variables which are cues for continued smoking. These cues can be grouped into three types: (*a*) the physiological, (*b*) the sociopsychological, and (*c*) the situational. Physiological cues are any possible bodily changes brought about by the deprivation of cigarettes. We assumed these particular cues, whatever they are, to be independent of social class. The sociopsychological cues refer to feelings of anxiety and of social pressure, both of which are reported to be sources of a desire to smoke. Situational cues are simply the actual sight and smell of another person smoking.

To inquire into how these stimuli for smoking relate to social class, we translated the occupational roles into behavior which might affect smoking. Social pressures to smoke regularly were very strong on our young blue-collar smokers. While for both of our class groups the importance of social pressures to smoke decreases with age, this change affected the smoking consumption of our blue-collar smokers more than that of our white-collar smokers. One might conjecture that this is because the blue-collar habit is more intimately entwined with social pressures.

The other major sociopsychological cue is anxiety. Since blue-collar jobs tend not to change, advancements in terms of the complexity of the work are rare. Thus, in terms of jobs there is less likelihood of increases in stresses coming from new demands of the job with increasing age. In fact, the degree of stress on routinized jobs may decrease with practice, diminishing the amount of threat a blue-collar smoker feels from his work as he gets older.

As white-collar smokers assume jobs, they find themselves more and more in new and challenging situations, since their type of work is more likely to be oriented toward increasing their powers and responsibilities. While increasing responsibility accounts for increasing stress, the very nature of white-collar jobs tends to be more anxiety arousing than are blue-collar ones. Because white-collar professions and occupations usually involve working with other people, and since blue-collar trades more often involve working with things, a white-collar worker is more likely to be threatened by the kinds of unpredictability which people cause and which things rarely do.

It appears that situational cues also help sharpen the distinctive patterns of blue- and white-collar smokers. Many blue-collar jobs, either because they involve physical work or because there are only certain periods when smoking is permitted, dictate and limit the amount of smoking possible during working hours. This means not only that the blue-collar smoker himself can't smoke, but also that he does not perceive the sights and smells of others smoking.

This routinization and limitation on smoking imposed by much of blue-collar work leaves room only for variations in smoking behavior during leisure time. There are suggestions, however, that periods of social leisure decrease with age for the blue-collar group. Partying, drinking, and talking give way to television. The more solitary the activity, the less opportunity to be stimulated to smoke by other people.

Because white-collar smokers tend to work with other people in a more interpersonal manner, and because there are rarely external restrictions on amount of smoking, white-collar smokers can expect to be bombarded by smoking cues during a day in an office. If advancement in a particular job means increased interactions with other people, we would expect an increase in the situational cues. Finally, an increase in accomplishments is often accompanied by an increase in social life, which generally means an increase in smoking cues.

Undoubtedly there are alternative explanations which could account for this observed interaction of social class and years smoked upon smoking rate. The one just presented is of interest because it is an attempt to articulate occupational roles with stimuli to smoke. A good test of its usefulness, however, is to determine if the phenomena outlined here can help explain the observed relationship between occupational class and difficulty in quitting. One possible theoretical explanation is presented here.

Social Class and Difficulty in Quitting: A Theory of Self-Selection. It seems possible that the more resistance to smoking which a smoker encountered initially, the more committed he would be to his habit. The critical period seems to be the transition between the first attempts and the formation of the habit. During this period, the smoker who persists despite many objections must find something particularly rewarding in the cigarette not found by individuals who stop under pressure at this point.

Since continued familial complaints and a serious concern with the recent reports on health hazards are less common among blue-collar families, it is probable that a greater percentage of blue-collar smokers do not stop smoking at this transitional stage compared to white-collar smokers.

This analysis suggests that since an individual who smoked against odds initially is more devoted to the cigarette, he is going to find it more difficult to give up than smokers who never questioned, or were never questioned about, their smoking habit. Since most white-collar smokers have tried to quit or inadvertently experienced periods of deprivation, they are cognizant of the difficulties in stopping. Presumably many of those who did not suffer during abstinence or deprivation, responded long ago to this information about themselves by quitting.

Because of the greater pressure against smoking in white-collar groups, the percentage of white-collar smokers who have difficulty giving up is higher proportionately than the percentage who have difficulty among blue-collar smokers. This could well account for the fact that our white-collar smokers who tried to give up smoking were more likely to report suffering than were our blue-collar smokers. One could therefore hypothesize that a higher percentage of blue-collar smokers, because the habit was initiated without objections, would find it easy to quit, at least temporarily.

The hypothesis would continue that white-collar smokers have "selected" themselves as people for whom the smoking habit is important enough to sustain even though it causes interpersonal problems. Thus they are people for whom cigarettes have great value. Blue-collar smokers are not as likely to share the same commitment to cigarettes.

18

SMOKING BEHAVIOR
1953 AND 1970:
THE MIDTOWN MANHATTAN STUDY

Leo Srole and Anita Kassen Fischer
College of Physicians and Surgeons,
Columbia University

The Midtown Manhattan Study was the first, and thus far the only, epidemiological investigation of mental health in the general population of a metropolis. A probability sample of 1,660 adults, representative of 110,000 age 20 to 59 residents of the high-density Midtown study area, were the objects of inquiry in a home interview conducted in 1953-54.

The main mental health findings from this 99% white sample have been reported in two volumes (Srole, Langner, Michael, Opler, & Rennie, 1962; Langner & Michael, 1963).

The two-hour interview yielded a large corpus of information from each respondent, relating either to symptomatic specifics of his current mental health status or to somatic, behavioral, and sociological corollaries and antecedents of his mental health status. Such corollaries and antecedents have since lent themselves to secondary analysis in which mental health figures peripherally rather than centrally.

For example, we secured height and weight information from each respondent. These data subsequently made possible an epidemiological analysis of obesity, the first of its kind in a general population, that has been reported in two articles published by the *Journal of the American Medical Association* (Goldblatt, Moore, & Stunkard, 1965; Moore, Stunkard, & Srole, 1962).

As another example, the psychiatrists participating in the study were interested in excess intake of food and liquor, as manifestations of deficiencies in self-management and ego functioning. The questions on onvereating and overdrinking were accompanied by what at the time were intended to be filler questions on two other areas of oral intake, namely, "Do you smoke?" Do you drink coffee?" In each case a parallel probe was made, for example, "Would you say you smoke more than is good for you?"

In no instance had we anticipated that smoking behavior might later warrant intensive analysis as a phenomenon in its own right. Hence, because of the length and tightness of the interview, we did not inquire about the form of tobacco used, nor the number of units consumed.

Despite these limitations, I was invited to present a paper on the Midtown smoking data to the Conference on Smoking and the Heart sponsored in 1968 by the New York Heart Association, and subsequently published in the *Bulletin of the New York Academy of Medicine* (Srole, 1968).

This chapter presents the second installment of that analysis, plus panel information secured in 1970 as well. As a preliminary, it is essential to emphasize several points about our original smoking variable.

1. The original interviews were conducted between the fall of 1953 and summer of 1954, just *before* the first of the large-scale epidemiological investigations of the health consequences of smoking had been reported in the public press. Thus, knowledge of these reports could hardly have significantly influenced the responses to our smoking questions.

2. Since our lead question was "Do you smoke?", affirmative replies, at least from men, referred to cigars and pipes as well as cigarettes. Accordingly, the smoking frequencies of Midtown men cannot be strictly compared with the results of other studies focused exclusively on cigarette consumption. Marketing research people have reported a lack of evidence as to the proportion of all smokers who consume only pipe or cigar tobacco. We therefore lack any empirical basis for estimating the representation of the latter among Midtown's male smokers. However, we would make an educated guess that exclusively pipe and cigar users number roughly 5% of the total of male smokers, and are largely concentrated in the upper third of the socioeconomic range. We will return to this point later.

3. On the basis of our two interview questions, we can divide our sample of 1,660 Midtown adults into two main categories: (*a*) nonsmokers, and (*b*) smokers. The smokers in turn can be subdivided into:

(*a*) moderation smokers (replied "no" to the query, "Would you say you smoke more than is good for you?"); and

(*b*) problem smokers (replied "yes" to the above question).

Obviously, replies to the "more than is good for you" question entail subjective judgments which can be assumed to reflect that the average amount of smoking in the Moderation group (M) is less than the average in the Problem group (P). Another study (Elinson, Padilla, & Perkins, 1967) supports this assumption. Cigarette smokers were asked the number of cigarettes they consumed daily in whole and fractional packs. They were then asked the judgmental question of whether they thought they smoked "too little," "too much," or "about right." Men replying "too much," on the average smoked about 10 cigarettes more per day than those replying "about right." As expected, women of both judgmental groups smoked fewer cigarettes than their male counterparts, but the difference between their "too much" and "about right" groups was in the order of 15 cigarettes per day.

Although our P and M smoking groups within each sex could probably be considered as "heavy" and "less than heavy" smoking-rate categories, we shall in this paper make only limited use of them. (When so used, we will calculate the "problem rate" as a proportion of the total of smokers, expressed as P/S.) Our primary emphasis will be rather on the smoking rate figured as a proportion of all smokers to the combined total of smokers and nonsmokers, expressed as S/T.

To turn first to the sex variable in the Midtown sample (see Table 1), males and females as always distribute themselves differently on the smoking continuum. The nonsmoker percentage among women is twice that for men. Women also have a somewhat small P/S rate. Clearly, the sex factor will have to be controlled in all subsequent intergroup comparisons.

Our age variable has been divided into eight 5-year intervals across the sample's age span of 20 to 59. Among the males, both the S/T and P/S rates are essentially flat across the entire age range. Among women the P/S rates, although lower than those of the males, are also flat across all eight age groups. However, their S/T rates are flat (around the 60% level) only through age 44, and then descend in the three oldest groups to 52%, 44%, and 38% respectively. It should be noted that these three oldest groups are matrons who were in their 30'S and 40's at the beginning of World War II, the period in which female smoking accelerated greatly, primarily among the younger members of the sex. All in all, however, there is no apparent need to control for age differences in subsequent group comparisons.

To operationalize respondents' socioeconomic status (SES), we have combined scores on four quantitative status indicators, namely, years of schooling, occupational rank, family income, and rent. The distribution of the sample's combined scores was cut into six more or less equally populated strata. The S/T rates of Midtown men are more or less inversely related to socioeconomic status. More specifically, in the top stratum (A) the rate is 64%, in both B and C approximately 76%, and in all three of the lowest strata (D to F) approximately 82%. Conversely, the nonsmoker rates vary from 36% to 18% at the two extremes.

However, it is probable that men who are exclusively pipe or cigar smokers are mainly represented in the A and B strata. If these could be subtracted, to give us *only cigarette* smoking rates, then their inverse relationship above the midpoint of the SES range would be even sharper than our figures above suggest.

In the huge corpus of sociological research on SES, there are exceedingly few behaviors in which the sexes show contrary trends on the socioeconomic

TABLE 1

Percentages of Male and Female
Smokers in the Midtown Sample

Category	Males (N = 689)	Females (N = 971)
Nonsmokers	23.2%	46.7%
Smokers	76.8%	53.3%
Moderate	36.9%	28.9%
Problem	39.9%	24.4%

TABLE 2

Female Smoker Percentages by
Socioeconomic Status

Strata	Nonsmokers (%)	Smokers (%)	
A	31	69	= 100%
B	33	67	
C	47	53	
D	51	49	
E	53	47	
F	64	36	

continuum. As Table 2 demonstrates, smoking prevalence joins these rare exceptions.

In brief, the top-level females (A) have almost twice as many cigarette smokers as do the women at the bottom of the scale (F). In fact their 69% smoker rate exceeds the 64% of their stratum A male peers. And, as already suggested, the latter figure is itself inflated to some degree by the presence of pipe and cigar smokers. Moreover, only in this top stratum is the female P/S rate larger than the men's, by a significant margin of 65% to 53%.

The above data have been partially reported elsewhere, and are presented here as foundations for newly analyzed data we have prepared for this report.

From the Midtown interview information, we are also able to classify the SES of the respondent's family during his childhood, as derived from his father's schooling and occupation, scored and divided as before into six categories. By comparing respondent's present SES stratum with his father's during childhood, we can classify those who, relative to father, have risen (upward mobile), fallen (downward mobile), or remained the same in social class position (nonmobile).

When we extract the smoker rates for these three mobility types among men, we

TABLE 3

Male Smoker Percentages
by Status Mobility

Category	Nonsmokers (%)	Smokers (%)	
Upward	32	68	= 100%
Nonmobile	23	77	
Downward	19	81	

find the results shown in Table 3. This trend to our knowledge has not been previously reported in the literature. We must now proceed to clarify it by fixing the mobility types within each stratum of respondent SES separately.

A cross comparison of the male respondents' present SES levels with their SES mobility antecedents yields the following observations:

1. S/T rates of men continue to vary significantly with the mobility variable on all SES strata.

2. Male S/T rates vary to a much smaller and less consistent degree among SES strata within *like* mobility categories.

Stated more precisely: (*a*) the highest nonsmoking rates of about 36% are found among the *upward*-mobile men of *all* SES strata; (*b*) the lowest nonsmoking rates of approximately 12% are found among the *downward*-mobile men of almost all SES levels; (*c*) an intermediate 26% of the nonmobile men on all SES strata are similarly nonsmokers.

Thus, the earlier reported correlation of male S/T rates and SES has been uncovered as largely spurious. That is, it is a product of the fact that the high SES groups are progressively more heavily loaded with upward-mobile males, and the lowest SES strata are more heavily loaded with downward-mobile men.

The situation among the women is more complicated. Their S/T rates in the upward-mobile and nonmobile categories show the same kind of difference as among the men, namely, 52% and 60% respectively. The downward-mobile women of the upper SES levels, further, have still higher S/T rates of about 64%. But in the lower SES strata, the S/T rates of such downward-moving females plunge to about the 39% mark, bringing down the S/T rate of total down-moving female group to 47%. The effect is to be found in Table 4.

There are several possible explanations for this SES-localized deviation from the expected trend among downward-mobile women as compared with their upward-mobile and nonmobile counterparts. This deviation may warrant focused exploration at a later date.

If further exploration of these SES mobility relationships should support the parallelism in the male and female smoking-rate trends as suggested here, it will force reconsideration of a long popular stereotype, namely, that smoking is most characteristic of successful, upward-mobile people. In Midtown, at least, this

TABLE 4

Female Smoking Percentages by
Socioeconomic Status Mobility

Category	Nonsmokers (%)	Smokers (%)	
Upward	48	52	= 100%
Nonmobile	40	60	
Downward	53	47	

characteristic seems to be more predominantly associated with nonmobility and downward mobility.

A second noteworthy finding has recently emerged from the analysis for this paper. We asked each respondent the number of siblings he had grown up with and his birth-order position among them. We have thus been able to sort our respondents into four categories—the eldest (of one or more siblings), the middling (of two or more siblings), the youngest (of two or more), and "only child." The smoking rates of this birth-order continuum are shown in Table 5.

Although the differences among the women are of smaller magnitude, the same consistent trend is observed as among the men, namely, increased smoker frequencies downward on the scale.

We have not yet encountered other smoking studies that used the birth-order variable. Therefore we are unable to judge the generality of the above trend.

Had we formulated an hypothesis before the above data emerged, we would have predicted highest smoker rates among the eldest children and among the "onlys" both of which groups are the first born and therefore, we would assume, would have been especially close to the probably smoking father. If the "onlys" stand in support of this hypothesis, the eldest children, male and female, do not. The latter appears to be an anomaly worthy of further attention.

We propose next to make a long jump in time from the original Midtown interviews. We are now preparing plans for a twenty-year follow-up study of a subsample of the original sample, to be conducted in 1973. To this end, in 1970 we sent a Study *Newsletter* to the 1,060 respondents then still alive and at a known address. (At the date of this writing we have been able to locate, dead or alive, about 1,260, or 76% of the entire sample.) Accompanying this letter was a return postcard requesting changes of address and a number of other items of updated information, including current (i.e., 1970) smoking status, trichotomized into: (*a*) now-smokers, (*b*) ex-smokers, and (*c*) never-smokers.

Cards were returned by 400 of the respondents, of whom 370 answered our smoking question. It is not claimed that the latter are representative of the total sample. In terms of age at the time of the 1953 interview, they were largely between 25 and 55; and therefore, at the mailing they were between 42 and 72. In average years of schooling, they were higher, as expected, than the total sample, but in sex and marital-status composition (at interview) they were strikingly like the

TABLE 5

Male Smoker Percentages by Birth Order

Birth order	Nonsmokers (%)		Smokers (%)		
	Male	Female	Male	Female	
Eldest	30	50	70	50	= 100%
Middling	24	47	76	53	
Youngest	16	43	84	57	
Only	12	40	88	60	

whole sample. And in their now-smoker rate of 35%, they were close to the 33% rate reported for the national population over the age of 45 by the Current Population Survey of August, 1968, conducted by the U.S. Census Bureau.

In any case, the 370 smoke-reporting respondents of 1970 are a perfectly representative sample of themselves 17 years earlier. In this sense, they are of great interest in terms of their changes in smoking behavior over so long a span of time, a period marked by unprecedented turns in scientific knowledge and in the lay opinion-climate about the risks of smoke ingestion.

As a first step, let us compare in Table 6 the gross sex-specific distributions of our subsample when both their 1953 and 1970 smoking statuses are dichotomized into (a) smokers, and (b) abstainers.

TABLE 6
Smoking Status Distributions

Category	Males ($N = 150$)		Females ($N = 220$)	
	1953	1970	1953	1970
Nonsmokers	33%	61%	43%	67%
Smokers	67%	39%	57%	33%

During the 17 year interval, the abstention rate among the subsample of males almost doubled. Among the women, on the other hand, the 1970 abstention rate had increased by about one-half over their 1953 figure.

Historically, of course, our Midtown men moved into the smoking practice far faster than did their sisters, and now almost two decades later, they are clearly moving out of the practice at a rather faster pace.

As our next step, we can trace directions of change among the trichotomous smoking categories of 1953 and those of 1970, as set forth with sex-specific rates in Table 7.

To start with the nonsmokers of 1953, large majorities, especially among the women, over the intervening 17 years have remained nonsmokers (64% of men, 85% of women). This is as would be expected, since life styles and supportive values emerge and stabilize in early adulthood.

From the earlier (1953) base of abstention, 36% of the men (20% + 16%) and 15% (9% + 6%) of the women had at some later point moved into the ranks of smokers. But in both sexes, more than half of these particular movers subsequently shifted back into the ranks of abstainers, leaving a net shift to current smoking of 16% of the original male abstainers and 6% of the original female abstainers. (Regrettably, these movers are too few in number to sustain further analysis.) This suggests that a cross section in time of the population of smokers consists of a sizeable proportion of "in-and-out" transients.

Now let us look at the respondents who in 1953 were smokers. Among the men, half of both the moderate and problem smokers in 1953 were nonsmokers in 1970. Among women, however, 60% of the moderate smokers and 32% of the problem smokers were nonsmokers in 1970. Among both sexes the conversion to nonsmoking was of course substantially larger than the reverse conversion from nonsmoking to smoking.

When we dichotomized respondents into age groups (under and over 40), we were surprised to find that the male smokers' conversion rate to nonsmoking is higher among the younger men (58%) than among the older (42%). For the comparable female age groups, the rates of conversion to nonsmoking are not significantly different. Overall, in this subsample the 17 year frequency of moving out of the ranks of smokers is, among the younger people, the same as or higher than among the older.

The movement results as analyzed by socioeconomic status are shown in Table 8. The high concentration of conversion from nonsmoking to smoking among the

TABLE 7

Turnover Movements
Between Smoking Categories

1970 smoking category	1953 smoking category		
	Nonsmoker	Moderate	Problem
Males			
Never	64%		
Ex-smoker	20%	54%	47%
Now-smoker	16%	46%	53%
(N = 100%)	(50)	(43)	(57)
Females			
Never	85%		
Ex-smoker	9%	60%	32%
Now-smoker	6%	40%	68%
(N = 100%)	(94)	(70)	(56)

TABLE 8

Conversion Percentages by Socioeconomic Status
1953 to 1970

SES	Smoking to nonsmoking		Nonsmoking to smoking	
	Men	Women	Men	Women
Low (E-F)	50%	40%	57%	15%
Middle (C-D)	50%	50%	12%	16%
High (A-B)	50%	47%	8%	0

Low-SES men stands out conspicuously. Both sexes are quite similar on all three SES levels in their smoking-to-nonsmoking conversion percentages.

We would add that on all three male SES levels, the 1970 ex-smoker rates are identical among the moderate and problem smokers of 1953. However, among the women of all SES strata, the ex-smoker rates are consistently higher among the moderate smokers of 1953 (±60%) than among the problem smokers (±32%).

At least among women, therefore, moderate smoking is a predictor of subsequent conversion to nonsmoking, whereas problem smoking is a predictor of long-range continuity of smoking. Why the men do not show this differential pattern of conversion to nonsmoking may have to wait upon our 1973 reinterview study for answers.

The remainder of this chapter will look more closely at several other characteristics in a larger array distinguishing the 1970 ex-smokers of both sexes.

More likely to be ex-smokers in 1970 are those with the following characteristics in 1953:

1. Those who were worriers.
2. Those who were sensitive to "what others think of me." One might conjecture that in those circles where smoking is becoming part of an unfavorable social image, those averse to such self-images apparently tend to change their behaviors accordingly.
3. Those in 1953 who were separated, divorced, or widowed, rather than single or married. However, there doubtless have been considerable changes in marital status since that year, calling upon us to reassess this 1970 finding in the light of marital status to be reported in the 1973 interviews.
4. Those with an appetite for food that was "good" rather than "fair" or "poor." If quality of appetite proves to be a more or less long-term personal trait, this would suggest the hypothesis that smoking is a substitute gratification that is more likely to persist when gratification derived from food, whatever the reason, is less than optimal.
5. Those who had "trouble sleeping" were more likely to give up smoking. This may be part of the worrying syndrome we have already seen associated with abandonment of smoking.
6. Among men, the lower the alcohol imbibement in 1953, the higher the rate of conversion by 1970 from smoking to nonsmoking. Stated in reverse, the greater the alcohol consumption, the greater the persistence of smoking.
7. However, among women the trend was somewhat in the opposite direction: the greater the alcohol consumption the greater the shift from smoking to nonsmoking. Hypotheses to account for this sex difference in the linkage between drinking and smoking continuity will be formulated for the 1973 investigation.
8. Respondents' mental health status (degree of symptom formation) in 1953, as globally judged by the Study psychiatrists, is unrelated to subsequent smoking continuity-discontinuity among women. However, among men there is a direct relationship, with the highest ex-smoking rate (61%) among "the well" (the asymptomatic).

CONCLUSION

In his chapter on methods, Dr. Dunn has emphasized the limitations of post hoc research designs. We have gone one step beyond in this chapter by dealing with what may be called "post hoc nondesign."

Two simple questions on smoking were asked in the Midtown Study interviews, without benefit of an hypothesis or even a rationale, beyond the accident that we needed filler items to disperse respondent attention from questions on more sensitive areas of intake behavior. Because of competing analytic demands, it was not until a decade later that we focused down on our Midtown smoking data, and then largely by the promptings of newly intensified scientific and public interest in the smoking problem.

At that point we had four things going for us:

1. We were committed to the comprehensive, comparative approach of social anthropology to the entire spectrum of social behaviors.

2. We had applied the methods of medical epidemiology.

3. We held title to an accessible data bank of hundreds of items of individual information, secured in 2 hour interviews with 1,660 Midtown adults. Each item had been included to test its hypothesized relationship, independent or interdependent, to mental health as the Study's dependent variable.

4. Albeit belatedly, we now grasped the nettle of opportunity to upgrade our crude, trichotomized smoking variable to the status of a dependent variable, and to test against it essentially the same large matrix of hypothesized independent and interdependent factors as we had screened against the dependent variable of mental health.

Without expertise, without hypotheses, without prior design, we took this post hoc opportunity and, so to speak, took off on a "go-for-broke" netting expedition for correlations. The analysis is not yet complete, and with this paper and its predecessor we have reported only a part of our catch.

With acute awareness of our limitations in this particular fishing ground, we have not generalized beyond our particular sample population. We consider that the findings we have reported so far at the very least have illuminating descriptive value in their own right.

In most cases, we are not even able to explain the dynamics behind these correlations. Their ultimate value, by no means a humble one in science, is to stimulate new hypotheses for further, more sophisticated research designs. After all, Gregor Mendel only described what he had found in his rather crude hybridization experiments with sweet peas; and if memory serves, the speculations from these findings, which launched genetics on its spectacular scientific career, did not follow until many decades later.

As social scientists committed both to the natural history observational approach and to its more controlled variants, we have invoked Mendel here only to suggest that the post hoc design, and even the "post hoc nondesign" exemplified in this paper, have their own modest place in this march of science.

In effect, therefore, we are arguing not in defense of the particularistic Midtown smoking data but, more broadly, for a sociological view of the pluralisms essential to compensate for the limitations in what C. P. Snow, in an anthropological vein, has called "the culture of science."

REFERENCES

Elinson, J., Padilla, E., & Perkins, M. E. *Public images of mental health services.* New York: Mental Health Materials Center, 1967.

Goldblatt, P. B., Moore, M. E., & Stunkard, A. J. Social factors in obesity. *Journal of the American Medical Association,* 1965, **192,** 1039-1044.

Langner, T. S., & Michael, S. T. *Life stress and mental health.* New York: Free Press, 1963.

Moore, M. E., Stunkard, A., & Srole, L. Obesity, social class and mental illness. *Journal of the American Medical Association,* 1962, **181,** 962-966.

Srole, L. Social and psychological factors in smoking behavior: The Midtown Manhattan study. *Bulletin of the New York Academy of Medicine,* 1968, **44**(12), 1502-1513.

Srole, L., Langner, T. S., Michael, S. T., Opler, M. K., & Rennie, T. A. C. *Mental health in the metropolis: The Midtown Manhattan study.* New York: Harper & Row, 1962.

19

ETHOLOGICAL AND BIOCHEMICAL INTERACTIONS AND THEIR RELATIONSHIPS TO SMOKING[1]

Richard J. Hickey and Evelyn B. Harner[2]
University of Pennsylvania

It is hypothesized that tobacco-smoking behavior for many people is in part symptomatic of, or an effect of, one or more underlying problems of metabolism, particularly glucose metabolism. These are thought to occur with varying degrees of severity in different individuals in human populations, and are influenced in part by the genotype and in part by environmental variables, including various stresses which affect individuals. It is further hypothesized that most smokers smoke, to a large extent, to obtain nicotine and its pharmacological effects which are perceived by the smoker as beneficial.

SOME EFFECTS OF NICOTINE AND GLUCOSE

Nicotine has been reported to demonstrate many effects on the living subject. The dosages or levels of use in the smoking context are quite small. Small doses are reported to stimulate the ganglion cells of the peripheral nervous system directly, and to facilitate impulse transmission (Volle & Koelle, 1965). Nicotine stimulates the CNS, excites respiration, and has some antidiuretic action (Volle & Koelle, 1965; Royal College of Physicians, 1971). Cardiovascular effects of nicotine are also reported, but are related in part to adrenal discharge of catecholamines.

Of the various effects of nicotine (Volle & Koelle, 1965), those of particular interest with regard to examination of the bioenergetic deficiency hypothesis involve (*a*) elevation of blood glucose concentration, (*b*) elevation of blood epinephrine concentration, (*c*) the relationship of these changes to blood insulin level alterations, (*d*) the relationship of insulin concentration changes to changes in

[1] This study was supported by a Special Project grant of The Council for Tobacco Research–U.S.A., Inc.

[2] We are indebted to Caroline B. Thomas, Carl C. Seltzer, and Richard C. Clelland for constructive criticisms. Any errors are, however, our own.

glucose penetration into cells, and the consequences, and (e) CNS and systemic "stimulation" by nicotine and by epinephrine. Also significant are (f) the interrelationships with endocrine regulatory mechanisms and (g) the relationships of all these processes and their effects to behavior.

It has been known for many years that nicotine intake often leads to elevation of blood glucose levels in man and in certain experimental animals (Volle & Koelle, 1965; McCormick 1935). Glucose is the principal product of carbohydrate metabolism and the principal circulating sugar. The blood glucose level increases following a meal and then drops off as it is absorbed by the cells. The normal fasting level of glucose in peripheral venous blood is 60 to 80 mg per 100 ml. In arterial blood it is 15 to 30 mg higher per 100 ml. When the blood glucose level becomes excessively high, glucose is excreted by the kidneys and appears in the urine. This is often a sign of a metabolic block, often of diabetes mellitus.

Glucose is the main source of metabolic energy and the primary fuel used by the brain. As blood glucose level falls, there are various responses. Hypoglycemia produces nervousness, tremors, and palpitations, probably due to sympathetic nervous system activity. As blood glucose levels fall below normal, brain areas are affected starting with the cortex, which has the highest metabolic requirement. This is followed by the diencephalon and finally by the medulla. Ganong (1969) states that "the blood glucose level at which symptoms appear is variable. A rapid decline to 20-30 mg/100 ml in humans does not cause symptoms until the cerebral carbohydrate reserves are depleted, but a slow or sustained decline usually causes symptoms at blood glucose levels of approximately 50 mg/100 ml [p. 282]." People with clinical hypoglycemia experience a variety of undesirable behavioral effects whose severity tends to be related to the severity of the hypoglycemia (Bondy, 1969; Volle & Koelle, 1965; Marks & Rose, 1965; see also the next section of this chapter).

The various metabolites under consideration are part of complex cybernetic mechanisms that regulate metabolic functioning. Elevation of blood glucose leads to pancreatic release of insulin while increases in levels of epinephrine and norepinephrine tend to suppress insulin secretion. Excessive insulin induces hypoglycemia, which tends to depress insulin release and stimulate glucagon release. The latter stimulates hepatic glycogenolysis leading to elevation of blood glucose. The suppressive effect of epinephrine on insulin secretion can be abolished by drugs that block α-adrenergic receptors (Ganong, 1969). Direct and feedback effects on the pituitary might be expected but have not been well worked out. Secretion of ADH (antidiuretic hormone) has been observed, however (Royal College of Physicians, 1971).

Based on considerations of molecular genetic variation and of concomitant phenotypic variation, it would be expected that variations occur among individuals in populations with regard to (a) influence of blood glucose concentration on pancreatic release of insulin, (b) influence of concentrations of catecholamines individually on degree of suppression of insulin secretion, (c) efficacy of "excess" insulin in inducing hypoglycemia, (d) efficacy of hypoglycemia in depressing insulin release and in stimulating glucagon release, and (e) efficacy of insulin in mediating glucose entry into cells.

To further complicate an already highly complex metabolic system, it should be noted that reduction of circulating insulin concentration is associated with elevation of concentrations of circulating free fatty acids and of amino acids which are also catabolized to produce energy under some circumstances (Ganong, 1969).

Epinephrine affects phosphorylase and maintains it in its active form, phosphorylase-a (Ganong, 1969; Kalow, 1962). Phosphorylase converts glycogen to glucose-1-phosphate. Ganong (1969) has shown that phosphoglucomutase converts glucose-1-phosphate to glucose-6-phosphate, which is converted by glucose-6-phosphatase to glucose in the liver. It should be noted further that epinephrine stimulates adenyl cyclase, which "causes activation of the phosphorylase in liver and skeletal muscle [Ganong, 1969, p. 230]." This action brings about a rise not only in the blood glucose level, but also in blood lactic acid. Such descriptions as the above involve exceedingly brief parts of the very complex glucose metabolic system. It is important to recognize that, at every enzymatic step in the glucose metabolic sequences, it is to be expected that clonal variations can exist among individuals regarding the structures or "quality" of the enzymes (i.e., variations in amino acid sequences) and in quantity produced per kilogram body weight of the individual. Amino acid sequence variations or polymorphisms could be expected to arise in large part from variations in the individual genotypes in populations (Harris, 1966). This would also apply to polypeptide hormones, for example, insulin and glucagon, to some extent. Disfunctional variants would, of course, be selected out. It could also be expected that under the influence of cumulative somatic genetic degeneration, alterations might also arise in amino acid sequences of both enzymes and polypeptide hormones. Behavioral consequences could ensue.

The effects of nicotine could be expected to be different from person to person. Perhaps from the same amount of nicotine some persons may react with an appreciable increase in blood epinephrine and blood glucose levels, while others may respond less, and still others hardly at all. The question of influence of nicotine on blood glucose *utilization* and its variation among individuals also needs study.

A few instances have been reported in which smoking led to an aggravation or induction of hypoglycemia (Berry, 1959; Bohan & Berry, 1953). These were largely males who had smoked from 25 to 40 years. The one female cited with this problem was 24 years old, and had smoked for nine years. One might speculate about whether some instances of the presumably smoking-induced hypoglycemia could be a result of processes of senescence on metabolism, with the smoking behavior having become established before the metabolic modifications occurred.

Living things tend to exhibit behavioral characteristics that have survival advantage. Hamburg (1968) observed that "tasks that must be done (for species survival) tend to be quite pleasurable; they are easy to learn and hard to extinguish. Their blockage or deprivation leads to tension, anger, substitutive activity, and (if prolonged) depression [p. 254]." When hungry, people tend to eat, and tend to enjoy good food. What is "good" varies from one culture to another. When thirsty, people tend to drink aqueous products with great relish if the thirst is great.

Eating is, of course, a behavior which has survival value, though it can be, and sometimes is, indulged in to excess. One result of the ingestion of food is to obtain the necessary "fuel" for various essential energetic metabolic functions which may or may not involve behavior. One basic source of energy, once it enters the blood, is glucose. Low blood glucose, or hypoglycemia, can impose a limit on certain types of biological energy available for various functions, including bioenergetic respiratory functions of the brain.

It has been estimated (Ganong, 1969) that brain metabolism consumes about 18.4% of the glucose metabolized by an "average" human adult. In the human child, "the brain may account for 50 per cent of the total oxygen consumption during the first four years of life [Cheek, Migeon, & Mellits, 1968, p. 549]." In what ways do nicotine, insulin, and catecholamines affect glucose utilization in the brain directly or indirectly? Is monoamine oxidase affected by nicotine directly or indirectly?

There are various causes of hypoglycemia, and varying degrees of severity (Sayers & Travis, 1965). Very severe hypoglycemia can result in convulsions and coma. We are, however, concerned presently in part with much more limited hypoglycemia in "normal" individuals. It can result, for example, from "failure to eat, unaccustomed exercise, and too large a dose of insulin [p. 1588]." Among the symptoms are "lethargy and yawning, confusion and impaired mental function as judged by ability to execute simple calculations [p. 1588]." According to Bondy (1969), initial manifestations of hypoglycemia in individuals whose blood glucose levels drop slowly may include hallucinations, confusion, bizarre behavior, depression, and neurological manifestations, along with "subjective tension or a feeling of impending disaster [p. 244]" and more serious effects. Apprehension, dizziness, blurred vision, and fear of falling have also been reported (Berry, 1959). Related physiological effects (Bondy, 1969) of hypoglycemia, involving body response including secretion of epinephrine, are tachycardia, vasoconstriction, piloerection, and perspiration. If the basic functional problem of hypoglycemia is bioenergetic restriction, then it might be possible that somewhat similar symptoms may occur where glucose metabolism is limited by enzyme or hormone inadequacies, or by both, in the presence of adequate blood glucose. Such inadequacies or anomalies might in fact tend to result in "normal" or elevated blood glucose levels *because* the glucose is poorly metabolized.

In this connection, pheochromocytomas, which are catecholamine-producing tumors (Levine, 1969), can lead to rather permanent hypertension. It is curious that among the symptoms of patients with pheochromocytoma are some which have been reported for hypoglycemia, including dizziness, perspiration, anxiety, and blurred vision. This is particularly curious since these tumors tend to lead to *hyper*glycemia (Levine, 1969). But high blood concentration of epinephrine tends to suppress or inhibit insulin release (Bondy, 1969), though the "major control of insulin secretion is exerted by a feedback effect of the blood glucose level directly on the pancreas [Ganong, 1969, p. 284]." With regard to diabetic hyperglycemia, Ganong has stated that the "plethora of glucose outside the cells in diabetes contrasts with the intracellular deficit [p. 277]," and that inasmuch as the catabolism of glucose is usually a primary source of energy for metabolic functions of cells, these energy requirements in diabetics are shifted to utilization of protein and fat sources. Preoccupation with blood glucose levels rather than study of its utilization can be of only limited value. It is well to keep in mind, however, that it seems inescapable to conclude that "no single cause can be postulated for all cases of diabetes [Pathogenesis, 1971]."

The lower bound of "normal" blood glucose is considered to be about 60 mg/100 ml (Bondy, 1969), with hypoglycemia considered clinically significant below 50 mg/100 ml, though obvious symptoms may not occur until the level is lower. Older people particularly, however, tend to exhibit mental difficulties at glucose levels below 50 mg/100 ml (Bondy, 1969). In the event that there are specific regions of the brain in which cerebral blood flow is reduced (e.g., due to atherosclerosis), there may be visual and other disturbances; and if the hypoglycemia attack lasts long enough, local damage or death of brain cells may occur (Bondy, 1969).

Marks and Rose (1965) observed: "The cerebral manifestations of hypoglycemia have been likened, largely as a result of morbid anatomical studies, to those of anoxia and attributed in each case to the same cause, namely a reduction in cerebral respiration [p. 56]."

Kalter (1968) included withholding of food, and hypoxia, among the teratogens, among which was also, interestingly, insulin. Ingalls, Avis, Curley, and Temin (1953) reported on the genetic basis for hypoxia-induced congenital anomalies, and Smithberg and Runner (1963) described the teratogenic effects of hypoglycemic treatments of mice, which included the use of insulin. Mazess (1970) observed that high-altitude hypoxia is associated with "increased perinatal mortality, increased birth defects, cardiovascular defects, retarded growth and development, particularly of the brain and nervous system [p. 275]," and reduced or impaired mental and physical performance. Adequate energy would seem obviously necessary for DNA synthesis and mitosis.

POSSIBLE CONSEQUENCES OF THE RELATIONSHIP BETWEEN NICOTINE AND GLUCOSE

Cattell (1967) observed: "The recorded history of tobacco smoking, going back to the discovery of America, and its rapid spread thereafter to all parts of the world, suggests that it provides something of value to the human race [p. 1]." He noted further that although controversy exists regarding the various effects of smoking, it seems essential that "why we smoke" must have its origins in the central nervous system.

Having discussed briefly some of the deleterious and sometimes dangerous effects of hypoglycemia and hypoxia, as examples of bioenergetic deficiency diseases, consideration of possible means of alleviation seems obviously necessary. A particular recommendation often made to hypoglycemics, for example, is that they employ high-protein diets. The intake of glucose can lead to temporary alleviation, but this can be followed fairly rapidly, especially if the dose is large, by elevation of insulin concentration of the blood followed by a recurrence of hypoglycemia.

Alleviation requires assessment of the causes of the problem, and there are numerous causes of hypoglycemia. Bondy (1969) lists two primary causes:

(a) excessive glucose removal from the blood, and (b) insufficient secretion of glucose into the blood. Among the causes of (a) are excessive release and accumulation of insulin for a number of reasons including induction by drugs, presence of certain tumors, and induction by glucose feeding. A high degree of muscular exercise can lead to excessive glucose utilization, also leading to hypoglycemia. Among the causes of (b) are chronic starvation or malabsorption, reduced gluconeogenesis (e.g., from amino acids), and inadequate release from glycogen stores. Alleviation of feelings of hunger may well have been one of the significant factors in the rapid worldwide spread of smoking.

Only a few examples of the numerous exceedingly diverse and complex origins of hypolgycemia have been mentioned. Involved also are various glycogen storage diseases (Bondy, 1969; Childs & Der Kaloustian, 1968). Some of the problems, such as von Gierke's disease, have heritable components. Defective hepatic glucose-6-phosphatase metabolism is involved in this disease. Genetic variation in glucose-6-phosphate dehydrogenase is also well known.

However, if, for many hypoglycemic people, the use of nicotine leads to alleviation of the hypoglycemic state through elevation of blood glucose concentrations, which may lead to the smoker "feeling better" and being able by objective observation, for example, to handle mathematical problems more efficiently and to drive an automobile with fewer driving errors (Heimstra, Bancroft, & DeKock, 1967), such subjective and objective benefits of smoking may be considered as possibly involved in the acquisition of the behavior.

Hypoglycemia and hypoxia have been discussed as two fairly well-known conditions producing bioenergetic deficiency. The concept of bioenergetic deficiency must obviously encompass a much wider scope than is contained within hypoglycemia and hypoxia. In particular, it must be recognized, as already noted, that merely because a chemical, such as glucose, is *present* in "adequate" concentration in the blood, it need not follow logically that it is being *utilized* properly or efficiently.

In diabetes, one of the basic physiological defects involves reduced or limited entry of circulating glucose into the cells of various "peripheral" tissues or more specifically, into, for example, (a) skeletal, cardiac, and smooth muscles, (b) the aorta, (c) adipose tissue, (d) leukocytes, (e) pituitary tissue, (f) fibroblasts, and (g) the mammary gland (Ganong, 1969). Insulin elevation increases glucose uptake into the cells of these tissues. In contrast, insulin elevation evidently does not affect glucose uptake in certain tissues such as (a) the brain, except perhaps for part of the hypothalamus, (b) kidney tubules, (c) red blood cells, (d) intestinal mucosa, and (e) possibly the liver (there is disagreement on the last) (Ganong, 1969). The "typical" insulin half-life in circulation in man is approximately 30 minutes. Based on genetic theory, it might be expected that variations could be observed among individuals regarding insulin formation and/or release, and also regarding its breakdown. It seems likely that there are individuals in a population whose typical blood glucose levels appear "normal" or even higher than "normal," but who are in fact bioenergetically deficient because blood glucose is improperly metabolized. Both structural and functional metabolic variations could, of course, affect observed blood glucose levels and also, importantly, intracellular glucose levels. This variation is, perhaps, why we find an appreciable range of "normal" blood glucose levels rather than a single expected level.

Businessmen have been observed to show fasting blood glucose levels which were significantly higher among smokers (74.3 mg %) than among nonsmokers (69.6 mg %) (Blackburn, Brozek, Taylor, & Keys, 1960). Secretion of epinephrine and increased blood glucose levels are part of the individual's "fight or flight" response. In a recent study of middle-aged men in Sweden, smoking tended to be more prevalent among diabetics than among controls (Nilsén & Persson, 1972). Thus, here are two observations of greater prevalence of higher blood glucose among smokers than among nonsmokers. Since diabetics evidently tend to smoke more than "normal" controls, the glucose elevation response to nicotine use would not appear to be the needed response. But diabetics suffer from intracellular glucose deficiency. Epinephrine elevation could, however, be significant. Innes and Nickerson (1965) state that epinephrine, in pressor doses in man, increases both cerebral blood flow and oxygen consumption without modifying cerebrovascular resistance. Increased blood glucose also tends to lead to insulin release. If smoking can serve to induce an increased metabolic rate somewhat related to the energetic function of the "fight or flight" response, or to prolong its duration, it may be not only of subjective but also of operational benefit in meeting the challenges of contemporary living.

NICOTINE, BIOENERGETIC DEFICIENCY, AND THE BIOLOGY OF BEHAVIOR

Tinbergen (1968) has pointed out that "the ignorance of ourselves which needs to be stressed today is our ignorance of our behavior—lack of understanding of the causes and effects of the function of our brains. A scientific understanding of our behavior, leading to its control, may well be the most urgent task that faces mankind today [p. 1411]." The structure and biochemical functioning of the body's control mechanisms, the endocrine hormones and the central nervous system, are extremely complex. Behavior is a dynamic, ongoing process. Certainly behavior is to some extent malleable. Man's capacity for culture—which can be defined as a set of learned behaviors and their products—is his major adaptive modification. What is possible to learn, however, is limited by the structural and functional nature of the learner as well as by his history, as has been shown by numerous experiments in comparative psychology.

This discussion is largely theoretical. It is based in part on the concept that life is a dynamic chemical process that requires energy for its reactions to proceed. If essential energy-supplying sequences are suppressed or lowered in efficiency, for whatever reason, there will be disadvantageous or debilitating consequences. Hypoxia and hypoglycemia are simply two examples of this situation which can be examined. Unfortunately there are those who reject bioenergetics as essential to biology. Caplan observed in 1971 that "the claim that thermodynamics is not relevant to biology (believe it or not) has recently been advanced in certain quarters with such vehemence that the innocent biologist may be forgiven if he begins to be convinced [p. 1123]."

It seems curious that rather little has been made of the likelihood that nicotine may be of benefit to some people in the alleviation of hypoglycemia or other problems of glucose metabolism, though it has been known for many years that nicotine can lead to elevation of blood glucose levels (McCormick, 1935). If the presence of some degree of hypoglycemia, or other bioenergetic deficiency involving glucose (whether recognized clinically or not), is an important factor relating to tobacco smoking, one might inquire whether the hypoglycemic state or other glucose-related biogenergetic deficiency is of any significance in experimental animal studies concerning tobacco usage. Most studies on effects of smoking on experimental animals have not considered this question as relevant to the problem. Further, the use of inbred lines or "races" of experimental animals for such studies is hardly representative of genetically heterogeneous human populations. Neither individual nor group variation seems to have been adequately appreciated.

Is nicotine usage, or tobacco smoking, symptomatic in part of the presence of some degree of hypoglycemia or other glucose-related metabolic deficiency in some smokers? Are many of the behavioral and health effects attributed to smoking in reality the effects, or partly the effects, of bioenergetic deficiency, either chronic or transient, with cigarette smoking being merely one of the effects? There is some circumstantial evidence which is not inconsistent with the smoking-bioenergetic deficiency hypothesis, but experimental evidence from properly designed biochemical and other substantive experiments is essential for proof.

A further complexity in the relation between smoking and metabolism concerns the question of smoking as a displacement activity. The concept of displacement activity was envisioned originally by Tinbergen (1952, 1960; also, Eibl-Eibesfeldt, 1970; Manning, 1967). A displacement activity may be a rather irrelevant activity or behavior which serves simply as an action that relieves tension or inner conflict. Tinbergen (1960) has referred to an angry man"whose action is restrained by fear of social convention. In such states of inner conflict the impluse to attack may also be redirected against inanimate objects or displaced by some irrelevant activity such as the nest-building head flick in the gull or the lighting of a cigarette in man [p. 122]." Not all tensions threaten violence, of course. Some may be considered subjectively, as Manning (1967) observed: "We all know that when we are ill at ease we are apt to do completely irrelevant things without much conscious thought. People rarely sit peacefully in a dentist's waiting room or outside an examination hall. They fidget, making minor adjustments to necktie or hair, light cigarettes and talk unnecessarily fast and eagerly [p. 100]."

Eating may be a displacement activity for some persons, including, perhaps, persons who have recently quit smoking. Eating may also tend to alleviate bioenergetic deficiency problems in some ex-smokers, temporarily, at least. Metabolic changes have been reported associated with cessation of smoking (S.C. Glauser, E.M. Glauser, Reidenberg, Rusy, & Tallarida, 1970), including weight gain. Hunger contractions of the stomach have been shown to he reflexly abolished by smoking one cigarette; the effect may persist for 15 to 60 minutes (Volle & Koelle, 1965). But eating may not always be feasible. There are cultural constraints on behavior with respect to food. In Western society it is considered rude to eat in the presence of others without offering to share. Smoking is not similarly considered, though sharing may occur. Moreover, food sharing has a bonding function that may be inappropriate in mass society, where the individual must interact with far more people than in a face-to-face group, not all of whom could possibly be maintained as friends.

It may be difficult or impossible to separate that part of cigarette-smoking behavior which may be influenced by hypoglycemia or other bioenergetic deficiency from that part influenced by a tensive situation. Both variables may be positively related to smoking. A tensive situation may itself produce changes in blood glucose level. Hypoglycemia is known to be associated with feelings of anxiety. The neural mechanisms involved are obsecure and require further examination.

We can hardly presume, as already noted, that over the vast reaches of time involved in the evolution of man there was evolved something ridiculous like a "gene for smoking." But there are physiological variations among individuals which may be significant. Moreover, in order to develop the smoking habit, one must first experience the use of tobacco. There is a tendency, particularly among the young, to desire to learn something new and to experience new circumstances. There also appears to be a certain enchantment about that which is forbidden, or is perhaps "anti-establishment." Claims regarding the dangers of certain materials, if subsequently shown to be exaggerated or false, can also lead to lack of confidence in the perpetrators. So, among those who try cigarettes when young, there are evidently those who like them and derive some pleasure from smoking. Among smokers the degree of usage varies. No doubt cigarette advertising and antismoking propaganda both have their influences. But tobacco smoking has existed for many years. The South American Indians who first discovered tobacco smoking must have found something in its favor, without the influences of advertising. Anthropologist Ralph Linton (1924) has pointed out that "at the time of the discovery of America, tobacco was in use over the greater part of the continent. It was not used in the sub-Arctic regions of North America or in the extreme southern part of Southern America [pp. 1,2]." He stated further that in the Andean highlands and on the west coast of South America tobacco was replaced by coca *(Erythroxylum coca)*, from which cocaine may be extracted. Little (1970) has shown recently that coca, used as the Indians use it, has physiological effects that would allow it to serve to alleviate fatigue and cold, just as the ethno-pharmacology indicated.

The antismoking propaganda (cartoons, exhortations, threats) has evidently had a rather limited effect on cigarette consumption. How much of the earlier reported declines in cigarette consumption, if real, were due to antismoking propaganda, and how much were due to the rise in popularity of other activities such as the use of marijuana and other drugs? Could there be persons, influenced by the antismoking propaganda, who found tobacco to be less satisfying in advocated products of lower nicotine content, or who quit smoking altogether and substituted materials of an illegal nature? The ethnographic explanation for tobacco smoking was, in part, that it alleviated hunger and fatigue.

If a particular biological basis for use of nicotine is that it contributes to the alleviation of glucose-related bioenergetic deficiency for many smokers, it might be expected that smokers would be greater users of sweet products than nonsmokers.

Thus, statistical examination of appropriate population data might demonstrate some observable positive association between the tendency to smoke and the tendency to consume sweet food and drink. Murchison and Fyfe (1966), Bennett, Doll, and Howell (1970), and Elwood, Waters, Moore, and Sweetnam (1970) have provided observations which demonstrate a positive relationship between cigarette smoking and the consumption of sugar-containing materials.

Among the popular drinks used by many people, some of which may include sugar, are coffee and tea. Further, cigarette smokers tend to be coffee drinkers (Paul, Lepper, Phelan, Dupertuis, Macmillan, McKean, & Park, 1963; Royal College of Physicians, 1971; Yerushalmy, 1971). It could be of importance if coffee, which contains caffeine, or tea, which contains caffeine and theophylline, can lead to elevated blood glucose based on physiological effects of these xanthines, and/or to improved glucose utilization. It has been reported (Ritchie, 1965) that methylxanthines, especially theophylline, do in fact lead to glycogenolysis, or glucose release from glycogen stores. Interestingly, injection of theophylline in rats leads to elevation of plasma insulin (Robison, Butcher, & Sutherland, 1971). Elevation of insulin leads to increased intracellular glucose, which can permit intracellular utilization. Methylxanthines competitively inhibit phosphodiesterase, an enzyme which inactivates cyclic $3', 5'$-AMP (AMP = adrenosinemonophosphate), or cyclic AMP. Thus, the concentration of cyclic AMP rises in tissue under the influence of these xanthines. But cyclic AMP is critical in promoting glucose release from glycogen stores, leading to blood glucose increases with increases in the concentration of cyclic AMP. It is also reported (Robison *et al.*, 1971) that methylxanthines enhance a number of hormonal effects, including insulin release, amylase release, and smooth-muscle relaxation in relation to catecholamines. In addition, caffeine is reported to suppress monoamine oxidase (MAO) activity (Galzigna, Maina, & Rumney, 1971), which is involved in metabolizing catecholamines. The complex metabolic interrelationships among catecholamines, xanthines, insulin, glucogenesis, cyclic AMP, and other factors are beyond the scope of this chapter. For further information, see Bondy (1969) and Robison et al. (1971).

TESTS OF HYPOTHESIS

Three types of observations are presented in this section which can serve as conceptual tests of the bioenergetic deficiency hypothesis. Such tests cannot establish that an hypothesis is true. They could, however, reject it to the extent that the observations were in conflict with the hypothesis. Substantive evidence is, of course, essential to proof.

The first test of the bioenergetic deficiency hypothesis deals with the repair of deoxyribonucleic acid (DNA). Repair of damage to DNA is essential to the continuing integrity of the cell. The chemical reactions involved in repair require energy to function. Where *intracellular* glucose concentrations are deficient because of hypoglycemia, or because of inadequate insulin (which affects glucose entry into cells, as discussed above), then even though *blood* glucose is adequate or even high, as in diabetics, DNA repair efficiency (intracellular) might be expected to be impaired. Repair could also be impaired by defects in DNA repair enzymes. Of possible significance is the report of Koch and Kruuv (1971) that the presence of hypoxia, following irradiation of mammalian cells, led to a decrease in the recovery or repair of damage following radiation exposure. Also of significance are reports of Cleaver (1968, 1969), who described a defect in a genetic repair mechanism in the human autosomal recessive disease, xeroderma pigmentosum, in which patients are at high risk of developing skin cancer when exposed to sunlight. Cleaver (1969) stated that "carcinogenesis in xeroderma pigmentosum, and perhaps in some normal individuals, may be the result of somatic mutations caused by unrepaired damage [p. 428]." Since enzymes are evidently involved in genetic repair processes, structural polymorphisms of the enzymes could be expected which could affect repair efficiency clonally among individuals in populations. Differences in inherited levels of DNA repair efficiency in man have been reported by Bootsma, Mulder, Pot, and Cohen (1970). If reduced DNA repair efficiency, via genetic deficiency in xeroderma pigmentosum, is functionally involved in increasing risk of contracting cancer in man, it might not be altogether unreasonable to expect that reduction of DNA repair efficiency through bioenergetic deficiency, if chronic, might also be involved functionally in increasing the risk of contracting cancer. Inadequacy of intracellular glucose might be one of the foundations for this increased risk. Are some smokers hypoglycemic? Are there other smokers whose blood glucose levels are "normal" or above normal, but whose intracellular glucose levels may tend to be subnormal because of enzyme or hormone anomalies, or both, of genotypic origin?

Of course, genetic repair implies that mutation is involved. But mutagenic damage could mean damage by mutagens of environmental origin, along with accidental mutations occurring during DNA replication. Are there important environmental mutagens? Can they accelerate the rate of cumulative somatic genetic degeneration? Is this a partial basis of progressive senescence? Cancer and heart disease are largely diseases of senescence, or, at least, they increase in frequency, statistically, as age increases. We have considered these questions elsewhere (Hickey, Boyce, Harner, & Clelland, 1970), and it does appear, for example, that atmospheric SO_2 is a mutagenic hazard (Mukai, 1970; Summers & Drake, 1971) via bisulfite. It was first suggested (Miller & Todaro, 1969) and later demonstrated for xeroderma pigmentosum (Veldhuisen & Pouwels, 1970) that cells from several categories of persons at high risk of contracting cancer underwent malignant transformation by the SV40 virus much more readily than did normal control cells. Such an outcome could be expected if deficient DNA repair were involved.

This material does not appear incompatible with the concept that bioenergetic deficiency, whether due to inadequacies of glucose metabolism, or to heritable inadequacy of DNA repair processes, may contribute to increased cancer risk. Cancer mortality rate is known to be positively correlated with heart disease mortality rate in metropolitan populations in the United States (Hickey et al., 1970).

A further test of the nicotine-bioenergetic deficiency hypothesis might be derived from the statistical relationship between cigarette smoking in women and birth weights of their children. If cigarette smoking tends to be symptomatic of hypoglycemia, or of other bioenergetic deficiency involving glucose metabolism, and since hypoglycemia imposes bioenergetic deficiency or limitation on metabolic processes (Smithberg & Runner, 1963), it might be expected that a more or less chronic bioenergetic deficiency condition during pregnancy could lead to limitations of growth and development of the fetus, i.e., a kind of stress, leading to a tendency for birth weights of infants of smoking women to be lower than birth weights of infants of nonsmoking women. This might be observed statistically. Such an inverse relationship between birth weight and smoking habits of the women has indeed been reported (U.S. Public Health Service, 1964, 1967, 1968, 1969; Royal College of Physicians, 1971; Yerushalmy, 1971, 1972). Could insulin deficiency related to reduced intracellular glucose in the presence of adequate blood glucose be involved among some of these women?

Yerushalmy (1971) reported that while the incidence of low birth weight among infants of smoking women was higher than the incidence of low birth weight among infants of nonsmoking women, "the neonatal mortality rate and the risk of congenital anomalies of low birth-weight infants were considerably lower for smoking than for nonsmoking mothers [p. 443]." Might it be possible that bioenergetic deficiency could be involved in increased risk of spontaneous abortion of fetuses with some kinds of congenital anomalies (Smithberg & Runner, 1963), thus leading to reduced risk of congenital anomalies among the live-born survivors?

Very recently, Yerushalmy (1972) reported that the prevalence of low-birth-weight infants was higher for nonsmoking women who later became smokers than for women who never smoked. This is suggestive that the low birth weight was due more to the *smoker* than to *smoking,* in accord with Fisher's (1959) genotype hypothesis.

Yerushalmy (1972) also observed that low birth weights were significantly less prevalent among infants of smoking women who later stopped smoking than among infants of regular smokers. The birth weights of infants of smoking women who were to become ex-smokers were rather comparable to the higher birth weight prevalence among infants of nonsmoking women. This is also compatible with the theory that low birth weight is more a consequence of the smoker than of smoking. The possibility should be examined that smokers who can stop smoking easily are constitutionally, perhaps genotypically, different from smokers who encounter difficulty in stopping smoking.

To examine the bioenergetic question still further, we may also examine the relationship between birth weight and *hyper*glycemia, or diabetes, in the mother. The diabetic women should tend, statistically, to demonstrate blood glucose concentrations higher than "normal," and certainly higher than blood glucose concentrations in hypoglycemic women. If there is a higher level of glucose and thus of available potential energy, it might lead to higher than "normal" birth weights of the infants of diabetic women. This has been observed; diabetic women do tend to produce relatively large infants (Bondy, 1969; Pederson, 1954). It might be added that, with such considerations, it is important to recognize that the genotypes of the infant and its mother are different. It is to be expected, of course, that metabolic complexities are vastly greater than are suggested by the preceding observations.

It was observed by Scarr (1969), and by others whom she cited, that low birth weights—i.e., less than 2,500 grams—and particularly birth weights less than 2,000 grams, are associated with "permanent deleterious effects on later intellectual performance [p. 249]." It would seem imperative that authentic causes of low birth weight be established in order that effective measures might be undertaken for alleviation of developmental problems to the extent that this might be possible. The costs to society, and to the victims of reduced intellectual capability, are very great. It is necessary, however, to distinguish between problems originating with the genotype, e.g., phenylketonuria, and problems resulting from the gestational environment, as from maternal malnutrition. Environmental alteration can alleviate the second kind of problems, but has no effect on the first. Man can manipulate nature only when he understands her correctly.

SUMMARY

A hypothesis has been presented in this chapter which considers cigarette smoking to be an acquired behavior that is influenced by the presence of bioenergetic deficiency, by its severity, and further by the effectiveness of its alleviation by nicotine. Considerations of population biology suggest that considerable variation exists in glucose metabolic characteristics among individuals and in individual responses to nicotine. Since a bioenergetic deficiency such as hypoglycemia leads to deleterious behavioral consequences, through metabolic deficiencies in the brain, and since nicotine usage leads to glucose release from glycogen stores in many people via epinephrine release, nicotine may function in part as an antihypoglycemic agent. Nicotine, via epinephrine release, may also lead to an increased rate of metabolism via enzyme-hormone mechanisms in the presence of adequate glucose. Behavioral reinforcements for smoking appear possible through (a) alleviation of hypoglycemia or other bioenergetic deficiency and the behavioral effects, (b) CNS and other systemic stimulation via epinephrine released by nicotine, (c) more direct CNS and other effects of nicotine, and (d) smoking as a displacement activity under tensive conditions. It is hypothesized, therefore, that cigarette smoking is for many people a symptom or an effect of bioenergetic deficiency and/or a displacement activity under tensive circumstances, and that the tendency toward hypoglycemia and other glucose-related bioenergetic deficiency, such as intracellular glucose deficiency, is influenced in part by the genotype.

REFERENCES

Bennett, A. E.. Doll, R.. & Howell, R. W. Sugar consumption and cigarette smoking. *Lancet*, 1970, **1**, 1011-1014.

Berry, M. G. Tobacco hypoglycemia. *Annals of Internal Medicine*, 1959, **50**, 1149-1157.

Blackburn, H., Brozek, J., Taylor, H. L., & Keys, A. Comparison of cardiovascular and related characteristics in habitual smokers and non-smokers. *Annals of the New York Academy of Science*, 1960, **90**, 277-289.

Bohan, P. T., & Berry, M. G. Hypoglycemia and the use of tobacco. *General Practitioner*, 1953 (November), **8**, 63-64.

Bondy, P. K. Disorders of carbohydrate metabolism. In P. K. Bondy (Ed.), *Duncan's diseases of metabolism.* (6th ed.) Philadelphia: Saunders, 1969. 2 vols.

Bootsma, D., Mulder, M. P., Pot, F., & Cohen, J. A. Different inherited levels of DNA repair replication in xeroderma pigmentosum cell strains after exposure to ultraviolet irradiation. *Mutation Research,* 1970, **9**, 507-516.

Caplan, S. R. Review of H. J. Morowitz, *Entropy for biologists. An introduction to thermodynamics. Science,* 1971, **172**, 1123-1124.

Cattell, M. Introductory remarks. In H. B. Murphree (Ed.), The effects of nicotine and smoking on the central nervous system. *Annals of the New York Academy of Science,* 1967, **142**, 1.

Cheek, D. B., Migeon, C. F., & Mellits, E. D. The concept of biologic age. In D. B. Cheek (Ed.), *Human growth.* Philadelphia: Lea and Febiger, 1968.

Childs, B., & Der Kaloustian, V. Genetic heterogeneity. *New England Journal of Medicine,* 1968, **279**, 1205-1212, 1267-1274.

Cleaver, J. E. Defective repair replication of DNA in xeroderma pigmentosum. *Nature,* 1968, **218**, 652-656.

Cleaver, J. E. Xeroderma pigmentosum: A human disease in which an initial stage of DNA repair is defective. *Proceedings of the National Academy of Science,* 1969, **63**, 428-435.

Eibl-Eibesfeldt, I. *Ethology: The biology of behavior.* New York: Holt, Rinehart & Winston, 1970.

Elwood, P. C., Waters, W. E., Moore, S., & Sweetnam, P. Sucrose consumption and ischaemic heart-disease in the community. *Lancet,* 1970, **1**, 1014-1016.

Fisher, R. A. *Smoking: The cancer controversy: Some attempts to assess the evidence.* London: Oliver and Boyd, 1959.

Galzigna, L., Maina, G., & Rumney, G. Role of ascorbic acid in reversal of the monoamine oxidase inhibition by caffeine. *Journal of Pharmacy and Pharmacology,* 1971, **23**, 303-305.

Ganong, W. F. *Review of medical physiology.* (4th ed.) Los Altos, Calif.: Lange Medical Publications, 1969.

Glauser, S. C., Glauser, E. M., Reidenberg, M. M., Rusy, B. F., & Tallarida, R. J. Metabolic changes associated with the cessation of cigarette smoking. *Archives of Environmental Health,* 1970, **20**, 377-381.

Hamburg, D. A. Emotions in the perspective of human evolution. In S. L. Washburn & P. C. Jay (Eds.), *Perspectives on human evolution.* Vol. 1. New York: Holt, Rinehart & Winston, 1968.

Harris, H. Enzyme polymorphisms in man. *Proceedings of the Royal Society, London,* 1966, **B164**, 298-310.

Heimstra, N. W., Bancroft, N. R., & DeKock, A. R. Effects of smoking upon sustained performance in a simulated driving task. *Annals of the New York Academy of Science,* 1967, **142**, 295-307.

Hickey, R. J., Boyce, D. E., Harner, E. B., & Clelland, R. C. Ecological statistical studies concerning environmental pollution and chronic disease. *IEEE Transactions on Geoscience Electronics,* 1970, **GE-8**, 186-202.

Ingalls, T. H., Avis, F. R., Curley, F. J., & Temin, H. M. Genetic determinants of hypoxia-induced congenital anomalies. *Journal of Heredity,* 1953, **44**, 185-194.

Innes, I. R., & Nickerson, M. Drugs acting on postganglionic adrenergic nerve endings and structures innervated by them (sympathomimetic drugs). In L. S. Goodman & A. Gilman (Eds.), *Pharmacological basis of therapeutics.* (3rd ed.) New York: Macmillan, 1965.

Kalow, W. *Pharmacogenetics.* Philadelphia: W. B. Saunders, 1962.

Kalter, H. Teratology and pharmacogenetics. *Annals of the New York Academy of Science,* 1968, **151**, 997-1000.

Koch, C. J., & Kruuv, J. The effect of extreme hypoxia on recovery after radiation by synchronized mammalian cells. *Radiation Research,* 1971, **48**, 74-85.

Levine, R. J., The adrenal medulla and catecholamines. In P. K. Bondy (Ed.), *Duncan's diseases of metabolism.* (6th ed.) Philadelphia: Saunders, 1969. 2 vols.

Linton, R. *Use of tobacco among North American Indians.* (Anthropology Leaflet No. 15) Chicago: Field Museum of Natural History, 1924.

Little, M. A. Effects of alcohol and coca on foot temperature responses of highland Peruvians during a localized cold exposure. *American Journal of Physical Anthropology*, 1970, **32**, 233-242.

Manning, A. *An introduction to animal behavior*. Reading, Mass.: Addison-Wesley, 1967.

Marks, V., & Rose, F. C. *Hypoglycaemia*. Oxford: Blackwell Scientific Publications, 1965.

Mazess, R. B. Cardiorespiratory characteristics and adaptation to high altitudes. *American Journal of Physical Anthropology*, 1970, **32**, 267-278.

McCormick, W. J. The role of the glycemic response to nicotine. *American Journal of Hygiene*, 1935, **22**, 214-220.

Miller, R. W., & Todaro, G. J. Viral transformation of cells from persons at high risk of cancer. *Lancet*, 1969, **1**, 81-82.

Mukai, F., Hawryluk, I., & Shapiro, R. The mutagenic specificity of sodium bisulfite. *Biochemical and Biophysical Research Communications*, 1970, **39**, 983-988.

Murchison, L. E., & Fyfe, T. Effects of cigarette smoking on serum lipids, blood-glucose, and platelet adhesiveness. *Lancet*, 1966, **2**, 182-184.

Nilsén, R., & Persson, G. Smoking habits of diabetics. *Lancet*, 1972, **1**, 1283-1284.

Pathogenesis of diabetes mellitus. *British Medical Journal*, 1971, **3**, 594-595.

Paul, O., Lepper, M. H., Phelan, W. H., Dupertuis, G. W., Macmillan, A., McKean, H., & Park, H. A longitudinal study of coronary heart diesase. *Circulation*, 1963, **28**, 20-31.

Pederson, J. Weight and length at birth of infants of diabetic mothers. *Acta Endocrinologica*, 1954, **16**, 330-342.

Ritchie, J. M. Central nervous system stimulants (continued). II. The xanthines. In L. S. Goodman & A. Gilman (Eds.), *Pharmacological basis of therapeutics*. (3rd ed.) New York: Macmillan, 1965.

Robison, G. A., Butcher, R. W., & Sutherland, E. W. *Cyclic AMP*. New York: Academic Press, 1971.

Royal College of Physicians. *Smoking and health now*. London: Pitman, 1971.

Sayers, G., & Travis, R. H. Insulin and oral hypoglycemic drugs. In L. S. Goodman & A. Gilman (Eds.), *Pharmacological basis of therapeutics*. (3rd ed.) New York: Macmillan, 1965.

Scarr, S. Effects of birth weight on later intelligence. *Social Biology*, 1969, **16**, 249-256.

Smithberg, M., & Runner, M. N. Teratogenic effects of hypoglycemic treatments in inbred strains of mice. *American Journal of Anatomy*, 1963, **113**, 479-489.

Summers, G. A., & Drake, J. W. Bisulfite mutagenesis in bacteriophage T4. *Genetics*, 1971, **68**, 603-607.

Tinbergen, N. "Derived" activities: Their causation, biological significance, origin, and emancipation during evolution. *Quarterly Review of Biology*, 1952, **27**, 1-32.

Tinbergen, N. The evolution of behavior in gulls. *Scientific American*, 1960, **203**(6), 118-126, 128, 130.

Tinbergen, N. On war and peace in animals and man. *Science*, 1968, **160**, 1411-1418.

U.S. Public Health Service. *Smoking and health: Report of the Advisory Committee to the Surgeon General of the Public Health Service*. (USPHS Publication No. 1103) Washington, D.C.: U.S. Government Printing Office, 1964.

U.S. Public Health Service. *The health consequences of smoking: A Public Health Service review*. (USPHS Publication No. 1696) Washington, D.C.: U.S. Government Printing Office, 1967.

U.S. Public Health Service. *The health consequences of smoking: 1968 supplement to the 1967 Public Health Service review*. (USPHS Publication No. 1696) Washington, D.C.: U.S. Government Printing Office, 1968.

U.S. Public Health Service. *The health consequences of smoking: 1969 supplement to the 1967 Public Health Service review*. (USPHS Publication No. 1696-2) Washington, D.C.: U.S. Government Printing Office, 1969.

Veldhuisen, G., & Pouwels, P. H. Transformation of xeroderma pigmentosum cells by SV40. *Lancet*, 1970, **2**, 529-530.

Volle, R. L. & Koelle, G. B. Ganglionic stimulating and blocking agents. In L. S. Goodman &

A. Gilman (Eds.), *Pharmacological basis of therapeutics.* (3rd ed.) New York: Macmillan, 1965.

Yerushalmy, J. The relationship of parents' cigarette smoking to outcome of pregnancy: Implications as to the problem of inferring causation from observed associations. *American Journal of Epidemiology,* 1971, **93,** 443-456.

Yerushalmy, J. Infants with low birth weight born before their mothers started to smoke cigarettes. *American Journal of Obstetrics and Gynecology,* 1972, **112,** 277-284.

20

THE SOCIAL SCIENCES AND THE SMOKING PROBLEM

Paul F. Lazarsfeld
Columbia University

In his analysis Dr. Dunn (this volume) has described four phases of a general smoking cycle. In each phase a different type of motivation is dominant. Most contributors to this volume think of motivation in either psychological or physiological terms. Dr. Dunn correctly points out that in the initiation phase social factors do play a role—imitation of age peers and desire to copy adults. These factors have been studied in the literature but are not touched upon in this collection; therefore, I shall not deal with them. Rather, I want to emphasize those social factors which not surprisingly—have been objects of attention in recent years. I refer to the effect which the larger social environment has on people's smoking habits.

Most of the time this larger environment is taken for granted and affects us only very slowly; as a result most people are not aware of it. There are, however, situations where more rapid changes occur, and then we have an opportunity to uncover processes which otherwise would remain unspecified. Research experts have always known that they should heed such opportunities. John Flanagan (1948) has created the term "critical incidents technique." Some of us like to talk of "firehouse research." Events like the Orson Welles broadcast on the Invasion from Mars; the numerous studies of natural catastrophes; the outbreak or riots—these are examples of events which occur very suddenly. Other episodes are more extensive in time but still stand out as unusual. The depression of 1930 has yielded considerable research literature. The emergence of social movements of election campaigns have similarly served as natural quasi experiments. The intensified controversy over smoking belongs into the same group.

Two papers in the present collection are firehouse research in this sense. The most drastic example is Mr. Ryan's report. He describes the intensity with which a nonsmoking campaign was conducted in Greenfield, Iowa, and how little effect the whole effort had left 7 months later. Ryan's careful analysis makes two major contributions to my topic. One is an extension of Dr. Dunn's emphasis on synergy. While Dunn speaks of it mainly in terms of a combination of physiological and psychological factors, Ryan extends it to the combination of external efforts with individual personalities. It is known that concern about smoking is greater in upper socioeconomic strata. It is therefore understandable that it was with this group that the Greenfield campaign had an incremental effect. We also know that intended change comes about, if at all, very slowly. The sudden introduction of a new mathematics curriculum does not make school children love mathematics immediately; a new health facility does not cure overnight the distrust low-income people have toward bureaucratic institutions. Therefore, again it is understandable that a one-time effort, however vigorous, will not change a habit as ingrained as smoking. But that still leaves open the question of whether change might not come about by other routes.

This broader question is approached in a tentative way by Meyer and his Columbia associates (this volume). Their idea was to discover processes of change or of resistance by detailed interviews with a relatively small number of cases. The study was originally conceived as a study of conflict. The authors expected that the rather strong government propaganda would have created much turmoil among individual smokers. They did find much less such conflict than they had anticipated; in this sense the Columbia study corroborates Ryan's findings. On the other hand, the study sheds light on a number of processes which the broader campaign set in motion and which raise a set of new questions. Thus, for example, school teachers found in the antismoking movement a welcome topic for discussion with children. Children in turn brought the issue to the home. In many cases this invasion was resented by parents. But it is not inconceivable that once the questioning of the smoking habit has become part of the school routine, it will persist longer than the intermittent efforts of government agencies. The authors also found that smoking had become a much more explicit criterion by which people classified one other. A possible polarization of the population along the smoking habit is another trend which is worth watching. It should be a very worthwhile research investment to come back to the 200 families involved in the Meyer study after a year or two, to see how certain of these cases, such as spouses with conflicting habits, or people who at the time of the study had resolved to give up smoking, have played out their roles afterwards.

Scholars who have reviewed the literature on smoking have usually expressed justified skepticism toward simple questionnaire studies asking people why they do or do not smoke. In contrast, the interviewers in the Columbia study went into considerable concrete details that permitted interpretations well beyond what the respondents themselves could verbalize. This raises the broad question of whether social scientists have added new techniques to the study of smoking. Two developments are worth noticing.

One is the introduction of sociological attributes different from the psychological characteristics such as Ryan reported. Thus, in the Meyer et al. study, people are characterized not only by their general socioeconomic status, but also by the social characteristics of the work they perform. Many differences between white-collar and blue-collar workers can be explained by the fact that the latters' schedule and type of work leaves much less opportunity in individual behavior, and therefore habituation to smoking is less likely. Leo Srole found in his study reported in this volume that an important determinant of smoking behavior is not just where people stand socially at a certain time, but also whether they are upwardly or downwardly mobile. This may raise new questions for the impressive longitudinal studies which Dr. Thomas has conducted and on which she reports in this volume. It would be interesting to know whether the total career patterns of subjects in these two studies are related to their smoking habits.

In addition to introducing new variables, the anthropologists among the social scientists contribute another valuable new tool: the comparative method. An example is Dr. Damon's report (this volume), which shows how rapidly smoking is adopted by primitive tribes once they get acquainted with it through contact with other cultures. His study still leaves many interpretations open. It is interesting to find how anthropologists and sociologists have exchanged roles in this volume. Traditionally sociologists reproach their anthropologist colleagues because they do not support field observations with statistical procedures. Inversely, anthropologists admonish sociologists that they do not pay enough attention to the rich details of concrete situations. It can only be hoped that Dr. Damon's findings will be further analyzed in the light of his background knowledge about these tribes. I want to emphasize a remark which Dr. Damon makes only parenthetically: tribes who are converted to Islam do not take up smoking. How does an ideology make such abstention possible? The Columbia study has made some preliminary suggestions by interviewing a few orthodox Jews. They are not permitted to smoke on the Sabbath, and somehow are able to push away the temptation for this one day. Incidentally, this somewhat mysterious mechanism also permits smokers to continue their habit by "pushing away" TV commercials with their health warnings. In this connection, it should be very helpful if this Islamic tribe were studied in more detail.

In addition to the contributions of empirical social research, one should not overlook the guidance available from the social theorist. He would look at the smoking issue as part of a larger "system." At least two alternatives should be considered. Smoking could get linked with trends like the women's liberation movement and therefore could increase; but an opposite effect could ensue if smoking got involved in the antipollution drive. Both alternatives deserve future research attention.

The main contributions in this volume are made by physiologists and pharmacologists. Their experimental design is impressive to a social scientist, even if he has difficulty understanding all the details. He can raise questions only with diffidence. Some of the measures mentioned, such as change in blood composition, seem to be of a strict biological character. Others, such as pulse rates, or perhaps even brain waves, might be affected by the presence of others, by the way the individual interprets an experimental situation, or by social experiences just prior to an experiment. Could the study of smoking give rise to something like sociopharmacology? And if these examples are too farfetched, let me raise a more concrete question addressed to one contributor of this volume. Since Professor Miller has joined the Rockefeller University, he has concentrated on physiological work, a turn which many other psychologists have taken in recent years: Kretch, Festinger, and even Köhler. Professor Miller has in former years done pioneering work in the theory of imitation, a topic which in my opinion has since been badly neglected by social scientists. Is there a place for still another synergy: to look at imitation in the field of smoking as a combination of social and physiological factors? I found in the literature that light smokers are more subject to external influence in their smoking behavior than heavy smokers, who seem to be more regulated by internal patterns. Would the light smoker deserve the joint attention of the social scientist and the physiologist?

I want to end my remarks with the topic which has concerned me through most of my academic career—the relation between what is usually called basic research and public policy. None of the studies reported in this volume, including those by psychologists and social scientists, are either influenced by or take a stand in the present controversy about smoking. This is as it should be as far as objective findings go. But I consider it extremely important—and important from a theoretical point of view—to study what the relations are between objective research findings and the contributions they make to pragmatic decisions. I personally have no opinion as to the merits and demerits of smoking. And I have never felt that my own work is affected by the sources of support. But I always have been very curious as to what men of action do with objective findings. There is no direct road from knowledge to action. Guesses as to unintended consequences, assessment of possible external events, and opinions on social and psychological costs have to be added to factual information before a practical decision can be made. I would find it fascinating if two competent authors taking very opposite positons on the smoking controversy would review the present volume as to its policy implications.

The distinction between basic and applied social research is vague and often overdone. Much basic knowledge has been derived from studies done for practical purposes—remember what public opinion polls have done for the study of attitude change. Or take the basic contributions of Stouffer (1950), a consolidation of all the management studies done by the Army during World War II. Inversely many a laboratory study turns out to be useless when its results are applied to concrete situations—educational broadcasting provides well-known examples. To study the rich content of the present volume from the point of view of practical implications would be a major theoretical contribution.

REFERENCES

Flanagan, J. C. The aviation psychology program in the Army Air Forces. *Army Air Forces Aviation Psychology Program Research Report I.* Washington, D.C.: U.S. Government Printing Office, 1948.
Stouffer, S. A. *The American Soldier.* New York: Free Press, 1950.

21

THE MOTIVATIONAL FACTORS IN CIGARETTE SMOKING: A SUMMARY

Seymour S. Kety
Harvard Medical School and Massachusetts General Hospital

In examining the multifaceted question of what drives the cigarette smoker to continue smoking, and in attempting to resolve what, superficially at least, are contradictory lines of evidence, I had an interesting déjà vu. I saw myself attending a conference like this about 50 years ago in Lyons, France, sponsored by the Société des Restaurateurs de France. The conference, which was attended by many of the famous gourmets of France, was called "Motivational Mechanisms in Gastronomy."

One of the early speakers began by pointing out the ubiquity of the habit of gourmandism and yet the variety of forms in which it has existed. He started, of course, with France, but acknowledged that even in England some gourmets had been discerned. They had also existed in China, in ancient Rome; and then later on in the proceedings, a well-known anthropologist had just been across the Atlantic and exhibited some examples of what purported to be gastronomy even in the American colonies. It was apparent that the phenomenon existed in many cultures, but took different forms, and even in the same culture there was considerable variety. There were gourmets who liked their steaks rare, medium, or well-done. There should be, insisted the speaker, some common ingredient in all of these habits, throughout these different cultures; and that common ingredient he had narrowed down to food. With the development of even more sophisticated analytical techniques, someone later suggested that an active ingredient of food could be isolated which was "calories." He concluded with the hypothesis that the motivation which drives gourmets is a craving for calories.

That conclusion was immediately challenged by another speaker, who showed two slides. In the first slide (Figure 1), he plotted the number of visits that

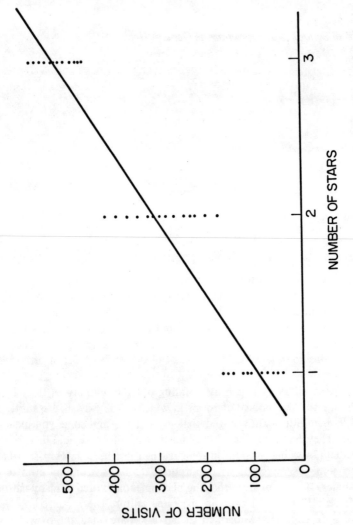

FIG. 1. Visits to restaurants by members of the Epicurean Society, as a function of the number of stars awarded in the Guide Michelin.

members of the Epicurean Society had made to various restaurants in France. On the abscissa were the numbers 1, 2, and 3, representing the number of stars in the Guide Michelin. What he found was a compelling correlation between the number of stars and the number of visits. He showed another graph (Figure 2) on which were plotted the calories served per meal at various restaurants against the number of visits by the members of this gourmet society, and there was no correlation at all. Therefore, obviously, calories were not the important motivational factor, but rather some function of the stars. He coined an expression, "Astronomy leads to gastronomy."

As if the situation weren't complicated enough already, some experimentalists entered the picture and began to do experiments which even further confused it. They got Le Grand Vefour, one of the great restaurants of Paris, to cooperate by preparing meals with all of the sauces and flavors but without any calories. These meals were served blind, of course, in exactly the same ambience, with the same elegant service, the same great wines, and, though all of this was unbeknown to the clientele, it was soon found that there was a steady drop in attendance until the proprietor was forced to discontinue the experiment to avoid bankruptcy. Thus, it appeared that calories must be important after all.

Then someone reported another experiment. If calories are important, he and his associates surmised, why not administer calories while a gourmet is indulging his habit. If the hypothesis is correct, he should decrease his intake of food. They gave some gourmet volunteers intravenous infusions of glucose while they were dining at a great restaurant and found that there was some reduction in eating but not a complete reduction, and that the amount of glucose they had to administer was extremely high.

While all of the experimentalists were struggling with their results and interpretations, others were performing their own studies in the field. Anthropologists, psychologists, sociologists, epidemiologists, were making extremely interesting comparisons between gourmets and nongourmets and finding highly significant differences. They found that gourmets are of a different body build—tending to be on the portly side. They also found that gourmets tend to run in families, that there is a high concordance rate among monozygotic twins, that they separate on the introversion-extroversion scale and on neuroticism coordinates. These results appeared to point to a conslusion that there are constitutional factors in being a gourmet.

But, wait; others point out that some of the effects could be results rather than cause. Obviously, being portly must be an effect of being a gourmet and not its cause. In addition, they point out other important discriminants: social class, income, age, and a wide variety of cultural characteristics. Therefore, obviously, gourmandism must be an environmental phenomenon. Other characteristics appear. A distinguished experimental psychologist points out that it is very difficult to teach a rat to be a gourmet, somewhat easier to teach a monkey the trait, but that really only human beings can become dyed-in-the-wool gourmets, and these largely in the more sophisticated and cultivated societies. Therefore, some peculiar human quality appears to be required, and he suggests that perhaps it is man's ability to conceptualize, to symbolize, to learn to develop associations.

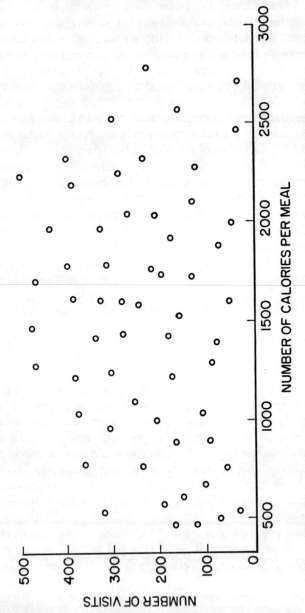

FIG. 2. Calories served per meal by various restaurants, plotted against number of visits by the Epicurean Society.

Others report on studies of withdrawal symptoms among gourmets in which two types are immediately recognized: there are the hard-core gourmets, and then there are the fellow travelers. These are largely women who go along for the ride and, if they are wives, are continually complaining about the cost. Fellow travelers find it very easy to abstain. The others find it extremely difficult. More sophisticated and compelling experiments are performed to discern why gourmets act as they do and what are the specific effects of deprivation. They find that gourmets are more relaxed at a good restaurant and more irritable at a bad one. They count the number of complaints at a restaurant and find that gourmets will tolerate a large number of insults at a good restaurant but fewer if deprived of eating or at poor restaurants. They also find that gourmets will use all sorts of mental mechanisms to continue the habit of gourmandism even against their doctors' orders.

There is a remarkable parallelism between the evidence which was presented at the older conference on gastronomy and that which was reported in this book on cigarette smoking. There is reason to believe that plausible hypotheses can be constructed about gastronomic tendencies on the basis of current knowledge about appetite and the development of the apperceptive, cognitive associations with primitive drives, to which Schachter (this volume) has so significantly contributed. Perhaps we can use the same kind of reasoning in approaching the more difficult problem of cigarette smoking which nevertheless has so many interesting similarities to being a gourmet.

Therefore, let us develop a hypothesis about cigarette smoking which assumes, first of all, some common active factor in cigarette smoke. We have heard good evidence that nicotine is that factor, and it is likely that nicotine satisfies some biological need of the smoker and yields some fundamental reward. On the basis of that assumption, we may reason that with the repetition of the process in a wide variety of diverse situations, and in association with many different types of rewards, there will develop a huge perisphere of accompanying symbolic, appetitive, gratifying, rewarding associations until a puff of cigarette smoke gives rise, in the smoker, to an unbelievable array of olfactory, gustatory, visual, and respiratory sensations which may be sources of gratification or even "pulmonary eroticism," to quote one of the more psychodynamic thinkers in this area. That is not to mention a large number of even more remote associations such as self-image, status, all of the consciously or subconsciously recalled pleasant associations of prior situations.

Once that aura of positively reinforcing components has been established, it is easy to see how the primary biological need may not then be always necessary and certainly is no longer sufficient. At that point it would be like attempting to satisfy a gourmet with mashed potatoes.

Let us go back now to nicotine, which has been implicated with great likelihood as the active agent, and attempt to formulate some hypothesis about the basic need which nicotine develops and satisfies. For one thing, nicotine is known to activate the peripheral adrenergic system via presynaptic cholinergic stimulation. I find it a parsimonious hypothesis that, just as it operates in the periphery, a cholinergic action acts to stimulate a central adrenergic system in the same way. Domino (this volume) presented evidence that nicotine causes cortical arousal. There is a fair amount of evidence, although the case is hardly proved, that the adrenergic system of the brain may be involved in the phenomenon of arousal. Domino also reported experiments indicating that an intact midbrain is required for the arousal induced by nicotine, and it is in the midbrain that the neurons of the central adrenergic system lie. He also adduced evidence that argued against the involvement of the central adrenergic system in the arousal by nicotine, i.e., that this activation is not blocked by reserpine. I don't find this a completely compelling argument, however, since one cannot be sure that the reserpein completely depleted the adrenergic endings of their transmitter; and even so, without a blockade of its synthesis, the transmitter may still be produced and released in sufficient quantities to permit some adrenergic function. So I think there is still a tenable hypothesis that nicotine, by its cholinergic action on the adrenergic system of the brain, is stimulating that system and causing arousal. If it causes arousal, it may also be producing some of the other effects of adrenergic stimulation. The effect which I find particularly relevant to this discussion is the possible effect in the reward system. I am thinking here of the work of Stein and his associates (Stein, 1964) who have lately amassed a great deal of evidence which I, for one, find difficult to disregard, that norepinephrine and the adrenergic system are crucially involved in the pleasure or reward system of the brain.

It is interesting that other habituating drugs are geared to act on the adrenergic system, either by increasing the concentration of transmitter at synapses, as is the case with amphetamine and cocaine, or by acting postsynaptically, as does caffeine, on the destruction of cyclic AMP. This does not necessarily imply that all habituating drugs act through the adrenergic system. For example, I do not know where the barbiturates act, and there is only the beginning of evidence that morphine may involve the adrenergic system. Other experiments reported by Domino argue against the involvement of the reward system in the action of nicotine. For example, he finds that self-stimulatory behavior is blocked by cholinergic drugs, whereas this hypothesis would predict that such behavior would be potentiated by cholinergic drugs or at least by nicotine. However, the self-stimulatory behavior was achieved by stimulation of the medial forebrain bundle, which carries postsynaptic adrenergic fibers. To test the hypothesis adequately would require presynaptic stimulation, but the hypothetical cholinergic input to the adrenergic system cannot be so easily specified. Nevertheless, Domino did find that potentiation of self-stimulation with nicotine occurred after the blockade. With large doses of nicotine, he found that before the behavior returned to normal, there was a period of reinforcement occurring at a time when the concentration of nicotine might have passed from one which was paralytic to one which was stimulating on the cholinergic synapses.

There are some other intersting features of the reward system. Miller and his colleagues (this volume) have used it as a positive reinforcement in conditioning experiments. Drugs which stimulate the system—amphetamine, which certainly does, and nicotine and caffeine, which may—appear to favor acquisiton in certain experiments. Drugs which block the reward system, such as alpha-methyl-paratyrosine or reserpine, appear to depress acquisition, and I have speculated about the possibility that the adrenergic system in the brain somehow represents a special adaptation which favors acquisition by action on cyclic AMP and through it on protein synthesis and consolidation. That is why I was interested in the results that Essman (this volume) reported in which nicotine and one of its congeners appeared to stimulate special types of protein synthesis in the brain. Thus, there are a number of ways by which the reward system of the brain could facilitate the elaboration of the complex neural network on which a cognitive superstructure rests, and a number of reasons why, then, stimulation of the adrenergic system by a drug would be especially adapted to creating a habit or a dependence upon the agent which produced it.

Now we come to another interesting question. I have assumed that there is some basic appetite which nicotine satisfies. How is this need established in smokers? I can think of at least three hypotheses. There could be a simple genetic defect in the reward system in some individuals requiring an artificial boost by a drug which can compensate for it. On the other hand, one could postulate that the need, even though biological, is an entirely acquired one, representing a biological change induced by the repetitious use of an agent. In addition to the extreme genetic and environmental hypotheses, however, one could formulate a hypothesis that one or more genetic factors operated in some individuals to predispose them to smoking or to the acquisition of a smoking habit. Let us look at these hypotheses in the light of evidence which can be adduced relative to them.

In the absence of data obtained from a large sample of adopted individuals and their biological and adoptive families, which serve to disentangle genetic and environmental factors better than any other device I know, let us look at studies on populations of twins. Most of these find a significantly higher concordance rate for smoking among monozygotic than dizygotic twins, which is often used as evidence for a genetic basis of the tendency. Such data are not conclusive, however, since it is well known that monozygotic twins share considerably more of their environment and life experiences than do dizygotic twins, so that a higher concordance among them is not necessarily evidence for the operation of genetic factors. On the other hand, Shields (1962) has reported on the smoking habits of 42 pairs of monozygotic twins reared apart, and his results are summarized in Table 1. Here the observed frequency of concordance and discordance for smoking is presented along with the frequency of these characteristics of the pairs expected on the basis of chance alone. The observed frequency distribution is significantly different from

TABLE 1

Smoking Habits in 42 Pairs of Monozygotic Twins
Reared Apart

Characteristics	Observed number	Number expected by chance
Both nonsmokers	18	12
One smoker, other nonsmoker	9	21
Both smokers	15	9

Note.–From Shields (1962). $p < .001$.

the expected, with a *p* value of less than one in a thousand. The presence of a substantial number of discordant twins indicates that genetic factors do not operate exclusively to determine smoking tendencies, and an estimate of the amount of variance with regard to smoking in this sample which can be accounted for by genetic factors is somewhat less than 33%. It seems reasonable to conclude that genetic factors operate significantly, but by no means exclusively, in the tendency to smoke; and they may do so in a wide variety of modes, including personality characteristics, and social and psychological needs and values, rather than simply by producing an inborn craving which nicotine satisfies.

Thus, the genetic evidence does not rule out the probability that the craving for nicotine is induced and intensified by repeated exposure and a variety of positive reinforcements. The genetic factors may operate in determining the likelihood of exposure, the frequency or intensity of those exposures, and the number and power of the positive reinforcements. We know that the repeated administration of other much more potent agents can induce dependence; and, although no one would suggest that nicotine had anything like the habituative properties of morphine or other narcotics, yet it is likely that its slight habituative properties are enough to contribute to the perpetuation of this complex biological and psychosocial characteristic.

It is an interesting property of many drug effects that compensatory processes occur within the organism to counteract them. Therefore, we might expect a certain amount of tolerance at the cholinergic synapse or at the adrenergic endings of the reward system with repeated administration of nicotine. In that way, an insensitivity of the reward system could be produced which would be just as potent and effective as a simple genetic defect and which would also require continued use of a substance which acted upon the reward system. If nicotine induces some tolerance in the reward system, it may also do the same for the arousal system. I found it interesting that according to the findings in Barbara Brown's (this volume) report, the EEG changes in chronic smokers were quite the opposite of those changes which are produced by an acute smoking of a cigarette. Instead of arousal in chronic smokers, she found a tendency toward increased synchronization. Although I am sure Dr. Brown is much too cautious to interpret it in this way, yet it is exactly what one might expect from the continued use of an agent which causes arousal and which induces tolerance in its target system.

Are there any practical inferences which emerge from this interpretation of the evidence which has been presented? If a physical dependence on nicotine, however acquired, is important but not sufficient in maintaining the motivation for cigarette smoking, the administration of nicotine in small doses should lessen the motivation, but only partially, unless the administration of nicotine is accompanied by a broad variety of other inputs comparable to those found in cigarette smoking. The taking of a capsule or some chewing gum containing nicotine or an active congener would not be nearly as effective a replacement as the smoking of a pipe or cigar. Many cigarette smokers have been able, with little difficulty, to switch to these modes of administration when they found it extremely difficult to stop smoking entirely. It is quite possible that this occurs because, in addition to providing a certain amount of nicotine, pipe or cigar smoking embodies enough ritual, flavor, and many other forms of sensory and psychosocial feedback to substitute almost completely for cigarette smoking. If, as much evidence appears to indicate, these other forms of smoking are associated with fewer hazards, they may represent a satisfactory and appropriate substitute.

Although it may be premature to propose specific hypotheses regarding the pharmacology of nicotine in the central nervous system, it is probably useful and compatible with most of the observations to regard the motivation to smoke, like many other motivations, as a multifaceted problem, with some genetic components but largely acquired, depending upon some simple biological mechanisms but with a massive input and modulation which is cognitive in nature, molded by culture and individual experience.

REFERENCES

Shields, J., *Monozygotic twins.* London: Oxford University Press, 1962.

Stein, L., Self-stimulation of the brain and the central stimulant action of amphetamine. Federation Proceedings, 1964, **23**, 836-850.

AUTHOR INDEX

Numbers in italics refer to the pages on which the complete references are listed.

G

Gale, A., 73, 76, *79*
Gale, S., 117, *143*
Galzigna, L., 276, *280*
Ganong, W. F., 268, 269, 270, 272, *280*
Garg, M., 124, *143*
Gatti, G. L., 123, *142*
Geller, I., 67, 77, *79*
Giannitrapani, D., 73, 74, 75, *79*
Gibbs, E. L., 77, 78, *80*
Gibbs, F. A., 77, 78, *80*
Gilman, A., 9, *30*
Ginzel, K. H., 20, *30*, 122, *143*
Giunta, F., 122, *144*
Glass, A., 73, 74, 75, *79*, *80*
Glass, L. H., 96, *109*
Glauser, E. M., 274, *280*
Glauser, S. C., 274, *280*
Glick, S. D., 7, 8, 9, *30*, 35, 36, 41, 43, *49*, 89, *91*, 130, *144*, 194, *195*
Goldblatt, P. B., 255, *265*
Goldfarb, T. L., 7, 8, 9, *30*, 41, 43, 44, *49*, 130, *144*
Goldstein, L., 123, *144*
Gollub, L. R., 194, *196*
Golod, M. I., 51, *65*
Goodman, L. S., 9, *30*
Goodyear, J. M., 123, *145*
Gray, J. A., 75, *80*
Green, D. E., 98, *109*, 137, *144*, 148, *155*
Griffiths, R. L., 8, 25, *30*
Grossman, S. P., 213, *214*
Grover, F., *30*
Grunewald, G., 73, *80*

H

Haag, H. B., 8, 9, *30, 31*, 36, 42, *49*, 100, 103, *109*, 191, 194, *195, 196*
Hake, D. F., 174, 177, *195, 196*
Hall, G. H., 9, 16, *29*, 56, *64*, 67, *78, 80,* 85, 90, *91*, 99, 100, *108*, 122, 134, 135, 136, *142*
Hamburg, D. A., 269, *280*
Hamilton, B., 8, 25, *30*
Harlan, W. R., 6, *30*
Harner, E. B., 277, *280*
Harris, H., 269, *280*
Hartmann, R., 67, 77, *79*
Hauser, H., 67, 68, 77, *80*, 126, *144*
Hawryluk, I., 277, *281*

Heath, C. W., 68, 74, *80, 167, 170*
Heimstra, N. W., 199, 200, *207*, 272, *280*
Heldman, E., 54, 60, *65*
Hendrickson, E., 117, *144*
Hendry, D. P., 194, *195*
Herrington, R. N., 125, *142*
Herxheimer, A., 8, 25, *30,*
Herz. A., 122, *144*
Hickey, R. J., 277, *280*
Higgins, M. W., 95, *109*
Higinbotham, C. Q., 157, 158, 159, *170*
Hinkle, L. E., Jr., 73, 76, *80*
Hofer, M. A., 73, 76, *80*
Hoff, E. C., 9, *31*, 191, *196*
Holland, H. C., 124, *143*
Horn, D. A., 98, *109,* 137, *144,* 148, *155,* 191, *195*
Hovland, C. I., 213, *214*
Howarth, E., 114, *144*
Howell, R. W., 276, *279*
Hull, C. L., 93, 95, 96, *109*
Hunt, G. M., 174, *196*
Hunt, W. A., 97, 105, *109,* 113, *144,* 233, *240*
Hunter, N. A., 177, *195*
Hutchinson, R. R., 89, *91*, 174, 177, 184, 189, *195, 196*

I

Ianni, F. A., 95, *109*
Ikard, E. F., 98, *109*
Ikard, F. F., 137, *144,* 148, *155*
Ingalls, T. H., 271, *280*
Innes, I. R., 273, *280*
Inoki, R., 130, *143,* 194, *195*
Itil, T. M., 67, 77, *80, 81*
Izard, C. E., 197, 198, 206, *207*

J

James, W. H., 68, *80*
Janku, I., 123, *142*
Jarvik, M. E., 7, 8, 9, *30*, 33, 35, 36, 41, 43, 44, *49*, 51, *65*, 89, 90, *91*, 102, 103, 104, 105, 107, *109*, 122, 130, *144*, 194, *195*
Jenkins, D., 94, 96, *110*
Jennings, J. R., 197, 198, 206, *207*
Jiminez, J., 34, *49*
Johnston, L. M., 8, *30,* 73, *80,* 130, *144,* 191, *196*
Jones, A. L., 125, *145*

Woodruff, A. B., 68, *80*
Wooley, D. W., 52, *65*
Woolf, M., 68, *79*
Wurm, M., 94, 96, *110*

Y

Yamamoto, K. I., 16, *30, 31,* 90, *91,* 122, *146*

Yeager, C. L. 74, *80*
Yerushalmy, J., 276, 278, *282*
Young, G. A., 174, 177, *196*

Z

Zimmerberg, B., 89, *91*
Zotterman, Y. A., 89, *91*

SUBJECT INDEX

A

Acetylcholine, 16, 18, 51, 85, 90, 213
Actions of nicotine, 9
Addiction, 2, 168, 211
Adrenergic systems, 213
  and nicotine, 291
Aerosol particle size, 89
Aggression, 2, 213, 215
  EEG patterns, 75, 164-169
Alcohol, 2, 8, 164-169
Amphetamine, 8,14
Anger, 3, 159-162, 167-169, 210
Anxiety, 3, 73, 159-162, 167
  EEG patterns, 74, 75
Arousal (*see* Emotional activation)
Autonomic nervous system
  effects of smoking on, 147-152

B

Bar pressing responses in animals, 11, 85
  and barbiturate rewards, 210
Barbiturates, 8
Behavior therapy, 140
  and stopping smoking, 140-141

Benefit-risk, 2
Bioenergetic deficiency hypothesis, 267-279
Blood clotting time in smokers, 96
Blood pressure, 6, 16, 34, 45, 48, 87, 159
  effect of cigar and cigarette smoking
  on, 87
Body weight, 159
Brain coding
  muscarinic vs. nicotinic, 213

C

Caffeine
  behavioral effects of, 177-178
Catecholamine hypothesis, 51
Catecholamines, 34
Central cholinergic system, 51
Central nervous system
  actions of nicotine on, 9, 117-122
  hippocampus, 16
  reticular formation, 14, 16, 18
  reward centers, 34
Channeled drive, 212
Chlordiazepoxide, 14
  behavioral effects of, 178
Chlorpromazine, 10
  behavioral effects of, 178

Smoking, *(Cont'd.)*
  cigarettes, *(Cont'd.)*
    and mood changes, 234
    and nervous mannerisms, 234
    factors related to, 234-239
    effect of nicotine blocking agents upon, 43
    effects on central nervous system, 67, 117-122, 147
    effects on mood change, 197-207
    etiology, 78, 83, 294
    genetic determinants of, 101, 275, 293
    habits of, 67, 102
      initiation of, 197, 251, 283
      motives and phases, 106-107
    in man, 34
    in monkeys, 34, 35, 45, 89
    in primitive societies, 219-230
    motives
      physiological, 103-104
      psychomotor, 104
      psychosocial, 104
      sensory, 104
    nicotine as reinforcing agent, 48
    personality and, 113-142, 157-169
    phases of, 102-107
    rate determinants of, 7, 9, 93, 130-134, 256

Smoking, *(Cont'd.)*
  cigarettes, *(Cont'd.)*
    resistance to extinction, 48
    synergism of determinants of, 101
    variability of effect, 67
Stress, 1
  and jaw contractions, 191
  and nicotine, 125
  effects on protein synthesis, 63
  reactions to, 157-169
Surgeon General's Report, 147

T

Tetrahydrocannabinol (*see* Marijuana)
Tobacco
  chewing, 33
  historical use, 33
Tranquilizer, 10
Tranquilizing action, 3, 216
Triglyceride level in smokers, 96
Trimethidinium, 11, 12, 16, 18
Type A vs. Type B behavior, 96

U

United Artists, 231